Doctor Olds of Twillingate

Portrait of an American Surgeon in Newfoundland

Gary L. Saunders

BREAKWATER

all from Dad... love, Angie 7/95

Breakwater
100 Water St.
P.O. Box 2188
St. John's, NF
A1E 6E6

*The Publisher gratefully acknowledges the financial support of
the Canada Council, which has helped make this publication
possible.*

*The Publisher acknowledges the financial support of the
Cultural Affairs Division of the Department of Municipal and
Provincial Affairs, Government of Newfoundland and
Labrador, which has helped make this publication possible.*

Canadian Cataloguing in Publication Data
    Saunders, Gary L.

        Dr. Olds of Twillingate

        ISBN 1-55081-092-8

    1. Olds, John McKee, 1906-1985.   2. Surgeons —
    Newfoundland — Twillingate — Biography.
    3. Twillingate (Nfld.) — Biography.   I. Title.
    II. Title: Doctor Olds of Twillingate.

RD27.35.043S38 1994   617' .092   C94-950139-5

Second Printing

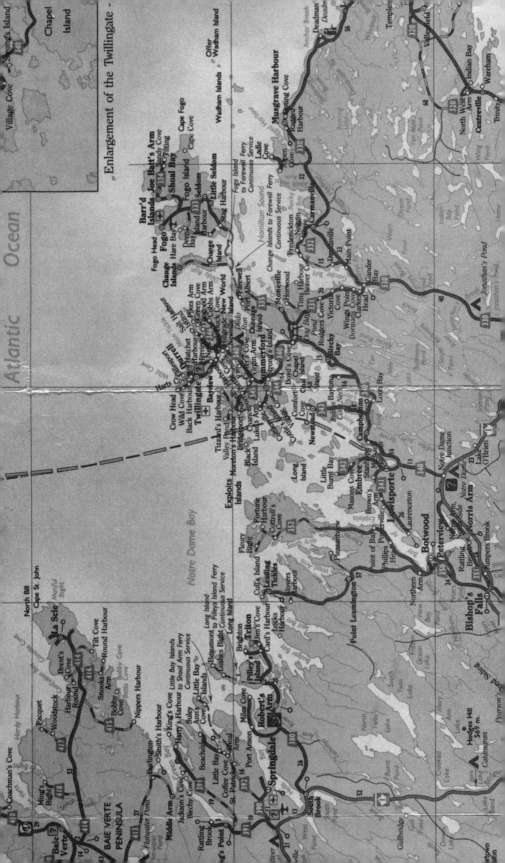

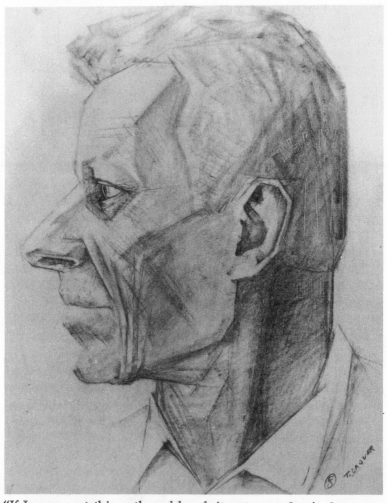

"If I carry out this oath and break it not, may I gain forever a good reputation among all men for my life and my art; but if I transgress it, may the opposite be my portion."

—Part of Hippocratic Oath

[Ted Drover drawing of Dr Olds, credited to Twillingate Museum]

To the memory of Betty Arms Olds

Contents

Foreword

Louis E. Lawton, MD, CM

On the morning of the day I was to leave for Twillingate—August 7, 1945—the St John's *Daily News* and other newspapers all over the world reported a literally earth-shattering event. The headlines heralded President Harry Truman's announcement of the dropping of a new explosive device, an atomic bomb, on a place called Hiroshima. It would be several years before the full impact and significance of that event would be understood. But there could be no doubt that six years of bloody war would soon end and that the world had entered a new and uncertain phase. Shortly before my arrival in Twillingate, Nagasaki was also bombed. So I can accurately date the beginning of my relationship with the town and with John M. Olds.

Both great wars directly affected the community of Twillingate. Following the 1914-1918 conflagration its people, after considerable debate, had decided to build a hospital as a memorial to those who died in the fighting. Funds were to be raised by public subscription—this at a time when Newfoundland was about to enter economic depression and financial ruin. Amazingly, the funds were found and the Notre Dame Bay Memorial Hospital was proudly erected on the South Side of Twillingate Harbour.

World War II also affected Twillingate. There were material deprivations, and lists of young men dead in faraway places. One of the people directly affected was the chief physician and surgeon of the Hospital. Dr John Olds and three other young American physicians, graduates of world-famous Johns Hopkins Medical School and perhaps inspired by the Grenfell legend, had set up a hospital-based health care system for thousands of residents of the coasts and islands of Notre Dame Bay. After the United States' entry into the war in December 1941, three of the doctors returned home for military service. John Olds was left to do the work of four while maintaining the extensive surgical service he had developed. With a few dedicated and devoted nurses, nursing aides and hospital staff, he became all things medical to all the people of the area.

By July 1945, however, the situation had reached a critical state. Hospital directors and others had repeatedly expressed their concerns to officials of the Department of Health and Welfare in St John's. Dr Leonard Miller, a senior official of the Department, asked me if I would go to Twillingate to assist Dr Olds, even if for a brief period. He also stated that he and the

Commissioner of Public Health, Sir John Puddester, would be going to the area to discuss the Hospital's future.

As we approached the island on August eighth in the Hospital boat *Bonnie Nell*, I naturally wondered about the place and about the physician with whom I would be working. On the boat I had learned that there were few automobiles (mostly taxis), and no electric power at the Hospital except from a DC generator that was being replaced by a modern one capable of supplying the whole town. There was a single telephone line. Mail came once or twice a week depending on the coastal boats.

As we entered the Harbour and neared the South Side wharf, a welcoming committee could be seen. All the men were dressed in business suits except for one, who wore a white operating room jacket, white trousers and canvas sneakers. Captain Elijah Dalley identified this person as Dr Olds.

We landed and there were introductions all around. Thus began a professional association which lasted a short two years—and a friendship which spanned forty years and only terminated on the night he died in St Clare's Hospital.

Dr Olds was younger, thinner and less formidable than I had anticipated, friendly but not immediately warm—that would come later. He had scheduled a full day in the OR and was now between cases. As we made hospital rounds and saw outpatients over the next few weeks—during which we acquired another doctor—I recognized that John Olds had achieved the art of appearing calm and in charge in the face of potentially serious medical problems and great anxieties on the part of the patients— the "Aequanimitas" of Sir William Osler. This was no doubt part of his legacy to the young physicians who came to the Hospital over the years.

But the years of stress and isolation had taken a physical and psychological toll. He was not the only doctor working alone at that time. Newfoundland in 1945 had fewer than two hundred doctors, some of them in remote areas providing services for large numbers of people. But the volume and scope of work in Twillingate made his burden unusual.

Already, stories of his healing skills were forming the nucleus of the John Olds legend. Physicians who remain in communities for long periods are often recalled with affection by the people they have served. In John Olds' case the affection may be unique in the annals of Newfoundland medicine. The degree of trust and the dependence by thousands transcended the ordinary doctor-patient relationship.

John did not establish a firm relationship with other members of the medical profession in other places, so his contribution and skills remained largely anecdotal for many of his colleagues. It seems clear, however, that as a young physician he had already begun to develop his thinking on the economics of medicine. His introduction of a patient-supported prepaid medical plan to the Bay in the early thirties may be one of the earliest examples of health insurance in North America. The concept of a large, well-equipped medical center augmented by a travelling clinic boat was a pioneer effort to be copied in other areas. He wanted to enlarge the service with an airplane; but those who might have provided one, including his father, knew his indifference to danger and wisely declined.

He was interested in research. In his early years he tried to develop an animal research laboratory, but increasing clinical pressures made it impossible. Nevertheless he remained a keen observer. His study of "Seal Finger" and his identification of Tetracycline as the proper treatment advanced the understanding of this disabling condition.

Those of us who worked with John frequently used instruments which he had devised and constructed. However, it must be stated that many of his devices owed as much to the spirit of Rube Goldberg as to Thomas Edison's.

Dr Olds' service during those war years and for many years afterwards has firmly established his name in Newfoundland medical history and in the memory of those who worked with him. But the picture of John Olds the man has remained somewhat two-dimensional. In order to understand this complex person it is necessary to explore what motivated a young man of superior intelligence, the product of an affluent family and two great universities, to leave a promising future in the United States to spend the rest of his life in a faraway country. And to give his story depth it will be necessary to examine his weaknesses as well as his strengths. Gary Saunders has provided those missing facets of John Olds—physician and surgeon, scholar, visionary and human being.

St John's
September, 1993

Introduction

David D. Olds, MD

My first memory is of lying face down on a sled, being pulled along over crunching, squeaking snow, with the faint smell of horse dung permeating the crisp cold air in my nostrils. I was probably being pulled by my nursemaid, Mamie Hale, and I was probably about three years old. Growing older, I noticed that my father was a doctor and that we lived in a hospital, while my playmates were the sons of fishermen and sea captains. It did not escape me that my father and mother were both revered in the town of Twillingate, my father as the "greatest doctor in the world"—as one old seaman he had treated for burns from a gasoline fire put it—and my mother as a generous, saintly nurse.

John Olds grew up in Connecticut, sailed on Long Island Sound, played polo at Yale and went to medical school at Johns Hopkins. As a third year medical student he went on a summer's adventure to an unheard of hospital in the equally obscure town of Twillingate in Newfoundland, at that time Great Britain's oldest colony. The summer's experience was offered to Hopkins students, as an elective, to show them medicine as practiced outside the metropolitan medical centers. It also gave them more hands-on experience than medical school could offer a junior student. Most came for the summer and then relegated to memory their novel experience with the hospitable, gentle people, the chance to do deliveries and appendectomies, and the rustic maritime beauty of the place. My father liked it so well that upon graduation in 1932 he returned, bringing my mother, whom he had met there in 1930 as a Hopkins nursing student, as his bride. They decided to stay a year; the year turned into their lifetimes.

When they arrived the world was in the depths of its Depression and Newfoundland was no better off than anywhere else. Poverty and malnutrition were widespread. Most years there was indeed plenty of fish, but this provided a diet not much better than that on the scurvy-ridden ships of two centuries before. Vitamin deficiencies of all kinds were prevalent. The fish was meant also to provide the fruits of international trade. But since no one could afford it, the fishermen were in hock to the local fish merchants, who themselves hovered near bankruptcy.

John and Betty settled in, having no doubt that they were in a place where they were truly needed. They were an enthusiastic and attractive couple. He was about six feet, thin and wiry with small bones and elegant hands, handsome but with a congenitally dour visage. Betty was also tall and thin with a pretty, innocent, but intelligent face. They had the energy and wit to deal with innumerable difficulties and to see the humour in it. Their life was not all hardship; there was a heady sense of opportunity and power, a lively sense that great things could be accomplished.

Dr Parsons became ill and incapacitated and left Twillingate in 1934. So John found himself, at the age of 28, the chief physician and superintendent of this 90-bed hospital, his post-graduate training being nine months of surgical internship at Hopkins. The most emergent need was for surgery; he had been a talented student and intern, he learned quite a bit from Dr Parsons and eventually he developed a reputation all over Newfoundland as a superb practitioner.

An equally urgent need was for money. Although patients often paid in quintals of fish or bushels of potatoes, such items would not pay salaries or buy equipment. After much agonizing John came up with what was then a revolutionary plan, possibly the first such plan in North America, called the "Blanket Contract," a forerunner of Blue Cross. Each subscribing man, woman and child paid 44 cents per year. For that they got the right to virtually *gratis* care. The system worked so well that the Hospital was solvent in about two years. It was viewed as a kind of a miracle. One reason it worked was that medical care was technologically primitive and relatively cheap. A second factor was that the people were extremely hardy, and afraid of doctors. They would pay their contracts but only come to the Hospital in dire emergencies.

The fear and awe of doctors was instilled early. The outport families were impoverished, most of them on the Dole; parents felt they would need much help in their old age and tended to have many children. They often got an early start by being well along in pregnancy before marriage. Most parents were lenient with children. At times—and inconsistently—they would enforce obedience with the ultimate threat: "If 'e don't mind (obey) I'll take 'e to Dr Hose (Olds)." In this spirit of apparent laxity, large decisions were often left to young minds. One woman was reported to have said to her eight-year-old-son with a ruptured appendix, "Do 'e want ta go to d'ospital for a hoperation, or will 'e bide 'ome and die?" This child chose to stay home and fortunately survived. As a result of such customs, the survivors of childhood were usually quite self-reliant.

Another good idea was a floating clinic. Many of the villages were born in the seventeenth century and were hidden in obscure coves, supposedly to escape the notice of sea-borne government tax collectors. Since there were no roads beyond cow-path grade until the late 1940s, they were also isolated by land. In summer the only way to the Hospital was by boat, and in the winter, when the ice was solid, by horse-and-sled or dogteam. When the sea ice was soft or unstable there really was no way. The Hospital found a sturdy 55-foot vessel named the *Bonnie Nell* and fixed up the after cabin with an examining table, dentist's chair and an X-ray machine. On board was a crew of three, plus a doctor, a nurse, and often a medical student.

The *Bonnie Nell* made one complete circuit of the Bay each summer. Her arrival was always a major event; the only other ocean-going vessels to visit were the coastal steamers which brought mail and freight once or twice a month in the summer. Novelty overrode fear, and the doctor and nurse would sometimes be deluged by people who had seen no doctor for a year. The most used item was the dentist's chair. Dental care was non-existent, tooth brushes were unpopular and most people by middle age were toothless. I went on the boat several summers and I remember the stream of people arriving with blackened, rotten teeth and leaving with handkerchiefs held to their faces and spitting blood. The X-ray machine was also busy. In the '30s and '40s tuberculosis was endemic, aggravated by the circumstance of malnourished people spending long winters in close quarters. There was no antibiotic treatment available; one whole wing of the Hospital was devoted to long-term TB patients. Many had been first diagnosed by the *Bonnie Nell*'s X-ray.

Winters at the Hospital tended to be quiet, but this was the time of adventures with the elements. Exhausting and unpredictable trips were routine. I remember frequently hearing a knock at the door late at night, then a plaintive, urgent voice, some grumbling by my mother and muttered oaths from my father, howling wind and a slammed door. The standard means of transport was the dog team pulling a rather sturdy but heavy wooden cart used for hauling firewood. The teams of the impoverished fishermen were often half-starved; their owners seldom had enough food for the family, let alone the dogs.

Eventually John quit relying on local teams and perfected his own means of travel. Sport, a heavy, adopted mongrel, along with another unlikely sled dog, an Irish Setter named Jake, became fast and reliable at pulling him on skis. He was quite proud and rather boastful of this method, for he could be at the patient's home long before the dog team that had been sent to fetch him.

As a surgeon John was extremely skillful with his hands, and prided himself on making the smallest possible incision. He would often view with derision a three-inch scar made by some other surgeon during an appendectomy. He took on very ambitious surgery—pneumonectomies, nephrectomies, even brain surgery—which were beyond his training, but which could be done by one adept in basic surgical principles and very patient. He would persevere in making a piece of surgery perfect long after his helpers were ready to sew up. He was patient, which is not to be confused with serene.

Gary Saunders

Like many surgeons, he was authoritarian. Frequently he fumed with rage at the assistant who held a retractor the wrong way or who got in the light. In the Operating Room there was often a steady flow of insult and cursing, sometimes aimed at a hapless medical student. Most learned to take this abuse as part of their dose of learning—especially when after the operation the person who had been led to believe he was incompetent, worthless, and should give up medicine, would be greeted with a warm smile as if nothing was wrong. John even claimed not to remember any of the dreadful names he had called his assistants.

Looking back, one of the most striking things about him, and about the people around him, was an amazing do-it-yourself mentality. On one occasion in the middle of winter a patient in emergency surgery had lost so much blood that he needed a transfusion to survive. The Hospital had no blood bank and only John had the patient's blood type, so he interrupted the operation long enough to give a pint of his own blood.

John's inventiveness made him a local curiosity. He had an extremely well equipped workshop with lathes, a drill press, and numerous other fairly sophisticated machine tools. He could grind a crankshaft for a fisherman's motor boat or replace the hammer on a muzzle-loader. Naturally I saw little of him at home; our most extended periods together may have been in the workshop, where I built my own crossbows and toy sailboats and later helped with some of his projects.

One which I remember was a hand-washing machine. This thing actually worked, and according to him saved time in scrubbing for an operation. It squirted hot water and a green soap solution into a maelstrom of revolving brushes; into that you stuck your hands and waited till they were clean. I believe no one was ever injured by it; strangely enough, his colleagues and assistants seemed reluctant to use it. Another time I helped him with a "suture cutter." This was a ring the surgeon could slip over his little finger; it had a piece of hinged razor blade inside. (My job was breaking razor blades into a suitable size to fit in the slot — it isn't easy.) With your fourth finger you could push a little nubbin on the ring, the blade would emerge and you could deftly trim the suture you had just tied. I also remember a steel reamer for hip joints, and a number of devices for holding incisions open during surgery.

His most quixotic and prolonged quest, and one on which I spent many hours, was a project to generate electricity from the motions of the sea. There were many versions of this machine. They had in common certain obvious essentials: a float which would move with the rapid action of the waves as well as the more prolonged movement of the six- to ten-foot tides, and a lever arm which would transfer this movement to a generator. I believe such devices now exist. The main problem we encountered was that nothing would survive even a medium-sized northeast gale. Our designs may have been adequate, but not our engineering technology.

There was a small team of regulars who eventually learned to work smoothly with him. One legendary scrub nurse, Rose Young, was able to function as third and fourth arms for him, able to anticipate every possible demand. Several Hospital employees showed similar responsive dedication. Two of them became loyal assistants and worked with him for over forty years. George Ings, the hospital's chief orderly, was always on the job when John was, at any hour. George knew where everything could be found, and if it could not be found he could jury-rig something that would work. Bud Young began working at the hospital at the same time as John, a local boy of 17 with an 11th grade education. He started in the clinical laboratory under Dr Parsons, learning how to do blood smears, urinalyses and the like. He became quite good at that. Then John asked him to take over the pharmacy, which was simpler then than now except that much medication had to be dissolved or proportionally mixed before dispensing. By the time he mastered that, the Hospital got its first X-ray machine and Bud became the X-ray technician. He got most of his education from studying operating manuals and learned an extraordinary number of skills.

An important addition to the small medical staff was the summer group of visiting medical students. During the War the student internship program, which had brought John to the island in the first place, stopped functioning. But in the fifties and sixties a similar program was operated with the Harvard Medical School. Each summer two shifts of three students would arrive and soon find themselves doing appendectomies, delivering babies and going on house calls. Usually in their third year of medical school, they had never been allowed to do more than watch such procedures. Their arrival each spring was eagerly anticipated by the staff, who yearned for new faces; John and his resident doctors were grateful for the helping hands as well as having bright young people to teach. For most of the students it was a powerful and important experience which they never forgot.

The period when his mettle was most severely tested and nearly broken was during the War. For the last year and a half he was the only civilian doctor in the Bay. This meant he was *always* on call. Rarely was there a meal, or a week-end at our little cabin on the back of the island, that was not interrupted by some emergency. On many occasions he did not sleep for two or three days. This was the period that marked him as a hero—and which no doubt helped to confirm him as an alcoholic. The alcohol probably assisted him through the grim, endless vigils and numbing fatigue. But by the end of the War he was a physical wreck. He had also apparently contracted tuberculosis, for which there was still no treatment except rest and fresh air. He was beginning to spit blood with ominous frequency. He refused all advice to slow his pace; he kept going like an automaton that was gradually winding down.

My mother Betty had been his primary emotional support through all of this. In those days doctors did not stay very long in a Newfoundland outport. It was usually a kind of way station between the doctor's urban home in England or the States and an urban practice to the south or west. If the usually male doctor brought with him a wife, after a year or two she would wilt like a flower in a snow storm, or leave. Betty was as unusual as her husband in that she was willing—not always happily, but devotedly and courageously—to put up with the many difficulties of that life. She did so out of fondness for the people and her love of him. But in 1943 she suffered an attack of erysipelas, a streptococcal infection which (as it often did in the pre-antibiotic era) led to glomerulonephritis, a progressive kidney disease. Over the next ten years, her health slowly deteriorated until in 1954 she died the gruesome death of renal failure. During her last years John could barely function: he drank incessantly and was chronically ill.

After 1945, working conditions were improving and there were usually one or two doctors willing to come and stay. However, even with other doctors in place, he refused to take time off. After Betty died the drinking increased and he became virtually incapacitated. He finally capitulated and spent a year in a tuberculosis sanatorium. There he managed to master both ailments, the TB with streptomycin, the alcoholism gradually over the ensuing years.

In July 1948 Newfoundland had to choose between responsible government or union with Canada. It became known that Dr Olds strongly favoured the Canadian option. Since his opinion was valued on all matters, Notre Dame Bay contributed an overwhelming majority for Confederation. Under its ebullient young premier Joey Smallwood, Newfoundland joined Canada and the 20th century. After this it became my father's challenge to adapt to a much better supported and more bureaucratic medical system. He grumbled a bit as things changed—even as his salary tripled to become a normal Canadian doctor's income. In his fifties and sixties he gradually left the administration to other able hands, first to Alfred Dennison and then Fred Woodruff from England and later to the current medical director Georgie Chaulker. He focused more on being a general surgeon.

He married again, first briefly to local nurse Stella Manuel and subsequently, until he died, to a nurse from Nova Scotia, Gloria Chisholm.

His interest in gadgetry remained high, and he greeted all the new technological marvels with enthusiasm. In 1966 he became a Canadian citizen. By 1974 the Hospital had celebrated its 50th anniversary. At 68 he could and did look back with immense pride at what he had built. His crowning honour was the Order of Canada, bestowed on him in Ottawa in April 1970. His own peculiar response to the ceremony, of course, was to grumble that he had to go to Ottawa and suffocate from exhaust fumes, that he had to rent a tuxedo and that he would have to give some sort of a speech. Public speaking was his only known phobia.

What happened to me? I became a psychiatrist. While I did not always want to be a doctor, I had a core feeling that being one was a kind of natural thing. During most of my childhood I had lived in a hospital with its attendant smells of steam heat, ether, antiseptics and pharmaceuticals. I felt that medicine was an essential part of an education, almost like learning to speak my native language or to drive a car. I would not have felt safe without it. I did prefer what I considered to be the more philosophical aspect. I was not sure whether my father, the surgeon, the man of action, would warm to this decision. Somewhat to my surprise, he responded by saying, "Hmm...probably not a bad idea. The way medicine is going these days, psychiatry may be the one specialty where you really get to know your patients." Remembering how he had always made it a point to know the life history of just about everybody in the town of Twillingate, I took that to be his blessing.

New York City
March, 1994

Acknowledgements

My first debt is to the many Notre Dame Bay people who talked and wrote to me about Dr J. M. Olds. My second is to his son David, a busy New York psychiatrist who took time to show me around his father's home and haunts in Connecticut, lent letters and photographs, proofed the manuscript and wrote the Introduction. Eric Facey's help has also been indispensable. He arranged legal access to hospital records, provided Oldsiana and answered many questions.

I am grateful to Lorna (Bradley) Stuckless for letting me peruse the Twillingate Museum's *Twillingate Sun* collection, and to her husband Gordon for explaining many of Dr Olds' inventions.

At least a score of doctors, nurses and former aides provided insight and information. Although all are named in the text (except those who requested anonymity), I want especially to thank Jessie Drover and her daughter Margo Evans, Edith Manuel, Thelma Christie, Elfreda Dalley, Irene Pardy and Linda Facey.

MUN's medical historian John Crellin, MD not only proofed drafts of early chapters but convened for me an informal seminar with St John's physicians who had known or worked with Olds. Other physicians who granted interviews or provided information were Drs Louis Lawton, Fred Woodruff, John Sheldon, Edward Shapter, Nigel Rusted, George Battcock, Cyril Walshe and Eileen St Croix. Drs Mike Maguire and Jesus Austria were also generous with hospitality and stories. Dr Gordon Thomas kindly proofed Chapter Twenty-One.

Among Dr Olds' co-workers, patients and friends I must single out Grace Sparkes, Marie Facey, Ivy LeDrew, Raymond ("Bud") Young, Hubert Vincent, Angus Dalley and especially Nellie Pardy for lending her late husband Frank's diaries and photographs. Others include Muriel (French) Small, the late Melvin Woolfrey, my niece Heather Saunders-Compton and her husband Larry, Uncle Donald Saunders, my brother Calvin and my late uncle Harry Layman.

Books like this seldom get written without the special skills of librarians and archivists. From start to finish, Angela Jenkins of Notre Dame Bay Memorial Hospital has been my capable guide. Others who helped were Anne Hart and Bert Riggs of Memorial University, Anne Slakey and William R. Day Jr of Johns Hopkins, Mrs June Schachter of McGill and Elizabeth Sutherland of Dalhousie University. Archivist Marillyn Loomis of Windsor's Loomis Chaffee School filled in details of John Olds' prep school years and proofed Chapter Three. Bonnie R. Waddell tracked down several of Dr Olds' medical papers. Norman Bethune's biographer Roderick Stewart helped clarify a point about Dr Charles Parsons' China excursion. Physicians Robert Ecke, Clement Hiebert and Jim Pittman, by granting permission to quote at length from their writings, added depth and flavour to the text.

The Hospital's 40th and 50th anniversary publications were useful, as was a well-thumbed 1960s copy of C. W. Taber's *Cyclopedic Medical Dictionary* from Notre Dame Bay Memorial's library. Among the scant literature of Newfoundland and Labrador medicine, I drew comfort from Gordon Thomas' *From Sled to Satellite*, Hedley Rolfe's *Water Down My Neck* and Tony Thomas' *Labrador Doctor,* and Richard Selzer, Eric J. Cassell and Lewis Thomas fed my soul.

I was pleased to receive Gloria (Chisholm) Olds' permission to quote from her book *In Green Pastures* and for her useful critique of Chapter Nineteen.

Finally, I thank the Canada Council, and my sponsors Grace Sparkes, Eric Facey and David Quinton, for the Non-Fiction award which helped buy me six months' leave to draft this book. This, with the help of Gerry Joudrey and Eric Robeson, moved it ahead at least two years.

It should be noted that any identified personal medical histories cited herein came not from hospital records, which are confidential, but from my own research and deductions. Admittedly some cases are atypical; by the same token they have become public property.

Gary Lloyd Saunders
Clifton, N.S.
May, 1994

Part I

Offing

Chapter One

Guts and Contentment:
Peter Troake's Story

"Belief in a doctor, any doctor, that's the thing."
— Captain Peter Troake

D r Olds and Twillingate Hospital were the last things on Captain Peter Troake's mind that chilly June morning in 1947 as he weighed anchor for Labrador and another summer's fishing. Standing in his greatcoat at the *Minnie B.*'s helm as she moved out into Durrell Arm, the short, energetic 38-year-old was thinking instead of his family, his crew, his vessel, of his provisions and what he'd forgotten, of whether the wind would breeze up, of how much ice they might meet above Cape John and if he would secure a good fishing berth this year.

Had all gone well with Captain Troake, Dr Olds might have glanced out the east windows of his second-floor Operating Room later that morning and seen the *Minnie B.* clearing Burnt Island with two or three other schooners. He had known and liked Peter a long time. The Troakes of Durrell and Hart's Cove were rough and ready fishermen and sealers—among the best. Peter was only six when he jigged his first quintal of cod. When he was nine, his father took him down to the Labrador with the Summerville floaters, where, in the long subarctic days, the boy quickly learned to split fish on deck and salt it below. Pete liked to tell John how, beating up to St John's that stormy fall, hull down with green Labrador Number One, he had been seasick all the way. After Grade Five he quit school to help his father. At sixteen, eldest of ten children, he was a full shareman on the *Lone Star* and proud of it.

Now as then, Peter Troake relished this moment of leaving a safe harbour, the moment when his boat began ever so slightly to lift to the ground swell, when the rigging started its faint, rhythmic creaking like a fiddler tuning up. But he would feel better once Burnt and Gull Islands were astern, when he could sling overboard like old ballast all the petty vexations of gearing up for a long voyage and fix his mind on the days ahead. His eyes twinkled in a smile. In nine days he would be 39. He had his own new schooner. Jim Hunby the builderman had finished her in four months two winters past. Last summer she fetched home 850 quintals in one trip. This year they might even fare better.

He had other cause to smile. Last winter he had installed a new 10 HP *Atlantic* auxiliary engine in the *Minnie B*. All his life he'd worked under sail; there was nothing like it. But Labrador was a far piece and the competition was too keen to let the wind call the tunes. Peter Troake was in a hurry. As his sleek black schooner clove the grey wind-lop and sent the scattered ice pans wallowing turquoise in her wake, the *Atlantic*'s pulsing bass stole under the treble cries of gulls and terns to sweeten his joy.

Experience had taught him caution, however. Five minutes of neglect could cook a new motor. Better check it one more time, he thought.

"We had about a 15- or 20-knot wind and the schooner was lickin' along pretty good, seven or eight knots. I went below to screw the grease cups down to make sure there was plenty of hard grease for this new motor. 'Twas on the starboard side, and the grease cups were on the inside, so I had to reach over. I had on a pair of Army pants from when I was in the Home Guard overseas. And when I leaned over, the coupling set-screw on the shaft caught and hooked on those pants.

"And it turned round and broke my left leg in half. I went down between two timbers about two feet apart. If my leg had brought up *on* a timber he would have broken again. As it was, my pant leg went around and around the shaft until it stalled this new motor.

"When I got clear of the shaft, my foot was up there by my shin, bottom up. I took my foot up in my hand and had a look. Right on my instep there was something sticking up about the size o' the top of my thumb. This was the small bone o' my leg, but I didn't know it. So I took hold of that and pulled it out. It was broken off and ship-lapped—sticking out so far on one side, less on the other.

"I got savage mad then. It was spite kept me from fainting, perhaps. I don't know what fainting is. I've been in a lot of trouble in my time, but never felt like I was going to faint. A person can't brag about it though, because tomorrow I might see something to faint about.

"Well, when they saw I was in a mess—feller at the wheel looked down and got frightened to death—I bawled out and told him to tell Herbie Weir, my second hand with me, to run her in to the Arm. There was a nice swell on, a nor'east wind. 'And when you gets in,' I said, 'you sing out for someone to take me off.'

"Just at this time my brother Allan was going up in the trap skiff, and as he come abreast, the fellow who had the wheel sung out and told him the skipper was killed. Frightened Allan right to death! So when Allan passed us by, he jumps onto the schooner—didn't tie 'er on or nothin'! Away goes skiff! Another fellow had to shut the engine off. That's how excited Allan was.

"Anyway, they got the boat alongside for to bring me to shore. 'Boys,' I said, 'take me up.' But when they went to handle me they didn't know how. Because there I was, my leg all torn away, and the foot lodged so that when they went to pick me up it just about fell off. And there it was, swingin' right off on a thread, and they afraid to touch it.

"I said, 'Boys, take ahold! If 'twas a fifty-six-pound weight on there it wouldn't stop you, would it?' But they were afraid. I reached down then and picked it up and put it to one side. Because you couldn't hurt me no more than I was already hurt, understand. I had all the hurt that I could have.

"Well, they put me on a handbar, with a mattress under and blankets over me, and they carried me over to Gillett's shop where there was a phone. There was not so many phones around then as now. Joe Elliott he come in, had a look at my leg and almost fainted off. 'Twas a Freeman man come and took me over to the Hospital. He belonged to the Hospital, was working there. He come and picked me up in a truck.

"Now, if you had a seen the blood! I never tried to stop it. I was going to, but said to myself, 'tis on the left side, and I might do damage. I've heard say that if you clamp it and didn't wrap the bandage right you could have trouble. So I said, 'Let 'er bleed.'

"But if you saw the blood that run out of Peter Troake you would not have believed it.... You should see the mess you can make with blood! When I hoisted my leg up I'd put blood the length of myself every time my heart would beat.

"Going over to the Hospital, coming up the hill, I was starting to feel a bit comfortable.... There was a light too, a dazzle, like when you rub your eyes too hard.... I started to feel right comfortable. Oh yes, that's how you die, you know. I haven't been dead yet, but I know how it is.

"They carried me in off the truck into the Hospital. And Dr Olds comes in. 'Doc,' I says, 'I got me leg broke.' He pulls back the blanket and takes a look.

"'Yes,' he says, 'and a damned good job you did on it too.'

"'Doc, you're goin' to have to cut off my leg, ain't you?'

"'Pete, I don't know. I want to try to save it, send you home on crutches with both your legs. But one thing I know for damn sure—if I try to save it, the ponds will be cracking before you get out of here. Are you game for that?'

"'If you are,' I says.

"'Good enough.' We shook hands.

"Then he says, 'One thing I'm afraid of—there's a piece of bone missing.'

"Right away I knew what he meant. It was the piece I took for a splinter of wood and hove down in the bottom of the boat. I told him and he sent an orderly who fetched it and cleaned it up. And with that we made for the Operating Room. On the way, one of the doctors said, 'We'll take off that foot before Christmas, Dr John.' Dr Olds only grunted.

"So they got me ready. My first cousin Rose Cooper was in the OR up there then and she said, 'Pete, b'y, when Dr Olds comes in he might have to cut off your leg.'

"Now I don't know much about Heaven, but I know all about taking this ether. In my life I was put to sleep nine times. I know about going to sleep, know how to sleep good, go to sleep comfortable. And I know how to go to sleep for punishment too. Get so much of the ether in you, get crazy too, sometimes. The last time they put me to sleep with that, the nurses had a job to hold me on. There was none of this modern anesthetic then.

"Anyway, when Nurse Manuel put the cone over my nose she said, 'Take a deep breath, now, and do this, and do that.' Finally I started to get comfortable again. And all the pain leaves me.... I said to Nurse Manuel—I was just as sensible as could be—'If there's anything any better than this, 'tis too good for Peter Troake.' Every pain was gone, see, every last twinge.

"Now Dr Olds liked me; I don't know why. I don't know why, but he loved me. And I loved him. Nobody was ever better to me than him; my mother and father could be no better. He was my old bosom friend. And there was no man around the Newfoundland coast he'd sooner do a job on than me.

"I wasn't timid, see. One time up there I said, 'Doc, if you was to tell me, "Pete, I got to take your head off and slew it round and you can walk backwards," I'd say, 'Sir, you do it.' I believed that much in he. Belief in a doctor, any doctor, that's the thing. They can do all they can for you and if you don't believe, it won't do a peck of good.

"'Twas a woman named Betty who belonged down there to Change Islands, she took me out of ether. After a while I heard somebody calling 'Mr Troake, wake up.' Now, I didn't want to hear anybody call me that. Never liked this "Mister" stuff. Mother called me Peter and that's what I wanted. Anyway, it was 'Mr Troake, wake up!' Seemed like I was quite some time listening to this. By and by I opened my eyes.

"'Has Dr Olds got my leg taken off?'

"'No.'

"'I don't believe it.' I was lying flat now, after taking that ether. 'Naw, I don't believe it.' I tried to sit up.

"'Oh, Mr Troake,' she said, 'you can't rise up, you got to 'bide flat.'

"I said, 'I got to see if that foot is taken off.' So she gives me a hand and lifts me up.

"The first thing I saw was my big toe sticking out of the bandage. Right there and then I knew what I was in for. I thought my leg would be taken off. I'd seen what a mess it was in, see. There was hard grease in this wound o' mine, there was pieces o' cloth, there was part of my sock—everything. I had picked out so much of it, but a lot still wasn't.

"Well, now, for Dr Olds to put this together for me to have to rear this leg again.... I thought, 'This is it. I'm in this hospital for a good long time.'

"I was there 11 months and 24 days; nine months on my back, never moved one inch only when the nurses moved me. All this time my leg was hoisted about three feet, and there was a shot bag, a twenty-five pound bag of shot, on the bottom of my foot down there, and sandbags on one side. The lobster pot, I used to call it. And there was a light—it gave off heat—that was shining on it.

"At first I was tormented. Then I said to myself, 'You were stupid enough to get into the net, so now you've got to 'bide here.'

"Sometimes when the nurses come in, I'd say, 'My dear, 'tis no good for you to look in that lobster pot now 'cause the feller got that pot robbed for long ago.' That's how I'd be.

"Dr Olds he'd come to see me three or four times a day. And at first he thought I was going to give up, that he'd have to take my leg off for to save my life.

"So the summer passed, and the fall. And the next spring Dr Olds goes to the ice again to look for the cause of Seal Finger. And when he went, every guy in the Hospital from one ward to the other was saying, 'Well, Dr Olds is gone, now we'm gonna die for sure....' I didn't think I was gonna *die*; but don't you think that we liked to see Dr Olds go. It was a selfish thing.

"Now I don't know who the other doctor was that took his place. I know McGavin was there. It was another one, just before Dr Olds come back, that X-rayed my leg. I didn't much care whether he did it or not; I wanted Dr Olds. I shouldn't have been like that.

"He wasn't gone very long before he comes back. 'Skipper,' he says, 'your leg is gonna come out good. Yes, Dr Olds will be pleased when he comes in.'

"By and by, Sir, in he comes. Don't know if he even went home when he come from the ice; up he comes.

"'Pete,' he says, 'you're gonna walk again!'

"I said, 'Doctor, I hear you. And I believe you.' I was sat up now; it was the only way I could think to keep going. And he says, 'Take the cast off and have a look. You're gonna cut that cast off.'

"'Can I?'

"'If you want to.'

"'I can do the job,' says I. 'But Doctor, don't you think it's going to be another operation to take that off?' I was half afraid of what I might see. They had it packed in tarry oakum for to keep down the stink. Before they did that, people couldn't hardly stand to walk by my room.

"'You've got to have it soaking wet first.'

"Well, he gave me something like a putty knife and they soaked the cast and there I was now, cutting it. I split it open all the way up. Probably I would have cut like blazes—I was so anxious to have it off—but Dr Olds warned me my leg might be ulcerated. Anyway, I cut it open from my big toe right on up.

"Now somebody had to pull that cast around for to bend it abroad, because it wouldn't soak wet right on me; 'twas fastened. And when my leg come out of that cast—if you were haulin' out me heart it couldn't have been no worse.

"And oh, if you had seen what I saw then! The X-ray didn't show what the flesh was like underneath; 'twas only the bone that showed up. When they took that cast off, even Dr Olds he got disgusted. It had been on so long, the cast ulcers were everywhere. And the linen that was wrapped around my leg under the cast—those ulcers had even grown out into that...arggh!

"He got down-hearted, the doctor did. I suppose he never thought it would be so bad.

"Well, we had to wait so long for those ulcers to heal up. For a while it was all one sore, then finally it was two. Three or four times he operated. The last time, the sore was down to the size of a fifty-cent piece. When he put the bones together that last time, he had to cut and ship-lap them.

"One day, after he got it to his satisfaction, he asked me to try my leg. But I was afraid to put my weight onto it. He said, 'For Christ's sake, Pete, put it to the floor. Put it whichever way you feel comfortable.'

"I did; it seemed okay. And after dodging round the bed once or twice I said, 'Doctor, why did you turn my foot in a little bit like that?'

"'Pete,' he said, 'I thought it would be better to have it turn in than turn out.'

"'Well,' I said, 'that sounds sensible too. Because if I'm goin' to the woods I won't need so big a path!' We had a good laugh.

"'Pete,' he said, 'that's better than an artificial leg.'

"'Yes, guaranteed, brother.' Your own leg is always better, even with a limp.

"After I was all better he said one day, 'Pete, who do you thank for your leg?'

"'Doctor,' I said, 'I thanks you and the Lord, Sir.'

"'Pete,' he said, 'guts and contentment.'

"'Well, no; I wouldn't say that,' I said. 'Because I could have all the guts I like and if you hadn't done the job you did do, I'd have lost my leg from gangrene.'

"So I got out of there with only a limp and a cane and a bill for $360.38. 'Twould have cost me $946.38 but I was on the Blanket Contract and that took up the slack. A patient don't want to get better and then get a bill that will kill him."

"Now if there was a meter put on that leg to measure the miles that I've a-covered on he since then, a person would be amazed. I had over fifteen vessels in my time. I was forty-nine years on the Labrador, up and down the Labrador all my life. And in 1950, when I lost the *Lady MacDonald* in the ice up in the Straits of Belle Isle with a heavy load of seals, we had to walk down the Straits nearly five miles to the *Linda May*. And after that I was on the *Christmas Seal* for twenty years.

"I'm not saying no other doctor could have done what Dr Olds did; I couldn't say that. I'm not saying he was the best. Nobody is the best; there is no *best*. I'll say *one* of the best, because he would try what another doctor wouldn't. There were people come from Montreal to get cured by him. There were people on the mainland that were told they couldn't be cured and they come to him. A lot of people he took chances on. They had to die anyway, but a lot are living today thanks to him. And I'm one of them.

"Because I guarantee you no doctor in Newfoundland would ever *try* to do what he did for me. Because I only had one inch—one inch—of good flesh left on my leg when I went in.

"That's why I say he and me and the Lord done it.

"But all Doctor Olds said was, 'Pete, guts and contentment.'"

Chapter Two

Connecticut Childhood

"Yesterday was sunday I dident go to church tho'."
— J. M. Olds at age eleven

The small, full-lipped blond boy stood haloed in April sunlight at the stairhead, fastening his grey woollen coat. As he mastered each button he lifted his head and bawled toward the bedroom: "Mama! John want downstairs now!" John McKee Olds, recently turned three, was ready for his afternoon walk. On this particular day in 1909, however, Mary Olds finally felt like spring cleaning. As she began to scrub a closet floor, another high-pitched summons echoed down the hall.

"You wait, John," she called. "There's nobody down there now. We'll go down pretty soon." In the ensuing silence the dark-haired woman's thoughts roamed the tall frame home she and Alfred had bought in 1903, the year they married and came to Windsor. Much as she liked Clark House on the Green, its steep stairs worried her. John couldn't even reach the handrails. And ever since that second bout with summer complaint last July, he had seemed sickly. Certainly he fell oftener than normal children. A doctor's daughter herself, Mary feared *Cholera infantum* with its diarrhea, vomiting, fever and dehydration. Several babies had died in other Connecticut towns last summer. It was a mercy she hadn't lost John.

Puzzled by the long silence, she stepped into the hall. John was coming toward her, head bent in thought. He stopped and looked up. For a long moment his blue eyes held hers.

"If *John* went down somebody would be there," he said gravely.

Mary put aside her mop, helped him down the stairs, got her coat and took her son for his walk.

The year John was born, America was falling in love with the automobile. It was said that young Henry Ford meant to produce thousands of identical, affordable horseless carriages just as Eli Whitney had done with guns. Alfred and Mary liked going to the New York auto show every January; everyone bought cars then because the autumn roads were so awful. That

Lichtman's
news & books & news & books & news

year they had fancied a roofless *King* roadster but couldn't afford it and came home disappointed. Alfred decided to build his own. On the way home he justified it to her: it would save them money; he wouldn't have to commute by train to the farm in Bloomfield six days a week; he was after all an engineer and a draftsman; two or three fellows in Hartford and Springfield were building their own.

For weeks the lean, dark 29-year-old had scoured Massachusetts for parts. From Boston he shipped home enough angle iron for the chassis; from Springfield and Worcester came wheel hubs, tires, a gas tank, a radiator, brass head lamps, a steering wheel. At Pittsfield he found sheet metal for the body. By November 24th he was ordering the engine from Continental Motors in Muskegon, Michigan.

That winter the garage had echoed to the clank of ball-peen hammer, whine of drill press, sputter of soldering torch. It was the music John Olds learned to walk to. By the boy's first birthday on March 27th, 1907, Alfred was bolting on the big headlamps and brushing on a second coat of gleaming black body paint. A fortnight later he took his wife and son for a spin around the Green, trailed by a noisy posse of dogs and children enchanted by the throaty braying of the car's rubber horn. Except for some overheating, the *King* had chugged along beautifully. They had never heard John jabber so much before.

Back home, laughing about the impromptu parade, the young couple heard a familiar honk. Frantically they looked around. Where was John? Then a car engine coughed. Alfred reached the *King* first, to find the boy grasping the steering wheel, his round face contorted in terror and delight. After the rescue, Alfred discovered that, when overheated, the engine *could* be started by pressing a cylinder buzz coil button. But what possessed the boy to do it? They thanked God the hand brake was on.

After they had all calmed down, Alfred photographed his son at the wheel. The boy named the monster "Ch-honk-mobile" and for weeks imitated the blat of its horn. It was John Olds' first of many adventures with machines.

Though not much for talking to people, John conversed easily with flowers, insects and stars. In 1910 Halley's Comet was impending. By mid-April the *Hartford Daily Courant* was running astronomical trivia next to advertisements for nostrums to guard against its supposed baleful effects. Evangelical preachers terrified their congregations with tales of Armageddon. In far-off Nova Scotia a woman drowned her two children in a well and dived in behind them. Mary shuddered and hugged the boy and his little sister Lois close; Alfred calmly explained it all.

At last, on the night of Tuesday, April 26th, the comet appeared. Amid a trilling chorus of spring peepers, Papa took his sleeping son, blanket and all, out to see the celestial visitor swing its mane in the solar wind. Gazing skyward, the boy shivered all over but not from cold. For weeks John couldn't sleep without this ritual. One night, fearing for his lungs in the damp night air, Mary went to rescue him, but retreated in silence at the sight of him rapt and warm in his father's arms. By early May the comet flared halfway across the heavens, its silvery hair entangling a thousand stars. In June it began to wither like a fading lily. Alfred broke the news of its departure gently, but for several nights the boy cried himself to sleep. The part about the comet's return in seventy-six years did nothing to console him.

That year the Olds bought forty acres of pasture and woodlot at Windsor Heights a mile north of town. They sold Clark House and moved to the country. Their property ran from Broad Street down to the railroad tracks and had an old tree-shaded farmhouse, a barn and outbuildings. To a small boy accustomed to street lamps, carriage traffic and velvet lawns, it was like going far away. But soon his memory of town playmates, of the daily visits of mailman and milkman, of ice cream from the corner store, were overwhelmed by the aroma of spicy hayfields, the loud dry whirring of cicadas, the warm moist breath of cows eating apples from his hand. His lifelong aversion to city life had commenced.

That fall a neighbour brought the newcomers a bushel of ripe Bartlett pears. A few days later Mary handed him the empty basket, saying, "John, I want you to return this. And son," she said, brushing hair out of his eyes, "remember how you enjoyed those pears and be sure to thank her very much." With a nod he ran off. Meeting the neighbour a few weeks later, Mary asked if her son had thanked her. "Oh yes," she said. "And more."

"Oh, dear—what did he say?"

"'And we'll have another bushel next week!'"

When John was five, Mary's legs crumpled with paralysis. Her doctor knew nothing of the minute polio virus that strips the spinal cord of insulation, scrambling its billion signals; but he knew its destructiveness. There was no cure, he told her. Privately he told Alfred that if it reached her lungs she might die. Complete bed rest and mild massage were all the defence he could offer.

For an active 31-year-old mother of two, this was a hard sentence. Albert helped with cooking and cleaning and laundry, but the farm demanded most of his summer days; town affairs kept him busy in winter. He telegraphed her mother, Ruth Hazen McKee in New Castle, Pennsylvania. The sixty-year-old Presbyterian widow was on the next train east. Mary Eva was her only child.

Mary resolved to walk again. First she would learn about her attacker. She got Alfred to comb the Hartford and New Haven libraries for medical books and she read them all. One day he bought her Mary Baker Eddy's

Science and Health, with Key to the Scriptures. It was a revelation. Mrs Eddy's calm and reasoned expositions on the spiritual nature of healing resonated in her weary soul as no Presbyterian or Episcopal preaching ever had. Having watched her doctor father John Cairns McKee heal the sick with little more than faith and love, she became a willing convert to Christian Science. The Olds had a pew in Grace Episcopal Church on the Green, but they were not strong churchgoers. For Mary's six remaining decades, Mrs Eddy's well-thumbed book would rest beside her Holy Bible. Slowly, over the next few months, through daily exercise and earnest prayer and by fending off well-meaning helpers, she learned to hobble about, first on crutches, then on canes. John would always respect her religious convictions, for he had seen the results.

About the time when she thought she might discard her canes, however, spinal meningitis struck. Bedridden again, she had to hire a live-in maid. Ruth McKee, having come for perhaps a year, was to remain in Windsor for the rest of her life. She was there for the birth of the Olds' third child in January 1914 and only left Mary's side for a pilgrimage to the Holy Land in 1919, the year before she died.

Among the worst effects of Mary's new disease—apart from recurrent fever, severe headaches and bowel problems—was intolerance to sunlight and noise. Her world shrank to one dim, quiet, downstairs room with drawn drapes. Reading had to be by dim light only. Her children's natural exuberance had to be curbed. John knew that his mother was fighting for her life. When the doctor came he listened intently; sometimes he asked questions.

On New Year's Eve, 1912, the year in which Joseph Lister the father of antiseptic surgery was to die, the year in which Harvard's great surgeon Harvey Cushing would publish another brilliant paper on the brain, Mary McKee Olds scored a medical triumph of her own. She went to a party. Alfred noted in his diary that she came home bone-weary but happy.

Neither the great Lister nor Dr Cushing could have explained it, but Mary somehow got better, did light housework, resumed shopping and tea and bridge parties with her neighbour and good friend Mrs Chamberlain, even took in the New York car shows again. When John caught lobar pneumonia in 1916, with coughing and high fever and delirium, she rallied all her strength to save him. She eased his chest pains with hot oatmeal poultices and on the critical ninth day she prayed all night by his sweat-soaked bed. Before dawn, his temperature suddenly fell to normal. When, a month later, he regained his strength, she breathed a prayer of thankfulness. During the influenza epidemic of 1917 she tended the children of her neighbours the Motts until their parents recovered.

That April, with the newspapers full of the *Titanic* tragedy, the Olds hired a contractor to build a two-story frame house on their new property.

Set well south of Broad Street, it overlooked a sweep of pasture and hardwoods and the Connecticut Valley beyond. In September they moved out of the farmhouse, which was later torn down. Until John's teens this pleasant house, standing alone amid woods and fields, was to be his home, and for years afterward a haven until it was sold around 1975.

Before the plaster was dry, he had left his mark. With Lois he sneaked into the ground floor pantry and they pressed their right hands with outspread fingers into the cool moist stuff. Using a nail, he inscribed their names below in careful block letters with the date, September 18, 1912. John's hand was smaller than hers but sported a thick ring on the middle finger.

His mother would never fully overcome her disability, nor be able to cope without domestic help. Yet so steely was her spirit—so much stronger than his father's—that he could never think of her as an invalid. To him she was a slow-moving, vibrant woman, a lovely lady of impeccable taste and mien, a warrior whom he admired immensely. Not until 1950 would she accept a motorized chair to help her up and down the stairs.

When Lois and he were little, they liked best the long winter evenings when the great river glistened like a pewter serpent under the cold stars and their parents told them stories. Sitting before the many-paned south window, Mother would point out the glow of Hartford five miles away and tell them about the big hardware store where Gramp Olds and Uncle Frank Whipple worked. Papa would tell them about the Amazon and the Seine, and the Nile where the Israelites once toiled in slavery. If they were too lively to sleep, or there was no school the next day, Papa would sometimes spin the tale of their twelfth century ancestor, the worthy thane Roger Wold, neighbour of Cedric the Saxon in Yolthorpe of Yorkshire. He would lead them down the long line that included John, a minstrel to King Richard the Lion Hearted, and John Le Old, manucaptor for Sir John de Langlelye, knight of the shire of Gloucester. He would mention another Roger Wold, the soldier who married Mary Talbot, niece perhaps of Sir John Talbot.

By now Lois would be asleep and Mary would take her to bed. Roger's and Mary's son John, Papa would continue, married Jane Eyton and in turn had a son named John. This John had become a priest and reformer and the friend of Bishops Latimer and Cranmer, but was disinherited by his angry father. Finally, said Papa, after much persecution the family abandoned Catholicism for the Church of England. Years later in Dorsetshire there was a Robert Ould who must have crossed the Atlantic, for his name appeared in Windsor, Connecticut in 1667 as an apprentice to one Jacob Drake. Prospering there, he was granted fifty acres of land in 1670. After recounting female lines—the Hanfords, Grangers, Walkers, Barnes and Webbs—Papa always ended with Archibald Olds and his son Nathan, father of Grandpa Alfred Allen Olds.

When John turned six, Alfred hired a private tutor so Mary could keep him home a while longer. Then for the next six years he attended Stony Hill school, a sturdy little brick building just to the east. He helped raise and lower Old Glory on its stubby staff and later took turns lighting and stoking the wood stove. Later, he walked Lois to and from school.

John's artistic ability was soon noted. Like Alfred he could visualize, draw and construct. One day he brought home a coloured pencil drawing of a squirrel in a tree. Mary treasured it all her life. In 1914, the year Mary Alfreda—"Tutie" to family and friends—was born, Papa built a workshop garage. Here he and his son would spend many happy hours. One day in 1916, watching Mother try to whip cream with a clumsy hand beater, John was startled to hear her yell, "Oh, I hate this thing!" and to see it fly across the kitchen. He picked it up and wandered off, absently licking the cream. A few days later he gave her a mechanical beater made from copper wire and a wind-up motor off his toy truck. When Grandma Lizzie and her husband Alfred A. Olds came and built a new house next door that year, he made one for her too. Mary used hers for nearly ten years.

They had a Victorian upbringing. One day when John was misbehaving, Alfred made him cut a switch from the hedge and whipped his bare bottom. The boy did not bawl, but hated the double humiliation. "The husband and father ruled the family and his word was law," said Tutie. "It was as Mother and Papa had been reared by their parents. We accepted it, never felt threatened or held back or warped by the strict rules. The standards they set were always reliable guidelines."

To his sisters John could be irritatingly aloof. So dour and intent was he that Lois and Tutie treasured their rare moments of closeness with him. Lois remembered his teaching her to play golf on the nine-hole course beyond Grandpa Olds' property, and letting her ride his pony. Tutie would cherish the winter afternoon when he taught her how to build an igloo. Most of the time he preferred hunting frogs with other boys in the nearby marsh or playing trapper in the woods. One day he brought a dead skunk into the house and wanted to skin it there. When his parents ordered him out, he was disgusted and went and buried it in the woods.

In summer John saw little of his father. Most mornings Alfred had left for Bloomfield before he was up, usually even before Grandpa Olds and his chauffeur left for Hartford. Papa supervised the Negro mule drivers who cultivated his long rows of tobacco plants, and he watched over the moveable shade panels and the irrigation pipes. Too much or too little rain, he said, or a touch of frost, could ruin the crop. Often he got back late.

His father once told him with a hint of pride that Grandpa Olds and Lizzie's brother Frank Whipple had helped pioneer shade-grown tobacco in Connecticut. Even after nearly forty years, he said, Olds and Whipple still ranked among the State's top growers of the thin leaves used for wrapping cigars, and they ran a big fertilizer business besides. Sometimes during summer holidays John would work on the farm, but to Alfred it always seemed his son was more interested in toads and beetles than in farming.

Alfred also attended a lot of meetings. He was a trustee for Windsor's new prep school, the Loomis Institute, from the time it opened in 1914. He was on the local Library Board and a Justice of the Peace. John noticed that whenever Papa was hearing a case, he was distracted and no fun to talk to. He was better company in the workshop. There, amid the smell of varnish and lumber, with saws, planes and hammers gleaming along one wall and wrenches, chisels and drill bits along another, they were content. The boy watched, chin in hand, as his father expertly planed pine wardrobe doors or inserted intricate mother-of-pearl flowers into rosewood jewellery chests. Best of all, he liked to watch Papa paint scenery backdrops for the local Drama Study Group, and then go see him act in the play. Years later, people who had seen both John's and his father's workshops would remark on the similarity.

Sailing was another of Alfred's passions. From the 1880s on, the Olds and Whipples had owned a cottage—or rather two, later combined—on Long Island Sound. Moneyed New Yorkers and Bostonians had grabbed the choicest properties long before, so the families had felt lucky to get a shore lot from local farmer Norman Bond. Black Point, halfway between Old Lyme and New London, became their summer reprieve from the Connecticut Valley heat. For Alfred and his younger siblings Edith, Frank, Edna and Herbert, the Point *was* summer. Wiry and strong, he soon became an able sailor.

While Papa and Uncle Frank and their brothers and sisters sailed, Johnny spent whole summer afternoons swimming and sunning on the nearby beach. He lolled for hours with a glass of lemonade, reading a penny novel or watching Papa's homemade windmill creakily lift cool water from the well. On clear days he could barely see, far to the east, the thin blue line of Long Island's Montauk Point. He wondered what lay beyond. He couldn't wait to go sailing with his father.

Mary enjoyed the Point too, but she noticed that the males had the most fun, while the womenfolk spent a lot of time in the hot kitchen, often in each other's way. Moreover, she did not share her husband's passion for salt water. She mistrusted her cane on the often slippery docks and decks, and she disliked being helped up and down. When his mother sailed it was out of wifely duty.

Truth to tell, she much preferred trains. On a train, even with the children along, she could escape housekeeping and troublesome maids, be waited *on* for a change. She especially liked to bundle them and her mother into a Pullman and go home to New Castle.

The overnight journey to western Pennsylvania was arduous for her, but always, as the train gathered speed and leaped the Delaware and thundered across the keel of New York State, she felt a girlish elation. She would show the children landmarks. They would sing silly verses to the rhythmic clack of wheel on track, wheel on track. She exulted in the mournful howl of the whistle, the thoughts of lamplit farms bearing other lives, the cradle-like sway of the softly lit night coaches, the sudden midnight roar of bridges and tunnels, even the gritty taste and acrid sting of coal smoke when someone opened a window or a door. It was an adventure.

She never felt truly embarked until they had left the Susquehanna's sinuous valleys and swung southwest again toward Lake Erie. Then she sometimes sat back and told John and Lois about her three years at National Park Seminary in Washington, D.C., about the magical Easter vacation of 1900 when she'd met a dashing young Yale engineer at the Old Point Comfort Resort in Virginia. Alfred was supposed to enter the family business, she said, but became instead a draftsman for a Newport News shipbuilding firm. She sighed when he told how Dr McKee's death that year at fifty-four had halted her schooling. Three years later, at her mother's church in New Castle, she and Papa had married.

To John's young eyes, Mother never seemed so happy as on these Pennsylvania trips. Privately Mary grieved that Alfred could not accompany them, but she was glad he wasn't peddling dusty bags of phosphorus and lime around New England for his father. Perhaps soon he could sell the farm. Meanwhile, they would summer in Pennsylvania without him.

Thus for John a pattern formed. As soon as school was out, Mother took him to New Castle. Then in mid-August, when the cornfields shimmered in white heat and sleep became an ordeal, they escaped to the Point until school began. If the boy wondered why an engineer spent his summers growing tobacco, he never asked.

It was during those vacations that John began to write letters home. Infrequent and brief as they were, these writings became his journal, mirroring year by year his unfolding life. The first ones were written to Alfred around 1915. His trademark directness is already evident [spelling and punctuation unedited throughout]:

Dear Papa

I am on the train now it is seven oclock we have been 160 miles, The paper man didn't come through all day. We had a good supper. I had fish and mother and Lois had meat. Tutie is rather cross tonight. We are going by the hudson river now, we have passed Albany the car rocks so I can't right desent I just didn't want you to forget that you ow me a dollar

Lovingly
John

One can imagine Alfred, absent on a Caribbean business trip to sell tobacco, smiling at this: "I wish you wouldn't send any more of cocanut [sic] cards if you half to do anything I wish you bring me a cocanut."

In 1917 Alfred bought his first real sailboat, a 30-foot ketch. Discarding tradition, he named it *Joloma* from the children's first names. As New London on the Thames River boasted a long jetty and a store, it became his base for sailing to Block Island and both sides of the Sound. When Johnny reached the age of eleven Papa took him along, as he would later take Lois and Tutie. John disliked having his sisters aboard because Papa seemed to pamper them. One morning when he heated water for Tutie to wash in, John spat over the side in disgust.

One of Mary's New Castle cousins was Fannie Hazen Harbison, who with her husband Charlie had a farm near town. Johnny helped Uncle Charlie stack hay and milk cows and in his spare time swung from a rope in the barn. Mary's favourite cousin, Oliver Shannon, an insurance broker with Dougherty and Shannon, took him swimming and golfing, and on rainy days let him use the office typewriter.

Toward the end of July in the last year of the Great War, Alfred was puzzled to receive an envelope marked "United States Underwriters' Policy, Crum and Foster, General Agents, New York." Inside was John's first typed letter. It overflowed with news of the Harbisons' crops, of setting out cabbage plants, of swimming at the YMCA with "Uncle Ollie," and of Gammie McKee's "rumetisim." A week later, on the letterhead of Milwaukee Mechanics' Insurance Company (German Underwriter's Department), he told Alfred "Mother wants some letters." He went on to describe a near drowning, told how burglars stole 23,000 cigarettes from a nearby store, and recorded his first purchase of two science magazines that would remain his lifelong favourites, namely *Popular Science* and *Popular Mechanics*.

John's use of Uncle Ollie's business letterheads revealed a curious liking for impressive stationery. All his life John never used plain writing paper if he could help it. As a child he was fond of his mother's decorative notepaper. In prep school he was to have his own printed notepaper; it showed a boy driving two yoked oxen towing a disabled Model T, followed by a crowd of irate passengers. At Yale he would affect a fine rag paper letterhead, reprinted with each change of address. Travelling, he always used hotel stationery. During his four years at Hopkins he seldom wrote on anything but Medical School letterhead. It was something more than thrift.

In the Pennsylvania countryside his interest in natural history blossomed. That August he spoke of making a butterfly net for each of the Harbison kids. "They have caught 70 butter-flies this spring, I caught about half of them." He also saw many horses and loved them all, especially "one around town that I would like to have to ride, it was about as tall as I was."

That fall his parents bought him a Shetland pony named "McDuff," and a few years later a western bronco.

His letters began to display an eye for human foibles.

Uncle Ollie wants to use the typewriter, so I have to let him.... Gammie found a bedbug in our bed at the hotel and she killed it.... Yesterday was sunday I dident go to church tho. In the after noon we had planed to go to Stoneboro but it rained about noon and scared Gammie so she wouldent go....Ruthe Harbison is trying to teach me how to play the violin it is some job.... I can milk a cow now I did it twice out at Uncel Charlies. Tell the rest of them I will write when it gets cooler.

There is also a growing pride in physical courage. "Yesterday I swam about half a mile without stopping," he told Alfred. He talked of learning to play tennis with his friend Jim Gordon over at the Afot's farm. Discovering that one could slide down the hay fork rope and land harmlessly on a load of hay, he dared Jim to try it.

I did it several times and then he tried it (Jim weighs 135lb.) he let the roap slac so he wouldent have to slide so far but when the roap titened it gave him a gerk and he couldent stop him self and it took all the skin off his hand and made a couple of blisters on his hands and I guess he was kind of mad at me for telling him to do it; he asked me if it hurt and I told him it dident....

During the summer of 1919 he discovered Aunt Essie's library. Pleased, she lent him *The Harvester*, Gene Stratton Porter's recent novel about a wise herb gatherer and a kindly physician. He read it all morning in her parlour and finished it at the hotel after midnight, sleeping in so late the next morning that Mother thought he was ill. Mary and Alfred had fostered a love of reading, but it was Aunt Essie who opened the treasure chest. Ten years later when she died, he would be well launched on his habit of reading a book a day.

"Gee, I wish my Loomis marks would come," he wrote Alfred in August. "Please send them as soon as they arrive." For the first time, he signed himself "J. M. Olds."

Chapter Three

Loomis and Yale

"We need leaders. You ought to make a good one."
— William Card, Loomis Teacher

As John trudged down Windsor Avenue and took Island Road across the tracks to the Loomis Institute in September of 1919, he was following a well-worn career path. His parents weren't openly shoving him toward Yale—though "shove" was the word he would later use—it was a tacit understanding. Hadn't Papa and Uncle Frank gone to Yale? The expectation was simply *there*, like a mountain on his mental horizon, a peak to be scaled before any real life could begin.

If it is hard to discern Twillingate's fiercely independent Dr Olds in the quiet, blazered boy who entered Loomis that autumn, it is because we have forgotten the power which Victorian families exerted over their offspring in such matters. They sent their sons to prep schools expressly to groom them for great universities like Harvard, Yale or Princeton. They packed their daughters off to finishing schools like Wellesley (where Lois would later go), Smith and Vassar for similar reasons. God willing they would all become a credit to their families, and, if not leaders, then intelligent followers.

It seems odd that John Olds took so long to rebel.

Although Loomis had opened its doors only five years before, to John it seemed oddly familiar. Before and during its construction, Papa had kept his family informed of the school's progress. Rustling his *Courant* for silence, he would recite items about "a school of much prominence for Windsor," "Windsor's building boom" and so on. He liked to talk about Windsor's famous Civil War colonel and native son John Mason Loomis, the Chicago lumber baron whose fortune, with that of his brothers and sister, had made the school possible. Papa had once or twice taken his son to the campus on "The Island"—so named, he said, because the Farmington and Connecticut rivers met there and sometimes flooded the surrounding land. All John remembered were the bellowing steam shovels, the shouting workmen and the smells of mud, lumber and wet cement.

Now as he descended Island Road, the campus spread before him seemed like one of Papa's more elaborate backdrops, a model town in red, white and green with raked paths, manicured lawns and toy buildings. Through the trees a cupola glinted coppery in the sun. He knew by heart how the New York architects Murphy and Dana had "transformed the old run-down Loomis farm into a gem of Georgian architecture," and how the heirless Loomis family had in 1874 successfully petitioned the State for a college in its name but couldn't build it until the Colonel's wife Mary died in 1910.

If John was nervous it was because he disliked being late. Sprinting the last hundred yards, he quietly joined over two dozen other freshman boys as they shuffled through Founder's Hall, peered into the administrative offices and chapel and examined the third floor classrooms that would be their headquarters for the year. He was surprised that the inner quadrangle was larger than a football field. It was enclosed on either side by a three-story dormitory and to the south by the William Loomis Dining Hall. John was more impressed with the towering furnace stack, which until now he had seen only from Windsor. Past the dining hall, workmen were finishing the Infirmary. Beyond that were fields of corn and potatoes being tended by students from the Institute's agriculture program. "Victory Gardens for the war effort," their guide explained, "soon to be resown to alfalfa and hay."

Like most New England prep schools, Loomis was a scion from older roots. Transplanted across the Atlantic, the English boys' school system had fortunately shed much of the caste-like cruelty described by alumni like James Joyce, C. S. Lewis and George Orwell. New World schools embodied more of the original ideals, which G. K. Chesterton described as "a rich sense of romance...a strong sense of the absolute necessity of some significance in human life." The Loomis family motto, "Ne Cede Malis"—roughly, "don't give in to evil"—preserved some of this knightly ring.

However, blood and money still fed the ancient roots. The school's first student was a Loomis from Virginia. In John's first year, five Windsor families alone donated $53,000. A. A. Olds and Frank Whipple likely gave substantial donations too. A prime reason for building such schools in the first place was the swamping of America's public school system by immigrant children. While tuition at Loomis was free, board and lodging and books and lab fees all cost money. This and the expectation of donations effectively excluded most immigrant families. And when non-Christian children enrolled, they felt uncomfortable. Even the best New England private schools had what Dr Hans Zinnser called "a deep Anglo-religious atmosphere" that was focused in the compulsory morning chapel service.

By speech and apparel, any Boston charwoman would have labelled Johnny "Upper Crust." In fact his parents were of fairly modest means. But as a day student living at home, he escaped the hazing and other dormitory abuse which sometimes plagued newcomers. An outgoing, sports-minded boy, within a fortnight he had made several new friends and knew dozens of students by name. While most were from Connecticut, he met boys from New York, New Jersey and Massachusetts, from Minnesota and Georgia and even one from Cuba. Johnny was enrolled in the college preparation course, but other boys were taking agricultural science, business and manual training such as carpentry and plumbing. The few girls on campus were offered the same options plus Domestic Science, but had their own preceptress, classroom and dining area.

His teachers impressed him from the start. Headmaster Nathaniel Horton Batchelder, a Harvard alumnus with eight years experience, taught English and Physics and coached football and tennis. Dr John Edmund Barss, a tall, austere Classics scholar who arrived the same year as John, shared Mr Batchelder's belief that "if the time comes when you can recognize a Loomis boy by his speech, by his clothes, or, still more fatally, by a standard attitude of mind, on that day we shall have failed." Though John disliked languages, Rene Cheruy's colourful French lectures were a treat. "Monsieur," a decorated war hero and former secretary to the great sculptor Rodin, loped about the campus in all weathers swinging a cane which students learned to respect. Ulrick B. Mather taught Mathematics and Manual Training. John's favourite was music master William Cogswell Card, a Canadian organist who would become a mentor and lifelong friend.

Loomis offered incentives for good marks. "D" students had to attend all study periods and couldn't represent the school in any public contest; "A" students could skip study periods and visit the village alone any free afternoon. John's grades hovered in the Bs and Cs the whole four years he was there. In sophomore year he shone for a while at General Science, even attaining a short-lived "A" status. As a senior he managed some Bs in Biology, Algebra, Geometry and Chemistry. But in Latin, English and French he sometimes dived to D or E. Even so, Headmaster Batchelder noted on his Senior mid-term report that "Two weeks special work ought to bring John's Latin up to 60 as Yale requires."

While Mary saved all her son's report cards, few of his school compositions remain except a short essay written at age fifteen for English IIIA. It described a Welsh chieftain who, in the year 1400, led a successful uprising against English rule.

> Glendower the magician is what he called himself and gradually many people began to think that he really had magical powers. When he was born he says that his father's horses were found standing belly deep in blood, and that the sky was all aflame and that the earth trembled. He was a noble Scotchman by birth, and a soldier of much renown. He was muchly feared by most men, partly on account of his magical powers and partly on account of his physical powers.

Three times the king had led troops against him and each time he had, supposedly, called upon heaven and brought down such awful storms that the king's army was driven back. He was also warned by his magic that it was unsafe to help the Percies and the others who were rising against the king, until a period of about two weeks had elapsed. This was probably beneficial to him as he might have been beaten. His enemies often spoke of him as a fiend and King Henry at one time spoke of him as that "wild and irregular Glendower." Hotspur was about the only man who could talk frankly to him. Mortimer, his son-in-law, was much afraid of his anger and did everything to keep him from being aroused.

John's admiration for the embattled chieftain in his misty mountains is apparent. There is also recognition of the power which special gifts confer. And the last sentence might have been written by one of John's scrub nurses from the 1940s. English Master George Cherry gave him a C.

Like all good prep schools, Loomis also encouraged students to take part in social and cultural activities, and above all in vigorous sports. There was also an annual medal for "Industry, Loyalty and Manliness." However, John showed little interest in the Choir, Glee Club or Mandolin Club, or in Jazz Band and Orchestra. He steered clear of the prestigious Student Council and student publications like the *Handbook, The Log* and the yearbook *Loomiscellany*. There is no mention of his joining the drama group or of his helping with the school's efforts for charity.

But each autumn he faithfully tried out for intercollegiate football and hockey. Always he was consigned to the midget teams. "At Loomis," he said ruefully, "I never topped ninety-nine pounds." Still, on Phil Cobb's football team in the Junior League playoffs he earned a reputation for having a "quiet way of not letting down when the going was rough." He also became a skillful baseball and tennis player.

As a keen outdoorsman, Johnny's real niche was Cobb's new Darwin Club, which offered its fifty members radio, gun and natural history divisions. On field trips to nearby woods and marshes Johnny learned the wild flowers so well that decades later he could take Lois' little granddaughter Beth to the woods and name them all for her. The Club project he enjoyed most was making a model steam locomotive that ran on compressed air.

Often in ensuing years the Darwin Club and its alumni would raise sizeable sums for his beleaguered hospital.

In his sophomore year Papa gave him a .410 shotgun. Johnny would rise at 5:30 AM, take the canoe and hunt ducks in the Farmington marshes before breakfast. One November morning he and Bill Card upset the canoe and arrived at the school wet, shivering and empty-handed.

Though John was athletic and popular, it wasn't girls and partying that kept his marks low. He dated hardly anyone but Nancy Chamberlain, the girl next door. Their mothers hovered over the romance like watchful hens. In any case, Loomis girls were already a vanishing species when he arrived. Headmaster Batchelder had declared his intent even before the school opened: "It seems to me impossible to allow either boys or girls natural freedom if many of both sexes are living together on a sixty acre lot." By admitting females as day students only, he effectively barred them from living on campus and from using the gymnasium. Soon, young women stopped applying. The last few were graduated with John's class in 1923. Later the town sued Loomis for breach of charter and girls got their own Chaffee campus on the Green in 1927.

In March 1922, John's classmates and Bill Card gave him a surprise birthday party. He had begun secretly to smoke and one of the presents was a pack of Pall Malls. That week Mary invited Bill to dinner. When John left the table feeling ill, Card innocently remarked, "Maybe it's the cigarettes we gave him for his birthday." Mary was so angry that she scolded them both and hid the Pall Malls.

Days later, on his Easter break in Boston, John's teacher wrote him a long letter and offered some advice. "I hope you woke up yesterday with a better feeling in your abdominal cavity. Of course if you *will* lead a high life, staying up late nights, etc., etc., you must expect to be sick. Have you found your Pall Malls yet?" He again apologized and urged his protégé to put off smoking for a few years at least.

> Above all, don't try to deceive her. I took for granted that you were allowed.... Please consider [this] as good advice from one good friend to another.... You don't have to do what some other fellows in school do in order to be a good sport & keep their interest—*you don't.* It's *easy* to follow a custom, it's a damn sight harder to *lead* sometimes. We need leaders. You ought to make a good one.
>
> Sincerely your friend,
> W. C. (Bill) Card

John did not smoke again until well into his college years.

That spring of 1923, he studied hard for college entrance examinations. "Johnny did nobly!" Batchelder exclaimed on his June report card. Yale accepted him and Papa beamed. The next move in Papa's plan was the Sheffield School of Science. John did not object, and Mary swayed her son neither one way nor the other.

In his last summer before college, he drove Gramp and Lizzie Olds and Alfred's sister Edith on a vacation trip to northern Maine. In a long letter to Mary from Greenville Junction his lifelong impatience with "foolishness" is already evident.

The scenery is very beautiful here and everything is fine if you don't listen. Gramp can't hear so very well and Edie & Mamman are afraid to talk loud enough for him to hear. Then he says, "What are you whispering at me for?" Then they say "Never mind," and that makes him madder. You should see Edie & her spyglass. For the first two days she squinted through it at the menues but since then she has been continually jawing it and everything else. [Her glasses] wouldn't stay fastened very well and that makes her mad. Also the spring is too tight and the lenses too strong.... Yesterday we went on the boat to Capers, about an hour's ride on the boat.... A fellow brought in one fish that weighed 1/2 pound and the whole joint went wild....

Today we are going to the other end of the lake to the big dam. It ought to be a pretty ride and maybe we will see some deer. Aunt Edie says 'I don't see why we don't see any deer,' looking in some people's barnyard probably. 'John goes so fast no wonder we can't see anything.' Maybe she thinks deer are as stupid as she is.

One night I thought I would be nice and take Edie to the movies as they were very anxious to go. [The movies] were rotten but they dident seem to realize it for if they had they surely would have said so. A fire horn blowed out in the street when the new orchestra was playing their only piece. I dident mind the horn any more than the orchestra....I must stop now as it is exactly time for the dining room to open and I expect Gramp to come & hurry me up.

"Yale was a family tradition, so there I went," said John in 1974. The journey down to New Haven took less than two hours. The city seemed almost as sleepy as Windsor. With Pop going on about landmarks and fraternities and his own Class of 1900, they had to ask the way to the Sheffield residence hall. Striding to and fro across the sunlit flagstones with trunks and boxes, Alfred noted with satisfaction how remarkably alike their long-legged shadows looked. John thought the room smelled stale, and raised a window for air. He felt sorry for the dead flies trapped inside the screen.

His roommate was "West" Harcourt, a grandson of the Smith & Wesson Firearms people and a good fellow. On October 9th John wrote home:

Everything is getting more settled and I like it better. Today we had our first polo practice on horses. The horses weren't much. The one I had...would only turn to the left and would hardly gallop at all. The regular polo ponies are dandies though.

Polo was a breakthrough. In his words, he was "still athletically inclined, but lightweights were a dime a dozen—so no football, no hockey, no nothing until I found a way for the horse to do the work and made the polo team for 4 years."

For the rest of that year his letters are mostly reports about polo, watching football, grades, money, social engagements and thank yous for goodies from home. His favourite parcels contained candy, cookies and nuts. For a while he went home almost every weekend, but train fare cost too much and there were games he wanted to see. He dated Nancy and a few other Windsor girls. Occasionally he enquired about former Loomis classmates or about Lois and Tutie. Always he was concerned for Mary's health.

With colder weather and firmer turf the polo teams moved outdoors. "Yesterday," he wrote Alfred in November, "we played polo on horses without any saddle and…had to stand on the horse's back and turn around backwards and get on and off while the horse was running…." He kept trying out for contact sports like hockey. In pistol practice with Colt .45s that fall he scored 62 out of 70. A week later on the rifle range he plugged 91 out of 100. In December, dropped from the hockey trials, he found solace in making the varsity polo team with a good pony under him. The following spring, at 134 pounds, he would try out for racing shell crew and for track and field: "I passed…the 2-mile run, 100 yd dash, hand spring & a couple more, but have been up against 2 tough ones. I tried the 100 yd swim Sat. but hadn't been in the water since camp couldn't do it fast enough & the pole vault is also bad, seeing as I never tried it before. I hope to pass them though pretty soon."

His pre-Christmas grades were better than at Loomis—70 in English, 75 each in History and French, 80 in Chemistry and 85 in Math. "The [English] master said I surprised him…. There have been 17 fellows kicked out already on account of poor marks, so I think I am pretty lucky…hope you and Pop will be satisfied."

Writing home became a chore. "I haven't anything to say and it is late," he wrote after Christmas, "but I suppose I had better write something, n'est ce pas?" A month later he said, "I don't know what to say but I suppose if I don't write you will get mad." Or, "I am sorry I didn't write but I didn't realize how long it had been." Then, "I wish I could think of something to write about but I don't seem to be able to. Why don't you make me some divinity fudge or something, or make Lois do it?" Almost every letter he wrote Mary for the rest of his life would open with some such apology. Teasing five-year-old Tutie, he wrote, "I really hate to waste the paper to write to you but after such a nice letter as you sent me I feel I must." Birthdays he usually forgot, but with Mary's he felt especially guilty "because I know you wouldn't forget mine." That March his mother commanded him to write once a week, thus ensuring at least one letter a month. "Mother just lived for letters from John," Tutie would recall years later.

In mid-May Mary received a breathless three-pager which read in part:

This morning when I got the news on the front page was a paragraph of those who got numerals and the polo team got theirs and so I will be able to wear a crew hat with a 1927 on it and also a nice white sweater.

I can get a sweater can't I? Don't you think I will look swell? You had better tear up this letter, but I am so happy that I got them. There weren't many given this year and only championship teams got them. I suppose I will be awfully stuck up now.

Mary had not lost him to Yale. He relied on her for everything. Could she have some calling cards printed for him? Find him a job in the bank in Windsor? Get Pop to let him have the old car for the summer? Can she board three fellows for the prom weekend and advise as soon as possible? "Mother, could you send me $25.00 as soon as possible without mentioning the fact? I can pay you back when a fellow pays me.... "

He even let her choose his prom dates. "I wish you could tell me of a girl to take; Nan can't possibly come so I am rather in a mess." He admits to lining up a Loomis prom date for Lois so he wouldn't have to take her. "Will you please ask Lois to give me a good description of Gene Poindexter and to send me a picture of her if possible—I am awfully particular, you see."

Alfred, his own father unwell since early spring, missed his son. He would show up unannounced, prompting comments like: "I was rather surprised to see Pop down here. I asked him if he didn't have to go to Boston on business this week, but he didn't take it at all...." When Pop delivered his hockey skates in person, John grumbled, "I don't see any reason why he couldn't have sent them—I asked soon enough."

As expected, John passed the final examinations. Since Olds and Whipple had no summer job for him in Hartford, he took the bank teller job in Windsor. Weekends and evenings he tinkered with the old car. In August Pop and he sailed in *Joloma* to Long Island, Greenport, Sag Harbour, Black Island and Newport. Sometimes they took along one or two of his classmates. Later they would venture to Martha's Vineyard, Nantucket and Provincetown, and once as far as Christmas Island in Maine. These were probably their best adult times together, times when he learned much about the sea and boats that would stand him in good stead in Newfoundland.

No sooner had he resumed classes than he had to return home for Gramps' funeral. It was held at the Asylum Hill Congregational Church on September 17th. Then the pattern of his freshman year resumed, to be repeated with minor variations for the next three years. While his grades remained average, he seemed less worried about failing. He delighted in small triumphs like being chosen for the first polo team, but cheerfully swallowed his disappointment when another player took his place at an important game in Cincinnati. "The fellow deserves it more than I do," he told Mary. "Maybe I will get something just as good by not going...."

During the summer of 1925 he worked in Maine at Camp Winona, run by Loomis' Philip H. Cobb and his brother. His Christmas marks that year were "the best I ever got: Econ. A, Eng. B, Mil. Science B+, Physiology B, Anthropology B and Chem C+."

In the spring of 1926 he showed his first real spark of independence. Unknown to him, Nancy had tried to arrange a birthday party for him at her house. He was now seeing other girls—the names of Dorothy Styles, "Swiss" and Liz appear often in his letters—and probably saw it as a ploy. Mrs Chamberlain's involvement made matters worse. On the 20th he scrawled a note to Mary: "I would much rather be home all alone—no guests Sat. night. If Lois and I got any invitation from Mrs Chamberlain please say you want me to *stay home*.... Oh! these damn petty mix-ups." A few weeks later he explained: "You know I must be independent."

On April 1 the *Courant* carried this story:

HURT IN CRASH

John McKee Olds, son of Alfred Olds of Windsor, a student of Yale University, and Nancy Chamberlain were badly cut about the face when the car in which they were riding struck a telephone pole at Station 14, Windsor avenue, about 12:30 o'clock this noon. They were travelling towards Hartford when a truck driven by Harry Lerner of Bellevue street, Hartford, turned into a gas station just as Olds turned to pass the car in front of him. He could not avoid it. Both cars were damaged.

He spent until early August at a Reserve Office Training Camp near Washington, D. C. He liked battle tactics, map and compass and firearms, but despised parade drills and continual inspections. "Next Thurs we go on an overnight & have a sham battle on the way with the regulars. We camp about 15 miles from here and come back the next day. It is a tough job...." While the cadets were in Washington, he swam across the Potomac "to where a bunch of yachts were anchored but the people were not very hospitable & didn't ask us aboard for tea as we hoped so we had to swim back. The river is a little over a mile wide." An irrepressible side was beginning to emerge, one which would prompt him to swim across Twillingate's frigid harbour on a bet, send a silly telegram to Queen Elizabeth, and wear a top hat and tails on hospital rounds.

Back at Yale, he finished ninth among ten candidates for intercollegiate cross-country running trials, ignoring a bad stomach to make the team. Indifference to pain would become his hallmark. He was also learning how to do more than one thing at once. "This Physical Chem class is very boring—the proff [sic] is terrible & isn't saying anything, & of course I don't like to waste time, so if you can excuse this paper you will have a letter."

Under the pressures of Senior year, his letters became cursory and infrequent. Mary, coping with two daughters, an increasingly testy husband and his even testier widowed mother, felt neglected and she told him so. "You should know," he replied in February, "that you have not failed in any way & I think you by far the biggest success in the whole family. If I don't come, please don't feel badly as it will be because I have to play polo or study. Love, Johnnie."

After Christmas, his father and Uncle Frank both began to drop hints about medical school. John shrugged and said the thought of more university depressed him. If he had to go, he said, he would choose the Massachusetts Institute of Technology in Cambridge. Or, even better, take a year off and see the world. Pop and Uncle Frank harped on medicine all the more. Mary, remembering what it had done to her father, told them to let Johnny decide for himself. Alfred pointed out that he should apply anyway in case he later changed his mind.

At last, to placate Pop and Uncle Frank, John applied to the medical faculties of both Harvard and Johns Hopkins. When Harvard accepted him on April 24th he said, "I suppose if I really wanted to go I couldn't get in. I will be never gladder of anything than when graduation is over.... Two months to go yet." When Johns Hopkins also accepted him, medicine suddenly loomed as a serious threat.

That spring Alfred sold the ketch *Joloma* and bought a 40-foot boat. On the May 7th weekend they sailed *Joloma II*. "I like the boat very much," John wrote, "but I doubt if Pop will be able to handle it with just the girls...." Gently he was confirming what Alfred and Mary had already surmised: he wouldn't be in Connecticut, or even in New England, that summer.

The papers that spring of 1927 were full of Charles A. Lindbergh's solo flight from New York to Paris. On reading that the aviator was only four years older than himself, John felt a curious lift, a catch in his breath. When classmate John Metcalf casually invited him to come out West for the summer, without a second thought he accepted.

"The dance is June 21st & graduation the 23rd," said his last letter from Yale, "and we are leaving for Alaska on the 24th to catch a boat from Seattle the 29th. I think I will go to bed now, as the more one sleeps the faster time will pass and it can't go too fast to suit me."

Chapter Four

Alaska

"I certainly wish I could stay."

—J. M. Olds

In the Roaring Twenties, America was on a spree and damn the hangover. She gave the world Charleston dance marathons, sexy flappers, George Gershwin, Prohibition, speak-easys and Al Capone. Soon after Pittsburgh began the Jazz Age in 1920 with America's first scheduled radio program, two out of three American homes owned a radio. "Ol' Man River" and "Let a Smile Be Your Umbrella" became national hits. Louis Armstrong and Duke Ellington massaged the national mood with jazz; it helped people forget the Ku Klux Klan. The Barrymores strutted the stage, and for those who didn't know Lionel from John, the silver screen offered Charlie Chaplin and Harold Lloyd with popcorn besides. And when Hollywood added voice to the haunting images of Greta Garbo and Gloria Swanson, a million travelling salesmen from New York to San Francisco fell in love. America had Charles Lindbergh and Admiral Peary and Johnny Weissmuller, it had Babe Ruth, Ty Cobb and Gene Tunney. Soon it would take Amelia Earhart to its heart. In the White House, Presidents Harding and Coolidge rode a wave of nationalist sentiment and prosperity. Fifteen million Model T Fords couldn't be wrong. America felt unbeatable.

Such was the nation's mad virus and John Olds wanted to catch it. Yet as he sat in the swaying railway coach, idly watching the landscapes of Ohio and Indiana slide eastward, he felt as lifeless as the textbooks he had just flung aside. Was he foolish to throw away a safe summer job at home for this wild scheme of Metcalf's? Land of the Midnight Sun! Gateway to the Future! Then he recalled his eight long years of books and chalk and teachers and labs, of countless midnight cramming sessions and frightening examinations. Even if Metcalf's stories were half lies, Alaska was still better than Connecticut with its everlasting obligations. The farther away the better.

They reached Chicago, one-fifth of the way, on June 25th, 1927. Hungry for space and air, they swam through the crowds in Union Station and made for Lakeshore Boulevard. Lake Michigan seemed vaster to him, like an inland Atlantic. They explored the downtown, but the roar of elevated trains around the Loop and the reek of manure and blood from upwind stockyards and packing plants spoiled the fun. The ten-storey Auditorium Hotel had only one bathroom to a floor but the food was fair and the beds okay. Hoping for news of the New London races his father and Uncle Frank were sailing in, John bought a New York paper but there was nothing.

Only the next day, crossing the tawny croplands of western Ohio and South Dakota, seeing no towns for hours on end, did John finally begin to relax. Suddenly all his fretting over grades and careers seemed trivial, his excitement over polo and proms childish. Suddenly New England seemed small and irrelevant and not new at all. He felt like a bird escaping a stale cage.

They entered the gaunt dry foothills of Montana, toiled up the mountain passes of northern Idaho and Washington at almost walking pace. They inched across yawning evergreen chasms on matchstick bridges, plunged under the black roots of mountains, skirted blinding vistas of snow and ice. Standing between the cars, he gulped the balsamy air until he felt dizzy. That night the Pullman got so cold the pair had to sleep in their overcoats.

At last, on a drizzly June 28th, their locomotive chuffed down out of the clouds into Seattle's bowl of mountains and they were on the Pacific. They tramped the city's hilly isthmus between Lake Washington and the sea but Puget Sound was cloaked in fog and rain and Mount Rainier's snowy cone never showed itself. The noisy waterfront was crowded with ships from Canada, the western States and the Orient. They even saw a freighter from Rotterdam. All the city's timber and gold had long since been consumed, but the War's appetite for new ships and the Panama Canal's opening in 1914 had revitalized it. Outside a curio shop they found two giant sperm whale jawbones joined in an arch. The placard said they had once formed the "gateway to an Eskimo village."

Still on Eastern time, the boys rose hours too early to board their ship. Impatiently they waited for 7:30 AM. Once aboard, they stood on an upper deck and watched the loading. At 220 feet long, the SS *Admiral Farragut* was one of the Pacific Steamship Company's smallest vessels. The air vibrated with the rattle and screech of donkey engines and steam whistles, the hoarse shouts of stevedores and deck hands trading insults in three or four languages, the screams of wheeling gulls. They watched as bags of cement and coal, bales of hay and crates of cabbages were lowered into the forward hold, while back aft a crane operator skilfully swung bundles of sweet-smelling pink lumber onto the deck. Presently a jet of white steam issued from the vessel's sooty funnel and a deep organ note echoed and re-echoed around the Sound. The *Farragut*'s lines were cast off. They were heading up the Georgia Strait for Seward, fifteen hundred miles away.

John stood for hours at the forward deck rail, a slender figure with curly brown hair whipping in the moist wind, his unbuttoned jacket flapping about narrow shoulders. Soon the captain slowed to a few knots to pick his way carefully among wooded islands and tide rips. The water was so mirror-smooth that sometimes John fancied he was cruising the upper Connecticut, with starfish and spiny crabs instead of river clams and eels below. The channels were so narrow that he could see the ship's bow wave sway yellow rockweed along the shore. John admired the helmsman's skill in judging speed and direction in the strong and subtle currents. Now and then the ship veered sharply to avoid a floating log. John wished he could paint the ship as seen from one of the islands—two ships mirrored keel to keel against twin green hillsides of great Sitka spruce, Douglas fir and western cedar, graced by a double white sky.

This ocean seemed richer than any he knew. Rafts of mallard and teal bobbed in the ship's wake. Squadrons of green and grey eiders skimmed by so low they seemed to be tied to their reflections. In the coves, long-whiskered brown sea otters dove for sea urchins and clams. Dappled grey seals crowded the ledges. Someone or other was always pointing out a white-headed eagle overhead or an osprey flapping heavily homeward with a fish wriggling in its black talons. The novelty of porpoises faded when a pod of seven orcas appeared, breaching and diving in perfect sequence under puffs of steamy breath. Seeing their triangular black fins slicing the swells like shears through watered silk sent goose bumps up John's spine. Sometimes the *Farragut* passed a fleet of green and yellow salmon boats dangling odd net poles.

On deck everything dripped from continual rain and fog. When the weather turned altogether foul, John and his friend explored the engine room and they talked their way onto the bridge. Occasionally the mist lifted long enough to reveal, miles inland and gleaming like castle ramparts in the westering sun, the snowy Coastal Range.

The Inside Passage was well named: he never got to see the open Pacific. From Vancouver Island to the Queen Charlottes, the *Farragut* nosed along like a beetle under a tree's bark.

Every few hours they passed a tiny fishing village or a logging community, some with half-fallen totem poles drowning in rank growth. Farther northwest the dark hillsides bore fewer scars of fire and lumbering and became yet more sodden and lush. On the third day they reached the southern tip of what Metcalf called the Panhandle. At the fishing town of Ketchikan on Revillagigedo Island, John walked ashore in pelting rain to mail his second letter home. He had written it the night before, addressing it to Alfred at Black Point with instructions to send it on to New Castle.

It is nearly eleven o'clock yet almost light enough to read. The only news we have had is what the radio operator gets & he found out about the

Doctor Olds of Twillingate

Poughkeepsie race & the flight to France; but so far haven't heard whether Byrd got across [Antarctica] or not. I was much surprised to hear the results of the race at New London. I hope you enjoyed them though, and [that you] enjoy your cruise this summer and New Castle. We are getting along very well together so far....

At Juneau, the capital, they stopped for freight and passengers, and the same at Wrangell, Yakutat, Katalla and Valdez. Except for Valdez, which he called "the deadliest place imaginable," he liked what he saw. Coming abreast of the Columbia Glacier, the steamer hove to a quarter mile offshore. Using a megaphone, the captain stood on the bridge and boomed out the glacier's measurements: "Two miles across, 400 feet high, thirty-five miles long." Obviously enjoying his brief public appearance, he then said, "Watch carefully, please." At a blast from the *Farragut*'s whistle, several house-sized blocks of ice parted from the glacier's face and fell, turning in slow motion, into the jade-green sea. The ocean lifted in silent geysers and seconds later they heard a faint mutter of thunder.

Because the *Farragut* reached Seward half a day early and the weekly train left the next day, the boys had time to explore the town and a nearby mountain. "Up above the snow it was terribly hot; we stopped to eat some on our way down." Then they were rolling along the new Alaska Railroad to Fairbanks. Chatting with the engineer, he learned that their engine was a new gas electric rig built in Philadelphia. That night at the hotel in Currie a tame reindeer, the first he had ever seen, begged bread from their table.

They reached Fairbanks on the Chena River around noon the next day. The place was little more than an outpost of frame buildings with muddy streets, and dogs running everywhere. But Mr and Mrs Metcalf welcomed him like family. On Saturday they drove out to see "The Ditch," a man-made earth flume channelling water from eighty miles away to flush the gold dredges. A ruddy Irishman showed them around. "Fairbanks' little gold rush came in 1902," he said, between squirts of tobacco juice, "a little after Klondike and Nome. And when them Guggenheims in Phillie discovered our worked-over gravels could still yield $1.65 a cubic foot, they got up the Fairbanks Exploration Company and brought in dredges." He waved a beefy hand toward the huddle of great mud-caked metal monsters standing in coffee-coloured pools amid acres of brown gravel. "What those things do, my friends, is they swallow bellyfuls of gravel and spit out mouthfuls of gold. Sift it down from top to bottom on conveyor belts and screens they do, till the lighter stuff is all washed out and nothin's left but yellow pay dirt. Ain't it purty?" he said, fishing a pea-sized nugget from his vest pocket. "But it makes one divil of a mess."

"And what's our job?" said John Olds, eyes shining.

"Ye lads'll lay heat pipe to thaw the ground ahead o' the dredges," said the miner. "See, the ground up here is froze all year 'cept the top layer in the summertime. Your job is to poke pipes down ten, fifteen yards so's we can pump hot steam down there." Red paused to spit. "The worst part is haulin' them points back up again; damned hard work in the sun and the flies. Ye'll take turns. The hours are seven till five, six days a week. But the pay's good and the grub's almost fit to eat!"

Monday morning a company truck took them over rutted forest roads and across corduroyed muskeg alive with black flies to the Chatanika River, a southern tributary of the Yukon. Briefed at suppertime, they were tossed bundled canvas tents and told to cut their own poles. John and Metcalf slapped on more tar and pennyroyal against the whining clouds of mosquitoes and awkwardly felled and limbed seven straight spruce. Choosing a level place where they hoped the river breeze would keep the insects at bay, they erected two A-frames a dozen feet apart, laid a ridgepole across with the tent reefed to it and spread and roped the canvas to two side poles.

Later, in the long Arctic twilight, everyone lounged around a crackling fire and heard oldtimers talk and sing of banshees and rampaging grizzlies and fierce wolves and fiercer snowstorms until the newcomers were half scared to leave the fire. When the campfire collapsed to red embers, everyone crawled wearily onto bough beds and slept.

At 5:30 AM they were jolted awake by knuckles banging on a tin skillet. The tent village stirred as dozens of men, blinking against the already high sun, like bears leaving winter dens, stumbled outside, yawned, scratched themselves, farted and urinated and lurched to the river to wash. Oldtimers merely splashed their eyes and beards in the mountain icewater; greenhorns like John stripped to the waist until the flies forced them to cover up. Then everyone trooped toward the grub tent to consume bacon and beans, hot biscuits and scalding black coffee in enforced silence.

> Oh, there is too much to describe as I could wright [sic] for hours. We are having a wonderful time & the country is wonderful & later in the summer we have several invitations to go moose & caribou hunting. At the Metcalf's we had moose meat twice & it is fine. [The tent is] an awful mess, but maybe we will be straightened out soon.
>
> Love
>
> John
>
> PS: It is light enough to read alright but the sun sets about 10:30 & rises around 2:00.

They worked so hard in the next few weeks he scarcely had time to scribble two postcards. Not until the first Sunday in August did he manage another two-pager. "It is remarkable in what disorder one will live," he wrote, "but no one tells us to pick up anything or put it away & it is a great relief. So we hunt for things when we want them. We have an improvised shower out back to keep clean, but the water is very cold."

He soon tired of driving points. "Besides being very hard work, it is monotonous & very trying to the temper when they won't turn, or they hit rocks that have to be patiently cut through & then the point usually bends & has to be pulled up. My hands are terrible; they wouldn't be bad if I wore gloves but I don't like gloves and they are all cracked & the dirt won't come off." Had someone told him that he would spend most of his working life wearing rubber surgical gloves, he would have snorted in disbelief.

In the long Arctic evenings the men fished for grayling. The trout-like little fish with the oversized dorsal fins offered little challenge but were tasty. Then one evening they saw the fins and tails of great salmon in the rapids. Most of the fish had spawned and were close to death, but some looked healthy. John waded out and tried to grab one but it slithered from between his legs. Then someone tried shooting them with a bear rifle. Lashing a homemade wire hook to a pole, John waded out again, chose his victim and after a wild struggle during which he got soaked, dragged ashore a fine female. At twenty-five pounds on the cook's scale it was the biggest fish he'd ever caught. The sceptics claimed it wasn't fit to eat, but he cooked some and found it good. The rest he sent to Mrs Metcalf by the next truck out. "It is a lot of fun catching them, & they put up a good fight if alright." It was not the last time he would defy local wisdom concerning wild food.

Their two supervisors amused him. "If they both aren't drunk, one is sure to be," he said, and went on to describe how the older man had picked a fight, got trounced and sulked in his tent for three days until the foreman ordered him back to work. "They are all right, though, & very decent to us; a much higher class than any labourers you would find at home. There are a lot of Swedes & a few Russians and they only work in the summer & in the winter go out on claims of their own or trap or loaf around town if they have enough money."

The note of yearning was not lost on Mary and Alfred. Her husband, she could see, was bent on making John a successful urban physician. Yet if John became a physician at all, she thought, he could never be happy in a city; he would have to be a country doctor like his namesake John McKee. And if, like him, he had to lose sleep and travel in all weathers and work until he dropped, he too would end up dying young. Johnny simply hadn't the stamina or constitution for it. Alfred, sailing on the hazy Sound, entertained no such doubts, but he sensed another confrontation brewing. He would have to be firm.

By mid-August Chatanika's daylight hours were rapidly waning. Some mornings the tent's inner walls were white with frost. Often they had to chop through an inch of new ice to get water. Watching the Northern Lights late one night, John heard among the stars the excited yelping of southbound Canada geese. Metcalf and he decided they would quit on the first of September, hunt moose and caribou for a few days and leave on the tenth. "I certainly wish I could stay," he wrote in his final letter on Sunday, August 7th. "I could get a job for the winter & have a wonderful time." When Alfred read this in Windsor a fortnight later, his heavy brows knitted in a frown.

John's hunting trip took him into mountains whose beauty again made him wish he could paint. Although the land lacked New England's flaming reds, in the pale, raking sunlight it glowed with the gold of aspen and birch, the jade of larch and willow and the deep wines and mauves of sphagnum, bearberry and laurel. Along the steep valleys caribou drifted southward like grey smoke. In the river bottoms huge black moose fattened on the last water lilies before ice and snow drove them to browse on leafless willow and birch twigs. On September 8th they awoke to find a dust of snow on the high crags. Hare and weasel began to change colour, and the ptarmigan donned white epaulets. John bagged a fine black bear and Metcalf got a caribou. They shared the venison among their workmates and left a hind quarter with the Metcalfs.

Back in Fairbanks, a fox rancher named Guy Turnbow offered him work. Alaska was hungry for young engineers, he said. John was torn. He liked the land, the people and the hunting. Why not raise a grubstake, take mining at M.I.T. with Pop's help, and come back?

He wired Pop and asked permission to stay the winter. Two days later the postmaster handed him a Western Union telegram. With shaking hands he tore it open and read:

IF STAY ALASKA NO MORE MONEY

That scrap of paper decided John Olds' career.

Chapter Five

Hopkins

"All I know is I don't want to be a doctor."
—J. M. Olds

Twelve thousand miles of brooding had not reconciled John to medical school. Pop and he argued into the night, his father for Harvard, John for M.I.T. or nothing. Mr Chamberlain's advice to Nancy that "Johnny wouldn't amount to much," didn't help. At last Pop said, "Why not try medicine for a year and then decide?"

"Pop," he exploded, "if I go for a year I'll go forever!" and stormed up to his room. Two days later John announced he would go to Hopkins, adding defiantly, "At least I'll have no exams till second year." His leave-taking was on that note—the son angry, the father smug behind his newspaper, the mother sad for them both. Lois, enrolled at Wellesley College, wondered what all the fuss was about.

Baltimore was not quite an overnight trip. Changing trains in New York's Grand Central Station for the Baltimore and Ohio line, he wished he could submerge himself in the crowds and somehow surface in Fairbanks. On the train, his usual pleasure in the engine's rhythmic stroke, in unfamiliar landscapes, vanished. The Blue Ridge Mountains were a poor imitation of Alaska's Wrangells, the Susquehanna just a slow and dirty Chatanika. Yanking down the window blind, he slept until the porter's hoarse "Havre de Grace!" "Aberdeen!" "Baltimore!" roused him. He raised the blind an inch and gazed sleepily at Chesapeake Bay's marshlands and thought of duck hunting. Southward a sprinkle of lights haloed the waking city.

By Connecticut standards Baltimore was vast and untidy. "This city is the worst I ever was in," he wrote. "It will take months to find our way about & there is absolutely nothing to do & it is very hot...." Except for some new construction after the 1904 fire, the downtown was a warren of slums peopled by poor blacks. The rest of the city sprawled west, north and east like a beached octopus. After coffee and toast and a glance at the want ads, John took a cab to the Johns Hopkins Hospital complex at Jefferson and

Broadway on the downtown fringe, found a room within walking distance at 809 North Broadway and flopped on his bed exhausted.

His roommate was Fritz Middlefort from New York City. Son of a Norwegian physician, Fritz wanted to study music. Their mutual discontent was an instant bond. Baltimore that fall of 1927 was celebrating one hundred years of railroading, so they spent every spare hour downtown, exploring the "Fair of the Iron Horse." But for John the aura of adventure only conjured up Alaska, and a German exam oppressed him. He crammed desperately, failed, and had to hire a tutor. A friend of Fritz's drove them to a football game in Annapolis, but the city's immaculate beauty only heightened his distaste for Baltimore.

Once classes began, he noticed several things. The junior and senior students seemed to spend as much time on the wards as in class. Many poor people were looked after free. And there were a lot of female students. It was not how he had imagined medical school to be. Hopkins, he was to discover, was an unusual institution.

The knots of white-gowned students dogging the doctors on their rounds, he was told, were a legacy of Hopkins' first physician-in-chief, William Osler. The British physician had come from Montreal's McGill University in 1888 with the revolutionary notion that medicine was best learned at the bedside, not from books and lectures. This was why the School was not uptown with the university, but part of the downtown Hospital complex. Its blend of teaching, research and clinical medicine had since been imitated across the country, just as Dr Osler's 1892 work, *Principles and Practice of Medicine*, had become a standard textbook. As for the swarms of indigent patients, they were there because of the founder's Quaker philosophy: "If thee would help the poor," said old Johns Hopkins, "build thy hospital where they live." Though segregated between black and white, the wards were free. The young women on campus were mostly from the Nurses' Training School, though a few were medical students like him. Hopkins had graduated female doctors from the start.

They needed a map to explore the campus, it was so big. The square hospital complex itself filled eight city blocks between Jefferson on the south and Monument on the north, and the medical school off its northeast corner occupied two more. Here they found the Anatomy, Physiology and Pathology buildings where John would spend most of his first three years, and the old Hunterian Laboratory, almost a second home in his final two years. Walking west on Monument to Broadway, they came to the Hospital's old domed Administration Building. John liked the weathered inscription on the sun dial outside its Broadway entrance: "One hour alone is in thy hands, the hour on which the shadow stands." Passing the ten-foot white marble statue of Christ in the north rotunda, they chatted with doorman Bill Thomas, who told them how "Jesus He come in the north door after four stout horses drug Him all the way up Broadway!" Jesus' toes were black, he said, because so many students rubbed them for good luck. Laughing, Fritz and he did the same. They explored a dozen other nearby buildings, including the Children's Hospital and the Phipps Psychiatric Clinic. The Wilmer Eye Institute and the School of Hygiene and Public Health looked new.

Slowly the heat ebbed into a typically mild Maryland winter. Johnny's mood stayed sour. It wasn't his classmates—some were old friends from Yale—nor the upperclassmen, though "they never talk of anything but work, & most of it is over our heads." Granting that "nobody likes first year" and that "the novelty hasn't worn off," his letters began to mention "disillusionment" and "the daily grind" and that Hopkins' new schedule might prevent his coming home for Thanksgiving. On September 18th he told Mary, "I wish I was anywhere but here," and asked her to get Pop to find out about mining at M.I.T. When Nan offered to visit him over the weekend, he curtly refused.

Then, his tone changed. After writing Mary to hold onto his things until she heard from him, he took a long midnight walk, and wrote his father: "The truth is I hate this school more than anything I have ever tried. I don't know whether you consider it a fair trial or not, but to me it seems as if I had been here for months, and every time I think of the future I think it will never come. I simply cannot make myself interested in medicine in any way," he went on, "& I have tried. It is not the present work that I dislike so much. I am satisfied on that point now, but the whole idea back of it."

He didn't blame his teachers; he admired them. "But it is all very distasteful to me. I can stay here the whole year but…I think the time would be wasted." His roommate felt the same, he said, even though Fritz's father was a doctor and his brother a medical student. He hastened to add that Fritz hadn't swayed him. "In fact, I have had every inducement to stay— but I don't like it & feel I never can. Also I think I would feel nearly the same way about going to M.I.T." Then he revealed The Plan.

> We want to rent Dr Middlefort's farm in Wisconsin for the rest of the year & live there and do all we can to make it amount to something. We will get a leave of absence from the Dean, thereby not ruining ourselves from studying medicine next year if we want to. If I should return next year my mind will be made up that medicine is what I want…. All I know at present is I don't want to be a doctor. I will not want any more money & I don't feel the time would be wasted. It is exactly what I have always wanted to do…. Will you give me permission? So far I have worked as hard as anyone & I will continue to study till I hear definitely.

> Love
> John

The part about his love of farming must have pained Alfred, who was agonizing about selling the tobacco farm. If his son hated medicine so much, why not help run the family farm instead of gallivanting off to Wisconsin? With Johnny's brains and drive, they could surely succeed—if not in tobacco, then in something else.

Predictably, Dr Middlefort refused. Less predictably, John's desire to escape collapsed like a kicked tent. It was as if he had needed some sign. Perhaps Hopkins itself had already defeated his resolve, won him to itself. For if John McKee Olds had to study medicine anywhere, no other school could have suited him more. Its classrooms and halls were haunted by the spirits of men very like him. The tall, craggy-faced founder himself—called "Johns" after his mother's surname—was a tobacco farmer's son. Like John he believed in God but seldom went to church, was well-off but dressed plain and often went coatless in winter. The school's first professor of medicine, William Henry Welch, was the son of a country doctor and also started out hating medicine, studying classics at Yale instead. The brilliant surgeon William Halsted, the first to use rubber gloves in surgery, had suffered from drug abuse just as John would in middle life. And Howard Kelly, who would die the same year as Alfred, possessed the same lively inventiveness, devising among other things a special pad and a clamp bearing his name, a urinary cystoscope and self-absorbing sutures.

Before John's time Hopkins people had discovered adrenalin, mapped the role of the pituitary, devised the first tissue culture, introduced kidney dialysis and, only two years before, crowned the work of Canada's Dr Banting by purifying insulin. They had discovered the anticoagulant heparin and the master role of the pituitary, were mapping biorhythms, finding a way to measure red blood cells, curing rheumatic fever. In such a hive of excellence it was likely that one with John's ability would find himself. Hopkins' gruelling pace of lectures, lab work and hands-on diagnosis was exactly the right prescription for him.

"Well," he told Mary a few weeks later, "I am still here though I don't know why." Fritz caved in too, to be rewarded with a twenty-first birthday dinner to which Johnny was invited. As would so often happen when tensions were removed, John began to draw. Fritz said his work was "panoramic," that the drawings expressed modern culture and explained things for him. "I guess he sees more than I do in them," said John, and asked for photographs of *Joloma* to copy.

Having bullied his son into medical school, a wiser father might have given John his head, kept his pockets full of money, cooperated in every way. In the months ahead Alfred did the opposite. He had disliked Fritz from the start, provoking John to defend him to Mary: "He is younger than me but much wiser. Pop is afraid he is a radical or a Bolshevik or something & might have a bad influence on me. He is so different from all the rest that it is a pleasure to room with him. Among other things he is a fine musician & has composed quite a number of pieces. It is too bad he has to stay here as I am sure he would go far in other lines." A tangle of misunderstandings developed. None of Pop's correspondence survives—John seldom kept letters after answering them—but its central themes were the importance of building suitable friendships and careers and of respecting the institutions of marriage and family. As usual Mary was caught in the crossfire. At one point John angrily declared, "I know what my life will be from now on—better, I am sure, than Papa does!" That Thanksgiving John stayed in Baltimore. Snow came, reminding him of Christmas. He sent Chatanika photos to his Alaska friends. On the excuse that he was too busy, he began his lifelong practice of getting Mother or Lois or Tutie to do his Christmas shopping. When Christmas dinner was scheduled for Monday and not Sunday, he fumed because he had planned to go duck shooting. "A day wasted," he said, blaming both his father and Uncle Frank.

After Christmas he attacked his studies with determination. Alfred was slow with the tuition money and Mary confided that she could not afford to attend the Daughters of the Revolution Congress in Washington that year. John offered to save $50 out of his allowance, adding, "I certainly think you should go & make a speech. You can do it very well." She thanked him but stayed home.

In February of 1928, Alfred sold the farm. For some time, paper cigar wrappers had been reducing his sales. Rumours of a national economic collapse worried him too. His Board of Education and magistrate duties were taking more time, and with two children in college he was short of cash. For John the sale evoked mixed feelings, especially since around this time his Fairbanks friend Guy Turnbow offered him a partnership in his fox ranch.

Fortunately he was too busy to think about anything but advanced organic and inorganic chemistry, human physiology, neurology and histology—and German, which he still hadn't passed. Trekking halfway across the city two nights a week for tutorials annoyed him, "but I have to pass the exam sometime." He didn't even get home for Easter.

John now began to develop patterns of thought and productivity that would serve him well for the rest of his life. He came to despise any waste of time or energy. He began to question every conventional approach, to assume that almost everything could be improved, and to quietly seek a better way. A case in point was the killing of dozens of laboratory dogs during routine student experiments. He felt that some of the deaths were unnecessary. Although his exact contribution is unspecified, a 1930s *Loomis Alumni Bulletin* states that in his freshman year he had "worked out a method whereby the dog survived in good health." Next, tired of shaking blood samples by hand, he devised an electric pipette shaker. But the invention which first drew attention to him was his *Technitron,* an apparatus that would have earned him much money and some fame had Pop not let him down.

Ever since the nineteenth century, selective staining had been the standard method for identifying disease in human cells. In Clinical Microbiology, John and his classmates had to prepare numerous tissue samples for analysis. This entailed hand-soaking each specimen in different solutions at precise mixtures, all carefully timed. By microscopically observing and carefully drawing and labelling colour-coded healthy and diseased cells, the students learned to identify scores of pathogens and symptoms.

Unfortunately, the soaking could take hours. Students often stayed in the lab all night, watching a clock, dipping the specimens and trying to stay awake. John was sure a machine could do the job easier and better. He analyzed each step. Typically, the lab assistant handed him a cube of diseased tissue the size of a pea and asked him to embed it with paraffin. First he had to dehydrate it in increasingly stronger alcohol baths of different durations. Next he had to soak it in increasing concentrations of xylol to absorb the wax. Then he repeated the process with liquid paraffin until he had a solid block ready for slicing in the microtome. A difficult specimen might require ten or more separate immersions. Once the cube was ready, the rest was easy. He simply pared off transparent slices a few microns thick, floated them in water onto a slide and fixed them to the glass with heat. Using eosin for red, hemotoxin for blue and so on, he stained the slide to bring out specific structures under the microscope.

This part—seeing into the secret geometry of a nephritic kidney or a cancerous prostate, decoding the enemy's telltale marks—always thrilled him. It was the embedding he despised, the wasting of precious time while physician and patient hung in suspense. And a small human error could lead to a wrong diagnosis.

Within weeks he designed a self-timing, automatic electrical tissue embedder. His idea was simple: place the solution jars around a turntable's edge, insert the specimen in a pincered, overhanging metal arm, and use a clock-timed electrical switch to turn the carousel and to lower and raise the arm. The prototype carousel would be wooden and eighteen inches wide. His excited histology professor assured him no such apparatus was on the market. With a long letter about his hopes for the apparatus, John sent Pop the plans.

That spring of 1928, unable to face Baltimore's sultry summer, he turned down a bank job and went home to study, work on his machine, play golf, and perhaps drive Pop's car. After a month in Windsor, however, he returned to Baltimore. A New York instrument maker now offered to manufacture a few of his embedders if he would patent it and be prepared to defend his patents at all costs. "What medical student could do this?" he said. He asked Pop to build a proper prototype and to finance the patent. Pointedly he left the model on his father's workbench.

Alfred, busy working on *Joloma II* with a New London contractor, either ignored it or forgot. September came, and classes resumed. Pop now had carpenters working on the house. October passed with no sign of the crucial fee. In a "rather mean" letter, John insinuated that Pop must be planning to patent the invention as his own. After Christmas he lugged the unfinished apparatus back to Hopkins.

His studies became more troublesome; but tinkering with the machine calmed his nerves. His professors were losing their initial enthusiasm for the device, so with trepidation he told the New York firm to go ahead without a patent. Within six months the apparatus started appearing in most labs—"a more metallic and glass job but working exactly as mine in principle." It was cold comfort for him to see his invention become standard equipment in the Hopkins histology and pathology laboratories. Quite apart from lost income, this act of piracy would vex him for decades. He got some consolation, however, from being put in charge of tissue preparation, a position previously always held by a full-fledged MD.

At Hopkins the residents, interns and department heads attended gruelling daily conferences to discuss autopsy results. Clear, accurate photographs were important. A third-year student supplied these but often his images were poor. Concluding that better lighting would help, John designed and built a camera stand with adjustable electric lights. When Chief of Pathology Dr MacCallum saw it in Dr Langworthy's office he fired his junior assistant and hired John on the spot. Dr MacCallum was notoriously hard to please, but within weeks the daily conferences had much better images to work with. And since he needed to know what to shoot, John got to sit in. "It is a fine help in learning pathology, but I had to work all Wed. afternoon & also Sat. till 6:30 & one night & about three hours today."

During their sophomore winter term, students were allowed to work with patients directly for the first time. Initially it was only in the dispensary, but later they were invited on morning and evening rounds to learn minor procedures and to take notes. Until now John's feeling for medicine, soured perhaps by hours spent dissecting corpses, still wavered occasionally. Working with living patients that spring of 1929, he suddenly felt like a real doctor. There was no shortage of patients to see. As unemployment rose and downtown bread lines lengthened, Hopkins' free wards overflowed with misery.

That spring fellow medical student Marion Howard, who roomed with Mabel Grosvenor, daughter of the *National Geographic*'s editor, invited him to Herbert Hoover's inauguration. They stayed at the Grosvenor's Washington mansion and attended the parade and inaugural ball. At the parade they sat directly across the street from President Hoover's box.

Torrential rain soaked everyone, he wrote, "& some of the fancy uniforms faded & ran sadly. People [marched] in it from nearly every state. Conn. must have had the whole foot guard & they are a sloppy looking outfit but not as bad as some. There were dozens of politicians with big cigars—all in all a low lot. The Gov. of Wisconsin & wife came to the Grosvenor's box & Dr Grosvenor introduced me as 'Doctor Olds'—which doesn't matter but sounded funny."

Briefly a new girl appeared in his life, whether Marion or another he did not say. "Can you imagine it? I have found one girl who can walk. I have just come back at 1:30 AM; we started at 9:30 AM & didn't stop once & she can really walk as fast as a man. It was a splendid day here—almost too warm this morning & sunny & now it is cool & bright moon."

On March 23rd, 1929 he wrote, "Am I going to be 23 or 24? I really am not sure...." He was to be 23—and Pop bought him a new car. John was overwhelmed, but the expense worried him. Lois and Tutie mischievously sent cigarettes with Mary's usual nuts and candy. Bill Card drove down from Loomis and John drove him to Annapolis to play tennis. To celebrate his status as a car owner, he designed a new letterhead. Printed on soft blue rag stock, it bore the simple monogram "J. M. O." Annapolis was the only trip he could afford that spring, however, as Alfred either forgot or could not afford to increase his allowance. Even with his photography earnings he was unable to buy gas and oil. Perhaps it was a bribe after all, a foretaste of the wealth to come if only he would see the world Pop's way.

His letters home assumed a more relaxed, professional tone. When Mother complained of chest pains he wrote, "I want to listen to your heart as I know something about that now & have had quite a few such cases in the dispensary. I wish you would please rest & not overwork...." That Easter, his own increasing workload kept him in Baltimore, but in Clinical Microbiology he scored 18.5 out of 20. In April he began Obstetrics and after four deliveries he called it "somewhat interesting, but the hours aren't." Babies, he discovered, took their own sweet time. Even a year later he would write, "[Obstetrics] is one thing I decidedly do not care for," adding pointedly that it had convinced him never to marry.

Another specialty he disliked was "G.I." or gastro-intestinal—the messy workings of the stomach and bowels from mouth to anus."We have to give talks on diff. things & it is a nuisance. I have been trying to prepare a talk on Auerbach's & Meissner's plexuses & have read 8 books & no two anywhere near agree though that sounds almost impossible."

The sophomore year examinations, his first major hurdle, hung over him like a sword. They proved even tougher than he feared. "Everyone has been as nervous as an old maid & now they are all tired out. Neither Fritz or I could sleep much at all and the heat has been terrible." But he passed, and Dr MacCallum got him a summer job in the Pathology lab. On June

16th, the eve of the State Board Examinations, John sifted eight years of old Board exams and passed. His marks—Anatomy 89, P. Chem. 91, Physiology 88 & Materia Medica 68—displeased him, "but they are passed at least."

It is a remarkable mother, even a doctor's daughter, who will read with interest such letters as John, now carving cadavers every day, wrote Mary that summer. "Someone made a bad blunder during the [brain tumor] operation—if not intentional it was careless or stupid. [About] half the right frontal lobe...was removed, and to stop bleeding silver clips were put on the arteries. Only one side of the brain was affected by the tumor, but...the other side was [also] stopped by a silver clip—so that if the person hadn't died from the operation he couldn't have lived, as the left side, which was good, was shut off from all blood supply...."

He was also experimenting on animals. "Last Tuesday I took the spleen out of a dog & strangely enough...he was so well the next morning he jumped out of the cage before I could stop him & ran all around the room. I was afraid he would tear out the stitches & get a hernia but there was no way to keep him quiet & the stitches didn't give way. He didn't even get infected, which is remarkable I think. His blood count is very interesting...." His pipette shaker would have been useful but Alfred still had it in Windsor.

Again the sun smote the city with jungle heat. Down in the morgue it was cool, but he yearned to be on the salt water. With classmate Conrad Van Storch and two young resident interns, he borrowed an old open launch and headed out Chesapeake Bay. The rudder was useless, so when the rusty two-cycle engine consented to go, they steered with an oar. One day about six miles from home, the jump spark rod broke and he fixed it with a nail. It was the sort of makeshift repair he would perform many times in his long affair with boats. When he wasn't fixing the engine they frolicked in the cool, brackish water and explored the islands.

That July, when the assistant resident went on vacation, John was asked to take his place. He wore a white suit and was on call three nights a week including Sunday. "It is really a lot of fun & I am glad they let me do it as I didn't think they would. Living in the Hospital is pretty nice, but I seem to be on call most of the time...."

That month Conrad's wife Liza died of an infected tooth. John looked after her ashes and comforted his friend. At almost the same time his Aunt Essie died in New Castle. After the funeral Mary stayed there for a month. In August Alfred took her and the girls for an extended cruise on the refitted *Joloma II*, but the weather was foul and tempers flared. "I am sorry you didn't have a good time," wrote John, adding philosophically, "one often doesn't."

September came, his Junior year. After a brief visit home he plunged into Obstetrics, Surgery, Gynecology, Psychiatry, Orthopedics, Surgical

Dispensary and Dog Surgery. For pocket money he continued doing autopsies and photography for Dr MacCallum, who also let him do occasional conference presentations. Conrad became his roommate. They teamed up on dog research and were cited by Dr Rich in a lecture to sophomore year Pathology students. John was also working on a paper with Edward S. Stafford for the Department of Anatomy on the blood circulation of the liver, a matter then poorly understood. They hoped to clarify it by injecting dyes into dogs. John would illustrate the paper.

Although he must have been aware of world events, John seldom referred to them in his letters. When he did so, it was usually to point out something that intrigued or amused him. Despite the fiscal alarums of that October, he seemed more upset about the rash of weddings around him. Professor Baker tied the knot that month. His classmates Larry and Peabo succumbed. "It is great foolishness," he declared, "& too bad but they don't agree with me. I will say now that I never shall marry." When Lois also got engaged he exclaimed, "What a foolish thing to do!" That night he wrote Nan to say that he had "monopolized her too much already," and not to expect to marry him. Her gracious reply softened him enough to admit, "Maybe sometime I will, but at present I am doing everything I can to be independent.... When that happens I will consider myself old & entirely disillusioned." Within two years he would eat those words.

In late November the news came that several Hopkins physicians were accepting positions next summer at Duke University's new hospital in Durham, North Carolina. Dr Amos, Duke's future Head of Medicine, offered John a summer job there. Despite the low pay, he was interested. Far more intriguing, however, was a notice which appeared on the bulletin board announcing that Dr Charles Parsons, chief of a Newfoundland outport hospital, would be recruiting six third-year student volunteers next spring for a six-week summer practicum. Without telling even his mother, John put down his name.

In the last weeks of 1929, he had an idea for repairing malformed aortic valves. "No one has ever attempted anything like it," he wrote. "If it works it will really be a splendid thing." He got permission to use the laboratory and a supply of dogs and started in. His first operation on a dead dog was a failure. He made smaller instruments but still could not demonstrate his idea.

After the Christmas holidays the first thing he did was to check the bulletin board. His name was among the six. That same day he wrote his parents: "I am very glad to be going to Newfoundland instead of Duke."

For Alfred, it was Alaska all over again. He had not written his son in months but now fired off a rambling exhortation about family honour, the sanctity of matrimony and above all a man's duty not to squander God-given gifts. As a clincher he offered to use his connections to find John a more lucrative and respectable summer job.

"That letter of Pop's was certainly a long outburst," John mused a few days later, "but I am afraid he misses the point entirely. I don't care what you tell him."

Just in case, he did some checking. Dr Parsons, he learned, was a 1919 Hopkins graduate who had worked in Labrador with Grenfell, done post-graduate work in Vienna and was a respected surgeon. In six short years he had almost single-handedly built and equipped a frontier hospital that he hoped to enlarge from sixty to ninety beds the following year. Its clientele was so diverse, with so much scope for orthopedics, that John persuaded Surgeon-in-Chief Dean Lewis to let him skip his Junior Year's first quarter, giving him nearly six months in the North. In late January 1930, Alfred received the dreaded letter: "Everything is fixed up to go to Newfoundland for the summer.... This is a very depressing place."

To forestall his usual New Year blues, he studied as never before. Perhaps to impress Pop, his letters mentioned "a couple of lucky diagnoses in surgery which were rather unusual but happened to be right. And then I went to see Dr Firov about my heart operation & he was so pleased he gave me his laboratory & instruments to use for the next two months & all the dogs I want & a man to help me." With Pop's outburst still unanswered, he was glad Obstetrics kept him busy. Finally, at Mary's insistence, he replied:

> I don't know what to say to your letter. You are right from all points of reason. However I don't feel that way—probably because *I have no faith in any human being outside the family.* I do not dare to trust them & want to make myself mentally independent of them—though I realize no one can be physically independent as you have to buy food, clothes, etc.
>
> When I finish here—if ever—I want to go away as far as possible. The idea of settling down in a so-called civilized city is very abhorrent. Of course you will say that life will be as monotonous anywhere, but I want to find out. I do not want to marry because I don't want the responsibility. I have no sense of duty on that point—either for the perpetuation of the race or family. As you have said, all this is a perverted idea.... In college I did not feel this way, though I wanted to travel. Medical school has completely changed my ideas and views of life. If I had not come here I should probably now be married & in a complete rut for the rest of my life—so I ought to be glad I am here.

"All this may be a temporary phase," he concluded, adding in bold letters, "**but for the last five years I have been consciously trying to make myself independent & by the time I finish here intend to have no restrictions which will keep me from going anywhere I want.**"

His liver research with Stafford was ready to publish. He toiled over the drawing, but "Mr Broedel said it was rotten so I am just where I was at Christmas." No one, even the senior professors, questioned the verdict of German medical artist Max Broedel. A protégé of Howard Kelly's, he had started America's first school of medical illustration at Hopkins in 1911. Years later, when John had become a master surgeon and gifted painter, he still found Broedel's favourite maxim true for both scalpel and brush: "Full comprehension must precede execution."

By mid-March Broedel had accepted two new drawings and Dr Lewis Weed, Head of Anatomy, was reviewing the paper for publication. "On the Manner of Anastomosis of the Hepatic and Portal Circulations" was to appear that September in the *Johns Hopkins Hospital Bulletin* and to prove the textbooks wrong in some points. Broeder labelled John's drawings "camera lucida drawings from actual fields" and the budding artist was proud.

That spring his mother was plagued by toothache. John, recalling the fate of Conrad's wife and perhaps worried about possible complications from Mary's old illnesses, demanded full details from his father, then guided his parents through the extraction procedure. One letter ran to five pages. Just before the operation, she received a message scribbled on a prescription pad: "Rest & *rest* & *rest*." As he feared, Mary suffered post-operative speech problems. After another exchange of textbook-like letters he concluded, "I don't see how he hurt [the nerves] unless he put his knee on your throat when he pulled the tooth.... I think the dentist did a rotten job and something slipped & injured your tongue."

Pop began to have bad headaches. John at first suspected constipation but later put it down to nerves. "If he had 1/10 your strength of mind & character," he told Mary, "there would be nothing the matter with him." He advised a complete physical anyway, but Pop put it off as long as possible. Years later, when it was almost too late, he would discover that his blood pressure was dangerously elevated.

The Newfoundland countdown commenced. Dr Parsons arrived, briefed his summer students, gave them steamship tickets and told them to be aboard the boat Saturday morning at 9:00 AM sharp. The remaining days were a blur of intense study, interruptions and fitful sleep. Fritz came to see him off, talking about "abstracts of life in general. It is all interesting but wastes too much time." He insured his new car and put it in storage, got off two days early and took the train home. Lois and Nan, perhaps primed by Pop, tried again to dissuade him. John simply said, "I think Newfoundland will be splendid." His father was unusually quiet. Just before train time he disappeared into his workshop. John was about to follow but Mary shook her head. As they were getting into the car, Pop returned with his best fishing rod and shotgun and with brimming eyes pressed them on his son.

Part II

True North

Chapter Six

Twillingate Summer

"Three [patients] have died on me & none on the other 2
fellows so it looks like I better go in Pathology."
—J. M. Olds

Until the summer of 1930 the dour, bespectacled young man from Connecticut seemed headed for a career in pathology. At 24 he had put in so many hours plying scalpel, scissors and suction trocar on pickled grey corpses that the stink of formaldehyde was to him almost the fragrance of discovery. In Microbiology he easily decoded the Persian patterns of cancerous cells, the teeming leucocytes of blood poisoning, the malformed erythrocytes of sickle-cell anemia, the bacilli of typhoid.

The trouble with medicine in the thirties was that it still had so little to offer the patient. Except in Pharmacology, taught in second year, the stress was all on diagnosis not treatment. It was as though the medical profession, having discarded blood-letting and other spurious nineteenth century practices, having learned a great deal about microbes and the workings of the body, had forgotten that the patient still expected to be cured. Impressive as the GP's black leather bag appeared, it contained little but a scalpel with spare blades, a bone saw, a reflex hammer, a tuning fork for the ear and maybe a scope for the eye, a few needles and syringes. His only useful medicines were aspirin, tincture of digitalis, morphine, ergot, barbiturates and a few cathartics and ointments. Most of his healing power came from faith, kindness and common sense. He was an unarmed Lancelot.

Surgeons, on the other hand, actually *did* things for their patients. As far back as the Egyptians, they had known how to remove cataracts and ease pressure on the brain. Thanks to the work of Davy, Lister, Billroth and others, modern surgeons no longer dreaded the three bogies of pain, infection and hemorrhage, and could repair bodies without torturing or losing the owners to other causes. Surgeons were a strange hybrid of doctor, mechanic and egotist, but they knew how to pin a broken hip, rest a tubercular lung, and cure diabetes. They had even ventured into the sanctum of the abdominal cavity to fix stomachs, kidneys and colons, and would tackle the brain and heart next. John was a natural surgeon but did not know it until Twillingate.

When he and Conrad Van Storch boarded the *Nerissa* in New York on May 31st, John knew more about Alaska than about Newfoundland. What little he knew he had learned from Dr Parsons, who would join them there in a few weeks. He recalled disbelieving, until he consulted a map, that the island equalled New England in size and that if one added Labrador it rivalled Texas. Dr Parsons said it had been a British colony when the Pilgrim Fathers reached Plymouth Rock and a fishing station long before that. It had its own currency and stamps. The economy was tied almost entirely to cod, he said, and, like every other country's, had been devastated by the Depression, which had ruined overseas markets. Parsons had praised the people's intelligence and spirit, calling them the most hospitable on earth. As the ship dropped slowly under Brooklyn Bridge and passed the Statue of Liberty, John wished he were already there.

"This is certainly a wonderful day," he wrote the next afternoon. "No wind but considerable swell, so that the boat is rolling quite a lot & a few people left their breakfast rather hurriedly.... We went south of Long Island & didn't see Block Island or Martha's Vineyard. The breakfast fish horn goes off at 7:00 (we have already set watches ahead 1 hr), 3 babies in the state room next to us start bellowing & then the Steward pounds on the door. Tomorrow morning we get to Halifax. The play in New York was splendid."

Bowring Brothers' *Nerissa* was ten times bigger than the *Farragut*, but John was disgusted when several European steamers that left after she did overtook them in the night. Halifax he called "a poor place," but St John's was "a little more interesting," even in the rain. Their sixteen cartons of cigarettes slipped through Customs undetected and by 2:00 PM they were jolting northwest up the foggy Isthmus of Avalon. Gazing out on mile after mile of boulder-strewn, grey granite ridges, dark green scrub spruce and teawater ponds, he wondered that the island had people at all.

"The railroad is narrow gauge & the train goes all of 20 m.p.h. downhill & the roughest road bed imaginable. Impossible to sleep, tho. we tried." At 1:30 AM they detrained at Notre Dame Junction and waited miserably for the freight train to Lewisporte, the Bay's principal port, ten miles away. The town's physician, Dr Knapp, put them up for the night. "Bump" Compton, the third student, had already arrived by train.

At daylight, before the alarm went off, John woke to the patter of rain on the window. After a quick breakfast of bread and jam with black tea, the trio joined a huddle of passengers boarding a small motor boat for the 36-mile run to Twillingate. Already New York's smiling May weather seemed an illusion. Conrad and Bump soon dived down the fo'c'sle to play cards close to the little *Cod* stove. John went aft to the tiny wheelhouse to chat with the skipper and learn some geography.

Unlike the Alaskan coast, the country was low. He liked its ancient, worn-down look, its headlands brooding over the sea like sleeping giants. It reminded him of Maine. After Little Burnt Bay and Knight's Island the skipper had to weave through patches of rough ice. In Black Island Tickle an iceberg as big as a cathedral gleamed against the leaden sky. Along its fluted base, turquoise and cerulean surf played prettily, and seabirds wheeled like gnats above its glistening ramparts. Alaska's Columbia Glacier seemed somehow benign and theatrical compared to it.

Everywhere he saw rocky islands of every size and shape, the largest of them crowned with evergreen thickets fringed with the bony skeletons of dead trees. The captain called them resonant names like Silver, Cranpot, Yellow Fox, Gleed, Sugar Loaf, South and North Samson, Currant and Tinker and Cottle. For over an hour the low rumpled profile of New World Island kept them company to starboard. Under the rain's wet glaze its ochres, greens and purples glowed like stained glass.

Beyond Western Head, Twillingate North and South Islands hove into view with a dimple marking the tickle between. Around dinnertime the rain eased to drizzle, the wind backed into the west and shafts of sunlight pierced the cloud deck and slivered the horizon. Rounding Twillingate Long Point with its towering lighthouse, he saw at last, about two miles away, the town he had heard so much about.

The two things that struck him most forcefully were the Harbour's forest of masts and the beet-red hue of almost every waterfront structure. Anchored on either side were at least two dozen schooners. "Gettin' ready for the Labrador, my son," explained the skipper. "Feesh 'as been scarce round 'ere of late, so the Troakes and Whites and others goes down Narth as soon as the ice clears off." John liked the way Newfoundlanders put an "a" in North and dropped their Hs. As they drew closer, several white church spires caught the mid-day light. The rounded, lofty hills, purplish on top and moss-green below, were almost treeless. All along the kelpy shore they passed low clapboard buildings perched on close-spaced stilts, in front of flattish, weathered platforms of close-packed poles, also on stilts. Here and there were small gardens neatly fenced with grey pickets.

In a cove on the North Island a fire winked on the curving beach as men with pitchforks dunked nets in a steaming black cauldron. Children and small dogs darted along the narrow footpaths between houses and people plodded along the single road on various errands. He saw women hurriedly pinning washing on lines after the rain. In the gardens men were spading the dark earth into beds. John, shivering in his thin coat and noting the stranded ice pans still melting along the shore, shook his head at their faith.

His nostrils caught the mingled scents of rancid fish oil, coal smoke and cabbage cooking. They were closing on a cluster of premises marked "Ashbourne," with a long wharf cluttered with casks and still slimy with seal blubber. To his left, high on the South Side, he saw the long, dormered, grey stone building which he knew must be the Hospital, with Dr Parsons' house just above and to the east.

The next day, as he delivered some Hopkins mail to the doctor's Cottage, four great black Newfoundland dogs bounded out and frisked him with wet tongues and huge paws. "One weighs 150 pounds & is the biggest thing I ever saw," he wrote. He thought of the caribou that greeted him in Alaska and took it for a good omen.

"The town is most quaint. Small wooden houses with five-plus dogs around each & a little plot of ground fenced off in which they have their garden. Ponies, dogs, goats & calves roam thru the streets which are unpaved but fairly good. The ponies are taller than M°Duff but just as shaggy. The whole country is solid rock with high hills covered with moss.... The day we got here there was no ice in the harbour but the next morning it was jammed so that no boats can get in or out—therefore no mail...."

Used to New England's look of architectural permanence, at first John found Twillingate's antiquity hard to believe; it was nearly as old as Windsor, yet entirely made of wood. As early as 1650, Dr Parsons had said, Breton fishermen had named it Toulinguet after a place back home. For over a century it had been a major fishing and sealing centre, boasting its own magistrate, doctor, Customs House and even a weekly newspaper. Yet the Hospital seemed to be its most imposing and permanent structure.

Dr Parsons' assistant, Richard Blackwell, showed them around the building. It had been built in 1923, he explained, mostly with local labour, under a local contractor named Henry Rideout who had learned his trade in England and worked for years in the States. It was intended as a memorial to 242 local men lost in World War I, and to the wounded who returned. It was not, as some supposed, a Grenfell Mission Hospital. Dr Grenfell had raised $25,000 toward its construction and had helped choose the site. The remaining funds were raised around the Bay, he said, augmented by $5,000 from the British Red Cross and $10,000 from the Newfoundland government. At present they survived on government grants and charity—and the financial outlook was bleak.

Right away, John liked Notre Dame Bay Memorial. It was clean and well lit and had reasonably good equipment. A water-driven generator supplied some electricity. First Floor East contained rooms for X-ray, darkroom, drugs, outpatients and a lab; the West Wing housed the office, staff dining and living rooms, doctor's study and rooms for the resident surgeon and interns. On Second Floor West he saw two parallel wards twenty by forty feet long, one for men, the other for women. Asked why so many beds were empty, Dr Blackwell smiled and said they would fill up soon enough. "Just wait till the drift ice leaves and Dr Parsons gets back," he laughed. Second East contained the kitchen, linen storage, bathrooms, two semi-private and one private room. The Operating Room, about twelve by twenty feet, occupied the northwest corner with a sterilizing room outside. Spanning the west end of the building on both floors was a narrow solarium, the top for TB patients and the bottom for staff. The nurses lived just west of the Hospital in a two-storey house.

John wanted to see the whole Hospital. The dormered top floor was used for storage, apartments and a small medical library. Its rafters and wood work, he learned with pleasure, had been sawn from the timbers of a wrecked schooner. The basement housed the main kitchen and scullery, food and meat lockers, a laundry, linen closet, bedrooms and a small dining room for maids and nursing assistants. Large coal-fired boilers in the east end supplied steam heat. Outside, between the Hospital and Cottage, there were a concrete warehouse and workshop, turf-roofed root cellars and a small barn with half a dozen cows, some pigs and a flock of hens. To John's surprise two cows and one bull were thoroughbred Ayrshires. For some years, explained Dr Blackwell, they had been nearly self-sufficient in food while serving over 50,000 meals a year. Besides bottling wild berries they preserved rabbit, spinach and turnip greens, cut some of their own hay and sawed ice from the same pond that provided electricity.

Overnight, a westerly wind took the ice out to sea. The next fine Sunday, they woke to the *put-put-put* of small boats bringing patients. Then the SS *Prospero*, on her first weekly trip of the season, arrived with more. Many long-term patients went home but the new arrivals outnumbered them. After that the sixty beds were hardly ever vacant. That was why, said Blackwell, Dr Parsons planned to add thirty more.

The three students were immediately put to work, one each on Obstetrics, Outpatients and Surgery. John chose surgery, but Dr Parsons was not due back for a fortnight. Within a week he had fourteen patients with ailments ranging from burns and cuts to terminal pulmonary tuberculosis and cancer. Half of them had some form of TB, and he saw malnutrition diseases like rickets and scurvy. There was even beriberi, which his textbooks said was found only in China. He had been considering going to China; it seemed he might learn as much in Newfoundland. Neuroses and mental illness seemed rare and he saw less hypertension than at Hopkins. Syphilis showed up from time to time, a legacy of World War I.

A few weeks later, strolling back to the Hospital from a house call in Crow Head, John heard a commotion near the shore. In a shallow cove a crowd of laughing women and children were running about with dipnets, baskets and buckets, scooping up something. "The capelin has struck in," they told him excitedly. It was his introduction to the little fish that swarmed ashore each June under the full moon to become codfish bait, garden fertilizer and winter food for people and dogs. The swarming silver and olive capelin rose and fell with each wave, darkening the bottom in thousands. Just offshore a man stood in a punt, holding the skirt of a lead-weighted castnet in his hands and teeth, intently watching the water. When the surface dimpled, his net flew out in a graceful oval, dropped with a *shush* over the fish and sank around them. In moments he was wrestling a wriggling purseful aboard. By early July the stench of rotting capelin from Twillingate's gardens would be almost overpowering. Nobody seemed to mind; John ignored it too.

That month John was disgusted to learn that Lois had gotten married after all, and moved to a pretty house on Mohawk Avenue in Norwood, Pennsylvania. She was now Mrs Stuart Chapman. "Her life is my idea of nothing at all...." he grumbled. "I suppose I will get in a rut sometime but hope not for a long time."

The Medical Director got back on June 23rd. Dr Parsons looked older than John remembered, a prematurely balding man in his late thirties with a Chaplin moustache and sad eyes behind thick-lensed round glasses. He welcomed the students warmly. In the OR, however, the older man cut and sutured with a sureness borne of long practice. Yet during longer procedures his hands trembled and sweat beaded his forehead. And sometimes, scrubbing up together, John smelled alcohol on his breath.

"We get busier and busier," he wrote. "Most of the patients are TB...." He did examinations, wrote up cases, and assisted in the OR. He began to use doctor's short hand: "I had a pt. [patient], old man c [with] carcinoma [cancer] of the esophagus that almost died but I kept giving him glucose intravenously & he was alive when I put him on a little motor boat at 3:30 AM to go home. I feel sure he died on the way though." He interrupted the letter to attend a man delirious with terminal meningitis. "Three have died on me, & none on the other 2 fellows so it looks like I better go in Pathology." He sat up most of one night trying to save a dying gall-bladder patient with glucose injections and a blood transfusion. During one week he did five gastro-intestinal X-ray series, one gall bladder series and numerous chest and bone X-rays.

The week of July 20th was especially hard. "In one day I had a tough pair of tonsils which bled a lot & the pt. was very sick afterwards & had to be taken back & sewed up again. And then, giving a pneumothorax [injection of air into pleural cavity to collapse lung] I broke the needle off inside the person & hunted for 2 hrs & never did get it." That same week a pneumothorax patient either went into shock or had an epileptic attack and her heart and breathing stopped for about a minute. "She had violent convulsions c. screaming and laughing and biting her tongue. [Her heart] only resumed beating when adrenalin was put directly into it by needle." In addition, a little girl had died and another was dying. When tissue samples from a three-year-old boy's swollen lymph glands suggested Hodgkins Disease, he pondered how to tell the parents.

"This is the hardest place to get any sleep in I ever saw. If one doesn't have to get up with a dying patient, one gets called to go & meet the steamer, which is most irregular & usually comes between 2 & 3 AM, to meet or send off patients or supplies."

Pulling teeth in Outpatients, or "OPD," was a welcome change. It was uncomplicated and it brought the patient quick relief. "Great fun!" he exclaimed. But he never got used to seeing a beautiful girl smile and reveal a mouthful of rotten teeth.

A fortnight later he wrote to say he was "getting his first restless attack—it won't last long I suppose." Dr Parsons thoughtfully lent him his old 35-foot sailboat. On the first sail the wind died three miles from home. Rowing back in a downpour, he thought ruefully of Pop and Tutie cruising Long Island Sound in comfort on *Joloma II*.

"The people here are so religious you can do practically nothing on Sunday. I think we shocked many by going out in the boat this afternoon. They have a Church of England, Methodist, Episcopal, Catholic & Salvation Army—[the latter are] about the most powerful and parade with band on Sun.; the Pentacostals [sic] who are like Holy Rollers. They were supposed to have a baptismal dipping this afternoon but didn't, probably thought the water too cold. It was—as we found out when we went swimming."

An urgent telegram came saying Dr Knapp was seriously ill in Lewisporte. John had just finished repairing the X-ray unit when Dr Parsons told him to come right away. Around 6:00 PM they set out for Lewisporte. A half hour later the motor died. The engineer tinkered in vain for an hour while John, sculling with an oar to keep the boat off the rocks, looked quietly on. When the engineer gave up, John fixed it in about ten minutes, "which pleased Dr Parsons as he was getting worried." They arrived at midnight, saw to Dr Knapp and started back around 2:00 AM. By 7:00 AM, after two halts "because the engineer wouldn't leave the motor alone," they were in the OR doing a tonsillectomy. It was John's third; he did it in eighteen minutes and did it well.

One morning at six o'clock an accident case arrived by open boat, the crew having travelled most of the night from White Bay. Caught under a falling barn, the man had dislocated both hips and fractured his lower pelvis. He was also spitting blood. They put him under ether, eased the femurs back into their sockets, pinned his sacrum and gave him morphine. He was very sick for weeks, but in time went back to work.

On July 24th Governor Anderson arrived on the coastal steamer for a short visit. Dr Parsons arranged a reception with the town's business and church leaders and their wives. The students had to dress up and serve as guides. "Much fuss...all very silly & the governor is a fool," wrote John.

To relieve Dr Parsons and Dick Blackwell, the students undertook most of the house calls. For a time he was calling on five different patients. He performed a delivery and "got a very nice baby girl, named after the nurse that was with me." The mother wanted him to christen it but he refused. He checked in on a boy whose broken arm he had set the day before and found him comfortable. There was a typhoid fever case, an epileptic and a girl bleeding from a miscarriage. He was thankful they were all doing well.

The patients seemed to like him. He certainly liked them. Walking back home to the Hospital from these house calls, swinging his black bag, he felt such a lift of happiness as he had not felt since Alaska. He decided he loved this place—the sea, the land and the people.

August was a month of hot afternoons and chilly nights. Whole families took to the bogs and hillsides to pick bakeapples and blueberries for the coming winter. On the flakes, women in shawls and bandannas turned the pale golden triangles of salt cod in the sun and whisked them under cover at the least threat of rain. In twos and threes, deep-laden schooners with patched tan sails tacked in from the Labrador amid rejoicing and frantic activity around wharves and storerooms.

Every morning he swam before breakfast. The water was so cold, he said, you hadn't time to start shivering before you had to get out, and then you actually felt warm. Lobsters were cheap but scarce. "Once we had over 10 lbs for $1.05!" Bumps and Connie and three summer nurses left for home via Lewisporte. John, who had grown fond of the one named Betty Arms, saw them off in Lewisporte and met the three incoming students. Among them was Stanton Hardy, a Harvard and later Hopkins man who was to become a lifelong friend.

In August he lost two patients, but in surgery he scored a small triumph: "Last week I did an appendix myself & the pt. has the most beautiful scar & hasn't been a bit sick since.... It was encouraging." Doing this basic operation quickly and neatly would become a matter of pride with him.

He acquired an old sailboat, "hard to steer but better than nothing." One day in a stiff breeze Dr Blackwell, no sailor, bet him he could sail astern of an anchored schooner, come about and pass in front without colliding. John figured he could win if Dick didn't drown them both. On the first try, Blackwell nearly ran the boat on the rocks. On the second John barely prevented their capsizing. "I am sure we would have sunk as the wind was blowing hard and we were moving fast."

In September he took out two more sets of tonsils, this time using local anesthetic, "...more sporting than ether, and, I think, if the patient will keep still, you can do a better job." He did his second appendix and his first major operation. A girl thirteen years old came in with severe pain, which he correctly diagnosed as appendicitis and TB peritonitis. "There was the most extensive peritonitis c. dense adhesions binding down everything. I finally got the appendix out, which was affected, & sewed her up, but she has little chance of living long." During another appendectomy he found "the most amazing thing—a cancer of the tip, which is rare enough in adults & almost unheard of in people below 40-50."

An unwritten staff rule decreed a party for anyone having a birthday. John's wasn't due for months, but he began hinting it was September 27th. At first nobody believed him. Nurse Dot Blackman wrote Mary to get the truth; but by the time her reply came it was October and the laugh was on them.

Twillingate now began to show a harsher face. The memory of August afternoons on sunny hillsides faded as scudding storm clouds hid the sun for days. From the OR windows he saw mountainous grey seas blossom white as snow against Burnt Island's iron cliffs. By supper time it was already dark. When the generator died one evening they ate by kerosene lamps normally reserved for night rounds. Until the steamer brought a replacement part a week later, they had to operate by lamplight as well.

Near the end of September, his Twillingate sojourn more than half over, he wrote Pop a modest assessment: "I have done a lot of things I didn't expect to. I at least am getting some idea of the general course of a patient's illness & how long he is liable to be sick & when to do certain things, which is something." He said nothing about falling in love with Newfoundland.

It seems clear that Dr Parsons overloaded this talented young man. To allow a Junior student to perform fairly advanced surgery verged on recklessness. He may even have assigned him cases he should have handled himself. That summer, the patient load was particularly heavy, and the Director seemed to be ill a lot. In fact he was sometimes too drunk to operate. The Directors understood all this, and were certainly aware of John's ability. As for John, he simply helped all he could. Whatever Dr Parsons' failings, John knew how much the man had accomplished since 1922, when Dr Grenfell had released him from the Battle Harbour Hospital to supervise construction and fund-raising for the new Hospital. Dr Parsons had argued down those who wanted a small clinic, and had served as Chief Surgeon and Medical Director ever since Governor Allardyce had cut the ribbon on September 20, 1924. Since then he and his one assistant had routinely done four to five hundred procedures a year. Among the four residents who preceded Blackwell—Andrews, Wilszusen, Green and Abrams—not one had stayed three years. Even on his holidays to the States, Dr Parsons had to raise money.

One day the older man showed John his plans for the new 30-bed wing. Drafted by a Cincinnati firm from his sketches, they showed a two-storey, south-facing extension. Its basement level would provide new space for meat, vegetable and fuel storage and a new morgue; the first floor would give them new children's wards, a sewing room and diet kitchen; the second would give them five more private rooms plus a recovery room. And, for the first time, they would have a utility elevator. His next task, Dr Parsons said tiredly, was to find the money.

John pitied Charlie Parsons. He was too fond of women, alcohol and drugs for his own good. His drinking had alienated most of the directors. The nurses and aides no longer trusted him. More than one female patient had complained about his sexual advances.

November came, spitting hail against the OR windows. On the roads below, sheep and goats pawed for the last grass under the picket fences. As northeasters darkened the short afternoons and whipped Hamilton Sound to fury, the stream of Sunday afternoon patients in the OPD or Outpatients Department dwindled. Long-term TB patients wrote home saying they'd be in hospital till spring after all. Old women began to knit Christmas sweaters and socks.

Each day tempered John's steel harder. He began to speak the casual, heartless lingo of hardened physicians. "I just lost 2 more patients, one after operation for a large tumor & the other from an infection of the leg which went into puerperal infection as she aborted soon after arriving. The infection one died at 3:00 AM & I got her undertook about 4:00 (I am getting to be an expert at that & can make them look real lifelike)."

He found ways to dispel the tension. The night the woman died he never went to bed at all. At first light he and Dick walked two miles to Back Harbour to hunt. The little auk-like bullbirds were rumoured to be in from Greenland. John had Pop's twelve-gauge and Dick brought Dr Parsons' 10-gauge. Rowing out into a raw northeaster, the two oilskinned hunters suddenly found themselves in a maelstrom of whistling, tumbling birds. In an orgy of gunfire they downed twenty-two before running out of shells. They rowed back and got four more boxes, returning with seventy birds. The next day, there were so many boats that the birds were gun-shy and they got only ten. But a week later they bagged ninety-five. After a few feeds they put the rest in the Hospital cooler.

"The most I have gotten at a shot is 8. The old men up here shoot only muzzle loaders—bigger than your thumb & seven feet long. I shot one 3 times this morning & nearly went out of the boat each time...." To the fishermen, bullbirds meant fresh winter meat and soft pillows, a gift from the Almighty; for the two weary physicians they were a sacrificial offering.

"I hate to leave here very much," he confessed to Mary, "as I have been more at ease than anywhere for a long time." The night before they left for Lewisporte, Dr Parsons begged John to stay the winter. But he sailed from St John's on November 26th as planned.

Back in Baltimore, he found his classmates frantically trying to secure internships. John applied for surgery at Hopkins, with Pathology as a second option. A week later he wrote, "Every day it gets more obvious that I can't hope to even approach happiness in our 'civilized cities'.... I wish I were in Newfoundland."

All that winter he was glum. He designed a new stomach clamp, but "...no one was interested & it is too expensive for me to make & when made I would be the only one to use it so what is the use?" He fell behind in his Psychiatry case write-ups and presentations and despaired of catching up. "I don't like it half as well as surgery & I don't like surgery much," he moaned. When everyone started fretting about summer work, he said, "In Newfoundland everything was so simple. Here everything is so complicated." There was one bright note. A German author whose work on the liver Stafford and he had criticized wrote them a sarcastic letter. "He will have to do more work to prove us wrong—and if he does I won't believe him."

In March a fire removed the third floor and one side of their boarding house. This cheered him up. Then, two weeks before final exams, the Pathology students staged a play and celebrated with a cast party. "Everyone had a fine time...One broken arm (Stebbins), 3 black eyes, several damaged legs, 2 cut wrists & the ruining of many suits of clothes...The play was better than expected."

The final exams were tough and the heat again oppressive. "Never have I been so relieved or sweated so much over exams," he wrote. He was sure he had flunked Psychiatry. In early June, however, he told his mother, "You may now address my letters 'Dr.'"

That summer, after a short cruise on *Joloma II* with his parents, he worked as a youth counsellor with a hundred ten-year-olds at Camp Iroquois on Lake Champlain near Burlington, Vermont. "There are about 1000 other things I would rather do...none of which would result in a positive cash balance in the end however." The only medical crisis was a smallpox infection which he checked by vaccinating everybody, including the staff, some of whom had to be threatened with dismissal before they complied. In 1936 his decisive action would similarly avert a typhoid epidemic in Twillingate. He admitted to Alfred that he liked bossing people around.

In the fall of 1931 he began his internship in the Hopkins Neurological Service, passing instruments to Dr Walter Dandy, a world-renowned neurosurgeon and the first to use injected gas to X-ray brain anomalies. He had "the worse temper in the world & is proud of it," said John. In years to come, many would accuse John of the selfsame OR manners. "I don't want to stay here longer than this year—and for that matter I didn't want this appointment. But as always I have been completely conservative & done what was 'best.'"

Twillingate haunted him. His letters became scarcer and gloomier. A Christmas card from Dr Parsons saying, "Come on, John, and chip in for the winter," only deepened his malaise. He stayed in Baltimore over the Holiday and asked that nobody send him presents.

In January of 1932, Twillingate sent a telegram offering him a term residency under Parsons starting next autumn. In a confidential follow-up letter, they told him Dr Parsons was to take a six-month study leave next winter and might not return. As Dr Parsons would be paid while on leave, they regretted being unable to offer more than $50 a month and found, but promised to double that if he stayed a second year.

John slept on it and wired "Yes." On the 18th he told his mother: "I shall go up in November & shall stay ?? [sic] years." He knew what his father and Uncle Frank thought, for Lois had just spent most of a weekend in Baltimore trying to change his mind. "No doubt you have received a full report on my acts, actions & thoughts," he grumbled to Mary, "none of which are anything to be proud of. However...I shall not sink if I can maintain a sense of humour." Pop wrote one of his rare letters, ending with, "If only you'll not go up there and bury yourself, we'll send you to Austria to do more work; we'll send you to Vienna." Mary had guessed all along that Johnny would return to Twillingate. Clearly he had the ability to succeed anywhere; it was equally clear that he could never be comfortable in a leather studded chair in Boston or New York. Life in Newfoundland would test his health severely, but the people seemed to need him so desperately. She left it in the hands of God.

As he moved toward the brink, John himself hesitated. "I should be very pleased," he confessed to his mother, "were it not for the acute realization that it is professional suicide & a complete waste of my education. It is too bad, but life is not worth bothering with around here—and I might as well go as do nothing."

In March Alfred sold *Joloma II*. Tutie would call it a casualty of the Depression; it was equally a casualty of John's decision to leave New England for good.

But there was this Arms girl, a secret girl whom not even Mary knew about. Elizabeth Joy Arms of Grand Junction, Colorado had entered the Hopkins' School of Nursing from Colorado College in 1928 and graduated with honours in 1930. He had known her barely two months when she returned to Baltimore as an OR nurse. In that brief encounter the willowy girl with the luminous face had completely overturned his notions of independence. Her merry brown eyes, soft voice and impish humour inhabited his mind.

He had called her on his return and they had dated ever since. He had said nothing to her of marriage, however.

To further complicate matters, Hopkins' Surgeon-in-Chief Dean Lewis now offered him a one-year trial residency as his assistant. This he knew was a coveted position. But he could not work in Baltimore. He asked Betty to marry him and return to Twillingate with him and she accepted. Unable to postpone telling his parents any longer, he invited them to Baltimore to meet her. After the wedding Betty would confess to Mary, "I am so glad you came, and it was such a relief to meet you and know that you approved. All that year had been a strain, but after that I felt so much happier." Alfred was captivated by Betty, who in the coming months and years would salve his disappointment over John as only Betty could.

Lois felt smug. Tutie concluded that her brother had a heart after all. Dr Parsons, himself finally married that June, was delighted. As most of Betty's relatives lived in the East, the wedding took place in Groton, Massachusetts.

On Saturday, September 3rd, 1932, the day of the wedding, they left with Dr and Mrs Parsons to catch the New York boat to Newfoundland. Newfoundland had no medical reciprocity with the States, so the two couples had to stay in St John's three days while John and Mrs Parsons, a pediatrician, took the Medical Board examinations. John's were tougher even than the Hopkins State Board exams, but that Friday evening they celebrated success.

The next morning, mildly hung over, they embarked on the *Prospero* for Twillingate. For three days the little steamer was buffeted by the fiercest storm in years. Most of the thirty passengers were sick, but the newlyweds "felt like regular old sailors," wrote Betty on September 9th, "and all the crew even marvelled at us…. We really enjoyed the trip, but I was glad to arrive. John is fine and makes a wonderful husband," she told Pop. "I can't get used to 'Mrs Olds,' tho'. John is going to get wonderful experience and I think we are both going to find it a very profitable year."

Chapter Seven

Independence

"There are unlimited fields in all directions here."

— J. M. Olds

On New Year's Day, 1933, Dr Parsons left with his wife for a six-month study leave in Vienna. John had hoped to spend a few weeks on a sealing vessel that spring to earn some money, but the sudden administrative load and the amount of friction among the nursing staff made it impossible. After he fired two aides, things improved and Betty was able to take a month's rest.

Late in February the couple moved out of the Hospital and into the Cottage. The Directors had bought the two-story frame house from the widow Elizabeth (Churchill) Young around 1923 and launched it to a site just east of and overlooking the Hospital. Dr Parsons had endlessly remodelled it, tearing out partitions, adding dormers and a glassed-in sun porch, putting in a fireplace. John liked the long shed and garage under the porch with ample space for tools and a motorcycle—if he could persuade the Board to buy one. And he liked living closer to the workshop and warehouse.

The Cottage proved to be as cold in winter as it was pleasant in summer. With the gales of winter there were times when they expected the 12-paned verandah windows to give way in a shower of glass. The newlyweds draped the frost-feathered windows and stuck mats under the doors and laughed to see them billow in the draft. On nights when wind moaned under the eaves and sleet rattled against the panes, they huddled by the wood stove or one of the two large fireplaces, piling on coal and drinking rum toddy or hot cocoa. They postponed as long as possible undressing in the frosty bedroom and diving between freezing sheets warmed only by a hot stone in a sock.

They tried to save some money but it wasn't easy. As Charge Nurse she earned $75 a month; he received only $50. He had hoped the Directors would increase his salary but he would not ask. In April the sealing vessel returned with 56,000 pelts, the largest catch ever landed there. "I certainly lost money by not going," he grumbled. Yet the couple had saved $400 in

Newfoundland money. They kept it at the local Bank of Nova Scotia, where they hoped it would be safer than in Hartford. Besides, US interest rates were only two percent and the exchange rate only twenty. The rumour that the Bank of Newfoundland might collapse, and with it the Newfoundland Government, worried them considerably.

That winter they set up a well baby clinic. The flood of preventable childhood cases of rickets, scurvy and tuberculosis made it urgent. Backed by his Directors and Dr A. J. Wood, one of the town's two private doctors, John made a pitch to the local clergy. If the Hospital staff could teach mothers proper infant care and feeding in a free clinic, he argued, it would not only save many babies but free the doctors and nurses to serve more patients. On March 4th eighteen church women, representing almost the whole district, launched the Child Welfare Association. Mrs Hollands presided, Mrs A. J. Wood was treasurer and Mrs A. H. Hodge acted as secretary. Dr Olds would direct the Clinic, which was to be run by contributions. He put notices in *The Twillingate Sun* inviting mothers to bring their babies once a month on Wednesday afternoon from 2:00 to 6:00 PM for bathing, examination and any necessary operations.

At first nobody came. But when word spread that the Hospital was giving away baby food and clothing, the younger women began to show up until there were seven or eight regulars. Breast feeding, good personal hygiene and a balanced diet for older babies were among the lessons. Some of the sessions were humourous. One day after a talk on sterilizing milk one woman snorted, "Well, now I can't sterilize my nipples, can I?" Another stopped coming when she learned that turnip water had vitamins in it.

"A Dole baby was in serious danger after weaning," said Dr Olds. "So we dispensed an awful tasting concoction of cod oil—not very refined—in which was suspended dried brewer's yeast and calcium lactate powder. This hopefully took care of vitamins A, B and D and the calcium unobtainable from milk. A turnip with instructions for getting juice out of it took over the C problem from oranges. A pound of margarine supplied another part of the milk and a pound of prunes was good for the bowels and blood. The food—except probably the cod oil mixture—could be eaten by adults and there were rumours of midnight prune 'scoffs.' A fair diet for about $1 a month," he wrote in the *Twillingate Sun*, "and [we are] seeking contributions of food and money." Oatmeal was also provided.

Three days before his 27th birthday that March, as he had done so often in Uncle Ollie's office, John slowly tapped out a letter to his father. "The secretary is in bed with the 'flu, and I have decided to learn a little about running the typewriter as when she gets well she is going to be discharged." This letter, his first on Hospital stationery, was more symbolic than perhaps he knew. He had promised the Directors to stay for a year, and there was a chance Dr Parsons might not return. Clearly he wished to convince Pop of the importance of his work.

"Of course I enjoy being the boss, but it seems like a big responsibility at times. My baby clinic is doing well; 17 cases last Wed. We have examined nearly the whole island now from birth to 3 yrs of age. None are much to be proud of." Then he asked Alfred to find him a second-hand 10-20 HP engine for a 40-foot boat he was having built, "not fancy but dependable...not over $200 delivered." I might also experiment with it on a sled next winter," he added. His obsession with mechanized overland travel had begun.

With the opening of navigation in June, the *Prospero* brought back Dr and Mrs Parsons and delivered three Hopkins medical students. The Director seemed "improved in health but certainly not what he used to be.... He doesn't seem very popular any more & some people won't let him do anything with them." Board Chairman Frank Roberts and his Directors were faced with a dilemma. In the past they had overlooked Dr Parsons' behaviour because they had no one else to run the Hospital and because they hoped his marriage and study leave would help. When they saw little improvement, they knew he had to go, but hesitated to lay such a burden on one so young as John.

The summer influx of patients now commenced. Expecting little surgery out of Dr Parsons, John relied heavily on the Hopkins students and on the new resident assistant, Dr Goodwin. "Dr Parsons isn't so very well and doesn't do much operating," was how Betty phrased it.

That year the fishery was again poor, with weak markets and strong competition from Scandinavia. Merchants in Fogo, Change Islands and Twillingate felt the pinch, and that fall had to cut off credit to many fishermen. Newfoundland's treasury, already weakened by the Morris regime's reckless spending on branch railways, was almost bankrupt. People had hoped that Sir Richard Squires' Liberals, elected in 1928, would straighten things out; but the little Dominion's ills were larger than that. To their credit, the Liberals had brought in the country's first comprehensive health and welfare legislation in 1931—but the same party had offered to sell Labrador to Canada for $110 million, which rang alarm bells in London and Ottawa. The election of the United Newfoundland Party under F. C. Alderdice in June 1932 brought no improvement.

Watching these events unfold, John wondered how an institution such as the Hospital, which depended on Government grants, merchants' donations and whatever funds they could raise around the Bay and from the States, could survive. Would Britain allow its oldest colony and greatest fishing platform to be swamped like an overloaded skiff in a storm? Could Canada in good conscience let a neighbour and fellow Commonwealth member default on its loans? It was true that Newfoundland's per capita debt was smaller than Canada's, yet personal income in the country was so low that mass starvation was possible. In February 1933 a Royal Commission had been announced.

As the Depression tightened its grip, Twillingate's patient load increased, maintaining a summer level of 65 to 70 inpatients all that winter. The two town physicians, A. J. Wood and Isaac LeDrew, felt the pressure too. People would sign on to one doctor's books on credit, find out they couldn't pay, and switch to the other's. Then they would throw themselves on the Hospital's mercy. To save the situation, the Government granted private practitioners $1,500 a year to treat paupers free.

Dr LeDrew had never liked the Hospital. He had opposed its construction, boycotted its opening in 1924 and badmouthed it ever since. To him it was simply unfair competition. That fall he packed up and left. For the sake of his abandoned patients, the directors asked Dr Parsons to organize a new set-up. As November's first snow squalls swirled around the Hospital, his committee worked night after night on the details. In return for a fixed salary, "Doccy" Wood agreed to join the Hospital staff for two days a week and emergencies. All doctors agreed to take house calls on Twillingate and New World Islands. There would be one set of books, with the regular $5.00 doctor's fee going to the Hospital. While the payment scheme was to change under John Olds' Blanket Plan the following year, the house call provision would still be in effect forty years later.

Under the Liberals' Health and Public Welfare Act of 1931, relief committees had been formed in every district. Dr Parsons chaired the Twillingate Island Committee, and John became his vice-chairman in charge of censuses and food distribution, which included brown flour for the Dole rations. "I may have something to do if he gets drunk," John quipped that winter. "He made a big mess last weekend." When Parsons tried to merge the Child Welfare Association with Dr Olds' committee, John refused, reasoning that when the Government disbanded those temporary committees his Baby Clinic would be lost.

A few weeks before Christmas 1933, eight months into her first pregnancy, Elizabeth Parsons developed toxemia. A shaken Dr Parsons put her entirely in John's hands. One morning at 3:00 he performed an emergency cesarian section but her baby was born dead and her own survival remained in doubt. "It worried me considerably," John wrote Pop with typical understatement, "but I feel today that she will live."

Charles Parsons' courage, wasted by years of overwork, drink and morphine, was melting like a candle near a hot stove. Somehow he dragged himself to St John's in one last effort for the Hospital and the brown flour drive. A few weeks later he suffered a complete nervous and physical breakdown. On Dr Olds' advice, Mrs Parsons took him to a Boston psychiatrist. She had no sooner returned than Charlie begged her to come back, which she did. "I rather expect Dr P. will resign," said John, "but I hope to get the Directors to continue his salary for a year, though it will cut down mine." He would also miss Elizabeth Parsons' help in the pathology section.

With the summer students gone and only Dr Goodwin to assist, John coped as best he could. He amputated a woman's gangrenous leg at mid-thigh, successfully removed an old man's bladder cancer after a four-hour struggle and repaired numerous inflamed appendices, suspended ovaries and painful hernias. All recovered well. He confessed to his mother that he sometimes had to study a procedure in books before operating.

The number of house calls increased but he didn't mind. "It is good to get outside. The winter has been unusually cold—the oldtimers can remember nothing like it but the travelling has been good with horse or dogs. Mostly I ride horseback, & in that seem to be unique, but we have a beautiful new horse. It is a lot of fun."

He enjoyed his patients. They were so direct and open, entirely unlike the tense and suspicious people of large cities, more like the poorer blacks of Baltimore. He recalled laughing when the black porters on the *Admiral Farragut* couldn't understand their Japanese passengers. Now the joke was on him. If the OR was his boot camp, ward rounds and OPD became his language school. Understanding his patients was like trying the decipher Shakespearean English the first time one heard *King Lear*. They pronounced his surname in a dozen different ways, always with an "H" in front. He starting listing the variations, but stopped after eight or ten. "Dr Hose" and "Dr Holds" were the commonest. Almost every afternoon, barring emergencies, he and Dr Goodwin spent two or three hours in OPD. As he plied stethoscope, blood pressure cuff and reflex hammer, he discovered an even richer trove of unconscious wit. Humour might be the last thing on their minds, yet it rolled naturally off their tongues. Their prose—17th century West County English marinated in tears and sweat and rum for two centuries—sometimes baffled him. His Yankee drawl was equally incomprehensible to them.

A father would arrive with his ailing daughter and announce, "Doctor, I got a maid 'ere and I wants you to see to she." Before long Dr Olds began to scribble sayings on cigarette packs and prescription pads, and when they overflowed his desk drawer he bought a big ledger. Always he omitted the patient's name.

He discovered it was useless to ask outright what the trouble was. Invariably the surprised patient would retort, "Doctor, that's for ye to find out." The golden key was some variant of "What do you find?"

For many young women the cause of pregnancy seemed elusive. "Doctor," said one, "I got my feet wet picking berries in the burnt woods and my periods stopped." Another, asked when her last period had occurred, said, "I don't rightly know, but I think it was about bakeapple-picking time." A third, informed that she was pregnant and asked whether she was surprised, replied: "No, Doctor. I work in the fish plant and thought I caught a cold."

One day he stopped by the bed of a woman who had arrived by boat from Exploits the day before. Expecting her to have voided a kidney stone overnight, he said, "And what did you pass?" Without smiling or missing a stitch in her knitting she replied, "I passed a skiff with a punt in tow, Doctor."

Another day, querying a male patient about his recent prostate operation, he said, "Can you pass urine all right now?"

"'Yes, doctor.'

"'A good stream?'

"'Doctor, I could piss over to the North Side!'"And how are you today, George?" he asked another. "Not bad, Doctor; but I believe my memory has capsized."

On February 17th, 1934, as the Royal Commission had recommended, Newfoundland got a new government. To a Yankee like John, it seemed a pity that responsible government, so hard-won in 1855, should be dissolved in favour of a committee under the King's thumb. However, perhaps the new Commissioners could do something for the Hospital. Whatever happened, he thought, he would have to deal with it because Dr Parsons was resigning. In a month or so, he would be the new Medical Director. One of his first acts, he decided, would be to fire two more gossiping aides.

"It is apparently a fairly permanent job," he wrote Alfred and Mary after the appointment came through. "Of course that depends on many things, and to keep the place going I have to finance it as well as run the medical end. However, with the new govt in power I have hopes we will pull through. So, as far as I know now we shall be staying a long time." Betty and he moved back to the Cottage.

John wondered what the Commissioners would be like to work with. It would not do to approach them too soon. One hospital 250 miles away might seem unimportant when thousands of fishermen were seeking able-bodied assistance to feed and clothe their families, when strikes and riots loomed and massive debts had to be paid. The collapse of the Newfoundland Savings Bank had been narrowly averted by loans from Canada and Britain, but what of repayment? Besides, he thought, the Commissioners were not answerable to the voters and might be hard to sway. However, his Directors assured him that Commissioner John Puddester, a Newfoundlander and responsible for Public Health, would prove a friend. John resolved to make a strong case for him when the time was right.

Feeling more secure than he had for two years, he urged his parents to sell their home and move to Twillingate once Alfred's mother died. In a four-page letter he told his mother how easy it would be to find a maid, to make new friends and to avoid tiring social engagements. He tried to sell Pop on the lower cost of living, pointed out that he could have a boat as big as *Joloma II* built for $150 or less and "indulge in all types of experimental rigs at practically no expense." He mentioned spectacular scenery to paint and the prospect of opening a commercial machine shop. There was a nice house for rent near the Hospital, he said, and he could even give Tutie a job when she graduated in two years from Simmons College in Boston.

He closed with a list of the things he had done the day before:

7:50	Got up—day cloudy
8:00	Breakfast
8:15	Hosp. rounds (3 patients; discharged 2)
9:00	Opened safe—gave Martin money to get express packages
9:15	Pulled 2 teeth; examined and admitted 2 patients
10:00	Mail arrived but hadn't time to read it as a call came to go to Herring Neck. Drove across Tw'gate Island—then 3 miles in boat; saw man with apoplexy—seized while out fishing; a premature baby; bad case of asthma
1:00	Dinner
2:00	Answered mail; wrote a circular letter to heads of Hosp. committees
2:45	Examined patient. Dr Wood came in, said he was all wore out being up all night & was expecting a call to Summerford in evening; I said I would go.
3:00	Pardy (farm manager) asked me to castrate a pig. Examined a patient.
3:45	Went up to barn & pig wasn't tied up so came down & examined patients
4:45	Castrated pig
5:00	Examined patient
6:00	Supper; received message to go to Summerford
6:30	Made Hosp. rounds. Drove across island, boat had not arrived. Went to island 1/2 mile away to light lighthouse lamp with keeper. Discussed means of raising money to put a phone in his house for use of people in bay coming for Dr
7:30	Boat arrived
8:45	Arrived Virgin Arm Neck. Walked three miles to Summerford. Woman in labour, had a lot of trouble; baby born at 4:30 5:45. Walked to Carters Cove, 4mi., for boat, got home 8:30 AM & so on.

I am not up every night & don't operate on Saturday; otherwise it was a fairly typical day.

On the Hospital's tenth anniversary that September, John paid tribute to his mentor in the *Twillingate Sun*. "Under the superintendency of Dr C. E. Parsons [the Hospital has] given service of the highest quality.... It is recognized by the American College of Surgeons as [a] Grade A Hospital...on a level with the best hospitals in the USA.... I wish to pay tribute to Dr Parsons who has for four years been my friend and teacher, and who through his dynamic personality has been largely responsible for the well equipped institution which you have at your disposal today. He has contributed a tremendous amount of good to the Bay and shall never be forgotten."

While he felt sorry for Dr and Mrs Parsons, he had no regrets for himself and Betty. Only two years out of medical school and he had his own hospital; which of his classmates could say that? At twenty-nine, Betty was Head Nurse in that Hospital and scrub nurse in the OR. They had a home of their own. They had many new friends and loved the landscape and the life. He could hunt and sail. Twillingate's sounds—the bleating of sheep and goats, the vesper medley of dogs barking and howling around the Harbour, the throaty organ blast of Long Point's fog horn had become the background music of their lives. It was true that on his driver's test that summer the Constable had marked him only sixty percent—he would have to get used to the roads.

Betty felt as she had the previous Christmas, when in a long letter to Mary and Alfred she had said, "We both have had a perfect year together. I don't see how anyone could be any nicer than John is to me and I hope I do make him happy, as happy as he makes me."

As November's gales returned, John felt at peace. If his letters seemed to ignore ominous political events in Europe, it was not that he was unaware. Like many other bright young Americans, he was deliberately shutting that world out because he thought it had gone mad.

"There are unlimited fields in all directions here," he told Pop, "& while it may not seem to many a particularly brilliant ambition, it can amount to whatever I can make of it." He had just submitted a paper on anemia to Johns Hopkins and received an encouraging reply. He had plans to research the vitamin content of northern diets. He could see ways to improve the OR, the pharmacy, the workshop. He would go after the Commission for more money, and get it.

The father saw his son lost on a small bleak island on the edge of night. The son looked at the same island and saw a bright world that needed him.

Chapter Eight

Beriberi

"It was the Dole racket that brought it on."

—J. M. Olds

When Joey Smallwood was on the Confederation campaign trail, he won many voters with the slogan, "No more fousty brown bread!" Always a foxy politician, he was playing on emotions aroused twenty years earlier by an unpopular program of the Commission of Government that saved hundreds of outport fishermen and their families from a debilitating disease.

In the days before vitamin tablets and enriched flour, outport doctors often saw scurvy and rickets, but seldom if ever encountered beriberi until after 1931. Those who saw it tended to treat it as an infection, which did not help. Others, notably Dr Grenfell and Dr Charles Parsons, correctly blamed the ailment on malnutrition. And since by 1932 thousands of Dole recipients were surviving on a diet of mostly white bread and tea, they foresaw fearful consequences unless something was done and soon.

Beriberi, they knew, could be prevented by a modest daily intake of Vitamin B. Since this vitamin was readily available in whole wheat flour but not in the Government ration of white flour, they began to pressure Prime Minister Alderdice to substitute brown flour in Dole rations.

After Dr Parsons came back from his six-month study leave in the summer of 1933, letters and telegrams began to fly between St John's, St Anthony and Twillingate. Prime Minister Alderdice was sympathetic but cautious. "The matter was discussed by the Executive Government," he told Parsons that fall, "and it transpired that several members [thought that] a good deal of prejudice would have to be overcome before standard flour could be substituted.... Personally I...am in complete accord with your idea.... However, you remember the trouble that arose when cocoa, a nutritious beverage, was introduced instead of tea."

Finally the Government offered to pay flour shipping costs if the doctors would mix white flour with brown in the first year or two, and the program was launched. In November Dr Parsons was pleased to receive a telegram from Bay State Milling Company in Winona, Minnesota, copied to Prime Minister Alderdice, stating that 580 sacks of whole wheat flour had been cleared for shipment to St John's on the SS *Newfoundland*.

St John's merchants now began to grumble that they couldn't afford to stock both kinds of flour. Notre Dame Bay merchants were upset because they had already laid in their winter stock of 1,200 barrels of white. Prime Minister Alderdice was worried that welfare recipients might get double rations, some white, some brown. And many people still had to be convinced. In December Dr Parsons persuaded world nutrition authorities Dr Frederick Tindall of the University of Toronto and Dr E. V. McCollum of Hopkins to endorse the superiority of whole wheat flour. A few months later, Premier Alderdice's Government was set aside in favour of the six-man Commission of Government. The Commissioners, less cowed by political repercussions, stood behind Grenfell and Parsons.

When Dr Parsons left for good early in 1934, it fell to Dr Olds not only to distribute the hated flour to local merchants and relief officers, but to persuade people to use it. In the end it was largely due to his efforts that beriberi was conquered in the Bay. In November 1981 he told the story to the Parent-Teacher Association of Durrell, Twillingate Island. He called it "The Brown Flour Racket."

"When I was first here in 1930 we only had normal diseases like TB, typhoid pneumonia, diphtheria, et cetera. Two years later when I returned, beriberi had been added. Of course it was supposed to be an affliction of polished-rice-eating Orientals and maybe a few Boston drunks and had no place here. It was not an infectious disease—though some doctors thought it was, maybe something like polio—but was due to a deficiency of vitamin B in the diet. All that was known about it then was that it affected chiefly the nerves of the legs, leading to paralysis.

"What was the connection between Chinese eating polished rice and Newfoundlanders not eating polished rice and both getting beriberi? Although there were other factors, the basic cause was the economic depression which started in the US in 1929 and did not hit Newfoundland until 1931. It forced many people to go on the Dole, or public welfare, and these were the ones that contracted it.

"The beriberi here did not fit all the criteria of the Oriental type. Our type, when fully established, resulted in complete inability to walk. It started with tender calves, weakness and later loss of knee and ankle reflexes and delayed conduction time. Men were more often affected than women and young people more often than old people. There was no wet or cardiac manifestations as described in the Orient, there were no deaths and it was not painful. No sedatives ever had to be given.

"The diagnosis of beriberi was generally accepted and Dr Charlie Parsons and Dr Grenfell were working on the Government to improve the Dole diet by substituting brown flour for highly milled white and they finally succeeded in 1933.

"Dr Parsons and I introduced brown bread in the Bay. This caused considerable anxiety amongst the people. It was very unpopular and resisted as much as possible. The brown bread was 'not good'—it did not look good, did not taste good and was not white. There was also a social stigma—if you ate it you had to be on the Dole. It represented hard times.

"I have no idea who figured out the Dole diet, which was valued at six cents per person per day. He must have been an economist and he certainly was not a qualified dietitian even by the standards of fifty years ago.

"Vitamins were fairly well known even then. They had been hooked into the alphabet the same as now, but B was not split up into its various components and was simply thiamin. We were taught that A was for xerophthalmia [dryness and hardening of eyelids] and night blindness, B for polished-rice-eating Orientals, C for scurvy and D was for rickets. D was important in Baltimore, as the large coloured population tended to get rickets, causing contracted pelvis and obstetrical problems. E was mentioned; K had not made it.

"There was no widespread knowledge of vitamins, no vitamins on the market—even if we could have afforded them—and no big advertisements. The only affordable source of vitamin B for us was brewer's yeast and brown flour.

"I have no figures on how many cases of beriberi we had but I do know that up to 1945 we dispensed around 400 pounds per year of dried yeast powder which we got in 100-pound drums and gave to anyone with tender calf muscles. Once a person really had beriberi it took them eighteen months to get on their feet again.

"Before the brown flour hit the Dole diet, Dr Grenfell tried to help us out and arranged for a carload of wheat to be delivered to Lewisporte. It arrived in mid-winter and there was no way to get it here except by dog and horse teams over the ice. We did not have any money to pay the freight so we got it down on the halves. Most of the dog team owners were on the Dole and needed it as much as anyone. So they took half the load in payment and we gave out the rest to Dole recipients who applied.

"There was soon a big demand. I never heard of anyone eating it but it made fine free chicken feed. This would have been a good way of converting the vitamin B of the wheat to a more a palatable food, as eggs are high in vitamin B. However, it didn't work out that way, as any increased egg production was sold to buy white flour.

"I have no idea how many people were on the Dole—one got on and got off and got on again. To get on you had to convince your Relieving Officer that you were broke and could get no further credit from your merchant. I know that in some communities over 90 percent were on, and would guess that forty to sixty percent of Twillingate and New World Island were involved from time to time.

"To get Dole you received a note from the Relieving Officer entitling you to white flour, salt beef or pork, some molasses and tea. The flour was the main thing. The Dole diet couldn't have added up to more than about 1,200 calories—and no vitamins in the whole lot. It was about one-half starvation diet. So they had to get at least another 1,200, plus some vitamins, to keep reasonably well.

"Of course there was plenty of food available—no one was really starving. If people had a garden and a cow they would never get beriberi, and wild berries were plentiful. There were no rabbits on this island in those times, but there was plenty of fish. In those days, however, nobody would eat anything but salt cod. The old people were so set in their ways. They just ate what their grandparents ate and anything else be damned. They wouldn't eat the fresh cod, and they wouldn't look at a mackerel to save their life. Fresh herring was the same. At the Hospital we couldn't afford orange juice, so we got tomato juice, the next best thing. The barrels of that we had to throw away! They just wouldn't drink it.

"'Well, why not?'

"'Don't like it.'

"'Did you ever taste it?'

"'Nope.'

"And that was the end of that. If you didn't like it you didn't eat it. So the habit of bread and tea and more bread and tea got them into a B deficiency finally.

"Beriberi was not a problem in earlier times. It was the Dole racket that brought it on.

"Soon after I came back in 1932 I went on a call with Dr Wood. He had been the local practitioner for years. The call was to a house on New World Island and when we arrived no one was home except two boys about eighteen and twenty years old. They were cheerful and looked well nourished; but both were sitting on the floor, each propped up in a corner. Dr Wood asked who was sick.

"'We are, Sir.'

"'Well then, dammit, come over here so I can look at you.'

"'Can't, Sir; we can't walk.'

"It was true; their legs were absolutely powerless, yet they looked strong and healthy. We carried them to the boat, put them in the Hospital, and put them on a regular diet which included brown bread and a teaspoonful of dried yeast in a glass of water twice a day. They recovered in eighteen months. They could walk a bit then, but could not work for a few more months. This was typical of the well established cases. Sometimes the recovery wasn't complete. It depended on how long the condition had gone on.

"They lost all sensation in their legs. There's another type where it affects the heart; but ours affected the legs. The nerves became demelanated—the insulation came off them and this completely paralyzed the limbs.

"Some time after that, a young woman from Green Bay, four months pregnant and unable to stand, was admitted. She had recently married into a family of marginal fishermen who were on and off the Dole. Brown flour was mandatory for Dole recipients then. They were on the Dole at the time, but because of her delicate condition, they made a great effort to get white flour for her only and ate the brown themselves.

"She delivered a healthy baby at term, but the demands of pregnancy and no brown flour kept her in the Hospital for about twenty months.

"A puzzling case was that of a family of five—mother and father and three children aged five to ten. They were long-time Dole recipients and four of them had beriberi but not as completely paralyzed as those mentioned above. The father could stand but not walk, and the others could take a few steps holding on to something. The little five-year-old girl was as spry as ever. They supposedly all ate the same food—Dole—and they had grown their own potatoes. Finally, after a lot of questioning, the little girl shyly confessed that she was so hungry that she frequently ate the potato peelings after they were thrown out. Potato skins, and the skins only, contain vitamin B. Either because she was so hungry or happened to like them, they saved her from beriberi.

"It was always my impression the beriberi did not come easily; you had to work to get it. Bad leg complaints gradually became fewer and I cannot recall a real case of beri-beri after 1937 or 1938. Later, when Joey Smallwood made that remark, it did not matter, as white flour was reinforced with vitamins by then—but it seemed unkind."

Chapter Nine

The Twillingate Plan

*"It took tremendous initiative and drive to do
a thing like that."*
— Fred Woodruff, MD

*"It is a great comfort not to have to consider money when
you deal with a suffering patient."*
— Robert Ecke, MD

J ohn Olds lay sprawled on a bunk in a small room with metal walls,
wondering whether the throbbing came from inside or outside his
skull. He shuffled outside and found himself on a ship. He slouched
over the rail, blinking like an owl in the dazzle of July sun on the
Harbour, and then he remembered. The *Prospero* was leaving St John's and
he was on it, going back to Twillingate with bad news. As the little steamer
backed away from the waterfront's broken comb of wharves with its stink
of fish and tar, he glimpsed his reflection in the oil green water below.
Suddenly his gorge rose and he vomited. He wiped his mouth, straightened
his back and stared up at the green and ochre row-houses with their
thousand sooty chimneys rising step-like to the Upper Levels. As the ship
slowly gathered distance, the old city and its landlocked harbour shrank to
postcard size. The last landmark he saw as they passed Chain Rock and the
Battery was the twin-towered Roman Catholic Basilica on the horizon.
When the *Prospero* met the first ocean swells off Signal Hill, he recollected
his failed mission and the task ahead.

When Commissioner John Puddester had requested his presence "to
discuss the Hospital grant for 1935," John had been hopeful. He had
prepared his case well, arming himself with statistics on the Hospital's
patient load, its need for new equipment and the consequences of cutting
the grant. The Commissioner, a balding, energetic man about twice his age,
had assured him he had read Dr Parsons' 1933 submission. The young
physician had begun by saying that in such hard times a viable Hospital
was the Government's strongest asset in the Bay, which had fewer doctors

now than twenty-five years ago. He reminded Mr Puddester that, in 1933, donations had shrunk to $3,900 while patient-days had risen sharply to nearly 20,000. Even with the current annual operating grant of $32,000, he argued, next year's costs would put them $13,000 in the red. He told him that tuberculosis, beriberi and rickets were increasing in the Bay.

As he spoke, Dr Olds studied the Commissioner's slightly jowled countenance. Except for some self-consciousness about a wall eye, the face was impassive. Finally Mr Puddester had run a soft hand over his wispy hair, stood, and said that he was sorry but the grant would be cut by $7,000 to a permanent basic amount of $25,000 a year.

Dr Olds had muttered something about locking the Hospital's doors by Christmas, grunted his thanks and stalked down the steps of Government House. Once past the iron gates, he turned east on Military Road and strode down Cochrane Street toward the nearest tavern. After that he killed a bottle of Jamaica black rum with friends—and without their help never would have found the ship.

As Cuckold's Head and Quidi Vidi receded, he thought: Why wait till Christmas even? That would only strand patients in Twillingate when navigation closed. No; he would have to discharge all patients before the end of November and notify every community from La Scie to Musgrave Harbour to send no more. Notre Dame Bay Memorial, monument to the people's sweat and Dr Parsons' dedication, would die on its tenth anniversary. Saving it would take more than a magician like Prospero, he thought bitterly. And if it closed, he might as well go back to Baltimore or even Hartford with his tail between his legs. Pop would have proved him wrong.

Presently, fog drove him into the warm saloon, where he stood by a window and stared at the purple cliffs snarling with foam and yearned briefly for gentle Long Island Sound. Then his mind ranged ahead to the archipelago he had begun to call home. He saw the lean, wind-burned men of Exploits and Herring Neck toiling ten or fifteen hours a day with hand-line and jigger, bucksaw and pickaxe. He saw their women bent double on the fish flakes, saw them tending babies and aged parents, knitting or plucking seabirds by lamplight. Finally he thought of all the hollow-eyed victims of TB, hobbling on crutches, coughing and spitting their lives away on day beds by cold stoves.

After Cape St Francis the pounding inside his skull subsided and an idea came to him. Ordering black tea, he fished a prescription pad and pencil from his shirt pocket. As they steamed north, rolling gently in the Atlantic swells, he jotted and paced and ordered more tea and smoked and pondered. After supper he fetched a scribbler from the purser, lay on his bunk and, nipping from a flask of whiskey, transferred his leaning columns of figures and names into a neat report. He wrote swiftly, bridging his "t's" with sweeping lines. That night he hardly slept, rising several times to rewrite passages. By the time they passed Cape Bonavista he had the solution; by Cape Freels on the third day he knew it would work.

First he would have to sell the Directors on his idea. Pacing the tiny stateroom like a lion in a cage, he rehearsed his arguments. The Hospital would soon have to serve twenty thousand people in 98 communities scattered across four thousand square miles from Cape Freels to White Bay. Since all of these people looked to Twillingate for health care, it made sense that all should pay. Many could pay nothing; that he knew. Some could pay and would not; he knew that too. Enough could and would pay, once they comprehended the gravity of the situation.

The situation was simple. The Hospital needed $125 a day to survive. It could no longer rely on generous individual donations. Even big firms like the Ashbournes and Earles and Hodges were getting stingier. Government support might fall further. Ever since 1822, Twillingaters had enjoyed local medical care, right from Dr Tremblett down through the times of Drs Stirling, Scott, Chandler, Stafford, Smith, LeDrew and Wood. Since 1924 the rest of the Bay had looked to the Hospital. Losing it would be disastrous, especially now. With his scheme it could not only continue; perhaps they could even extend its care.

Surely, he thought, there was no need to remind his Directors that, unlike St Anthony, Notre Dame Bay Memorial had neither endowments nor wealthy patrons, nor a Dr Grenfell willing and able to work the American tiara and tuxedo circuit each winter, writing articles and soliciting funds while others did the doctoring. Dr Parsons had tried that. John had seen a 1929 *Sun* article listing over $7,000 in donations which he had collected—including $100 from some poor Millertown loggers. But a surgeon shouldn't be out raising money. *He* certainly wouldn't do it. Anyway, Twillingate had three times St Anthony's clientele. Already the new 30-bed wing was full.

One strong selling point of his pre-payment scheme, he would point out, was that even the poorest fisherman could contribute. An individual doctor expected cash—after all, he and his family could eat only so many turnips or potatoes. A hospital, on the other hand, could accept any amount of fish and vegetables or firewood, and could pay its staff with the money saved. The Plan would hurt no one's dignity.

With the kind of thrift and self-sufficiency practiced in Dr Parsons' day, it could save them. It need only cover the deficit for a few years until the country recovered. Didn't the oldtimers always say, "Many hands make light work"? Newfoundlanders thought nothing of hauling big houses with a crowd of men and a "Jolly Poker" shanty. They could save their Hospital too.

Back in Twillingate, he immediately called an emergency Directors' meeting. They weren't enthusiastic, wanted to stick with the old billing system. He argued that charging patients $1.50 a day for a ward bed, $3.00 for a private room and even a moderate amount for surgery would no longer work. Most people simply could not pay. That was why the whole Bay had donated only $3,900 last year. For that matter, he said, the old "Doctor's Book" system, under which each family entered its name and promised to pay $5.00 a year for unlimited office visits or house calls, would not work either. And people could not pay the extra charges for pulling teeth, deliveries and medicine.

After a long debate the Directors voted to try his plan for a year. They realized it would take enormous effort to gather the money. They would need a trusted individual in each community to collect the fees. Relief Officers were an obvious choice. So were parish priests such as Father Casey in Fortune Harbour and Rev. Felix Honeygold. It would also help enormously if they had a clinic boat to travel the whole Bay, much as Dr Grenfell's *Maraval* did on the Labrador.

Using Dr Olds' notes, the Directors drew up lists of people for every community. Through the late summer and fall they contacted all of them by letter, telegram and in person. By September John felt ready to unveil his idea in the *Sun*. He did not mention the Blanket Contract itself, because subscribers must be tallied before he could estimate the per capita fee. The article read in part:

> There are many people in the Bay who are in need of hospital care but are not receiving it. Why is that?
>
> First, because they can not afford it.
>
> Second, because they do not wish to apply for a government pauper's pass.
>
> Thirdly, because they don't understand what exactly the Hospital could do for them and are afraid to come.
>
> How can these situations be bettered? First, as regards cost. For the past two months I have been advocating [a] system whereby for the price of $10, a man can obtain a contract with the Hospital which will assure him of all necessary treatment for himself and his family at no further cost; and I have urged the formation of active Hospital Committees in all parts of the Bay which have a two-fold purpose: One, to [be] responsible for the health of the community by sending to the Hospital those who are ailing; and, secondly, to raise money....
>
> The Hospital is a most necessary factor in your lives as it will do all it can to keep you fit for work, and if you have the chance of work you have the chance of earning a good living for yourself and family. If you can't work you can't earn a living. To raise this money may mean a

definite sacrifice for some people; but remember, the Hospital is for you, and the Government is supplying about two-thirds of the money necessary to run it. You must for your own sake raise the other one-third. Let us then co-operate...so that the Hospital can maintain its service to you, and you can put your trust and confidence in the Hospital.

"I made out two kinds of contract," he later explained, "one for wealthy individuals and one for a community as a whole. The prices were based not on complicated actuarial studies but on hope and the absolute need to increase our income by at least the $7,000 cut. The expensive or Medical Centre one cost $10.00 per family and guaranteed all necessary hospital care, free. Only a few merchants' families bought these. The Blanket Contract was designed to care for everyone in a community.

"Committees were formed in all communities in the Bay that wished to participate," he continued. "The assessment in 1934 was forty-four cents per head. This was collected and forwarded to the Hospital office with the names of everyone in the community. It entitled them to the same privileges as the individual contract, except that operations, X-rays, lab work and medicines were half price. For example, a cholecystectomy [gall bladder removal] would cost the subscriber $10.00 for the operation, including the anesthetic; $3.00 to $4.00 for X-rays including chest X-ray; $1.00 for laboratory work—blood and urine: a total of $15.00-$16.00. And if you couldn't pay it, you didn't."

Melvin Woolfrey of Moreton's Harbour recalled a case like that. "There was a fellow came down from Dog Bay. He had his daughter with him; she was real sick. I was in the ward, right by Number Two. He came in the back door—that's the way they brought patients into Emergency—and stood alongside my door, talking. The old man said, 'Doctor, I got no money for to pay you.'

"'Skipper, don't you worry about that,' said Dr Olds. 'You've brought your daughter, and we'll do the same for her as if you could pay. But if you can bring a load of wood or something it would be appreciated.' The man went away smiling."

After 1936, when the Hospital bought the *Bonnie Nell,* the Contract also entitled people to one visit a year from the clinic boat. Captain Elijah Dalley thus became an able spokesman for the Plan in the thirties and forties, as did Captain Cecil Stockley in the fifties. Before them, Bert Butt helped for several summers, especially in Green Bay, and so did Gus Young of Gillesport. "He had a hard job to get any cash," said Mr Young. "A lot used to pay in fish and berries and lobster—whatever people could bring. If a man had ten or twelve children, that's what he would do. One man in Indian Islands—he wasn't destitute—said, 'Now Doctor, if I pays $10.00 for the Blanket Contract and I don't get sick, what'll you do about it?'

Gary Saunders

"'Well,' said Dr Olds, 'If you can get clear with $10.00 for a year and not get sick you ought to be thankful.'"

Once the idea was sold and the committees in place, money could be collected in each settlement before the boat arrived. The committees also supplied a "black list" of holdouts. "Some communities," said Olds, "had so many black sheep that the white sheep couldn't afford to pay for themselves and the black sheep as well. It was usually more lack of cooperation than inability to pay. To avoid penalizing a whole group, we offered an individual Family Contract costing $0.85 per person for the same privileges."

The Plan demanded great faith from the Business Manager. He never knew until autumn how much actual cash would come in."How often did we ask," mused stenographer Mayme (Roberts) Hewlett, 'What kind of money have you brought today?'" As secretary to five successive business managers between 1935 and 1958, she had received potatoes, beets, fish and diverse other products. "This payment-in-kind was taken to the storeroom, weighed, a slip sent to the office and the amount credited to either Contract, Hospital bill or Medical Centre—or the 'Middle Centre' as we jokingly termed it."

Nonetheless, cash income from the Bay rose by $7,600 in 1934, the Plan's first year. And although the Hospital gave a thousand more patient-days of care that year at just under $2.00 per patient, the books nearly balanced. In 1935 local income reached $16,000. By 1945, when the government grant had risen to $40,000, local collections exceeded it by $1,000.

"And that saved us," wrote Olds. "We started getting in a lot more funds from the people because for their pre-payment we gave them free care."

While the Plan solved the immediate financial crisis, fund-raising was a continual headache. Typical of the energetic self-help approach was that of the Notre Dame Hustlers Club, an amateur theatre group which some aides and nurses set up in 1937. In April 1938 this group, led by Joyce Scammell staged *Madame Majesty, a Comedy in Three Acts* with Mayme Roberts as leading lady. Another year they netted $500 with *Anne of Green Gables.* After the disastrous 1943 hospital fire, they took a play fifty miles to Botwood aboard the *Bonnie Nell* and made another $500. Between 1937 and 1958 the Hustlers raised $15,000 to buy bedside cabinets, electric stoves, children's cots, training aids and instruments.

As the economy improved, donations increased. Not all of the money came from Notre Dame Bay. Like faithful college alumni, former patients sent payments from afar. For years the Darwin and Junto clubs at Loomis in Windsor sent money. Every so often Dr Olds would launch a special appeal. In March 1937 he typed and mailed a letter which began:

It is always a disagreeable task to write a letter asking for money and it is even more so frequently to receive one. However...I hope you will agree that in this case the cause is justified.

He went on to document the Hospital's work, citing the 5,536 inpatients treated since 1924 and the 27,800 patient-days of care in 1936. The Blanket Contract, he said, had "greatly increased our obligations." What he specifically needed was "a new X-ray unit costing $2,500 landed. All amounts in excess of that would be returned with thanks," he said, shrewdly adding, "...unless they will kindly let [it] be credited toward...an engine for our travelling clinic boat." Pop received a copy like everyone else.

An extension of the idea of payment-in-kind was the donation-in-kind. Among their most reliable fund-raisers was the "Fish Appeal." It began as a one-time effort and became an annual autumn event throughout the Bay. Fishermen donated part of their catch to local collectors, who in turn reimbursed the Hospital.

Dr Olds launched the 1948 Fish Appeal in the *Sun* with these words:

> Five years ago the cost of running the Hospital for the year was $51,000—this year, $174,000. Income...is below last year's by $3,000, though much more work has been done. Government grants have increased, but there is a deficit of $26,000 for the year ending June 30, 1948. Bills owed by patients over the past six years have accumulated to $80,000 [with most being] under $50.00, there being 1,400 accounts.... Many of these could be paid and it is hoped they will be. But.... the Hospital [needs] funds for winter supplies as soon as possible.... Please give a few fish so that the Hospital can continue to help you when you need it.... If all [small bills] were paid we would be in a much better financial position.... *Maybe a fish a day will keep the doctor away!*

No matter what they did, however, increases in patient load and general expenses offset any gains. Hubert Vincent, who succeeded Allan Stoodley as business manager in 1953 and served until 1982, worked under the Contract system for over half his term. "Finances then were gruesome," he recalled. "Even with new hospitals in Fogo, Botwood, Springdale, Gander and Grand Falls [to relieve the patient load], Twillingate always had a deficit." In June 1952 it exceeded $20,000, which the Government promised to pick up. Ten months later when no cheque had come, Board Chairman Ned Facey went to St John's to demand it. A day or two later Vincent received this telegram:

COMING HOME TOMORROW OR NEXT DAY STOP
DEFICIT CHEQUE IN ASS POCKET

"This buoyed me up," said Vincent, "but that money was for the year *past*. I still had five months to go and the next audit to be done. Couldn't get the deficit payment until year-end anyway, because the Government had no money either. And *they* had to wait till year-end when the audited account went in. Our collections went up a little bit, but so did our expenses. But they always paid eventually."

To feed the more than one hundred people every day, they no longer relied on their own garden and livestock but bought from wholesalers. Sometimes Mr Vincent had to stall them. "We used to buy meat from Swift Canadian—fresh beef, so many quarters—and you'd get it on thirty days' grace. Well, when the thirty days were up and we couldn't pay, I'd go to Canada Packers and get another month's supply from them. Now then, when *their* thirty days was up, I had no money to pay *them*. But by now I had Swift paid off, so I could go back to them again. That's the way it went for several years. I don't think we were ever far enough out of debt that I could pay $500 at one time.

"Coal—we used to buy 700 to 800 tons a year. First we used to contract it from Ashbourne's; several years they had the contract. They'd bring it in late summer or early fall. Sometimes we'd have maybe 300 to 400 ton the one time in schooner. Ashbourne's *Bessie Marie* brought lots of it. Then Manuel's had the contract for so many years. They got it for about five cents a ton less than Ashbourne. John Manuel used to get the *Thomas B. Hollett* to bring it in; Manuel's had no vessel of their own."

They bought medicines in bulk direct from manufacturers in the States, Canada or even from Britain. One time they were so late paying the Canadian Liquid Air Company that it cut off further shipments except C.O.D. ones. Reluctantly Vincent paid up, even though other creditors had waited longer.

Having a friendly local editor helped. Over the years the *Sun* faithfully covered every Hospital tea and bake sale, benefit dance and play, and listed donors and amounts. In turn, Dr Olds supplied it with weekly lists of admissions, babies delivered and patients discharged by community, as well as occasional articles on difficult or unusual surgery. Anniversaries, such as the Hospital's twenty-fifth in 1949, were accorded special supplements. Every October the churches observed "Hospital Sunday" with special services honouring the medical staff. And of course any disaster, such as the fires of 1939 and 1943, produced a province-wide response.

From 1932 on, Dr Olds' ingenuity and thrift saved the Board thousands of dollars. He never bought anything he could make or improvise. He watched over every pencil and roll of adhesive tape as if it were his own. This frugality earned him the Directors' complete trust. When he asked them to buy something they knew he had exhausted all other avenues—even, in some cases, his own bank account and his parents' generosity.

Few but his closest friends knew that Olds gave and lent the Hospital large sums of money. "I know for a fact," said longtime colleague and friend Dr Fred Woodruff, "that in the early days, although he wasn't paid very much, he often gave money back to the Hospital. He was extremely generous." In December 1936, for example, he lent the Hospital $3,000 at five per cent interest. "And, you know," said Vincent, "for several years he didn't get even his interest on that loan. The Hospital couldn't pay it. But he got all of the principal back. The last payment was $1,500; I know, because I paid him."

Dr David Parsons, who worked with Olds in 1954, said, "Money had no interest whatsoever for him. So long as he could buy the tools that he wanted, the books, the magazines—that was enough."

In time, the initial 44 cents levy had to be increased. By the early 1950s the Hospital had 20,000 families subscribing at 85 cents a member. To this the government added $45,000. Until federal-provincial hospital insurance appeared in 1958 and universal Medicare arrived a decade later, the Plan gave Notre Dame Bay a workable system. After Medicare, said Olds, "you could worry but you couldn't do anything about it."

"Without the Blanket Contract," said Dr John Sheldon of nearby Virgin Arm Medical Clinic in 1989, "medical services as we know them would have ceased here. It's hard to believe that even in the mid-sixties, Twillingate people paid only $10.00 a year and those on this island only $13.00—the $3.00 difference being for house calls."

The success of Twillingate's scheme was not lost on the Commissioners. Young Dr Olds had proved that health insurance could work in Newfoundland. Although they studied British rural health care models such as Scotland's Highlands and Islands Plan, they almost certainly had the Twillingate Plan in mind in 1936 when they set up regional cottage hospitals on the South Coast. Their pre-payment scheme was essentially the same, though costlier. Dr Nigel Rusted, who worked on that coast in 1936-37, cited $7.50 a year for a family of seven. At Twillingate rates this would have serviced a household of seventeen; but then Twillingate's hospital was already paid for.

Despite all these economies and sacrifices, it was Dr Olds' Blanket Contract which saved Notre Dame Bay Memorial during the Depression years. In 1936, when Olds' scheme was catching on, the Canadian surgeon Norman Bethune was lobbying vigorously in Canada and the States for a form of socialized medicine similar to the Soviet Union's. The Establishment's rejection of his proposals played no small part in his decision to abandon Canada for Spain and later for China, places where he felt more useful. One of the ironies of his passionate career was that three decades later, Canada would adopt a similar scheme.

Like Bethune, Dr Olds put forward a form of social medicine—albeit on a small scale and administered by a hospital association, not the State. His philosophy, that health care should not be the prerogative of the wealthy, paralleled Dr Bethune's. The main reason John Olds' plan succeeded while Bethune's failed was that Olds' small kingdom had no entrenched medical and political hierarchy. Dr LeDrew had left and Dr Wood had joined the Hospital. The fish merchants considered healthy fishermen good business. Another factor in Olds' success was that his costs were low and the people shunned doctors. And although Newfoundlanders took their politics seriously, labels like "Commie," "Red" and "Pinko" meant little to them.

Was the Twillingate Plan North America's first true medical insurance scheme? Probably not; but it was certainly one of the first. American health officials knew that Europe had utilized health insurance since the late 1800s, and that Britain had since 1911. Some progress had been made in the US before 1914, but these reforms were undone by World War I. By 1929 Dallas Methodist Hospital had a health care scheme for teachers and in 1932 Sacramento's community hospitals offered local health insurance. However, fewer than half the States had such schemes. The only national programs were small concessions which women had won on behalf of the poor and insane. Even President Roosevelt's vaunted 1935 program for resettled Dust Bowl farmers was but a partial solution. Then, in the forties, the fear of Communism undid many of these reforms. As Bethune had discovered, most American and Canadian doctors would fight any form of government sponsored medicine. The model for Canada's health insurance program was Saskatchewan's Swift Current Medical Plan of 1946, but that came twelve years after Dr Olds' initiative.

Perhaps Moreton's Harbour on New World Island should take some credit for the introduction of medical insurance to North America. Around 1903, Newfoundland-born poet E. J. Pratt was teaching school there. When one or two local people died after trying in vain to get a doctor from nearby Twillingate, he raised enough $4.00 family subscriptions to persuade McGill University to send down a resident doctor.

"If medical care isn't available for all," John Olds once said, "it's no good." Old Johns Hopkins himself could not have said it better. The old Quaker would have been proud to read the rest of his young alumnus' *Sun* piece: "The whole of Newfoundland is in a state of economic change and old ways are being replaced by new.... The hospital is very intimately involved in this economic upheaval, in two ways particularly:

> First, the economic and social welfare of a community depends primarily on the physical and mental health of the inhabitants. If people were well off financially but sick physically they could not be considered a sound community because in time they would be poor. In most places...the people are poor as well as sick.

Are they poor because they are sick or sick because they are poor? Both situations exist and yet the usual complaint is, the community is poor because there is nothing to turn to profit. That is unquestionably true, but how many more people are really not well enough to work if there *were* profitable employment?

A sick community is a poor and unhappy one. A poor community may be happy if it is not sick, but the best community is one which is in good health—prosperity will then follow.... The worse the financial situation of a community, the more essential is...some sort of institution which can take care of the sick.

Dr Olds' closing words are as timely now as then: "You may consider that the cost of medical care is a burden, but it is infinitely less of a burden than the lack of care."

Chapter Ten

Horse Race

*"I met him on Twillingate Bight on horseback. It was
snowing at the time and he was holding a compass in one
hand and the reins in the other; he was travelling over
the ice to visit a patient on New World Island."*
— Ned Clarke, *Lewisporte Pilot*

In 1933 Dr Olds bought a saddle horse and began riding to house calls.
At first the Directors were sceptical. Then a pregnant woman from
North Side, about to miscarry, sent an urgent message. Dr Olds
saddled Jack, galloped directly across the frozen Harbour and was at
her side in six and one-half minutes. After this the Directors agreed to buy
two more horses and he trained his assistants to the saddle. A "Hospital
Horse" tethered to a fence meant things were being taken care of. It was a
natural development. John knew and loved horses, and hated wasting time.
House calls on foot took too long, as motor vehicles were scarce and roads
few and rough. A telegram from Herring Neck easily ate up a day in the
summer and not much less in winter. Thus for a few years, until motorcycles
and *Jeeps* came along, Dr John Olds on horseback was a common sight
around Twillingate, winter and summer. The image of him cantering along,
black bag bouncing behind the saddle, curly hair whipping in the breeze,
crackies yapping behind him, became the Bay's icon of mercy.

In 1935 Britain set aside the week of May 6-11th to commemorate the
twenty-fifth anniversary of King George V's coronation. Celebrations were
planned all over Newfoundland and school children got medals to wear.
John organized a horse race from Durrell's Arm up to Hospital Lane, a
distance of about two miles. Years later, when Mrs W. Ashbourne asked
him to recount some experiences from the old days for her church, he told
the story of that day.

"How many of you remember Jubilee Day and the festivities that took
place? Not very many! Well, one can't stay young for ever and I remember
it very well. Every town and settlement put on some kind of show. I was to
ride in a horse race with Herb Gillett and Rev. Mr Burden.

"My troubles started the day before. Soon after the telegraph office opened on May 6th I got a wire from Mr Fowlow at Fortune Harbour:

FATHER VERY SICK PLEASE COME IMMEDIATELY
BOAT AT SUMMERFORD

"In those days and at that time of year it was no trouble at all to get to Summerford if you had a horse, a boat and two feet. We had a fine horse named Jack, so I saddled him and rode to Kettle Cove. The roads were muddy and nearly clear of snow. The winter trail was melted out.

"No trouble getting to Kettle Cove, but they had kept a big bank of snow there. I ran into Gordon Whitt before that and he waved his arm and hollered something. I didn't pay any attention and the next minute Jack was floundering nearly up to his ears in snow.

"Gordon came with a shovel and we got Jack out. Gordon wanted to know what I was doing there. I said I had to go to Summerford and asked him if he could take me to Virgin Arm, which was on the way. His boat was in the water ready for lobstering when the ice cleared off, and he said he would try.

"I unsaddled Jack and put him in Gordon's barn. We poked out of Kettle Cove. There was some loose ice in Main Tickle which we weaved through till we were blocked just outside Virgin Arm Point. I went ashore and Gordon promised to walk Jack home to Twillingate (he wouldn't ride him) when he got back across Friday's Bay, as it was very obvious I couldn't tell when, how or where I would get back.

"I walked over to Summerford and I think got there about 2:00 PM. The boat was tied up at Ern French's wharf. It was manned by two Budgell brothers from Exploits who were trying to get to Lewisporte for mail and supplies. They had a telegram from Mr Fowlow that said there was no possibility of getting into Fortune Harbour, but as the wind was westerly we ought to be able to get into Northern Harbour and I could walk from there.

"We poked and twisted out of Summerford; the run was fairly clear of ice, though we jammed trying to go through Black Island Tickle and had to go via Samson's Island (I presume you are well enough acquainted with the local geography to follow me). Northern Harbour was ice-free with the westerly wind and we landed there about dark. No one lived there then or ever had, as far as I know. There was a woods road leading to Fortune Harbour, which is about four miles west.

"The Budgells' boat had a cabin on it and they said they would wait for me, but to be back by daylight as they wanted to get to Exploits in time to play in the band for the Jubilee. It took me over an hour to get to Fortune

Harbour. I went to Father Casey's to get oriented and he went with me to the patient's house.

"Mr Fowlow Sr was very sick, all right. He had far advanced carcinomatosis [cancer] of the abdomen and was unable to talk. There was nothing whatever to do for him, so I left some morphine pills to put under his tongue if he woke up and had any pain, and went back to Father Casey's.

"It was then around midnight and I said there wasn't any use in my going to bed as I had to leave around 3:00 AM to get to Northern Harbour so the Budgells could get rid of me as soon as possible. Father Casey was a Director of the Hospital at that time, so we sat up drinking rum and discussing how to get people who had no money to pay their hospital contracts.

"I made it back in time for some bread and tea and we moved out with little ice at the time. The wind was light and still westerly, and the ice was all packed on the New World Island shore. There was no point in going to Summerford, even if it had been possible. Bridgeport was jammed 'way out, so they finally landed me on the ice a quarter of a mile or so from Western Head Harbour.

"The ice was rough but safe enough and I got off near the bottom of the wooden steps they had built to get up out of the harbour and took the road to Moreton's Harbour. The road forked at the Salvation Army Citadel and I took the wrong one till I saw the houses in Bridgeport, then turned around and finally got on the right one.

"The Budgells had assured me that I would have no trouble getting a boat out of Moreton's Harbour, but I had a good view from the hill and decided not to stop there and ask foolish questions. The harbour was packed full and I remembered I wanted to go to Tizzard's Harbour anyway.

"Earlier that winter I had made a trip to Tizzard's Harbour with Arthur Locke who had a fine dog team. He had six, all brothers and sisters from one litter, so I hired him. We had just got ashore when they all started to fight. I was helping to separate them when Arthur said, 'Don't touch that one, he's a savage, and as soon as I get my wood hauled I'm going to kill him.'

"He didn't seem to me to be any worse than the others, so I said, 'If you're going to shoot him, will you give him to me?' and he agreed. Locke had a boat; maybe I could get out of there and take the dog as well....

"Tizzard's Harbour was ice-free, but Twillingate was blocked and the boat was up on the shore. After some bread and tea they agreed to launch the boat—and they were more than glad to get rid of the dog. Arthur tied a piece of six-thread rope around his neck and tied him to the gunwale and we finally got in nearly to Bluff Head. The savage dog and I climbed the face of Bluff Head and walked as friends to the Hospital. He was a big, stocky, very strong dog—90-plus pounds and short-haired. We were living in the old Cottage then and I wanted to bring him in; but Betty very firmly said no.

"There was still time to get to the horse race at 11:00 AM. I was a bit tired but as long as I didn't have to do the running I didn't mind. I tied the friendly, savage dog (I named him Sport) to the ramp rail at the Hospital, saddled Jack and went to the races.

"The course was from Hodge's Store to Preston's Store. I was never worried about Jack's not running, and he did easily enough going by Moore's Cove. I looked back to see how much of a lead I had and it was considerable. Then I looked ahead to see what kind of a ribbon they had laid across the road to mark the finish. I saw it, but not in time to realize it was a piece of one-inch manila rope tied tightly to the fence on each side. Jack didn't catch on either, and we both hit the ground hard.

"After I got picked up and got Jack up with no legs broken, I was advised that I had won a pair of shoes as First Prize. I really don't remember what I said about the prize and I often wondered if the shoes would have fitted me. Jack limped home. I put him in his stall, put Sport in the dog house and went to bed. Sport chewed out of the dog house sometime during the night, and was not to be found the next morning; but that's another story."

When Dr Ted Shapter, a leading St John's orthopedic surgeon, examined X-rays of Dr Olds' spine many years later, he saw a long-healed fracture. Then he understood Dr Olds' offhand remark, "Of course you know I broke my back one time."

Chapter Eleven

Dog-and-Sled Doctor

"I wish to put in a word for the dog."

— J. M. Olds

"**I**n the era of the horse and buggy doctor, the horse got all the credit for solving the transportation problems," mused Dr Olds in an article he wrote in the seventies. In paying his grudging respects to the sled dog he painted an almost loving portrait of one aspect of outport life before the snowmobile.

"Long ago when the world and I were younger," he wrote, "such as in the 1940s and 1950s, the dog still pulled some weight—but no more than he had to. In Newfoundland the dog played an important, sometimes essential, role—though he was usually thought of as a necessary evil. He went when and where the horse couldn't go and he could keep going longer. Before those old days are completely forgotten, I wish to put in a few words for the dog.

"At 6:00 PM, just as all the telegraph offices closed for the night, the last piece of business for the messenger boy was to deliver to me a pink telegram saying,

COME IMMEDIATELY WIFE VERY SICK

"It was not unusual to receive a telegram worded this way and the timing was often perfect also. There was, of course, the possibility that it could be true, and there was one way to find out: go and see her. Such trips were routine, frequent and compulsory. After all, the man had made a payment of $5.00 for all medical services required by his family for the year, and there was no use wasting his money. The incident I am referring to meant only about thirty-six miles travel through deep snow and over bad ice, and fourteen to fifteen hours' work.

"Recent snow and big drifts on land, and deep slob and possible open swatches on the ice, ruled out a horse. So I crank-phoned Max, who frequently taxied for me when he wasn't hauling firewood with his dogs. I enquired politely about their state of health (which happened to be fairly good) and asked him to take me to the place right away.

"'No! It was too dark; the trail was drifted out and it was bad on the ice.' So we compromised on 3:00 AM, when it would be getting light soon.

"The snow had stopped and the wind was dying out. With only mild protest from my wife, I got into bed before midnight in heavy underwear instead of pyjamas (it is much easier to add than subtract and then add clothing on a cold morning). I set the alarm for 2:30 and about five minutes later it went off. I added clothes, stomped on logan boots with seal skin tops, warmed up some coffee, ate a bowl of cereal and put my one-year-old thoroughbred Irish setter pup in a back room and carefully closed the door. He didn't like it, but I had no use for him that day and didn't want him to follow and foul up the working dogs.

"So far he hadn't found any calling in life except to be overly friendly with people and with other dogs—especially dogs. He had proven himself as a hunter—wild, noseless and worthless. With head high and barking cheerfully he ran over the countryside chasing songbirds and seemed especially pleased if he happened to hear a distant partridge whirring out of his blundering way. He appeared to be headed for a useless, ornamental playboy life.

"Hat on, earflaps tied down, double ball mitts and call bag in hand, I went outside to see if Max was coming. It was a still, cold morning—the first breath stuck my nostrils together with frost—and it was very quiet. Max was coming; I could hear him talking to the dogs, tapping on the cart with the butt of his whip; then a barely discernable, horizontally moving, vertical silhouette, the panting of the dogs and he had arrived.

"'Morning, Max.'

"'Morning, Doctor.'

"The dogs rolled in the snow, groaned, whined a bit and got generally tangled up. Max sorted them out and pointed them in the right direction while I held on to the two after horns of the cart, ready to jump on when Max opened the throttle. 'Hah, boys! Hist! Hist! Hat!' and we held on tightly for a rapid fifty yards or so. Perhaps a half-G [force of gravity] acceleration, followed by a one-G deceleration when we hit a patch of gravel. It felt good to get off, to walk and trot with the dogs, till we came to snow again. We needed to warm up.

"There were several of these 'breaks' going through town and we were comfortably warm when we reached the winter trail. Max was fully occupied with his driving duties: 'Hist, boy—Hiss, Hiss, Hah! Hold in, hold in—Hah! Keep off! Get out of that, you son of a bitch,' and the rope whip snapped near a dog that wanted to inspect something that interested only him.

"'Is that a new dog, Max?'

Gary Saunders

"'Hah…Hiss, Hiss—get over! Dash, get out of that—what did you say, Doctor? Hiss, boys, hiss!'

"The winter trails were as definite as the summer gravelled roads, and interconnected the same places but followed different terrain. Seeking the easiest path for these low-powered transporters of firewood and other freight, they followed level ground such as marshes and crossed as many ponds as possible.

"We were getting along reasonably well—five to six miles per hour, running, walking, riding, the usual routine pace—when trouble arrived in the form of my red, locked-in setter named Jake. He had come to play and the other dogs responded. They chased him sideways, got snarled up in their tail ropes, fought among themselves; and no amount of coaxing, swearing, snow and stick throwing would discourage Jake. He strictly wouldn't come near me. For the next half hour or so we got nowhere. Finally he made a mistake and I jumped him in a patch of deep snow. Now that we had him we weren't much better off. He wouldn't lead and he wouldn't ride. I didn't want to drag him three miles or so to the nearest house, nor did I want to tie him to some bushes and leave him all day.

"Max had brought along an extra harness, as one of his dogs had a bad habit of cutting his harness. It seemed the height of foolishness to put a harness on Jake and expect anything but more trouble. Dogs are broken in usually before they are a year old—and some take quite a while to get the idea. They either lie down and get pulled by the other dogs, pull in the opposite direction, won't pull at all and try to back out of their harness, or start a fight. None of these things happened. Jake immediately started to pull hard in the right direction and did as much work as any other two dogs all day. He converted instantly from playboy to useful labourer. I still don't know what happened to his supposedly inbred hunting instincts—which he certainly didn't have, anyway.

"Everything went well until we got to the ice—except for one small incident. One of the dogs vomited and we came full stop until he and the other dogs ate it up.

"The saltwater ice looked beautiful in the morning sun, white and smooth with a dark wet strip at the shoreline. As we expected, it only looked nice. Saltwater ice is porous and somewhat pliable. Water seeps up through it and wets any snow that falls; the mixture is properly called slob. The ballicatters (rough broken ice on the landwash) were small and no problem. Beyond them the cart sank to the beams and we to our knees. A few yards farther on the slob was only halfway to our knees, the cart stayed on the surface when empty and the dogs walked on the surface.

"As nothing happened for the next three miles or so except Max and I putting one foot slightly in front of the other after extracting it from the slob, I will describe our equipment.

"The 'cart' has no wheels. Other names for it are 'slide' or 'catamaran.' However, it is not a sled or a komatik. The cart evolved more or less locally for transporting freight by low-powered prime movers—dogs and horses. The horse cart is exactly like the dog cart except for being a bit larger and usually fitted with shafts. These may be omitted and the horse attached by 'slack harness.'

"The dog cart is always homemade. You never bought one from the merchant. If you couldn't make one for yourself, you bartered or bought one from someone who could. Being homemade in no way implies not well made. They were light, functionally excellent and unbelievably strong. Spruce was used exclusively, being available and tough. Trees with natural bends were sawed and cut into inch and inch-and-a-half planks.

"Our cart had two runners an inch wide, two to four inches deep and six feet long, shod with thimble iron (one inch wide, one-eighth inch thick) and fastened to the runners with counter-sunk wood screws. Two feet back from the upturned front ends, a four-by-three-inch strip was bolted to the runner and topped by a one-by-four-inch crossbeam twenty-four inches long and extending two inches beyond the runner on each side, spacing the runners twenty inches apart. A similar plank was placed one foot forward of the rear end.

"The crossbeams were kneed with natural bends fore, aft and, in between, fastened by wood screws and carriage bolts. Through the overhanging end of each crossbeam a square one-and-one-quarter-inch hole was cut, its inner edge flush with the outer surface of the runner, which was rounded and plated with a semi-circle of thimble iron. A stick (the horn), squared to fit the hole and tapered to a half-round, was stepped into a half-round thimble iron socket two inches above the bottom of the runner. From the beam up it was round and slightly tapered, the top being two and one-half feet from the ground or twenty-two inches above the crossbeam.

"The bridle, a piece of eighteen-thread rope, was passed through holes bored horizontally through the runners one foot from the tip. A knot at each end secured it as it fell in an arc between the runners. The passenger and crew seats (not used very much) consisted of three-quarter-by-five-inch boards loosely lashed fore and aft to the crossbeams. The four horns of the cart and its shorter runners differentiate it from the komatik. The komatik has two plough-like handles at the rear, and all driving and human assistance is done there.

"The cart driver assists by pushing or pulling on one of the forward horns. The four horns contain sticks of firewood very handily. Various articles such as tea kettles and lunch bags are tied to them and they are great assets (by holding on to one) when running with the dogs.

"These carts, given a coat of red or green paint, which soon wears off, last for years under heavy use and abuse. The shoes wear out on gravel and a horn may break. Replacing these, plus an occasional new bridle, is all the upkeep necessary. Old ones are preferred to new ones, as with age they become somewhat flexible and it is believed that they slip along better. The kids use them for sledding downhill.

"Max told me the dogs' names. The leader was Dash—a bit old, six years—didn't pull much but at least stayed in front of the rest and usually knew the difference between 'hold in' and 'keep off.' He was short-haired—a sort of greyish brown colour, long thin legs—around twenty-five inches tall and weighed about forty pounds. Number Two on the port side was Jib. Three years old, also short-haired, white with black spots, short legs, big wide chest, heavy wide head, short ears and long drooping tail, forty-five pounds. Punch was next to starboard.

"There was some resemblance between Jib and Punch but they were not known to be related. Punch had more black and less weight, but was willing and had his job for three years. He was the one most likely to succeed Dash when he would retire from old age in a couple of years. Fuzz and Perhaps, the next two regulars, in their first year at work, were litter mates, and had long dark brown shaggy hair. Fuzz was bigger and heavier than his brother. Perhaps got his name when he was given to Max as a very young pup, by the owner of his mother, who said, 'Perhaps he'll pull and perhaps he won't.' Perhaps he weighed twenty-five pounds.

"My long-legged, long-eared, long-haired, all-red Jake was pulling hard at Number Six on the port side. I thought he looked pleased and a bit surprised. I know I was both, and hoped it would last.

"Dogs' harnesses were always homemade and pretty much of a standard pattern. A piece of six-thread manila rope was doubled and bound together, making a small loop at the rear end. Two large loops were formed by splicing the two free ends into each strand six to eight inches in front of the rear loop. The two large loops were then bound together in two places to make a smaller median loop through which the dog's head was slipped—the two larger loops going between the forelegs, under the chest and up the back. Strips of old blanket, gunny sack, etc., were then sewn over the pressure areas around the neck and chest.

"A tail rope, same as the main harness, three or four feet long, was spliced into the rear loop. When all hitched up, each dog's tail rope was fastened by a rolling hitch to its proper position on the main line, which was twelve-thread rope, and roll-hitched to the bridle, ten to fifteen feet long, and the lead dog fastened to the other end. Each dog was supposed to stay on his own side of the main line—and sometimes he did for a while. There were other forms of hitching and I have occasionally seen fancier harnesses—such as each dog's harness ending in a little whiffletree, which can end up in some pretty wonderful snarls.

"The last piece of equipment, the whip, is optional. It is made from a round piece of spruce an inch or so in diameter and about fifteen inches long. A three- or four-foot piece of six-thread rope is spliced through a hole in one end of the stick. A double piece of fish line, six to eight feet long, is fastened to the other end of the rope and knotted in several places. When used, the whip serves as a conductor's baton, a pointer, a direction indicator, a maker of encouraging sounds (by tapping on the cart) and sometimes as a fear-inducer when it snaps near or happens to hit a loafing dog—not necessarily the one aimed at—but they all get the point, for a little while. It is something to hold in your hand, or you can tie it to the horn of the cart and forget about it.

"You have learned a bit about the dog and his equipment in a lot less time than it took us to reach the far shore. It came to us after an hour and a half or so, and Max ('Hist, hist!, Hold in, Keep off!') got us over the deeper shore slob and the ballicatters and onto a winter trail—still virginal from the recent snow. The mile or so across the neck was better than the ice and only took about twenty minutes. After that, there was only five and one-half miles of slob walking and one-quarter mile or so on land. We had the dogs tied to the patient's picket fence shortly after 9:00 AM. I got my bag off the cart, knocked on the back door and heard sounds in the house. We entered the back porch and smelt the wood fire burning in the kitchen stove.

"The sender of the telegram appeared in shirt sleeves and greeted us with: 'Good morning, Doctor, didn't expect you today; bad on ice ain't it?'

"'Uh! What's the matter with the missus?'

"'Oh, she's better now.'

"'Oh? Where is she?'

"'Up to bed.'

"I shed some clothes, got the steam off my glasses and went up. The history was straight-forward and the diagnosis not difficult. She had been constipated a bit more than usual and yesterday she had a pain in the back passage and there was a lump there. During the night the fruit salts had worked, there was blood on the stool, the lump was practically gone and it didn't hurt any more. She got some salve and a small bit of sympathy for her ex-pile [former hemorrhoid] and I went down to the kitchen to join Max, who had already started to eat. Grandma gave us some bread, biscuits, cake, cheese and tea. The weather, travelling conditions and the scarcity of rabbits were discussed.

"Grandma wanted her blood pressure taken. I took it and gave her a few of her usual pills as she was nearly out and promised to send her more first chance. Max had the dogs straightened out and pointed them in the right direction and we were on our way by ten o'clock. The sun was bright, the air warmer, the scenery beautiful and walking in the slob was the same, except we sweated more. There had been some travel on our home island trail, and we got a bit of riding on some of the ponds.

"If you have the opportunity to sit on the cart for a time, it is fascinating and hypnotic to stare at the dogs' trotting feet. They seem tireless (considering the diet of dried or frozen fish, which is all these dogs get to eat), and pretty damn near perpetual motion. When you ride, the dogs' speed seems terribly slow. The way to change your mind is to get off and run with them for a while. You soon start wondering how they can run so fast.

"For a short stretch Max got them into passing gear or overdrive—anyway, a higher speed. This can be done at intervals when the slipping is good by standing on the runners of the cart, calling out in a surprised and excited voice as though you hardly dared believe it yourself: 'Crow! Crow! CROW. Ho, boys! Crow, crow, crow! Look! See him? Crow, crow, crow!' Sometimes there *is* a crow flying up ahead, and if the dogs see it, so much the better—the speed will last longer. The word 'horse' or 'dog' can be substituted for crow if the word seems appropriate for the situation. 'House' is also used if one appears in the distance. The driver tends to stick to the facts as he sees them; maybe it makes him feel not a complete liar and saves face with the dogs. The dogs don't care; any word used in the right tone of voice and convincingly will do. They really like to strain after crows, though, especially if they are real.

"As the reader has no doubt gathered, these lowly haulers of wood and doctors are not the glamorous, well-bred, well-matched 'Mush, mush' dog of literature, of the Mounties and the Inuit. They are mongrels, fathered by their mother's whim or by necessity, but deserving of credit for their strength, guts and relative gentleness. I once saw a dog-powered komatik that had brought a patient to the Hospital from a distance of over twenty miles through deep snow. The two front dogs were half-breed Dachshunds with whiffletree harness. Numbers Three and Four were tall thin dogs and the driver told me he wished he had four like the first two, as they were really good.

"We got home about 4:30 PM. The dogs looked and acted just the same as when we started out. Jake had pulled very hard and was maybe a bit subdued. He was damned stiff for the next two days. Max undressed Jake.

"'Thanks, Max.'

"'Goodbye, Doctor.'

"It was nice the weather was good."

Chapter Twelve

Lady of Mercy

"The travelling clinic should be expanded, [preferably]
with our own boat..."
— Hospital Board Minutes, 1935

Every summer from 1934 to 1962, a small white motor boat with high deckhouse and two short masts could be seen in Notre Dame Bay. She appeared when the spring ice was leaving and stayed till new ice forced her retreat. Every fortnight or so she vanished for a few days, then resumed her slow, methodical circuits. Skippers of larger vessels saw her as something of a will-o'-the-wisp, out in all weathers and at all hours. Like a hound on a scent she tirelessly sniffed every tickle and bight of the Bay.

The clinic boat *Bonnie Nell* was John Olds' response to geography, poverty and disease. Geographically, Notre Dame Bay is a coastline that was drowned by the rising post-glacial ocean ten thousand years ago. It yawns nearly a hundred miles from west to east and plunges southward to mingle its brine with the sweetness of the Exploits and Gander Rivers. The shoreline of its filigreed capes and islands unwinds for thousands of miles. Like Grenfell's *Maraval* out of St Anthony, the *Bonnie*'s mission was to bring medical care to those who otherwise might never see a nurse or a doctor. She also served as ambulance, bill collector and early warning system for epidemics. Occasionally she took Dr Olds to St John's for a meeting or to Gander Bay for moose hunting.

In her early years, people sometimes mistook the *Bonnie Nell* for Elias Chaulk's passenger boat out of Carmanville and with good reason. Until 1935 that was her alter ego. After becoming the Hospital's full-time clinic boat in 1936, she retained the name, and would carry on until replaced in 1950 by a younger and slightly larger *Bonnie Nell II*.

Her arrival in any port seldom failed to attract attention. To wharf idlers she was a novelty, a link with nearby communities, an opportunity to ogle the new nurse or see this summer's handsome student doctor. To those who had endured aching teeth all winter, her coming meant blessed relief. The sick viewed her coming more fearfully. She might bring tidings of a cancerous breast or bowel, of a tubercular hand, of beriberi or typhoid. It could mean a sudden trip to Twillingate and a winter in hospital, or a clean bill of health and a deep sigh of gratitude.

Although in the first years Dr Olds went on the boat himself, after 1937 he assigned junior doctors to help the nurse. Thus the clinic boat became another training opportunity for scores of young doctors. Above all, the *Bonnie* was his strongest weapon against TB.

"Twillingate's geographical position had advantages for fishing," Olds wrote in 1974, "but there were many disadvantages in the location for a hospital attempting to serve the Bay. Although coastal steamers called here [and] brought freight, express and mail once a week, they did not necessarily stop at communities that had patients wishing to go to the Hospital, or take them home. Small passenger boats served for this in summer, but this was difficult in stormy weather, and ice usually stopped navigation for five-six months every year. When and if Bay ice was good, freight, mail and patients made it by horse and dog sleds."

Another problem was that in summer most people were too busy catching and curing cod to leave home for anything but major illness. This meant that minor ailments were often left too long. The only solution was a travelling clinic, an all-weather motor boat fitted with basic equipment, staffed by a doctor and nurse and skippered by a master mariner who knew the Bay.

In 1934 and 1935 Dr Olds had briefly tried the *Pauline*. He found it better to charter the *Bonnie* for $150 a month. The Board contacted the Bay's few practicing physicians about invasion of practice; all cooperated except Lewisporte's. They printed a schedule of fees: $2.00 for examination on board, $1.00 for prescribed medicine, $5.00 for a house call and 50¢ for pulling a tooth. Contract subscribers paid half these amounts.

During the summer of 1934 the hired clinic boat reached sixty ports. In 1935 the doctor and nurse saw 425 patients in twenty ports in three weeks, referring 104 to the Hospital. "[At first] there was some lack of understanding in certain communities," John wrote, "but this had entirely disappeared the next year when triple the number of patients was seen and ninety-six ports of call were established."

Board minutes for August 12th, 1935 state that the "travelling clinic should be expanded, [preferably] with our own boat...Dr Olds to organize." Captain Chaulk was not keen to sell, however, so when Deputy Minister of Health Dr H. M. Mosdell offered his *Minnie* for $1,000, they hastily accepted. But on the return voyage from St John's that fall, Dr Olds found her unsuitable. He stopped in at Carmanville, bought the *Bonnie Nell* then and there, and had Elijah Dalley fetch her home. An anonymous $1,000 donation helped.

The first task was to transfer the *Minnie*'s engine furnishings and other equipment to the new boat. As John and Lige Dalley worked together on this, John discovered that the older man possessed not only superb manual skills but a rare beauty of soul. In the ensuing years Lige would became an anchor for John's restlessness, a second father to replace the one he lost after Alaska. Lige would skipper the *Bonnie* until the day she was sold.

"Yes, my father used to do that work around the Bay," said Angus Dalley, "right down as far as Cape Freels. He'd be called at all hours of the night, gone for a month on the one trip. And if, say, he got back today, well, that night at twelve o'clock he might have to go to Gander Bay to pick up a patient, or to Nipper's Harbour or somewhere else. In the first years they had no ship-to-shore, but later they could call in twice a day. While the doctor and nurse were doing their work, my father collected money for the Blanket Contract, and later for the Fish Appeal too. In the winter time he did carpentry at the Hospital."

The first *Bonnie Nell* was a good sturdy ship with the desired shallow draft but her layout was less than ideal for handling patients. Dr Robert Ecke served on her in 1938 and could vouch for that. He discovered that the engine was weak, the clutch unreliable, and that the toilet sometimes backed up. "The boat is a good one," he wrote in an unpublished memoir of his years in Twillingate, "fifty feet long, twenty-five tons, thirteen feet in the beam. The wheelhouse is aft, as is the engine room and then a large wasted space. Its engine fairly eats gas. She carries the usual canvas—a big jib, a gaff-rigged mizzen, but a Marconi mainsail. She has a high billet bow that gives a large forecastle with plenty of headroom. Her draft forward is very slight and that fact, coupled with her high forward deck, makes her pound like fury in a head wind. The doctor and nurse have, respectively, two small staterooms off the saloon. The john is entered through a doorway four feet high, but you can stand up once you get inside. It has another entrance from the engine room.

"The saloon is inclined to be a bit of a jumble," he went on. "It is cluttered with the bottles and instruments and laboratory equipment and all the other materials that go to make a fairly complete doctor's office. If proper lockers were made it would be nice, but it's good enough—and in this country, anything that's good enough is plenty good enough and not to be fooled with. It is living quarters for all hands in the evening and a clinic during the day…. At the end of a rainy day, when fifty [patients] have tracked in the mud and the wet, our evening cocoa does seem to take on odd flavours…."

Besides the captain, doctor and nurse, there was an engineer-mate who also cooked the meals. Some days supper tasted of engine oil or gasoline, so Dr Ecke did the cooking whenever he had time. Each community knew of their arrival because the Hospital had telegraphed ahead. For the first few years people shied away. At Sansom's Island near Exploits, wrote Dr Ecke, "one old codger came 'way over to us in a motor boat to ask if I was a government doctor. When told no, I was from the Hospital, he allowed as how he wouldn't see me because it would cost. He didn't even give us a chance to bargain."

In a small community on a slack day they might see only eight or ten patients; in larger places they might work till midnight. The biggest visitations usually came after supper. To strengthen the contract system they charged twice as much for those who hadn't signed up. But as word got around that subscribers got a complete physical examination for a dollar and tooth extractions for only twenty-five cents, interest grew. Few infants were brought aboard, even though mothers were offered free baby clothes, examinations and medicines. Occasionally people brought a cow or a goat down to the wharf for examination or a needle. The doctor helped it if he could.

At Botwood on the 1938 trip Ecke and the crew arrived at 7 PM. and "the reception was slow…. We hung about for an hour before anybody much came; they were all home bathing and powdering; there was plenty of evidence of both on examination. Then from 8 to 11 I saw ten people."

The next day he "worked like a little beaver from 9 in the morning until 11 at night. I was dizzy by nightfall. We pulled very few teeth… [but] no end of bad backs, sides and stomachs."

Originally the boat had no X-ray equipment, but experience and skilled "sounding" with a stethoscope turned up numerous cases of TB. The doctor and nurse were always alert for signs of epidemics of typhoid or diphtheria. Unfortunately people mistrusted vaccination and needles, especially for babies. That year Dr Olds was especially worried about typhoid, locally called "Terrified Fever." Dr Ecke found some in Gander Bay that fall. He stood on a sawdust pile at French's sawmill in Mann Point and exhorted the workers to get shots. Most of the men feared the needle more than the disease and few came forward. The diphtheria epidemic of 1942, which sent the clinic boat scuttling to and fro all summer melted some of that resistance So did the post-war polio scare with its queues of school children and boats at every wharf. Nurse Irene (Young) Pardy, travelling the southern half of the *Bonnie Nell II*'s two-week circuit in July 1959, noted in her diary that she and lab technician Lou Osmond administered 450 polio shots in fourteen communities.

The best portrait of *Bonnie Nell*'s early years is found in Robert Ecke's diary from his 1938 voyage:

September 12

EXPLOITS ISLAND—We arrived at seven and after a long wait, pulled a tooth and made a shore visit to a one-room house where a 76-year-old pair are eking out the end of their lives—both fairly strong, but she with a shaking paralysis and he with a bad heart. The old man gets up on the table thinking he is still running his schooner. He says his feet are as cold as clay. I could only josh them a bit and give them a little false hope....

September 13

CHARLES BROOK—Here, two hours from Exploits, an ancient couple came aboard. The lady wanted a tooth out.... He said she had poor nerve and that "all smoothwater people had poor nerve." He said that "ar'a bit of work made his waters stop." The median lobe of his prostate was the size of a watermelon....

September 14, 15

BOTWOOD—I don't compare very favourably with the local doc. *He* can examine them through their clothes and tell them from the door what's wrong with them. *He* also gives much larger bottles of medicine.... After tea we walked down to the airport...[saw] the great concrete runway for hauling out the flying boats...went [up] to the weather station. They make the most complete weather map in the world—three shifts of twelve radio operators. The masts are 600 feet high. A German boat came in after lying-to all night waiting for news from Germany; she was afraid of being interned.

September 20

LOON BAY—No wharf, so we are at anchor for the first time. It is a deadly dark night with quite a breeze but no sea. The halyards slap against the mast and the anchor chain is rattling. We added a little rum to our usual cocoa in the fo'c'sle and the men got talking about their trips to the Labrador.

In one of his longest diary entries of that voyage, Dr Ecke creates a loving vignette of that era. "Every spring there is a competition among the captains to stake out the prime fishing berths as soon as the ice was gone. Lige told of races through the ice and fog and dark, six or seven schooners with lights out so they couldn't be followed. 'We couldn't see Tom White's schooner, but they could hear them swearing on deck,' he said. In the dead of night they ran into an iceberg. The boom was caught in the berg and snatched away and then back against the mast with a shock that threw them all onto the deck. [They were] racing along when the top half of the mainmast came down and hung in the rigging. They wallowed along all night before the gale. When they shot off some guns, the nearest schooner turned out to be skippered by Jim Gillett, lifelong enemy of their captain. But as soon as it was light, he dropped a line back.... The drag on the rescue ship put her stern under at every swell. They made harbour and both skippers embraced and cried and opened some rum. Stayed together nine days while they fitted a new spar. Lige recalled a time when 200 schooners were tied up side to side in Icy Tickle, icebound. You could step from one to the other for a mile. There were rough goings-on with the kind of girls making that trip."

September 23, 24

HORWOOD—Mr Horwood of the Horwood Lumber Company invited me to hear the news...an interesting sort of guy—black moustache, stocky and rather British. He talks very affably [but] the way he treats his workers is a crime. The news was very disturbing—all about the new war....

September 25

VICTORIA COVE—It hailed large hailstones. The "governor-general," old John Oake, who has the welfare of all at heart, came aboard and as usual showed me his varicose ulcers....

September 26

MANN POINT—The lop was rolling in there for fair, but a few braved it so I pulled a lot of teeth. These men have money. They work for French and he treats them right.... [Ray Hodder] came aboard, singing "I wish that I could diddle like the man who played the fiddle." I went ashore to see a woman who had been in the Hospital with beriberi three years before.

FREDERICKTON—Lots came aboard, including a poor wretch much scared because he had contact with Mary Dole and everyone in New-foundland knows she is in Twillingate for venereal infection.... One stinker with plenty of money came aboard and filled my hours with talk about himself and then announced he wasn't going to pay.... "Long may your big jib draw!" [said another] when I told him he didn't have diabetes.

September 27

LADLE COVE—We anchored 'way out because it was such a poor harbour.... One man couldn't pay, so he brought out a dollar's worth of potatoes.... Started up the coast to Carmanville. The breeze freshened but we made fair time until Alder Harbour. From there it's a wide indraft to Carmanville and we couldn't do a thing against that wind. The quick water from the propeller drifted ahead of us—we were going back-wards. With a mild curse Lige spun the wheel around to beat it across, wing and wing, for Seldom Come By... Porpoises played all around us in that ominous green swell. Seldom is a dream...twelve schooners in this little harbour, the *Bessie Marie* too....

September 30

CARMANVILLE—[The motor] stalls at the slightest strain.... You don't use Reverse unless you want it, and the moment until you strike what you were planning to miss is a long one.

October 2

TILTING—On a beautiful evening with a good, cold wind we wove in and out of buoys into this snug but tricky harbour. We put down the anchor though we knew it was pretty shallow. A man came aboard to tell us we were on "Mercury," a rock, and would strike at low water. ...I pulled one tooth on a [woman] who called on her pagan deity and vowed in a loud, clear voice that she "had to suffer in this world." It couldn't have hurt that much—I cocained it well.

October 4

CHANGE ISLANDS—Unable to get to Earle's wharf until they moved the schooner. Meanwhile, I was called out to see a congenital idiot with contractions and athetoid movements of the hands. He is going a little uremic.... Billy had us up to tea for a can of duck and one of lobster. The house is beautiful, called "Four Winds" and set high on a hill. Billy showed me around it; he is a simple, honest man. After tea I pulled more teeth. Thirty patients.

October 5

TWILLINGATE—Four times we had to stop the motor to drain water out of the gas. Without the motor going she really pitched. Everything came loose. I was happy to coast into Twillingate Harbour and get off.

After that trip Dr Ecke remarked, "I enjoy every minute of Dalley's company. He has been around a lot, has lived in the States and is a strong, fine-looking guy. He is very nice to me, gets me water and builds the fire in the morning. I approve of him highly. He was a little worried once, one stormy day off New Bay Head, when the cylinders of the engine kept filling with seawater through a leaky manifold and the RPM kept dropping. Another time, he dozed in the wheelhouse beside me as I manned the wheel according to his instructions—keeping Cape John Gull Island in the ring of the starboard bow anchor. I nudged him to say I saw what appeared to be smoke coming out of the engine room companionway. He moved fast and he could swear when the situation warranted. The hot exhaust pipe had set the wall on fire. Whether on the deep in a blow or ashore when the roof was blowing off the new Staff House, Lige lent an air of security."

In September 1940 Bob Ecke made another voyage on the *Bonnie*. They happened to be transporting a heavy *White* engine for someone and it nearly drowned them.

When we rounded Cape Farewell it was really something. I braced myself in the wheel house and at times it seemed I could put my hand on the top of a wave before it touched the boat. We turned into the lee of Baccalieu Island where we put on a little sail to steady us. A dirty darkness fell and through it I saw the *Kyle* bearing down on us. Lige ordered the lights on, but that was a coincidence as he hadn't seen the steamer.

Behind the island Lige and the Mate conferred, deciding to try for Twillingate. As we cleared the island the full force of the wind took us. We started to put the lee rail under and once or twice we floated the punt, which is on top of the rail.... We mounted a big lop and gave a sickening lurch to port, sliding sideways into the trough with our whole lee deck under. With a crash, that *White* engine on the stern hatch gave way, broke its lashing and at the same time our lights went out. I was more than scared.... The next three lops we took the same way. Two oil cans came loose.

That engine shifted with each crash until I thought the rail would go and with it part of the hull. I slid along the deck...tried to heave it overboard... could not budge the thing.... The skipper yelled to shorten sail and threw the helm over at the same time. I tried to get forward but the boom came at me. I ducked and it carried the [extra length of stovepipe] overboard.

Somehow we jumbled the mainsail down. We seemed to be riding easier. The geography was hard to make out but it became evident we were running for Herring Neck, listed to port with our tail between our legs. The following seas hurled themselves on us and sucked us back, but we made it.... Below deck the stovepipe had come out, the front legs were off the stove and soot everywhere. Chairs were upside down, broken glass everywhere with the soot. Medicine bottles all over the place, the microscope in the middle of the deck, bedpans, urinals, pails.... Doris couldn't get out of her room and when water had come through her funnel she had made herself busy with her prayers.... It is too deep in Herring Neck so we said to hell with it as we let the chain out past the weak link.

We got the stovepipe from the galley so as to have a fire in the saloon for drying ourselves and getting warm. I [made] an alcohol drink with seven cans of Malayan pineapple juice and we [had] a gay evening to celebrate our deliverance. There was something wrong with that pineapple. [We all] had a stomach ache which lasted three days.

Around 1946 Dr Louis Lawton did a stint before the mast. Among his most vivid images was that of a pretty 14-year-old girl from Triton or Pilley's Island who came aboard with a mouthful of bad teeth. "Look," he said, "why don't you go and get them filled, because..."

"No," she said, "I wants to get them out."

"Well," he said, "it means you're going to have false teeth."

"I don't care," she replied, "I'm not gonna put up with another winter of pain." He even pulled her two front teeth. She went away grinning.

By 1950 *Bonnie Nell I* was growing old. For fourteen summers she had been buffeted by winds, scraped by sunkers and growlers, lashed by rain and brine, hailed on, blistered by hot sun. As early as 1942 the Board had considered selling her but changed their minds and refurbished her instead. With a new combined wheel house and examining room back aft, and a more powerful engine, she simply carried on. But now it was time to get a new boat.

Dr Olds, recently back from his second US rest cure, huddled with Ted Drover to design the perfect replacement. It must have the first boat's shallow draught, but more space for patients, crew and supplies. It must be steadier in rough seas and have power enough to punch through the strongest gale. To resist spring ice, her belly would be sheathed in green-heart.

The new boat was built by Edgar Paul of Max Bursey's shipyard in Glovertown during the winter of 1950-51 and was ready for service that May. At Olds' request, they called her *Bonnie Nell II* and retained Elijah Dalley as skipper. Though six feet longer and five feet wider than her predecessor, she drew only seven feet, enough to enter the shallowest harbour. There was running water, an X-ray machine, a one-room clinic with examining table, a large store of pills and lotions, and equipment enough for minor surgery. Two years later, Dr Olds would get his friend Leslie R. Curtis to procure a refrigerator for storing drugs and an oil stove to heat the galley. Without a pause the *Bonnie* continued as before.

On the boat's maiden voyage in 1951, Harvard Medical School seniors Jim Pittman, Joe Wilber and John Shillito took turns on a ten-day circuit as assistant physician, full-time dentist and X-ray technician. "In the lounge on the main deck," wrote Shillito three years later, "we established the dentist's chair—a camp-stool well braced against the stove to prevent premature escape—and while one line of patients waited aft for the clinic, another curled around the fo'c'sle while we pulled teeth at fifty cents a yank. Some patients were stoic enough for eight or nine dollars' worth at one sitting! As the novice strained away to free the invariably large, firmly rooted tooth, spies peered through the lounge window and decided, from the relative distribution of sweat on patient's and physician's brow, who was winning. If it were the latter, a flood of patients; if not, retirement until the next port!"

Pittman's journal gives a vivid sense of the daily round on the new *Bonnie Nell*, this time in the western reaches of the Bay.

Wednesday, Aug. 1—Left T'gate at 11:00 AM. Went out the harbour and under the lighthouse, used up the last bit of movie film on some rough seas smashing against some rocks (but have since seen much prettier sea), then steamed northwest over around Cape St John and to Fleur de Lys, a little fishing village in a beautiful, nearly land-locked harbour....

Thursday, Aug. 2—Saw patients, pulled teeth, and took X-rays (2) in Fleur de Lys till after dinner (noon), then left and went over to Coachman's Cove. Saw a boy with otitis media [inflamed middle ear] and a man with a sebaceous cyst; pulled a few teeth; then left and steamed up to the little logging town of Baie Verte to pick up some test tubes and sponges from a Dr Edwards there....

Friday, Aug. 3—Steamed out to the Horse Islands where we had to drop anchor just outside the small ' bour. Watched a cod trader take some fish aboard as the people f͘   e village came out in skiffs to bring their dried and salted fish. ͘   nan with a mild follicular conjunctivitis.... We waited a while, hauled anchor (no fun), and went into Pacquet, a clean little place with two general stores and a whole little building (about 10 x 20 feet) devoted to the post office. Went ashore and bought some apricots and sardines, slept a while, saw some patients, pulled some teeth, read part of *An Essay on Morals;* to bed at 12:35. Diarrhea again today—good old paregoric.

Saturday, Aug. 4—Left Pacquet around 6:30 AM and steamed over to Harbour Round, which is just what it is named—a clean little round harbour. Anchored, since there was no large wharf, saw a few patients, hauled up a muddy anchor and steamed to La Scie, a little Frenchish town of about 300 families. Watched the schooner *Swile* leave, then changed mooring. Watched the great black-backed gulls and Arctic and common terns play around the harbour, saw some patients (including one little asthmatic girl with a remarkable pigeon breast—probably rachitic at one time), took some X-rays, suppered (cook made cake), talked with Herby and Capt. Dalley, Lawton and Ivy; went on call to twins' house. Now to bed.

For the next eleven years, first under Captain Dalley and for ten years under Captain Cecil Stockley, mostly with Martin Clarke as engineer and George Weir as cook, the *Bonnie Nell II* served the Bay. Toward the end of her career, Dr Olds experimented with radio medicine. For headquarters he chose tiny Herring Neck on New World Island's northwest side. Firstly, Joe White of Twillingate, a Hospital Director and one of its staunchest supporters, managed Carter's fishing premises there, and Herring Neck took an inordinate amount of doctors' time.

When the boat finished up the fall of 1958, Olds had the *Bonnie* moored there for the winter. He arranged for Nurse Irene Pardy, a veteran of both the Hospital and the clinic boat, to board at Boyd's Hotel with the boat as her base. He shifted the boat's radio-telephone up to Carter's store where there was always someone to answer. Pat (Whylie) Bartlett worked with Nurse Pardy that first winter, but afterward she was alone. Joe White kept a fatherly eye on her, even lending her winter clothing for cold trips. That first winter she did forty house calls, saw 140 patients on board and did 48 extractions.

Twice a day all winter, Nurse Pardy would radio the Hospital. George Ings, the orderly, looked after her general needs; for emergencies she called the OR direct. Every morning at 8:30 or 8:45, Joe White, then seventy years old but still bluff and hearty, would call George Ings. This ritual came to have special significance for Dr Olds. For one thing, it often saved Drs Halliday, Bruce or Smith a hard slog to Herring Neck and back for some minor complaint. For another, he enjoyed the exchanges of his two amateur radio operators.

Bonnie Nell II's call letters were VOJW, which some took to mean "Voice of Joe White." George would be in the scrub room outside the OR when the radio would crackle out, "VOJW calling Twillingate 'ospital, hover."

George would answer: "Twillingate 'ospital calling VOJW, hover."

"Marnin', Skipper Garge. Hover."

"Marnin', Skipper Joe. Hover."

"What's the weather like up dere dis marnin', Garge?"

George would step over to the window, take a look, and come back. "Twillingate 'ospital calling VOJW: Nuttin' in the 'arbour so far as you can see but hice, hice, hice. Any problems down there, Skipper Joe?"

"Yes, b'y. Mrs White got a pain in 'er stomach again. Hover."

George would put his head in the OR and say, "Dr Holds, Mrs White got a pain in her stomach again." Few knew more about the inhabitants of the surrounding communities than Olds and White—unless it was Malcolm Simms the telegraph operator. Between them they could diagnose and prescribe for minor ailments pretty accurately. When Olds had doubts he sent Nurse Pardy to investigate.

Olds would look up, think for moment and drawl, "Give her Mixture Number Two." He had equipped Joe with several standard medicines—aspirin, codeine and such, each in a numbered jar. George would repeat this to Joe, Dr Olds would keep on operating, and Mrs White would get relief.

The *Bonnie Nell II* was sold to Fred Chaffey of Lewisporte in January 1963. After 1964, when Twillingate was finally linked by causeway and ferry to New World Island and the world, there was less need for such boats, though the MV *Christmas Seal*, skippered by Captain Peter Troake, was to continue her important TB work until 1970.

For all her faults, Dr Olds had loved *Bonnie Nell I* like a daughter. When the time came, he had opposed selling her. But in 1951 he was sick and in no condition to protest. It especially pained him when she fell into the hands of prospector Jake Wolgar, a friend of Sid Fisher's and one of the few men he disliked. Wolgar, a handsome World War II fighter pilot, and war hero, renamed the vessel and used it for exploring and staking iron ore claims on the Labrador coast, where she was eventually lost.

Olds loved her skipper even more. One rainy evening near the end of October 1951, Lige Dalley brought the new *Bonnie Nell* down from Lewisporte. He'd been shooting turrs on the way and it was after dark. He made fast the lines and was walking up the wharf when someone hailed him. He tried to answer but no words came. They rushed him up to the Hospital, where, in spite of Dr Olds' best efforts, he died of a stroke forty-eight hours later.

On the morning of the funeral, John got Captain Andrew "Chum" Greenham to take him to Springdale on the *Bonnie Nell II*. It was long after dark when he got back.

Part III

Lee Shore

Chapter Thirteen

Consolidation

"[We have]...Not much to worry about except money."
— J. M. Olds

At the May 25th, 1936 Director's meeting, Dr Olds tendered his resignation as Medical Director effective August 25th. Chairman Frank Roberts had said something about "gross mismanagement" and Dr Olds had taken it personally. Magistrate Roberts apologized, saying he meant Business Manager Minty. Dr Olds agreed to withdraw the resignation only if his duties were better defined. After a long meeting the minutes declared that "Dr Olds is in full charge of the Hospital and works in conjunction with the Business Manager." J.W. Minty then resigned and E. J. Colborne took his place, which was an improvement.

The years from 1936 to 1939 were a time of consolidation and testing for John. While he had saved the Hospital from bankruptcy, revived the hospital committees around the Bay and introduced the clinic boat, he still had to put the Hospital itself in order. Charlie Parsons had left such a tangle of mistrust and confusion among the staff that it would take several years to rebuild a team spirit. John still craved his father's blessing; but not enough to beg for it. Despite repeated requests, his parents still had not visited Twillingate. Paradoxically, a fire and an illness would do much to resolve those problems.

Besides defining his role, he was trying to strengthen the OR. Before Dr Goodwin's departure in 1934, he had enticed summer student Stanton Hardy back as his assistant. For three years, with Dr Wood as back-up and Betty as scrub nurse, he had a strong team. When Dr Hardy left temporarily in 1937, Robert Ecke, a Hopkins student who externed in Twillingate with Hardy in 1934, was to take his place and stay five years. With Hardy back in 1938 for five more years, the OR became the heart of Notre Dame Bay Memorial's growing reputation. In January of 1936 John wrote Mary, "[We have] 25% more patients but lowest ever mortality rate. Not much to worry about except money."

Betty and John both needed a holiday, but there was still too much friction among the staff. Drs Hardy and Jacobs disagreed continually and their wives fought worse, and then some of the nurses joined in. Dr Jacobs didn't want to be stationed in Nippers Harbour with his wife pregnant, and Dr Hardy wouldn't relieve him because he "had a bad side."

"It is all right when we are here," said John, "but until some of the others leave we can't."

From February 1935 through October 1937 he was struggling to save the life of a young Carmanville boy named Cole who had accidentally swallowed lye. Dr Olds managed to graft him a feeding tube, but the boy also had pulmonary TB and died before the long procedure was a full success.

TB showed up everywhere. During that year he had to perform three thoracoplasties [removal of ribs to collapse TB lungs], three bilateral phrenectomies [crushing of nerve to immobilize TB lungs], six hip fusions— three of them of his own design—four spinal fusions, and a number of knee, ankle and hand operations. In all, that year he and his colleagues treated 435 inpatients, and Olds himself did 225 operations and deliveries. By 1945 the number of inpatients per annum would pass 1,100.

For relaxation he had many outside interests. During the winter of 1935-36 he built a small log cabin at Kettle Cove on the heel of South Island. Overlooking Friday's Bay, "The Tilt" would become the couple's favourite getaway and the scene of many happy staff parties. In 1938 he added a radio which Stan Hardy gave him and a little six-volt electric lighting plant, "so that it is quite a modern place."

Around this time Frank and Annette Olds shipped him a motorcycle. Besides being a symbol of Uncle Frank's approval, it speeded house calls on the Island and gave him a vehicle to tinker with. John promptly named it after them. "Gas up the *Frank and Annette*," he'd say to janitor Martin Young, "I've got a house call."

His long obsession with homemade travel contraptions and other hobbies had already begun with his construction in 1934 of the first of several snow machines. He was also having a sailboat built. "Tell Pop that all the boat makers here claim the boat would be no good for these waters, being too wide in the stern," he wrote. "I am having one built from a model that one of the builders and I designed." He wanted Alfred to send him a bow and some arrows, "but not too expensive or delicate as the weather here will be hard on them."

In July of 1936 an event which he had long desired but also dreaded came about: his family came to visit. As Pop now had a bad back and high blood pressure, it was a difficult trip for them too. Tutie, an attractive 22-year-old college graduate, wondered what her brother would say after not seeing her in four years. As she walked down the gangplank he shouted, "Too fat!" And "Where did you get that ridiculous hat?"

"All the charm of a brother!" she retorted.

The week they arrived, two Twillingate people came down with typhoid. John was about to vaccinate everyone, including his family, when he pin-pointed the source as bad water at a local hotel. He showed his parents the town and the Hospital, took them to see Long Point Lighthouse, and the North and South Islands by boat. They ate lobsters and blue mussels at the Tilt. They went to New World Island in the *Bonnie Nell* and visited his good friends the Frenches at their farm in Moreton's Harbour. Thoughtfully, the Frenches dispatched a driver with horse and carriage to fetch them from the wharf in comfort. Mary and Ern French's sister Muriel would become lifelong friends and correspondents.

Mary saw that her son and his young wife were doing fine things and that the people loved them. She saw too that Johnny was healthy and happy; she was content. Pop saw the same things but was not content. He felt that John was drinking and smoking too much, that he was wasting his life.

In the middle of this long visit, after midnight on Monday, July 27th, John developed acute appendicitis. It was later said that he had wanted to remove the appendix himself, which is probably true. Some said he did— which is not. There was some confusion at the time, and accounts vary. One story has a student doctor performing the operation, another states that Dr Wood did it. It seems likely that Dr Olds directed the procedure.

A former nurse's aide who claimed she witnessed the drama at sixteen or so described it as follows: "About twelve o'clock one night I was called to go to surgery. When I got there the first thing Dr Olds said was, 'I think someone should take my appendix out.' The pain had taken him all of a sudden and nauseated him. A scrub nurse, not Betty, had already arrived. 'Well,' said she, '*I* can't do it,' and turned to me. 'What in the name of God are we going to do with him?' she said. 'Twas only me and her now.

"'There's a student here,' he said. 'Get him in. Between the three of you, surely to God you can do something for me.' By this time he was really out of himself with the pain. It was so bad he didn't give a damn what happened to him. So we fetched the student and got Dr Olds in the OR and prepared him for the operation. He asked for a local anesthetic so we gave him a spinal needle. We marked him with a ballpoint pen right where he was going to be cut. I helped the student. Dr Olds showed the fellow how to cut. I passed instruments to the scrub nurse.

"'Now,' he would say, 'clamp the goddam artery. With the hemostat, dammit—you know the artery I'm talking about.' The student did as he was told. And Dr Olds would just bang at it, you know, to show us what he wanted. And you'd get the hemostats and flow packs and put them exactly inside where the appendix was.

"'Now,' he said, 'you have to go down this far, and you'll find something like a bean. Put your finger down there now, you'll feel it.' Now after that was done he said, 'You get that goddam Allis ready for the appendix, then you get two.' And then the student cut between the two and tied each corner and burned it with the cautery. And then sewed him up. Oh God, we were so frightened. We had no idea what was going to happen—he was our *doctor.*"

While her story is dramatic, what probably happened is that Dr Wood, summoned out of bed, arrived just as the student was about to operate and either assisted him or took over. Dr Wood was a GP, with little direct surgical experience, though he had assisted Olds since 1933. It is possible he had never performed an appendectomy alone—which would explain Dr Olds' directing the procedure. The students that summer were Jacobs, Pollock and French, one of whom was likely with Dr Hardy on the *Bonnie Nell.* In such a tense moment the presence of a calm and resourceful student could have been critical. This may be why he loomed so large in the aide's recollection. There was another reason.

"About five in the morning," she concluded, "there was another acute appendix case came in. So he got up and we took the other fellow's appendix out and he got back in bed again. And the next morning at eight o'clock he was back on rounds in his pyjamas—which were pretty fancy—and his white coat. That day there was no surgery 'til about twelve o'clock, because he had to have a little rest. Usually it was seven days before they took the stitches out. During that time, you wouldn't get out of bed. Tough is the name for him." Tutie remembered another detail: John wanted to take his usual morning swim that day. Dr Wood advised against it.

During one of the coastal steamer's last trips that fall, a young female passenger was seen sketching around the wharf while the ship unloaded. Dr Olds invited her up for lunch. Rhoda Dawson had taught school in Labrador for four years, had just spent two more in St Anthony and was just heading home to London, England. He immediately asked her to stay the winter and help, for free room and board. She agreed, and for two months worked with the children who were in plaster casts, teaching them to draw and paint and play games. In her spare time she sketched inside the Hospital and painted around the town.

"I had no idea what he was like," she said, "except that he was obviously brilliant and we got on quite well. Anyone I wanted to sit for me he would order to do so; he was monarch of all he surveyed. John could paint and had some paints. He asked me to give him a lesson. I did put up a very difficult still-life and he brought it off not at all badly.

"What struck me about him was his unwonted charm, his ability, his position in the town. He was King of Twillingate all right." She in turn was thirty-six, attractive and single, an accomplished artist. When he tried to kiss her, she simply reminded him that he was a married man. "He seemed kindly disposed toward women," she recalled, "but his real interest was his work." She recalled that he was very nervous because he had just imposed a two-person limit on Sunday afternoon visiting at the Hospital, a traditional pastime which he felt was getting out of hand. Miss Dawson departed in December by train from Lewisporte.

Whenever he felt daunted, his patients' wit revived him. All of them, male and female, adult and child, played with the language as sunlight played on a waterfall. Their attitude to calamity was a constant wonderment to him. They taught him humility and courage.

Doctor: "Do your bowels work all right?"

Patient: "I had diarrhea when I first went home, but they are more reconciled now."

One patient was so stiff she "had to help the nurse get [her] on the bed." Another said, "My back is so bad I have to get down on the floor to get up."

Loss of appetite, always worrisome, evoked many exchanges. Olds: "Is her appetite good?"

Patient's husband: "No, she only eats a little and not much of that." Another husband allowed that once in a while his wife came up with a good appetite "but not a ravishing one."

The pace of child-bearing was enough to confuse anyone. When asked whether she had any children, one woman replied, "No. Oh, yes, I had one two years ago."

Males brought their share of worries too.

Olds: "What do you find?"

Patient: "I am afraid my bird will get so small I can't make my water out of it. I want an X-ray on it and maybe you can strap it up and help me." Another was delighted by the supposed aphrodisiacal properties of his prescription that he said: "I wants some more of they pills."

Occasionally a patient dared to question Dr Olds' work. "I had my prostate gland out last month and now I can't hold my water at all; did you put my bladder back after the operation?" Sometimes they misunderstood the diagnosis: "The doctor told me I had water in my bladder."

Heart conditions were uncommon. "Anybody in your family with heart trouble?"

Patient: "Yes, Mother had it; but not during the last seven years."

"She was cured?"

Patient: "No—she died."

Mental problems were the least common. "And what is wrong with you?"

Patient: "I came to get cured of my shortmindedness."

A man confessed: "I was going to jump over the wharf and make away with meself but then I looked around and seed there wasn't any water—it was frozen over."

And hospital food produced its share of merriment. In those days Twillingate Hospital supplemented its food supply with wild meat and fish in season. This included the local autumn delicacy, turr or murre.

Doctor: "Was the turr tough?"

Patient: "Well, we could chew the gravy because we had some mutton along with it."

Another local delicacy was wild trout—if one could get enough. Said one patient: "The trouts they served us was so small it took fourteen or fifteen to made a dozen."

Much as they appreciated their wit, neither Olds nor Dr Ecke could understand one peculiarity. "Men will come twenty miles by dog team or boat," said Ecke, "to tell you that Mrs Bulgin has broken her leg. It is useless to tell them they should have brought her. We have to go back with them perhaps just to tell her we can accomplish makeshift repairs in the home and she will have to come to the Hospital. Like as not, she will refuse. Even if a six-year-old refuses to come it is final. Many a baby has lain home and died because it would 'fret' or 'grieve' in the hospital."

For a while after 1937, John wanted the Board to buy him an airplane. It would speed winter travel, he argued, and provide a year-round ambulance service. They pointed out that Twillingate had no suitable landing strip. He countered that he could use pontoons in summer and land on the Harbour ice in winter. With trepidation the new Chairman, Magistrate Beaton Abbott, authorized him to look into costs. In April of 1938 Dr Olds reported that a plane would cost $2,200 landed in St John's. They discussed selling the *Bonnie Nell* to pay for it, but nothing further was done. Some members felt that, while he might be able to service the plane, he was likely to crash it and kill himself.

The topic would reappear in modified form during the War. He feared that once Botwood's Military Hospital was no longer needed it would become a rival to Twillingate. He proposed setting up a satellite hospital there with a plane. They could use the seaplane base as headquarters and have their own pilot. Board minutes for March 26th, 1941 record that Magistrate Abbott authorized him "to go to Canada in the fall to negotiate purchase and investigate hiring a pilot for one year." Whatever transpired, his hopes were to be dashed by the 1943 Hospital Fire. Yet when Dr Louis Lawton was leaving in 1947 he would broach the satellite hospital idea again, urging him to be the resident physician.

"It always surprised me he that he didn't have a plane," said Gordon Stuckless, a Twillingate friend from the fifties. "He always wanted one. I wouldn't say he couldn't afford it. But by then I don't believe he trusted himself to fly it."

In November 1937, David Douglas Olds was born. Dr Ecke delivered the baby, recording in his journal that he and John sat up well into the morning hours celebrating. Happy as he was, John was still not fully reconciled to domestic life. Commenting on Tutie's recent marriage he wrote, "I hope [it] hasn't been a disillusionment as yet." Then he changed the subject and enlisted her chemist husband Doug Mott to analyze salt samples from two different Spanish mines to find out why local fisherman were having trouble drying their catch.

Around this time he discovered ski-joring, the Norwegian practice of using dogs to pull one on skis. By hitching his pure-bred Irish setter Jake and the mongrel Sport—the "savage dog" from Tizzard's Harbour—together, he found he could make better time on firm snow than with a full team. "Betty and I have been to the Tilt twice with them and I have driven them on calls when it is not good for the slide. It is a lot of fun."

In January 1938, Dr Parsons, in a desperate bid to make a new life, embarked from Vancouver for China with Dr Norman Bethune. The Canadian doctor, recently back from organizing a blood transfusion service for the Republican side in the Spanish Civil War, was setting up a medical unit for Mao Tse Tung's Eighth Route Army, which was defending north-central China against the invading Japanese. Within weeks the two disagreed. Dr Bethune labelled him "a drunken bum" and sent him packing. Two years later, while delivering a paper before the American Academy for the Advancement of Science in Philadelphia on December 31st, the founder of Twillingate's Hospital would collapse and die of a heart attack.

Meanwhile, in Winston Churchill's chilling phrase, the lights were going out all over Europe. While England slumbered and the Japanese bore down on China, Hitler annexed Austria and prepared to pounce on Czechoslovakia. In Twillingate all this still seemed remote, but John and Betty decided to take their long-planned US holiday sooner than later. On November 19th, 1939 they left on the SS *Clyde* for a three-month vacation in the States, their first in six years. They both needed a rest, especially John, who had recently undergone nasal and mastoid surgery. Leaving David in the care of their housekeeper Suzie, they visited both sets of parents, spent a week or so at the Hopkins and Duke University medical schools and even did some tarpon fishing with Uncle Frank in Florida. They returned on February 22nd, travelling over ice so bad that Betty called it the worst trip of her life.

No one knows for sure how the Cottage fire started. It happened a week after they got home. The night before, they had a few people over for drinks—a farewell party for Dr Rube Waddell and Nurse Joan "Tommy"

Thompson, who were leaving in the morning for St John's. They would marry there before Rube left with the sealing fleet. Harry Osmond, who was taking the couple to Lewisporte in the morning, was there, and Bob Ecke and his friend Marianne. Marianne did not drink, but on going into the Olds' bedroom with a lamp, she dropped it and broke the chimney. Her hand got nicked but no fire was started. The next morning, Waddell and Tommy said their goodbyes. At the last moment, Stan and Annette Hardy decided to accompany them to Lewisporte.

"It seemed very quiet when they had all gone," Dr Ecke recorded in his journal. "I was busy in the OPD, then at one o'clock sat down to dinner—meat pie. I was just putting a forkful in my mouth when Wyn Colburne stuck his head through the doorway and said something about 'getting to the Cottage.'

...Suddenly David's nurse ran in through the back door with David naked in her arms. She said the Cottage was on fire. I grabbed my favourite fire extinguisher and rushed up. John and Betty and ten men or so were standing out in front. There was a nasty loud crackling and flames were visible at the living room window.

I tried to get in at all the doors but it was impossible to do a thing. The fire gained rapidly. Mabel and a few of the women started to grab water to put it out, but there wasn't any sense to it. In two minutes the upper part of the house was a solid flame.

I went into the cellar with some of the men and we wheeled the motorcycle out. The doors were hard to move against the ice. We fooled around the porch window trying to get the radio. George Hawkins climbed into the porch but we hung onto him and begged him to come out. He had a wooden leg.

The windows were difficult to break. The hardwood bars were like iron. Someone had been right in the kitchen when the fire was discovered and had emptied John's closet which communicated from the bedroom to the back hall. The Olds had been at the dining room table when they heard a crackling noise in the cellar. They had gone down to investigate and had seen nothing. When they came upstairs, the room next to the dining room was in flames and as they left the dining room, [it] burst into flames behind them.

Betty had gone out of the front door and John to the back to shout up to David's nurse and the sleeping night nurses, Marianne and Hazel. By the time they had grabbed coats, it was hard to get downstairs. David and his nurse only just made it. Suzie lived in a basement room; men were able to get into her room through a window and save her possessions. Very soon a bucket brigade was formed and the fire was held. There was some concern that the Hospital, only a stone's throw away down the hill, would catch fire.

Melvin Woolfrey was in the Hospital at the time and saw and heard the commotion. "They didn't shift anybody out of the Hospital," he said, "because it was all concrete block construction." Even inside the storm windows, however, the glass got too hot to touch. And they had to throw water on the doors of the nearby storage shed to keep them from igniting.

"It is unbelievable how fast the house burned," John wrote his parents on March 2nd. "It was as though a pile of gunpowder was put on the floor of each room & lighted. There were hundreds of men here in no time but it was impossible to get in to save anything. I did get a few of my clothes—but Betty & the nurses got nothing. I certainly feel badly about the chairs you made & my watch." They also lost the antique furniture they had bought from Dr Stirling's mansion after the opera singer Georgina Stirling died in 1935. John's entire medical library was gone as well.

For weeks the couple had nightmares about the fire and how close they came to losing their little son. "David had been upstairs with Mamie & had been bathing about 2 minutes before the fire started. He was standing up in his high chair with only a shirt on. No one was burned but I got plenty of smoke & got my hair & eyelashes singed trying to go into the living room." He asked Pop to get Olds and Whipple to quote on a Gravely tractor that he hoped to rig for firefighting.

While the Cottage itself was Hospital property, most of its contents belonged to the occupants. "When the last wall had fallen," said Ecke, "they counted losses. Marianne and Hazel possessed only what they stood in... slippers, nightgown and coat. Betty didn't even have a coat: she was in a $1.50 utility dress. She had lost the first new clothes she had bought in six years. David was naked. Books, maps, silver, furniture, furs, guns—all gone."

Mayme Hewlett later recalled the mood over lunch that day: "We sat there, dumb with sympathy for Dr and Mrs Olds...until Betty looked up and said, 'It's a nice day, John.' This released the tension and the babble began." Even their Christmas presents, mailed home ahead to save weight on the plane, were gone. "And the damned Customs nicked us $100.36 on the stuff," said John.

"They were pretty brave," said Dr Ecke. "We assembled makeshift costumes for them and we all had a drink in my apartment.... The Hardys were certainly surprised to find the Cottage gone when they got back."

For John's birthday Pop and Mary wisely sent new and used clothes. Ivy (Baggs) LeDrew recalled shortening one of the coats for him. A relative of Betty's sent her a leopard skin coat. John described it as "very nice but funny looking." The housekeeper and the few nurses who had lived in the Cottage were taken in by local families. Until a new Cottage could be built, the Olds were given temporary living quarters on Third Floor West, vacant since Dr French had left. "It looks a bit slummy when we hang up washing to dry," said John, but it was now all they had. Nurse Thelma (Groze) Christie, a friend of Tommy's who arrived from Toronto only two weeks after the fire, called it her "second home," a place of music and laughter. With wartime shortages it would be four years before a new Cottage could be built.

Characteristically, John turned the disaster to advantage. The Hospital had long needed extra staff accommodation and storage space. The quickest and cheapest solution was to add a third storey to Dr Parsons' wing, which had a flat concrete slab roof. Lloyds of London paid a few thousand dollars insurance, but a local insurance company, miffed that a second company was involved, reneged. Letters flew back and forth between John and his father about asbestos cement wall board, plumbing fixtures and other building materials. The Board hired a Mr Primmer to supervise the work, and the nurses and aides finally had new quarters.

That spring, as War loomed in Europe, Edward VIII's successor George VI and his bride Elizabeth deemed it wise to visit their Dominions. Dr and Mrs Olds were invited to meet their Majesties at a Government House garden party in late June in St John's. Although the Board had voted $400 in March to buy the Olds new clothing, John and Betty had nothing to wear. "All I've got is my coonskin coat," John announced, hoping that would excuse him. Betty wrote the Olds and Chapmans in Windsor and Philadelphia but netted only Stuart Chapman's top hat which mice somehow chewed en route. John vowed to wear it with the coonskin coat. Betty took his measurements and sent them to their friend Grace Patten, who had worked in Twillingate in 1932 and was now married to John Sparkes, MD and living in St John's.

Out-flanked, John gave in. To save expense they would go in the *Bonnie Nell*, with Lige Dalley at the helm, and he would attend the annual medical convention that same week. When the Olds arrived in St John's, Maunder's Tailor Shop had the suit ready. It fit perfectly but John said, "This is a terrible waste of money. I'll have to wear it on rounds!" Grace noticed he was wearing a nice hat, not the earlier one with the chewed brim, and complimented him. "Shhh," he said, "Betty hasn't noticed it yet." While the women did last-minute primping in the bathroom, he sat and chatted with Dr Sparkes. But when they were heading out the door Grace said, "John, you *can't* go down there like that! The tails of your coat are wrinkled something scandalous!" "Well, I'm not gonna take the coat off now," he drawled. Grace put on her iron to heat, placed her makeshift board under his tails and, like Mammy Yokum in the comic strip *L'il Abner*, ironed them where he stood.

The young King and Queen of Old England charmed the crusty New Englander and his wife. After Betty and John had returned to Twillingate, Grace got a note from John saying, "What kind of an ironing board does a south-paw like?" And he made her a beautiful folding one. For years afterward he would wear his "King Suit" on Christmas morning rounds.

That August, with construction on the wing at last going well, he took Betty to St Anthony on the *Bonnie Nell* for a holiday. "I spent a very pleasant day talking with Sir Wilfred Grenfell," he told Mary. "He was most interested in our work, though could not promise us any financial aid. He is a delightful person but well past his prime both physically and mentally." After touring the Hospital, built in 1927 to replace the 1904 one, he remarked, "They have a fine set-up there & plenty of money to run it."

On the evening of September 1st, every working battery radio in Notre Dame Bay and all over the world crackled with the news that Hitler had invaded Poland. Two days later, Britain and France declared war on Germany.

"This war is terrible," Betty lamented as the Panzer divisions raced toward the Low Countries, "and I just don't like to think about it. We get reports from all the different countries & Holland seems in rather a precarious position.... I wouldn't want to be over there. I don't think John intends to go unless it seems necessary. He'd have a hard time getting away because they all depend on him so much. After all, he's doing a lot more good here than he would getting mixed up in this war. Rube was talking so much about it before he left that he got John all steamed up too—but lately I have heard very little about it."

Except to register David as an American citizen and get himself a passport, John continued as before. He wondered whether wartime blackout would be imposed on the Hospital. Mostly he was preoccupied with his patients, his Well Baby Clinic, the enlarged wing and the task of setting up a home for World War I syphilitics. Lately he had been worried about Jack, his horse: "He was sick for a while but is better now than ever. He is very wild lately & has thrown everyone except me."

Chapter Fourteen

Hospital Fire!

"In retrospect... the fire was of great benefit."

—J. M. Olds

For nineteen years Notre Dame Bay Memorial had stood above Twillingate like a medieval castle with a town under its wing, a Hotel Dieu ministering to its body as the churches ministered to its soul. By day its comforting bulk steadied the landscape; by night fishermen saw its rows of yellow lighted windows reflected on the waters and were glad. People knew those lights. On the Second Floor, if dim and in motion, they meant a nurse or aide or Dr Olds was checking the wards with lamp or flashlight. Lights in the basement might be Martin Young fixing the furnace, or the cook setting a giant pot of oatmeal porridge on the stove to simmer for breakfast. And if there was a gleam from the two OR windows on Second Floor East, it could only mean that Dr Olds was operating and they would bless him and go on about their business.

The winter of 1943 was no different, except that now the glow of dying ships sometimes crimsoned the horizon and people talked of spies and saboteurs. No blackout edict had yet been issued for the Bay, so the Hospital lights shone as usual. On the night of Saturday, February 27th no lights could be seen because a blizzard had swallowed all. Around midnight the gale veered northwest, the stars reappeared and a numbing torrent of Labrador air began to whip the new snow into high drifts.

Had Ned Facey looked over toward the Hospital from his North Side home just after midnight, he would have seen nothing amiss. Just before daylight, however, he would have noticed a ruddier glow in the topmost dormer windows. Knowing that John and Betty had gone to the Tilt that weekend, leaving their apartment empty, he might have been momentarily puzzled. But then he would have seen the strange glow brighten, burst through the roof and blossom above it like a giant orange and yellow marigold against the inky sky, spilling petals of flame downwind, lighting hillside and houses in its lurid glare.

Moments later, the bells of St Peter's and several other churches woke the town. As the few telephones jangled the news, huddles of men with buckets and axes and ladders, followed by horse-slide with barrels, began to hurry through drifted paths and across the Harbour ice to try to save their Hospital and the people in it.

That weekend Notre Dame Bay Memorial held the usual mix of winter patients, some sixty in all. More than a dozen lay immobile in plaster casts, some were on IV or stomach drip after GI operations, one was slated for tonsillectomy in the morning. A couple of children were recuperating from appendectomies. A few patients were fairly ill but only one or two needed emergency treatment. In the OR, Jean Anstey of Twillingate was in the early stages of a difficult labour and the anesthetist had administered ether to dull her pain while Nurse Edna Legge stood by.

Alison (Loveridge) Bartle, a former aide, was in a cast on the women's ward when the first firefighters arrived. She had heard something about a small fire in the library upstairs but figured someone had put it out. She thought no more about it until the lights went out and a nurse with a lamp came flying down the corridor, banging on doors and yelling "Fire!" and "Clear the building!"

After watching several patients being removed to safety, it occurred to her that she might have been overlooked. She hauled herself out of bed and over to a window. She had hoisted the sash and got one leg over the sill when someone pulled her back. On the second try she got through the opening. She fell more than ten feet but landed in a deep snowbank. As she lay there half buried, wondering what to do next, she heard overhead the crackling roar of flames and the cries of men, women and children. Men were wrestling ladders into position against the walls.

Frank Pardy, racing up the hill with two buckets of water and spotting her open window, stepped over her and disappeared inside. "He was the only one to take that route to the fire," she recalled. On his way back he picked her up, cast and all, and carried her to his home nearby. At the garden gate he stumbled and dropped her into another snowbank.

Dorothy Lambert was also among the last to be saved. "I was alone, and a burst of flame prevented my getting to the ground floor. I immediately returned to the women's ward, where I had to be rescued by the firefighters from the sun porch..."

By then the first and second floors were alive with hobbling patients, men carrying iron beds, bed clothes and pieces of equipment. The fire had spread to the Wing's new roof, blocking the building's only elevator. Terrified old women clasping pillows and Bibles were lifted bed and all by strong men in heavy boots and whisked away, the bedsheets flapping like sails in a wind, down the corridors and stairs and out into the winter dawn. On the roof, firefighters hacked away flaming timbers and flung freezing water at the inferno. The gravity-fed water supply from Stuckless' Pond gave little hose pressure on the roof, but a bucket brigade from the lower levels soon overcame the problem. To the east, downwind, men dashed water on the roofs and walls of the root cellars, warehouse and machine shop to counter the rain of flaming debris.

Like refugees from a war, a caravan of shivering night-shirted patients and uniformed nurses descended Hospital Lane with winking flashlights and lanterns. The sickest were taken to the nearest homes and to the town's two hotels. A few were discharged to their own homes. Frank and Nellie Pardy remembered the scene very well:

> David Olds was home asleep in the apartment with the housekeeper. He would be six years old then. George Ings the orderly brought him to safety first and put him down in Dr Hardy's apartment. Then around six o'clock in the morning George came down and called us to get ready to receive patients. I heard someone come in the house and say: 'The Hospital is on fire!'

> I didn't have time for anything that morning; just as fast as I could look after the patients that I had, and three small children of my own, another crowd would be brought in. By supper time I had to go to bed myself with a migraine. I had eighteen patients in all brought down to our house. I'll never forget—when the fire started a woman's newborn baby was brought here too. In the hurry, the baby's mother was taken with some other patients to the Harbour View Hotel run by Mrs Pynn.

> Other patients in the house that morning were Mr Coady, the bank manager; he had a bad back. His room in the Hospital was out of the way and they were so long coming he thought they had forgot him. He had covered his head in the sheet and said some prayers. There was one man with sandbags strapped to his legs; the men wondering what made him so heavy! Ned Anstey got out of the building by himself. But he was a bit delirious; they found him going the wrong way, up the hill. One patient with a ruptured appendix took out his IV needle and crawled up into the barn into the hay. He thought they would come too late, because the man beside him had a body cast and would have to go first.

That Sunday morning's dawn revealed a forlorn jumble of white enamelled beds and stacked mattresses covering the slopes above and below the Hospital. Men loaded them on horses and carts and took them straight across the Harbour ice to the Loyal Orange Lodge and the Society of United Fishermen Hall on North Side. The entire top floor of the Hospital was a blackened, steaming ruin. Cook Ivy LeDrew remembered that day. "They took about fifty patients over to the Orange Hall and Kate (Phillips) Churchill and I went and cooked for them there. We cooked in the Fishermen's S.U.F. Hall across the way—it had a bigger kitchen—and brought the food across the road to them. The patients were in bed with screens put up and all.

"It was hard on the staff, because most of them lost all their clothes. They all got some insurance money from the hospital. I had all my clothes burnt, except what I wore home that night. I had practically a new leather coat, and a new one for the summer and I got fifty dollars insurance toward my clothes—the most of any of the girls there. The only life that was lost was the little dog David had."

For nursing aide Elizabeth Burton, then sixteen, the near-tragedy of 1943 was still vivid after thirty-one years: "I remember one patient coming down the stairs in the Hospital carrying his drainage bottle and the end of the catheter in his teeth. After every patient was out and we all [were in] the L.O.L. Hall, the fun began—not for the good doctors, I assure you, or for Miss Gladys Dawe, acting Head Nurse—but for we eight girls who remained to help out.

"The men were divided from the women by a large schooner sail. Every night when they thought no one important was around, a man named Forsey would bring out his accordion and [entertain everyone]. Now that I think back, I'm sure we should all have been fired and most likely would have been, had we not been needed so badly."

Dr Olds returned from the Tilt in a hurry. "Early on the morning after the fire," he wrote, "the directorate met in no cheerful mood to look into the future." They had lost medical supplies, some of it insured but irreplaceable in wartime—as well as patients' clothing and belongings, much reserve equipment and essential winter supplies.

"We are glad you didn't hear it over the radio," John wrote Pop, "as the broadcasts from England & Canada were exaggerated. However, it was bad enough but we are very lucky that we still have a lot of room for patients—in fact just as much. Staff quarters and 2 yrs of supplies are gone.... There is no insurance on the building. We are cleaned completely. All the clothes we have are our heavy ones we had at the Tilt. Clock, high chair, pictures, all gone too. Betty is worse off for clothes & I got some given me that sort of fit. She can't get any shoes—& I suppose you can't send any with the rationing on. David lost his splendid puppy, but now has another one which is homely as the devil. The roof must be replaced immediately.

"The gloom lessened somewhat," he said after the meeting, "when a telegram was delivered to me from Mr Gerald Doyle of St John's, promising a $1,000 donation for reconstruction." On March 14th he confided to his parents, "More important than his donation is his gift of radio facilities...we are making a drive for funds—trying to get $100,000; we won't get it but so far have around ten." The Board appointed a rebuilding committee to solicit further donations. The citizens of St John's, including several business firms, sent $30,000. Dr Olds and his Directors were able to replace lost equipment and supplies. Later the Department of Health pledged to match dollar for dollar up to $90,000. The tally from all sources eventually reached $186,000.

As he had done after the Cottage fire, Dr Olds seized the moment to make improvements. "The chief loss in the fire was staff quarters and storage space, which had never been adequate. There were many other changes needed also. Mr W. D. McCarter of St John's, an architect, was given the job of rebuilding, which took three years; wartime lack of supplies made his work difficult and slow." Meanwhile, some of the staff moved in with those who had extra space on the ground floor, and others were housed in town. As Dr Olds wouldn't hear of putting the top storey back on, the Board opted for an inexpensive and speedy low-pitch roof. Ned Clarke and his crew had it on within a fortnight.

The Olds had for some time been looking forward to the new Cottage John had designed. Work had begun in 1941, but lack of funds made it intermittent and slow. They lived for a while in a house bought from Ned Facey and hauled it across the Harbour. Now that space had been provided for his nurses, aides and doctors, perhaps they might garner enough extra money to finish the Cottage. Board minutes for May reveal that both he and Chairman E. J. Colbourne donated their vacation salary to the fund. No one had much time for vacations that year.

"The $186,000 paid for a large, three-storey and basement concrete block staff house," Olds continued, "which included two apartments for doctors, storage rooms, workshops and garage in basement, single rooms for graduate nurses, multiple bedrooms for aides and dormitories for maids." Recalling his many stormy walks down from the Cottage, he had them connect Staff House and Hospital by a covered wooden ramp.

With Martin Young he also looked into the electrical situation. "The original idea of a hydroelectric plant was a very poor one. The water wheel generator was capable of an output of only 2.5 kilovolts, which put only a dull red glow in the bulbs if many were in use. When an X-ray was required for the Operating Room, a 10 k.V. gas-driven generator was cranked up. Lanterns and kerosene lamps were used by the night staff.

"The original X-ray machine was a very dangerous piece of equipment. [It had] a rotating disc supplying current to brass pipes suspended from the ceiling and leading to a moveable stand in which different, very large, fragile glass tubes were placed according to the type of X-ray required. During fluoroscopy the corona given off by the overhead pipes nearly defeated the darkness produced by closing the doors. More than one operator and patient received a severe shock while using the apparatus.

"The never adequate electrical plant, 220 V DC, was replaced by two *Vivian* diesel engines driving 50 KWH generators of 220-110 V 60 cycle AC. This not only gave us more light but for the first time made it possible to use standard electrical equipment. We also obtained a new high pressure steam plant of two 83 HP coal-fired boilers and a new laundry with much improved equipment...."

In the back of everyone's mind buzzed the question: *What or who caused the fire?* All during the War, outport people worried about clandestine German submarine bases and possible attack. Any stranger—especially one carrying a camera or any suspicious looking object—was dogged by whispers and glances. Many vowed the fire was set on purpose.

Staff physician Mariwald-Neild was a Viennese who had fled the Nazis during the 1938 *Anschluss*. She still spoke with a German accent and this made her immediately suspect. To the gossipers it made no difference that she too had lost everything. Kinder souls defended her and gave her clothing, but Board Minutes for October 22nd show that Dr Mariwald was fired that autumn. She moved to Eastport, where her emaciated prisoner-of-war husband rejoined her in 1946.

An enquiry was held. Ivy LeDrew was put on the witness stand, since she and Miss Eddy had been among the last to leave on Saturday night. Never inside a courtroom before, she was so nervous that she forgot to mention seeing an off-duty nurse and a soldier enter the Olds' apartment that night. She knew that Dr Olds and Betty sometimes lent their apartment to sweethearts. She had thought nothing of it and so never mentioned the pair. Later she wondered whether perhaps they had they dropped a cigarette in a wastebasket. In any case the hearing found no evidence of foul play.

Martin Young and others who knew the Hospital's innards had a better explanation. The fire had started in the library next to the Olds' apartment, a room lit by a single bulb enclosed in a large white porcelain globe. Water from a leak in the roof sometimes trickled down the wire into this globe; Martin had once found it half-full. He had fixed the leak but it could have filled again during heavy rain while the Olds were away. They concluded that the weighted globe pulled the wires apart, causing a short circuit.

"We had 220-Volt DC," said X-ray technician Raymond "Bud" Young. "That stuff could arc an inch anyhow—pure flame. And it would maintain itself. AC will break and snap; DC will arc like the devil." Such an arc, they reasoned, could have ignited the rubber insulation, causing the wooden ceiling to catch fire.

Edna (Legge) Hillier, who worked at the Hospital from February 1936 to September 1943, was senior nurse in charge the evening of the fire, with three nurse's aides assisting. "Our shift was from 8:00 PM until 8:00 AM," she recalled. "The evening started out very busy. In addition to routine duties, we had a seriously ill child requiring oxygen and continuous care, and a very pregnant mother already in labour. The baby was due sometime that night.

> Toward early morning there was a power failure.... We had to use flashlights, kerosene oil lamps and fortunately we had an emergency light in the Operating Room. I immediately notified the two doctors on call and also told Dr Swanker that the baby was on its way. During the delivery we were told the Hospital was on fire. Minutes later a little girl was born. The anesthetist had already left to assist...in removing patients. As soon as the doctor was satisfied the baby was all right, he also left to assist.... He told me to take care of the mother and child and that they would be back for us.

> Although terribly frightened, I knew I must stay calm and prepare the mother—who was semi-conscious—and the baby to leave the Hospital. I could hear voices in the corridor.... Smoke started to fill the room and the woman finally regained consciousness. Minutes dragged like hours. Suddenly I heard someone yelling that all patients had been safely evacuated from the floor. I groped my way through the smoke to the hall and cried, 'We're still in the Operating Room! Please come and get us!' Within minutes they had the woman and baby on a stretcher and we were all rescued. I almost collapsed from shock and exhaustion.

> What I find remarkable is the way the Twillingate people banded together to fight this fire. All patients were safely evacuated. Many volunteered their homes and fed the firefighters and patients. As a result there were no tragedies. Within a couple of weeks, it was business as usual.

In fact, even as the beds were replaced, three new patients arrived. They had left their homes by horse and sleigh three days earlier.

Jean Anstey herself only found out about the fire after it was over. Nurse Gladys Dawe had brought the baby down to Nellie Pardy's, saying before she rushed away, "If it stops crying, make it cry." Mrs Anstey, at the Harbour View Hotel, spent some frantic hours wondering where her baby was. "Finally," she said, "a nurse came, Mrs Arthur Hodge, and took both of us to her home and cared for us until I could go to mine."

Elaine Drucilla Anstey, the seven-pound baby born that night, knew nothing of the fire until years later when her mother showed her photographs.

"In retrospect," concluded Olds, "As there was no injury or loss of life, the fire was of great benefit to the institution."

Chapter Fifteen

A Sealing Memoir

"I predict that in ten years' time there won't be a seal to
go after if they keep on as they are doing."

—J. M. Olds

"**D**oc, what say you and me go swilin' next spring?" Every December over Christmas rum, Captain Saul White would ask John Olds the same question. John, he knew, liked everything about sealing: the ships and equipment, the seals and the methods of taking them, the icefields, the danger—especially the danger. But Dr Olds always shook his head sadly. He had no one to take his place, Betty wasn't well, he had staff problems—perhaps another year....

Tutie had once called Captain Saul White "a foul-mouthed old boozer"—but not to his face. Of course she was half right; but John knew a different Saul White. The Saul he knew was a master mariner, a skilled fisherman and sealer, a good friend, a man with a heart as big as his Jimmy Durante nose. It did John good to see Saul's shrewd, deepset eyes twinkle with ribald mirth, to hear him laugh and tell wonderful tales and curse with equal ease.

And Saul liked this lean, taciturn Yankee who ran his Hospital like a tight ship, who thought nothing of sawing off a rotten leg or teasing out a cataract. The Captain had once renamed a tug—the 59-ton *Exploits*, which he bought from the Anglo-Newfoundland Company—the *J. M. Olds* in his honour. They were two of a kind, fond of rum and ribaldry, suffering fools badly, leaders of men.

So when Dr Olds saw the Captain hurrying up Hospital Lane early in 1946, salt-and-pepper cap pulled down against the wind, long pipe clamped in his firm jaw, he had an idea what was coming. That year Saul's proposition was much stronger. The War was over, he argued; the Hospital and Cottage were rebuilt, the new Staff House finished. Betty was feeling pretty good, wasn't she? He had three young doctors—Louis Lawton, Bert Venables and Wade Hastings—to help him, didn't he? Dr Olds gave in.

Betty didn't object. Despite what Tutie had said, she could not deny that Saul White was a tonic to her husband. A few weeks at sea would do John good. He did look haggard of late, and he slept poorly. She knew John and Saul liked to drink together. She was aware too that even sober sealers perished in blizzards, that vessels bigger than the *Bessie Marie* got stove in and sunk with all hands. Well, she reasoned, their small hoard of rum would be gone in a night or two. She urged him to go.

Twillingate Harbour was plugged with drift ice that spring, but Captain White had wisely moored the 190-ton schooner over in Durrell. Even so, her 240 HP *Fairbanks Morse* engine had all it could do to punch a way to open water. On their first night out, the wind veered northwest and freezing spray enamelled her deck as slick as glass and glazed her masts and rigging with six inches of ice. When she began to roll to her scuppers Saul sent the crew aloft to swing hatchets with scrammed fingers until the deadly cargo clattered down and overboard.

Just as they were starting to see seals, John fell sick with cramps and diarrhea that would not clear up. Captain Saul had to land him protesting back in Twillingate. Embarrassed that his friend had lost time on his account, John vowed to go next year. The short sojourn at sea had buoyed his spirits unaccountably. He missed the long days amid the ice floes, the nightly yarns and poker games by swaying yellow lantern light in the snug fo'c'sle. At night he even missed the dull scrabble of ice along the hull, inches from his ear.

In January 1947 two events conspired to give him another opportunity. Dr Ecke wrote to say he was coming back, and Bowring Brothers of St John's asked Captain Saul to skipper the *Clarenville* to the Front. Dr Olds immediately signed on as fleet doctor and gunner. He also agreed to write a report for the Newfoundland Department of Fisheries, who were concerned about public criticism of the hunt and desired the views of an informed scientist. Dr Olds also wanted to investigate the mysterious sealers' disease called "Seal Finger."

He would have joined the *Clarenville* again in 1948, but Bowrings would not take him after what he had written in his report. That year he sailed for the Crosbies with Captain White on the *Bessie Marie*. In 1949 the Crosbies would pick Dr Lillie, and for the same reason. "I am out of favour," he told his mother that spring. "But I am proud to be so and I predict that in ten years' time there won't be a seal to go after if they keep on as they are doing." What follows is a blend of his accounts of the 1947 and 1948 voyages.

> For the past fifteen years it has been my good fortune to know quite intimately a character named Saul White, master of a Labrador fishing schooner for over thirty years. He recruited the sealers from Twillingate and adjacent islands, thirty-eight in all. He easily persuaded me to go as doctor for the fleet.

We left on March 6th, a very cold day, to join the train at Lewisporte. At about 2:30 AM we took the branch line to the junction, ten miles away, half an hour. After an interminable wait the 'Sealers' Special' came along—two day coaches attached to a way freight, hard wooden seats for the next thirty-six hours on the 240-mile trip to St John's. No diner, no food. Some of the men, having made the trip before, were smart enough to bring along food; but most of us had to fast, as the innumerable stops were always on a siding, well away from habitation.

When they arrived in St John's, the *Clarenville* was in dry dock being fitted with an iron bow shield and a new steel propeller. One of the Commission's "Splinter Fleet" of wooden coastal vessels built at Clarenville during the War, she was powered by a 350 HP *Vivian* diesel engine, 135 feet long, 325 tons.

"The next few days were occupied in purchasing personal needs and I had a considerable quantity of medical and surgical supplies to check from the list I had submitted, plus considerable bacteriological culture material as I was going to try and trace the etiology of the 'Seal Finger.'"

As men converged by train, boat and on foot on St John's, the old city came alive. For weeks its hotels, boarding houses and brothels were busier than usual. Taverns experienced brawls where chairs were broken over heads and blood had to be mopped up, but it was all in good fun and sales were brisk. Merchants rubbed their hands as hundreds of men made last-minute purchases of tobacco and whet stones and knives and sparables—[nails] for their boots—and blue eye-glasses guaranteed to prevent snowblindness. The *Daily News* and *Evening Telegram* ran profiles and photographs. The Sunday before departure, churches held special services.

On the great day, richly caparisoned clergy stood on crowded wharves to ask the Almighty's blessing on those who went down to the sea in ships to do business in great waters. Those who lined the taffrails waved to their friends and relatives. Then the motley fleet, flags and bunting snapping from every shroud and stay, hoisted anchor and cast off lines. Ships' whistles talked back and forth around the bowl of hills. The last vessel faded out of the Narrows in a squall of snow and those left behind turned to their radios.

"Our lines were slipped," continued Olds, "and we passed through the Narrows in a fresh northeast wind with the boat pitching enough to make about half the crew seasick." Like a dog indoors too long, John inhaled the cool moist breath of the sea. MacDonald Wholesale Drugs in St John's had lent him a camera and a few rolls of film. He also had several sketchbooks, oil pastels, pens and pencils and his oil paints. And he had his own .38-calibre rifle and ammunition. For the next few weeks their only contact with shore would be the *Gerald S. Doyle News* and the ship's new radio telephone.

"Very solid and seaworthy," Olds said of the *Clarenville*, but thought she should have been built to stand double the horsepower. "There were many incidents," he said in a 1947 report to the Fisheries Board, "when we were jammed and the Norwegians would go right around us picking up seals we could not reach. The *Ice Hunter, Blackmore, Lady McDonald, Linda May, Catalina Trader*, etc., are in the same category."

Ten miles off the Narrows they met heavy ice and had to turn back. The next day they reached Bay Roberts and took on ballast. Half way out of Conception Bay, they got jammed and drifted south for a while. Finally they got clear, and by March 18th were off the Funks, trailing the rest of the fleet. They made good time until Number 5 piston stuck one night. To ease the ship's rolling and hold her into the wind, they hoisted sails on the cargo masts. Replacing the piston took eleven hours, during which time they drifted many miles back. Freezing rain iced up the rigging and masts and only the crew's diligent chopping kept the ship from getting top heavy.

They aimed then for Belle Isle in the Straits. For hours they saw no floating ice. Captain Saul reckoned they would have to go well up the Labrador coast to find seals. Off the Horse Islands they met strings of ice, but no seals and no sign of the large flat pans three to four feet thick called whelping ice. All this time they maintained daily radio communication with several other ships, but everyone lied about their position. The Newfound-landers cursed the Norwegians because they couldn't understand a word they said.

Just north of Belle Isle they met the new *Lady MacDonald*, skippered by Captain Smith, and the *John Blackmore* under Captain J. Blackmore. All were in loose ice, so they exchanged visits. Each firm had a secret code for daily reports to the St John's office giving position, catch and such. There was another code for ships whose owners subscribed to the spotting plane service. Enthused over each other's company, the captains decided to adopt a code of their own for the voyage. However, once they got "in the fat" they abandoned it.

Next morning they again got in thick ice and went slower and slower. Finally, after a lot of backing and butting at full throttle, it became impossible to move at all. For six days and nights the *Clarenville* and *Lady MacDonald* were stuck fast. On the second day they saw, a couple of miles to the east, the *John Blackmore* reach a lead and steam north. This was the last they heard from her; "Captain Blackmore was never very chatty on the radio telephone." Several Norwegians passed, plowing through the ice at will, and Captain Saul and his crew cursed them colourfully. With much trekking the men managed to pile up a few hundred whitecoats.

At last the *Lady MacDonald* and *Clarenville* began to creep north again. Off the Round Hills—which John with his war surplus bubble astrolabe calculated at 59 degrees 31 minutes North, 52 degrees 45 minutes West—they picked up a few more seals. Killing had officially begun on March 13th. After ten days they still had little to show.

As seals had been reported off the mouth of Groswater Bay, they decided to return along the Labrador coast. Soon they met heavy ice again. As they went astern to take a run at it, a piece of ice smashed the rudder quadrant. The *Clarenville* lacked welding equipment but the *Lady Mac-Donald's* engineer brought his tanks and torch aboard, and, despite high winds and zero temperatures, repaired it using all his gas in the process. Three days later the quadrant went all to pieces. By now they had a couple hundred seals killed and piled and each pan flagged for retrieval. This method worked well in good weather, but in blizzards or heavy seas many pans were lost or pelts washed away. Helpless without a rudder, the crew began to mutiny. Two factions quickly arose: the regular salaried crew with nothing to gain by staying, versus the sealers with everything to lose. The former, led by the Engineer and Bo'sun, were for getting a tow back to St John's. The sealers demanded that the rudder be fixed. Soon the Captain and Engineer were not speaking. It fell to Dr Olds to mediate.

> The rudder was all right but the quadrant was completely smashed. The rudder post, three inches in diameter, protruded only six inches above deck—very little to get hold of without having a properly fitted, keyed hub. The Captain said it was not *his* job to fix it, but the Mate's; the Mate said *he* could not do it, the Engineer should; the Engineer said it was entirely out of his department.

> We continued like this for two days, watching our flags slowly disappear. One day some of us walked over to the *Terra Nova*, which was jammed about two and a half miles away due to propeller damage. On the return trip I was in the water for the first time. It is the custom when one does this to have a drink to thaw out. I had two.

The year before, radio telephones had been installed on sealing vessels for the first time. After some hesitation, skippers and mates were soon chatting and listening in on each other like gossips on a party line. Unknown to them, the colourful epithet of fo'c'sle and afterdeck was being picked up by battery radios ashore. Among the worst or best offenders was Captain Saul. Ship owners moved swiftly to tame the profanity and to make their seadogs practice radio etiquette, but not before some harm was done.

Like everyone else in Twillingate, Betty Olds was glued to the battery radio every evening after supper. One night she heard a conversation that electrified her:

Skipper: "An' 'ow be Doctor Hose dis evenin'?"

Saul: "Oh 'e's hokay now, me son. But we 'ad to put a rope round the sonovabitch's neck and pull 'en out of the water today..." Betty decided then and there to meet his boat in St John's and her friend Nurse Stella Manuel agreed to go with her.

Ernie MacDonald's new bellows camera fared much worse than the doctor. Though he picked it apart, flushed the works with fresh water and got it working again, the simulated leather was stained and warped and Ernie was later sorry he'd been so generous.

On the third day of stalemate, Captain Saul asked John to fix the rudder and assigned him some men. At first the Engineer refused him any tools, but after Saul threatened to fire him, he relented. John found two four-by-four oak beams and fastened them around the rudder post; he rigged two tackles, one port and one starboard, with a man on each. With a third man on the after bridge to relay instructions from the wheelhouse, he got the ship moving again. They even picked up a couple of pans before dark. As it turned out, the spotter plane dropped a new tiller assembly on the ice next day. While they had no more rudder trouble that season, they had to halt four times to "list her out"—tilt the ship—to repair sheathing gnawed dangerously thin by ice. That season nine other vessels were damaged and three were sunk, all of which the Gerald S. Doyle News reported. One can imagine Betty's state of mind.

"It is surprising what little illness or injury there is in a group of six or seven hundred sealers," wrote Dr Olds.

> Coughs and colds, not severe, are the most frequent; skin conditions, scabies and lice, probably next; minor cuts third; occasional sprained ankle or wrist; very rare frostbites or other thermal burns. In two seasons there were no fractures of any type. Gastric intestinal upsets are usual on first eating seal, usually too much. Snowblindness is common— among the gunners especially—and from personal experience I do not want it again. Though it can be reasonably painless with treatment, it is very bad without it (drops of 1% Butyn, cold compresses and protection from light keeps one quite comfortable; but none of the ships except the doctor's boat carried the local anesthetic). At this time physical examination was not required and I found a few cases of active pulmonary tuberculosis and bad hearts.

On his two voyages Dr Olds learned a lot about marine navigation—but not from Captain Saul. Before 1943, sealing vessels had not been required to carry a navigator. The old skippers sniffed their way along and did a good job of it. With a radio-telephone, direction finder (and later, radar) and a competent navigator, captains lost fewer men. Ships were still at risk, however, especially older ones. Captain Hancock, who had navigated a World War II destroyer, found John a willing student.

Eventually [he] pounded a little of his knowledge through my head. Of course, the Captain always claimed the Navigator was out in his position. It is unnecessary to say that Captain Saul did not know what end of a sextant to look through. There was considerable bickering but no definite hard feelings, as Captain Hancock had a very good sense of humour. We had a good time together. He helped me with dissecting and measuring seals and in what little doctoring I had to do.

As his report to the Newfoundland Fisheries Board was to make clear, Dr Olds was curious not only about Seal Finger, but about seal life cycles, population movements and the conduct of the hunt. As if writing an essay, he portrayed the industry with a clarity seldom seen before.

The location of these seal herds is off the coast of Labrador and northeast Newfoundland. In early spring when the pups are born, old and young ride the icefloes southward, carried by the Labrador current. As they reach the Straits of Belle Isle they split, part going into the Gulf of St Lawrence and part across the northeast coast of Newfoundland, as far [south] as the Grand Banks.

The seals are of two types, harps and hoods. For some unknown reason, hoods are found eastward of the harps thirty or forty miles and occur in family groups of two, bitch and pup, and never close to another family. Both types are hair seals. They are hunted primarily for their fat, though lately more use is being made of the skins in the manufacture of leather products and women's fur coats. There still is, however, a tremendous and sickening waste, as very little use is made of the meat. The flippers (front appendages) are brought in by the men and sold for their own advantage, but the rest of the carcass is always thrown away.

Young newborn harps are called 'whitecoats,' and at the age of two weeks—when killing begins—they weigh one hundred to one hundred ten pounds. Fifty percent of this weight is fat. They begin to shed their *lanugo* or baby hair at this time and then take to the water. Killing up to the time they "dip" is by hitting them over the head with a gaff. They make no effort to escape as the hunter approaches. After shedding, they become a dark grey in colour over most of their body (remaining white on their belly), and then are known as 'beaters'; i.e., they have had a ride on the ice for several hundred miles south and when they take to the water they 'beat' back over the route of the free ride. 'Ragged jacket' is a term applied to the few days during the molt. The next year they are known as bedlamers and mingle, more or less, with the adult herd. At the end of three years they are sexually mature, mate in the spring, and are then known as old seals.

He had long suspected that the regular issue of sealing rifles was inadequate, in particular the .30-.30 carbine. By comparing its performance with that of his own rifle he hoped to introduce a more powerful firearm. However, his methods put him in bad odour with the masters of some other vessels and even with Saul's own sealers. Shooting amid ice fields, he didn't always check the whereabouts of others or where his bullets might ricochet. Nobody was hit, but he scared and angered many crewmen. Not used to taking orders, he could be arrogant. He was an excellent marksman; many of the gunners were not. If he fired at an animal and it slumped, he claimed it even when another sealer had fired at the same time. Worst of all, he kept rushing up and firing his big .38-.40 over their shoulders. They regarded him as a menace and wished he would stick to doctoring.

Olds saw it differently: "...I signed on as a sealer and the crew, at least, expected me to do a bit of work in producing fat." The truth was, he enjoyed the hunting immensely. But the poor performance of many gunners irked him because hundreds of seals were being wounded and lost.

> There is [seldom any] proper selection of gunners and at best this is done on a man's local reputation as 'being good with the gun'—and that may be a shotgun. I believe that any man allowed to use a gun at the ice should pass a test [to ensure]...that not only [can he] hit something, but that he respect his shooting. Waste of ammunition is one thing, but waste of seals is another. Wounded seals are a dead loss; they leave the pan, are not found but probably eventually die.

> I heard one of the old sealing captains say over the radio that it was figured that one seal for five bullets was all right. If the other four had been misses I would not complain, but there are probably not more than two misses out of five. The other three are hit and one is recovered and two more die.... I speak of this from fair knowledge, as I was a gunner, and I had some ammunition for a good gun and unlimited poor ammunition for an inferior gun. I shot around 2,500 seals and gradually learned something about it.

> A seal has to be killed by the first shot and really killed. If it can give a jump it slides off the pan and certainly dies under some adjacent pan; very rarely does one hook one out of the rubble. To me that means a fairly high calibre expanding bullet. The best gun I have found is a .38-.40 with mushroom bullet.... A .45 is good, but unnecessarily heavy. I finally bummed some bullets for my gun...but I never had enough for much shooting. One day was checked; I had 150 (three boxes) of .38-.40s, and the pelters counted 142 seals recovered. I missed a couple and shot others twice. This ammunition was all gone in the morning and I took 250 .30-.30s out in the afternoon and did not get over ninety seals, and used all the bullets. It was most sickening.

Dr Olds thought the gaff a very useful tool, especially since, as a gunner, he could not carry one. "It is used as a vaulting pole, to pull or push pans together to make a passage, to kill wounded seals, to haul seals out of the water, to help in hauling the seals, for testing the thickness and safety of the ice, to haul men out of the water; it has been used as kindling to start a fire on a seal's pelt when men are out on the ice at night."

The anatomy and physiology of this close relative of the dog fascinated him. "The Hoods [are] so called because both sexes have a cap or hood which at will can be inflated with air. It is most marked in the old dog and is inflated in anger and in mating. Inflation is made possible by a series of valves.... This hood, though containing air, is nature's version of the self-sealing gas tank. Any number of bullets through it will not harm the seal or deflate the hood. Hitting it over the head with a gaff is utterly useless and very dangerous as these seals weighing a thousand pounds or more can get over the ice as fast as a man and have a vicious bite."

He had other observations—about the boats, the foreign competition, the cause of "sunburned seals," the need for better maps of ocean currents, and the utility of spotter planes (he didn't think much of what he saw in 1947). He also argued for more research and improved conditions for the men, including better equipped medicine chests. He especially admired the Norwegians:

> Their present boats are already better and more modernly equipped than any of ours. The *Polar John*, the smallest and an old boat, has an electric steering device which can be controlled from both barrel and wheel house. Also, the appointments are very superior. There is no covering of rough lumber, as in our ships, the men's quarters are CLEAN and WELL LIGHTED, the officers' quarters kept meticulously clean. The handling of the seals is extremely well done, orderly and clean.
>
> The Norwegians are well ahead of us in actual construction of their vessels, and in the care of their vessels and their crew. I can say this because I visited at various times (to see patients) all the vessels except the *Linda May, Eagle, Catalina Trader* and *Conrad*. Conditions aboard some of the Newfoundland boats are bad. The 'ice hoppers' are crowded, two to three in a bunk and in very dark quarters. The seals are handled sloppily, and the remainder of the boat is not clean. This is not true of all, but I saw none that could be compared with the Norwegians'.

He noted that in 1946 the *Polar John*'s 12-man crew netted $2,000 apiece. Shared among the *Clarenville*'s 40-man crew the same return would have verged on unprofitability.

He considered the lookout's job critical, but had misgivings about putting a man in an open barrel atop the foremast.

> Under the best set-up it is not good. The barrelman is the eye of the ship and it takes an experienced and responsible man to hold his post. Some skippers do most of the work, in other boats the mate does it; but no matter who it is, it is a miserable job—cold, lonely and exasperating. There is no reason why the barrelman should not be comfortable if he had a proper barrel to work in; and if he had that with other aids, he could be much more effectual.

I have considered the use of observation balloons with camera or with man and camera, and they seem rather impractical as to the added distance gained. I suggest a light aluminum barrel in the same position with a plexiglass dome with full-way vision and with sliding panels which would give open-air observation in all directions when required.

The barrelman [also] has to conduct the working of the men on the ice but also on deck. He should have a communication device as a radio extension from the present Marconi ship-to-ship apparatus with the men using a Walkie Talkie or loud speaker to direct them and a phone system to the bridge of the vessel and to the deck. What little I have seen is that the barrelman is chronically hoarse from trying to direct the men on deck, on the ice and the helmsman in manoeuvring the ship. In a modern ship the barrel could be steam-heated if necessary by simply adding a bit of pipe and a coil of radiator to the already present heating system.

To supply cracked ice for preserving pelts, as well as fresh drinking water, he suggested an ice chopper powered by the deck engine. By breaking the ice small enough to be run into the water tanks, he said, this would save many hours of work and end many gripes.

That spring was notable for storms. Heavy seas broke up the ice, scattering the seals and making travel difficult and dangerous.

There are several ways of improving the present facilities for men on ice getting around. The ice tends to push the pans abroad with men on them. It often takes a long time and a lot of oil to pick up men. If retractable lateral sticks with rope ladders of even ten- to fifteen-foot lengths were available, men could grab these innumerable times when they cannot get aboard by the ladders that were generally used this year.

We lost many seals in trying to get them aboard with the 'cats' supplied. The size of the hook was wrong and most ineffectual. The choker I made, which had a double purchase, worked well, but I think ordinary ice tongs would have been better, clipped into the skull. (The handles should be modified for this purpose.)

Two well-fed dogs will pull as much or more than a man, and they could be well fed on seal carcasses at no cost. This would cut down the number of men required, making less quarters to be provided, less food supplied and no expense for the maintenance of the dogs. (Most of the sealers have dogs and would be glad to bring their own if only to have them fed over this period.) I think a man and two good dogs would do more work than two men on ice, and be of considerable saving to the owners (I have tried dogs on ice).

He could not abide the waste of meat.

The old seals, even at that time of year, were quite fat, though I imagine not more than 30% of their total weight. It takes two men to throw over the rail the protein and minerals in one seal. This should be a most valuable product. It is edible protein for people or animals and the protein C nitrogen plus the mineral calcium is a valuable plant food. If all carcasses were left on ice and a ship followed the fleet and was informed daily as to the [location of] kills, could it not pick up tons of proteins and minerals very much needed for the growing of crops? And also, could not a great deal be canned for human consumption? This is an exceptional article of food and personally I prefer well-tinned seal to anything else canned in Nfld, except lobster.

By the last week of April 1947, with eight thousand young and old pelts below decks and room for only a few hundred more on deck, the *Clarenville* was pretty well filled. Another mild mutiny, this time over the crew's share of the profit, subsided as their thoughts turned homeward. The ship arrived in St John's May 2nd and discharged at Bowring's premises on the South Side. Betty and Stella were there to meet him.

His 1948 voyage on the *Bessie Marie* was similar except that it ended at Ashbourne's wharf in Twillingate on April 21st. The schooner had over six thousand pelts aboard. Under John's skilled navigation she came in through fog so thick he didn't even know they were home until the wharf and seal factory loomed ahead. A sizeable crowd stood on the wharf, including Betty and Stella.

Betty hardly recognized her husband. "His hair was quite bushy, but he looked well and tanned and it was great to see him. I can hardly believe he's really back. They had miserable weather, but enjoyed the trip and got a good load. The *Bessie Marie* is going out again next week. The first thing he did was take a bath...."

Dr Olds' report on the industry was ahead of its time. Most contemporary writing on the topic was commercial puffery about "stalwart men" and "veteran seal killers," not unlike the work of latter-day wrestling promoters. His preface alone could have given the reading public perhaps its first honest account of the industry in plain English. His recommendations, if implemented, would have made the hunt less wasteful and more humane. They might even have defused some of the public vexation which eventually killed the industry. For he too believed in not killing whitecoats. As several lovely pastel studies demonstrate, he admired their Bambi-like innocence. His suggestion was to tag and release them, not only as breeders, but as a source of important information about herd dynamics.

Unfortunately, he stepped on some merchants' toes, his report was shelved and he never got to go to the Front again.

Chapter Sixteen

House Call

*"Courage and cheerfulness will not only carry
you over the rough places...but will enable you
to bring comfort and help...."*
— Sir William Osler

I
n the horse and buggy age, a rural doctor's success often depended as
much on travel lore as on medical skill. Until the 1960s Notre Dame
Bay presented special difficulties to the traveller. Late fall and early
spring, when the sea ice was unsafe but boats could not move, were
the worst. The prudent stayed close to home; doctors had no choice.

"Dr Olds was sent for one night late in the winter when the ice was
breaking up," wrote Robert Ecke in 1937. "He walked endless miles through
a foot of slush, jumped from pan to pan of rotten ice, dragging a punt to
ferry the open swatches. Then more pans and swatches and slush. It was a
hazardous and dreadful trip in the pitch dark. He arrived exhausted to
confront Old Aunt Mabel comfortably knitting before her fire. 'I just wanted
to know if I should come down in the spring to be examined,' she said. The
twenty miles back to the Hospital that night left little time for bitter reflection on the behaviour of the upper class native.

"Many of course are the bona fide cases where you are only too glad to
drag your heavy feet through miles and miles of ten-inch-deep slob, the soft
salt water ice that gathers on the surface of the frozen bay. The dogs can
barely budge the komatik, even empty, so tenacious is the murderous stuff."

One house call in particular etched itself in John Olds' memory. It was
a nightmare journey in March 1949 from Twillingate to Fogo and back.
Going and coming, he travelled in sequence by snowmobile, foot, dog team,
foot, boat, foot, dog team and finally horse and slide. Twice he nearly
drowned, and he had to resuscitate the horse. He titled the story "A Child
Was Born" and submitted it to *Reader's Digest*, who rejected it as improb-
able.

"Even now that our electric technology has shrunk the world to the size of a village," he began, "it can still be difficult to pay a visit to your neighbour's house. On Twillingate Island we have instantaneous communication with the rest of the world via radio, telephone and television, but when springtime comes in April, we also have traditional bad weather. It is not unusual for the sky to celebrate for a few days with what the people call a 'glitter'—a foul mixture of rain by day and freezing fog by night that can put the next village a world away.

"One spring such a glitter began to tear down the telegraph lines and put our communications system out of business, to no one's great surprise. The last message to come over the wire was that Mrs Harvey Cobb, a nurse who had worked for the Hospital as well as in district nursing, had been in labour for three days without giving birth. Although she lived out on Joe Batt's Arm, Margaret had apparently trusted her knowledge of nursing to see her through the delivery.

"Joe Batt's Arm is 28 air miles from Twillingate, but air miles have nothing to do with it at all. There was one snowmobile in town at the time, and its owner Ned Clarke and his brother-in-law Frank Pardy said that, 'under the circumstances' they would come along. The ice was bad and they wanted to keep an eye on me and the machine. Twillingate and Joe Batt's Arm are on two separate islands and our route had to be roundabout—over stretches of saltwater ice, over islands and necks of the mainland, then more saltwater ice—roughly fifty-four miles.

"We left the Hospital about 2:30 PM on a Friday and crossed Twillingate Island and the bay ice to Tilt Cove on New World Island. At nearby Fairbank we picked up Captain Joe Gillard in case we needed more manpower or got lost, and headed across the neck to Dildo Run. About a mile or so from Fairbank, in trying to get off a pond, we got completely stuck in deep wet snow and had to send back for help to shovel out and push. Crossing Dildo Run the saltwater ice looked bad and there were many open places. But Joe knew his way through this maze of islands and we made it to Boyd's Cove on the mainland all right, and went on down the land to Port Albert. By then it was well after dark. Since the next leg of our trip lay from Farewell across more doubtful ice south of Change Islands, we waited for dawn in Port Albert.

"The next day showed no better weather. If anything it was foggier, and the ice had so much water on top of it that it was impossible to see a hole if there was one. In that particular twelve-passenger snowmobile there was no escape hatch in the roof. Expecting the worst possible trip, Joe cut two trees, which we lashed to the top, hoping that if it did go through they might hold it up long enough for us to get the doors open and escape.

"It was reasonably good going to South End on Change Islands, in spite of the impressive spray and wake she left behind. There the lighthouse keeper waded out onto the ice to find out where we thought we were going. Though doubtful we would make it, he pointed out the way to Stag Harbour. After we left him the fog got thicker and the water deeper. That snowmobile had the engine in the rear, and in one especially deep place enough water got on the engine to stop it. We got it started again by wiping off the plugs and wires; but this wasn't much help because there seemed no place to go.

"The snowmobile had a compass, but no calibration had been made for the effects the machine had on it. Since it would point North in different directions according to whether it was in the front or back seat or on one side or the other, no one had much faith in it. Nor were we any better off when I took the compass away from the snowmobile. It showed North, but there was no landmark in the fog and ice from which we could get our bearings. There was nothing to do but abandon its advice and drive on blind.

"After we spent a seemingly long time driving around, possibly in circles, the fog cleared some and off to port a man appeared driving a horse. We drove up and asked him if he knew where Stag Harbour was. He said he thought so as he just came from there, but as he left no track in the water, he wasn't too sure. However, he did find us the trail leading off the ice onto the island. But as soon as we reached the first pond, about half a mile in, we got stuck in the snow again. The houses were not far away, and soon we were pushed out and got to the village.

"Our next port was Seldom, called Seldom Come By on the map, because in the old days southbound sailing vessels would seldom come by without lying up to wait for a favourable wind to round dangerous Cape Freels. The men of Stag Harbour advised us not to go there by ice, as it was now considered unsafe—the mailman had lost his horse in the water a few days before. They were willing to help us on the "road" out of town, and their help was essential. To accomplish this, fences were taken down, trees chopped and one outhouse moved. After that, only trees had to be cut and rocks moved, with everyone walking and pushing except Ned, who was driving and had it worst of all.

"Another thing about the snowmobile was that it wouldn't steer when the front skis were off the ground—which they were most of the time in that kind of going. After a few miles of this, the novelty of land travel had thoroughly worn off. We were all exhausted, and, being close to the shore and some ice that didn't look too bad, we decided to try the ice again. This was at Little Seldom. Frank thought he would ride on the outside, behind.

"The ice held for about twenty feet and then it didn't. Ned had time to get the door open and we got out safely, but Frank was so interested in the sinking process he forgot he was involved till pretty late and then he had to wring all his clothes out. We had also forgotten my doctor's bag. With some difficulty we fished it out, and it was not very wet.

"We were now on Fogo Island—even if the snowmobile wasn't—and Joe Batt's Arm is on that island and the roads reasonably good. With the demise of the snowmobile, the others had finished their journey for the time being. But I still had fifteen miles to go. Presently a man with a horse and slide came by and offered to take me to Seldom, where the road to Joe Batt's Arm began. As there was no snow on the road, the horse pulled my bag while the owner and I walked behind. At Seldom there was no message from Margaret at the telegraph office saying the baby was born, and the operator couldn't send one to ask about it because the wires were still down.

"The horse pulled my bag another seven miles to Lions Den; the man and I continued walking behind it. At Lions Den I picked up a dog team and I rode for nearly half a mile over smooth wet ice until the terrain changed. After that I had to run with the dogs the rest of the way to Joe Batt's Arm through peat bogs and half-frozen marshes.

"When I arrived at Margaret's house late Saturday evening there were three tired people in it: the mother had been in labour five days, the baby I couldn't ask but assumed so, and, as for me, I was pooped. The two midwives, as usual after so long a labour, had little hope for anything. Margaret was so worn out that her pains had practically stopped.

"I didn't attempt to put her on a table and have the midwives hold her, because under such an arrangement the patient always slides off when I start pulling with the forceps. The alternative was to put boards under her sagging feather bed and work a few inches off the floor. It's no fun in either case, but better to have the safer arrangement and never mind your own back. Since I was still so soaked with sweat from the trip that I couldn't keep anything sterile, I changed into the husband's clothes. They turned out to be enormous—and I am not. After some discussion, one of the midwives admitted that she had poured ether once or twice, so she got the job of anesthetist.

"The baby came out eventually—a girl, and she was in the best shape of the three of us. The mother was in moderate shock and I was pooped and sweating again. After I had finished a quarter of a bottle of rum, all Mr Cobb had left, we were all three doing fine and only the midwives seemed a little shook up still.

"This should have been the happy ending to my story, but I was still far from home. The husband asked me if I would like to return the way I came or would I prefer going in a motor boat. Before dark the fog had lifted, and there had been quite a bit of open water visible; they would push a boat off in the morning if I wished.

"I wished, and after daylight Sunday morning, as mother and child were doing well and the midwives sound asleep, we dragged the boat out of its winter quarters with the help of some other residents. She was a twenty-six-footer with a small cabin forward and driven by a one-cylinder, two-cycle engine. On this occasion she carried a crew of four, and did very well on the open water between Joe Batt's Arm and Change Islands. Margaret's husband told me that these islands, which are close together, are named from their inhabitants' practice of living on the northern one in the summer, to be near the fishing grounds, then changing islands to the south in winter to be near the source of firewood.

"As we got closer to the islands the sea became more and more crowded with pans of ice. Occasionally we thumped one, and soon we had thumped a hole in the boat. Before she had time to fill up and sink we dragged her onto a pan of ice until the hole was clear of the water.

"There was a place for a stove on board but no stove, as this had been a rushed launching. All that was there was a piece of tin nailed on the side of the cabin to protect the wood from the heat of the stove pipe. Half of this would do for a patch. We pulled the boat farther up on the ice, and, with a few rusty nails that had been on board since shortly before the Flood, fastened the piece of tin over the hole.

"That hole was on the starboard side; within fifteen minutes there was a twin hole on the port side. We were forced to beach the boat on another ice pan and to repeat the patching process with the rest of the tin and some more rusty nails. After this, we had no more patching material. As the ice was closing in rapidly, it was agreed to abandon the voyage.

"I set out across the sheet ice on foot with one other man who offered to accompany me as far as Deep Cove, a mile or so away. The rest took the boat back. The weather started to improve. The walk ashore was terrible, because the ice under a few inches of water was so slippery and smooth that we couldn't keep our footing. Our rubber-soled boots had absolutely no traction and every little gust of wind sent us sprawling into the freezing slop.

"Once we made Deep Cove, I dried my clothes and located a man who had three dogs fit to travel. Not many good dogs are able to work so late in the spring. The sharp ice crystals, common at this time of year, cut their paws so badly that they won't stand up unless it is necessary to get into a fight. This leg of the journey could have been done nearly as well in a flat-bottomed boat. The dogs could pull us fairly well—in fact they had to, as we couldn't stand up on the ice. The water on the ice came over the beams of the cart, where one is supposed to sit, and made us crouch all the way to Port Albert, which we made at 2:00 PM. The dogs were too beat out to go on.

"I had heard that Alec, an ex-patient of mine, had a new horse and that it was considered a pretty good one. When I looked him up I had to dicker a good deal before he agreed to take me back to Twillingate, since it was a Sunday afternoon in the season of bad ice. But once we got under way, the travelling was easy and enjoyable. It was colder now and the ice a good deal drier, but still slow going for most of the way. Late in the afternoon, shortly before sunset, the sun came out and the temperature went down well below freezing.

"After leaving Tilt Cove, the seven miles back to Twillingate was about perfect for travelling. I was sitting on the back of the slide watching a full moon come up and talking a bit to Alec and enjoying the trip for the first time; the horse trotting along, his harness bells ringing and the church bells on shore chiming in.

"Suddenly we slowed up and I turned around in time to see Alec's horse sinking quietly through the ice. He had turned off the main path without our noticing and headed onto an old path leading to a nearer cove than the one we wanted. Since this cove was well sheltered, the ice had thawed until the path across it was no more than a fading winter memory.

"Horses don't panic when they go through the ice, but are completely incapable of getting out by themselves. The best technique for extracting a horse is believed to be this: you unhitch him from the sled, make a slip noose in his reins and pull this tight around his neck. In theory he will be able to breathe in but not out, and by thus inflating himself will float higher in the water. Then you haul him out on the ice on his side by pulling on the reins, and take him far enough away from the hole so that when he stands up he won't go through again. Alec and I didn't have the technique. We strangled the horse properly, but no matter how hard we pulled we couldn't get him out. Our feet slipped on the ice. Even if we'd had rocks to stand on, we wouldn't have been strong enough.

"There were several houses close to shore. We expected help immediately as Alec bellowed loud enough to be heard for miles in that thin, cold, quiet air—all the while bemoaning, between shouts, the $110 he had paid for the horse only a few months previously. No one came. As we couldn't budge the horse more than half-way out, I skipped ashore to see why no one was helping us.

"It turned out that everyone in the village, except those too old and feeble to leave their houses, had gone to church. I went farther and farther, and finally found a couple of young fellows and we started back. Meanwhile, several men had appeared from somewhere and dragged a punt down to the beach. Holding on to this and stamping, they had cut a channel out to the horse and were hauling him to shore. When he was dragged up on the rocks he looked done for—and the price had gone up to $150. His heart was beating but there was no pulse and he was making no attempt to breathe.

"Since it is generally believed that if a horse won't or can't stand he is bound to die, someone produced an old sail and he was rolled onto this and hoisted upright. It took several men to hold him upright, and with his legs folding under him and his neck drooping down, he looked deader than ever. Even his eyes looked dead.

"I got hold of his tongue, pulled it 'way out, and got a man on either side of him to lean their shoulders against his ribs, pushing together rhythmically. This bit of artificial respiration was surprisingly effective. Within ten minutes he was able to stumble around the rocks looking for grass to eat, although there wasn't any. We hadn't managed to prove the classical theory for rescuing horses that fall through the ice, but at least we had saved Alec's $170 investment. And at the present writing there is one more thriving Newfoundlander in Joe Batt's Arm."

Ned Clarke's snowmobile was rescued that July.

Chapter Seventeen

Alcohol

"I have no more griefs to tell."

— J. M. Olds

B y 1950 it was no secret. Dr Olds drank like a fish. "Who wouldn't?" said a knowing friend. People wondered how he bore so much without cracking. He did so because he had guts, a loving mate, a strong mother, faithful friends. He also had a crutch.

His drinking had started long before, possibly at Yale, certainly in medical school. At Hopkins he was a member of the Pithotomy Club, a name coined by Dr MacCallum, meaning "to pith" or tap a keg of beer. Yet that was but the tippling of young men, the liquid camaraderie of polo matches, football games, birthdays and Christmas. It was in Twillingate that he became an addict. This is not to say that Twillingaters drank more than other outport people. Rum was an outport tradition reaching back to Lord Nelson, to the seventeenth century fishing admirals, to the Dorset seadogs and beyond. Fortunately for Newfoundland, good liquor was both dear and scarce. To become a genuine alcoholic one almost needed a bootlegger in the family.

For a doctor in those days it was all too easy. Mix a few cc's of ethyl alcohol with canned fruit juice and you had a passable cocktail—inferior to Jamaican rum or Jim Beam or Glenlivet or Gordon's Gin to be sure, but producing the same glow with less stink on the breath and less thunder in the brain. Given this ease of access, their daily jousting with Death, the mind-numbing isolation, the lack of accustomed amenities, the oppressive weather, the incessant wind; given all this and the endless, dark, northern winter, heavy drinking was almost inevitable.

For these young doctors and nurses, parties became a way of life. "Everyone would get together," said one, "and have a drink and a bit of fun and maybe a feed cooked—stuff like that." There were parties up at the Cottage, in the nurses' quarters, at the Tilt in Kettle Cove, at the Staff House. They celebrated homecomings, leave-takings, birthdays and especially Christmas. The townspeople had their own drinking parties, which were censured by local Church leaders, some of whom secretly wished the

Eucharist could be half so much fun. Hospital Hill developed its own community and Dr Olds liked it that way.

Thus it began. At home, Dr Olds had cocktails before supper, perhaps a few more drinks over poker or bridge in Bob Ecke's or Stella Manuel's apartment after evening rounds, maybe a glass or two of wine with a book before bed. John was introverted—not exactly shy, but sociable only on his own terms. "He was boring until he had a few drinks in," said a friend. "Then he was a great fellow to be with."

Betty disapproved, but grudgingly accepted his drinking as a male prerogative. Early one morning during his family's 1936 visit, his sisters heard low voices outside the Cottage. "We looked out the window," said Tutie, "and there was John lying in the yard with Betty trying to rouse him. Apparently he'd slept there overnight. He had a terrible hangover and she was getting him going. Betty wouldn't let him stay there."

"If anyone had cause to drink," said Twillingaters, "surely it was Dr Olds." The Cottage and Hospital fires were merely the most spectacular of his calamities in the 1930s and 1940s. His mother's health had always concerned him. After the second family visit in 1940, he could see that his father was no longer well. Pop had high blood pressure, and bowel pains which John diagnosed as a hernia. On returning to Windsor, Alfred underwent an operation which left him strapped inside an ill-fitting truss. Soon he was to suffer one or more slight strokes, then facial numbness and loss of memory. By the spring of 1943 he was gone. And John was too busy to attend the funeral.

The patient load kept increasing. It became routine to have 80 to 100 inpatients even in winter. At most there might be three or four graduate nurses on staff, sometimes only one or two. For a year there were none; a dozen or so locally trained aides carried the nursing burden. There was only one orderly. In 1940 this small crew treated 849 inpatients, 89 in March alone. The TB epidemic of the mid-thirties now raged unabated in the Bay. With no reliable antibiotics to halt it, all he had was his scalpel and skill. That year he performed fifteen spinal fusions, six knee operations and numerous smaller procedures.

One by one, the War stole his best nurses and doctors. For example, Thelma Groze, an excellent RN from the Toronto General who arrived in March 1939 and who loved Twillingate, left in September 1940 to join up. Rube Waddell, a Virginian, left in 1939 and later fought in Italy. Stanton Hardy, for five years his assistant medical director, returned to the States in 1942 and entered the Navy. His dental technician Mr Henry went and Olds saw no chance of getting another. In 1943 John also lost Bob Ecke, his right-hand man and a kindred spirit. By the fall of 1943 the only remaining doctor was Wilson Swanker, whose three years experience in Twillingate made him valuable.

Though not everyone could work with John, John could work with almost anyone. Wilson "Bill" Swanker he found difficult from the start—though the two had collaborated on a paper on uterine malformation for the *Southern Medical Journal*. Before many more months had passed, Dr Olds would like him even less. The US Draft Board had ruled that only one of the Hospital's three American doctors could stay in Twillingate. All were willing to stay, but when Swanker said he would, Hardy and Ecke had left. Late in 1943, Swanker threatened to leave unless he got a raise. John got his salary increased to $300 a month—almost equal to his own. "We are still very busy," he told Mary in October, "& it may become worse as I can't make out whether Bill is going or not. Now he says he has a chance of a good commission in the Army." On March 12th, 1944, Swanker broke his word. John was now alone. "How much I can do by myself I don't as yet know," was all he said to Mary.

Meanwhile he was still troubled by the details of constructing the new Cottage and wing. In July he had to make a four-day trip to St John's about government funding. Like Dr Parsons before him, he was hampered by small thinking. On July 31st, telling Mary about the proposed Staff House, he wrote: "The Government is willing to help us substantially but the Association seems afraid to build a big enough building...."

John was still an American citizen. In the spring of 1944 the Draft Board fastened its eye on him. "No word yet if I shall have to leave," he told Mary. "Apparently the final say will be with the Windsor Board." Perhaps he was hinting for her to talk to them, if only to ease Betty's mind; no doubt she did.

"John is here alone," Betty told her in August, "and there are no definite prospects of help; but everything is going full speed ahead as usual. I don't know how he does it. The other night they had a special service in Church to pray for him. They are all so afraid he is going to give out, and I guess are beginning to realize that they'd never get anyone else who would keep things going as he has without sparing himself a bit. As soon as I can get up and about I'm going to try to get him out of doors more...." Betty's kidney problems had begun. When Mary wrote about having similar problems—perhaps a kind of sympathetic reaction—he worried until she recovered.

One autumn his friend Jim Strong, merchant and *de facto* mayor of Little Bay Islands, got stormbound in Twillingate for a week. He accepted John's invitation to come stay at the Cottage but hardly ever saw him. "There were 120 patients in the beds," said Strong, "and every morning he'd be down there about seven o'clock and go through the Hospital to see them. Then there were boats from all over the Bay. The porch would be full and a line-up down the road, waiting to see Dr Olds. The nurses would do what they could, but there were always so many...."

Gary Saunders

"As soon as he'd done his morning rounds, he went to the Operating Room. That week he averaged three operations a morning. Perhaps he'd have a cup of coffee in between. Then, it was down to see the outpatients. He'd be there 'til dinner time, come up and have a quick dinner—and down to the Hospital again. Some nights he'd sleep in the Hospital because there might be a woman in labour. Even when he was home, he couldn't rest. He'd lie on the couch and there'd be phone calls all through the night. And that's how it was for the seven days I was there."

In July 1944 Betty and David went away on holiday. "At that time Julie Parsons worked in the OPD," said Nurse Jessie (Troake) Drover. "One day she saw John just keel over on duty. He just passed out. And we discovered that, apart from being up for most of the night and a good many other nights, and coming on duty every day, he hadn't been eating. So Julie and I put him on four-hour feedings, and we threatened that if he didn't eat, we'd tie him down in bed and give him an intravenous. One way or another, we got him on his feet again. I don't know how Dr Olds survived the War years there alone. I consider that he did super-human work."

Fortunately, he still knew how to suck sweetness from his harrowing life. In April 1940 he had gone hunting seals on the ice floes with Ned Facey. Fall after fall he went moose and caribou hunting up the Gander River with Ern French, Ned Facey, Joe White and, later, Magistrate Beaton Abbott. Always he maintained a zest for his surroundings and the people in it. "They are hauling a house today," he wrote in February 1945, "& about an hour ago it broke through the ice & it is nearly half submerged—we can see it across the Harbour."

Dr Olds minimized his hardships: "I was about two years without any help," he said in 1974. "I refused to make house calls then. A pure waste of time; I could do much more for more people if they came to the Hospital. There were no more problems than usual. We were always short of things. Soon after the War, things picked up rapidly." Nonetheless, from 1943 to 1945 he was the Bay's only surgeon outside of Botwood Military Hospital. In 1945, working alone with only a trained orderly and a scrub nurse to help, he did, among other procedures, twenty-three spinal fusions and six multi-stage thoracoplasties. In all, the Hospital serviced 1,108 inpatients. He also supervised the school and well baby clinics, the *Bonnie Nell*, and District Nurse Drover who worked alone in Carmanville.

When Sir John Puddester attended the Hospital Association meeting in Twillingate that August, he was dumbfounded that one doctor had accomplished so much in one year. Shortly after this, Dr Leonard Miller, the Commission's Director of Medical Services, asked Dalhousie graduate Dr Louis Lawton to help Dr Olds out for a few months. By the time Dr Lawton arrived that autumn to join Bert Venables from the University of Alberta, Dr Olds was working like an automaton. Their coming should have eased

172

his task, but he had been alone so long that he did not know how to let up. On the contrary, he saw an opportunity to escalate his war on tuberculosis. Between 1946 and 1950 Hospital records would show that he performed 123 thoracoplasties, 40 of them in 1948 alone.

However, he did make a couple of trips to St John's. One was to extract $5,000 from the newly formed TB Commission for a third X-ray unit. In June 1946, he delivered a paper about his wartime work on pulmonary tuberculosis. He intrigued the city's medical community because until then many imagined Dr Garrett Brownrigg of the General Hospital to be Newfoundland's only surgeon doing thoracoplasty. "There are 46 persons (92 operations)," he told Mary, "and they are all alive except 2 that died from something else."

In 1946 Dr Wade Hastings arrived to stay two years. But Dr Venables, infatuated with a certain aide, quit when Olds wouldn't assign her to the *Bonnie Nell* with him that summer. Dr Lawton, having more than fulfilled his term, left in 1947, but Dr Ecke returned. Through all these changes John never paused. He could not; too many people needed him. On July 22nd, 1947, the Hospital overflowed with 139 inpatients.

As early as 1941 Betty had begun to suffer attacks of nausea and dizziness that sometimes laid her up for days. At first John diagnosed gallstones, "though X-rays didn't definitely show any." In November 1943 she had to go to bed for two weeks. Further tests confirmed his suspicions: she had acute nephritis or kidney disease. Their three-month "vacation" to the States that fall was really a mercy mission. He took her to the best kidney specialists at Hopkins and Duke University. They confirmed his worst fears. Successful kidney dialysis and organ transplants were more than a decade away, steroids further. When they got back, he insisted on having a vasectomy to prevent her getting pregnant, which they both knew would kill her. He did the operation himself under local anesthesia at the Tilt with Betty assisting, and told nobody.

Because of wartime shortages, the new Cottage was still without a furnace. Sometimes the single oil stove could not keep it warm. In March he wired Mary to say that Betty had suffered severe purpura or under-skin bleeding with "possible serious complication." They moved down to the Hospital where Betty would be warm and he could keep an eye on her. "What bad thing can happen next?" asked Betty in a letter to Mary.

He was running on caffeine, nicotine and will power—what Tutie called "that *will* of his." And in the background, quietly sustaining him with letters that he read and prayers he never knew about, was Mary the country doctor's daughter who had always feared the coming of this day.

Dr Olds began to hide liquor in his workshop, in his Jeep, in his call bag, even in the bathroom at home. "Mr Billy Earle was in charge of the Hospital furnace then," said a former housekeeper, "and Mr Dalley and them used to come up for drinks. And Dr Olds had a bottle of port wine behind the bathroom door. Nearly every day they'd take turns and come up and get a sip out of the bottle. I thought to myself, 'One of those days now you're going to get tricked.' I poured out the wine and put in molasses and water instead. Mr Earle came up to get a sip. 'What have you done?' he said.

"'What do you mean?'

"I never did tell Dr Olds; perhaps he knew anyway."

He took to keeping a half-gallon jug of ethyl alcohol in his office. The Hospital had stopped using methyl after an alcoholic patient broke into the Supply Room and drank himself nearly blind. Besides, the relatively harmless ethyl variety cost half as much, and for purposes of sterilization, body rubs and medicines was just as effective. During the thirties they usually bought one 45-gallon drum a year from the States. As the patient load and Olds' drinking increased, this was increased to four or five barrels. Although Customs duties went as high as $900 each, they could afford it because the Government rebated most of the money, leaving a net cost of about one dollar a gallon.

For a time, to discourage pilfering, the Directors had adulterated the ethyl with gasoline and methylene blue. When nurses and patients complained of the smell and Dr Olds objected to the taste, they stopped. Ethyl alcohol thus became his standard daily drink. Nobody complained about the cost because he had paid for it many times over in lost wages and cash donations.

Pharmacist Raymond "Bud" Young had strict orders from the Directors and kept all drugs under lock and key. "I came to Bud one time," said a former business manager, "and asked for some ethyl to make punch for a party. 'No, it was for medical purposes only,' he told me. But when Olds asked Bud to refill his jug every two or three days he had to comply. One day in 1952 a distraught Betty came and begged him to refuse John any more. 'I can't do that without a letter from the Board,' he told her. 'He's the big cheese.' So she got Chairman Ned Facey to write a letter. When John saw it he laughed and said, 'Oh, that's just Betty put them up to that!'"

Customs duties made it prohibitive for John to import his booze from the States. So if he heard of anyone travelling between St John's and Twillingate, he usually placed an order. Sometimes he didn't need to. When Lou Lawton was leaving St John's for Twillingate in 1945, a man handed him a bottle of rum and said, "Give this to my friend John Olds."

"I suppose we all contributed to the problem," mused Dr Lawton. "A bottle of rum could disappear very quickly in those days." The first time Captain Saul White took Dr Olds sealing on the *Bessie Marie*, Saul got Olds to stow his small stock of rum under lock and key at the Hospital. One February afternoon Olds said to Dr Lawton, "Let's go see how Skipper Saul is coming with his preparations." They set off down the hill on the hospital tractor with Olds driving and Dr Lawton perched uncomfortably on the three-point hitch. Once in the fo'c'sle, John produced a 40-ouncer of black Jamaican rum. Saul's eyes lit up. For the next hour, the three of them and two of Saul's sons passed it around. When it was empty Saul said, "That was some good. Where'd you find it, Dr Olds?"

"Up at the Hospital," said he.

"Sonovabitch!" cried Saul.

It was probably wartime scarcity that turned Dr Olds to beer. For a while in the mid-fifties he came to work each morning with two bottles in his pockets. "That's what he'd have for dinner," said a colleague. "And whenever the *Bonnie Nell* was going to St John's for dry dock work, he would order several hundred dollars worth from the Controllers. The beer would be packed with straw in sugar butts—barrels holding 300 pounds. Four or five barrels worth would be his winter's supply, and he'd keep it in the storage room at the Staff House. Or he would have fifty to seventy-five cases brought in by rail to Lewisporte and shipped from there. In those days the Hospital supplied each doctor with groceries. When Stevie Young delivered Dr Olds' groceries to the Cottage he had standing orders to add three to four cases of beer."

After long practice, John carried his liquor very well. By the late forties he was usually in a self-administered mild alcoholic euphoria, alert but feeling no pain, steady though irascible in the OR, serene on rounds, able to sleep at night. He dosed himself with alcohol—and sometimes Demarol—as deliberately as one would take a prescription drug. Seldom was he actually drunk, but seldom was he wholly sober either. His hunting partners said he would get drunk on rum the first night out, but stay strictly sober thereafter. He wore alcohol like a garment. When his employers at last comprehended the depth of his addiction, it would be almost too late.

He had a routine. In the forenoon when he did most of his operating, he was essentially sober. He might have taken one small drink before leaving home, nothing more. Toward noon he grew more irritable, especially if the operation was tricky or he ran into complications. Between operations he drank iced coffee and smoked cigarettes and took discreet nips from his jug if he had time to slip downstairs. At lunch he might have one or two bottles of beer to fortify him for Outpatients. After suppertime cocktails he returned, relaxed and convivial, for evening rounds.

"In the mornings he was like a lion," said Nurse Drover. "At night he was just like a lamb."

Although his friends and admirers turned a blind eye to Dr Olds' alcoholism, they felt differently when they themselves came under his knife.

One long-term TB patient, a friend of his, on learning he was scheduled for thoracoplasty at 8 o'clock the next morning, signed himself out rather than let Olds operate. The doctor was cool to him for three years. Sober or not, he would never endanger a patient. For this reason—and because he was well-nigh irreplaceable—he was never fired. And some Board members boozed as much as he did.

Inevitably, emergencies caught him under the weather. One Saturday morning around 1946, Nurse Stella Manuel told Dr Lawton she was having severe and increasing abdominal pain with vaginal bleeding. After a brief examination he gave her morphine and sent for John. Dr Olds quickly diagnosed a hemorrhagic ovarian cyst. Their only option was major surgery, and soon.

"Will you do it?" he asked Dr Lawton.

"No, you'd better," said the young resident.

Dr Olds hesitated, not only because Stella was his Head Nurse and anesthetist and Betty's best friend, but because he felt impaired. It was 4 o'clock that afternoon before he operated. With Lawton at his elbow and another nurse applying ether, he successfully removed a large ovarian cyst and probably saved her life.

Like any surgeon, Olds sometimes lost a patient; but never from carelessness. In thousands of operations spanning four decades, his record was exemplary by the standards of his day. "One should remember," said Dr Cyril Walshe of St John's in 1990, "that surgery forty years ago was a little bit harsher than today's." Dr Walshe worked with Olds from 1947 to 1951. "Yes, he used to drink a fair bit," he said. "But not to the detriment of his work."

Outside the Operating Room he was less prudent, especially after 1950. "If he put his old car or *Jeep* off the road," said a former drinking buddy, "nobody thought anything of it because he was a fine fellow, a fine man. If he was going somewhere in his *Jeep*—he usually drove some heavy machine—and if he put her off the road and the damage was slight, people would help him back on and off he'd go. Not many knew anything about this. Perhaps we'd pick him up next morning and have another drink.... He'd go on to work and I'd go on home. Stuff like that. But when he got older, he couldn't handle it."

One afternoon the Hospital van *Twilly* screeched to a halt opposite Ned Facey's home on the North Side and two doctors got out to have a leak on the landwash. In the back slouched Dr Olds, probably put there because they considered him too drunk to drive. While they were outside, he climbed into the front seat and drove off without them. Another time, half cut at a party, he lobbed a dart into the rear of a male friend who was bending over the punch bowl.

For a year or two in the fifties, people needed an ID card to get Government liquor. Dr Olds had one; so did many others in Twillingate. "They used to go to the graveyard and send in names off the headstones," said Hubert Vincent. Every week, he said, a Mr Tucker from Aspen Cove would bring down booze by boat from Botwood and people would go down on board with their own and others' cards. There was an element of shame. "Even in the 1960s," said another Twillingater, "if you wanted booze you got the driver of the wholesale truck to bring you down a case of beer from Lewisporte or a bottle of rum; you had to stop him on the road so nobody would see...."

Around 1952 Sid Fisher was in Twillingate to install the new federal telecommunications tower on Smith's Lookout for Montreal Engineering Limited. Always hungry for intellectual stimulation, Dr Olds insisted he stay up at the Cottage. The two men sat up till all hours talking philosophy and science. One morning around 3 o'clock when they were drinking milk and discussing geology, Fisher accidentally sipped from John's glass. It was pure gin with just enough milk to hide it. "John," he said, "you shouldn't be drinking that stuff."

"Why not?" said Olds. "Milk's good for you."

"It didn't bother me then," said Fisher years later. "I was awed by his intellect, his powers of conversation, his powers of reasoning. I probably ignored anything that interrupted the flow of ideas—even welcomed it because it brought him down to my level. By now his drinking was criticized in the town very much, but concerning his work I never saw John in any trouble at all." It put a strain on his family, however. For teen-aged David Olds, the worst thing was that he would get incoherent. "I used to find that extremely annoying. He couldn't finish a sentence any more."

In October 1953, during Newfoundland's second federal election, Premier Smallwood came calling with Twillingate District's new federal member for Bonavista-Twillingate, the Honourable John Pickersgill. When the coastal steamer anchored at the Government Wharf near the bait depot, Dr Olds went down with Fisher to greet his old friend Joey Smallwood. He was also hoping for a drink. They went aboard, and all save Mr Smallwood toasted the election several times. John told Jack Pickersgill he was a fool to be so much under Smallwood's thumb. Coming back down the gangplank, the doctor fell down between the ship and the wharf. There was a fair sea running and the ship was moving. Fisher's friend Jake Wolgar, a reformed alcoholic, lowered himself on a rope and fished Olds out. "I wish I could have caught a better man," he sneered.

Dr Olds' dislike for Mr Pickersgill was well known. During the second federal election in 1957 he took Joey and Mr Pickersgill on a tour of the Hospital. John couldn't fathom how a native of landlocked Manitoba could be Minister of Fisheries and said so. On a slab in the basement butcher shop lay a fine Atlantic salmon which the doctor had ordered for dinner. Pickersgill paused. Dr Olds, expecting some inane remark, was amazed when the Minister pointed to net marks on its flank and remarked about the mesh size. After this, John respected him more.

In 1954 the new Dental Clinic was officially opened, with Dr Michael Maguire in charge. Dr Maguire was to witness the final escalation of John's alcoholism and the events surrounding the crisis of 1954. In 1950 the Board had urged Dr Olds to take a rest. Suspecting pulmonary tuberculosis, they recommended a sanatorium. With many good ones in the States and Canada to choose from, they selected Summit Park in Pomona on the Hudson River, just north of New York City. Stanton and Annette Hardy lived nearby and it was close to some of America's foremost TB specialists.

That spring John did consent to see Summit Park's Medical Director, Dr R. L. Yeager. A month later he was back, still haggard. With his permission, they sent his X-rays to Toronto's Gege Institute for a second opinion. Toronto found no definite evidence of TB. Next June, as soon as the summer students arrived, they ordered him back to Pomona for ten months. Some of the time he spent writing a piece about hood seals for the American Museum of Natural History. It was published that fall in the *Journal of Mammalogy*. He came back improved, but drinking as hard as ever.

From 1952 on, Dr Olds knew Betty was dying. As she continued to fail through the winter and spring of 1953, his alcoholism deepened. After night rounds, too weary to sleep, he often lay awake and listened to her laboured breathing. Fishermen leaving for the grounds at 3:00 AM that summer saw the Cottage lights on and knew he was pacing with a rum or scotch. His eyes took on a haunted look, his breath stank of liquor, he walked with a stoop. Powerless to help, colleagues and friends watched their beloved doctor spiral down into darkness. Nothing but a miracle could save him, they said.

Ironically, her death in September 1954 broke the impasse. So erratic did he become that the new Board Chairman G.W. Clarke forced the issue. While no active tuberculosis bacilli had been discovered, he was now coughing up blood and his X-rays revealed a definite lesion on one lung. In January, 1955 they voted unanimously to send him back to Summit Park for as long as necessary.

For the Board minutes, the official reason would again be TB. But this time they must dry John out or lose him.

Chapter Eighteen

Betty and Stella

"John never cares what people think, does he?"
— Alice Arms

"Mother always said that when Betty went,
John lost his balance."
— Tutie (Olds) Mott

Twillingaters loved Elizabeth Arms Olds. "The best thing that ever came out of God's pocket," they said. From the day she arrived as Dr Olds' bride in 1932, they had taken Betty to their hearts. "Gracious," "warm," "an angel," "wonderful sense of humour," "a person whose *presence* was felt but didn't proclaim itself," were things they said of her. Like John she had worked tirelessly for them ever since. Her death at forty-nine plunged the little town into grief. It was as if the morning star had been stolen from the sky.

So when it was whispered only weeks afterward that Dr Olds was seeing another woman, they were outraged. They knew he was not always "true to her," that she "put up with a lot;" but this was different. For John Manuel, Hospital Board member and active churchman, the thorn of rumour bit deepest. His sister Stella had always been fond of John—too fond, in his opinion, and he had told her so. In the last two years of Betty's illness she had become his confidante and perhaps more. But the Hospital was a close-knit community, more like a big family than an institution, and who was to say? Besides, Stella had long been Betty's closest friend and of late her devoted nurse. Whatever the true relationship, it had been sanctified, encircled, by Betty's radiance. Now, with that light extinguished, Twillingate had become once more a small town on a small island, eyeing its own like a jealous lover.

Betty's ailment had begun around 1941, probably triggered by an erysipelas infection compounded by a chill. She had been out in boat, said Dr Lou Lawton, and had run up on the wharf in bare feet and stood around in wet clothes. The streptococcal infection invaded her kidneys and led to progressive uric acid poisoning. She suffered increasingly severe attacks of dizziness, sweating, nausea and headaches. By the time commercial antibiotics appeared around 1946, her enemy was entrenched. Nobody yet knew how to keep a patient with chronic, progressive glomerulonephritis in both kidneys alive, nor how to replace a human kidney successfully. For a surgeon like John Olds it must have seemed a cruel irony that only three months after his wife died, John Merrill of Boston would accomplish both, and that by the early 1960s the problem of tissue rejection would be solved.

In the winter of 1948, John and Betty had decided to send David to Connecticut after Grade Five. He would live with Mary, Tutie and Doug in Windsor and go to Loomis. They told people it was to give him better schooling, which was true; privately they had other reasons. John wanted to spare David his mother's slow extinction by renal failure, her coming agony of sweating and panting and vomiting, of the breath that stank of urine. Betty wanted to shield her son from the spectacle of John's increasing alcoholism. That summer Tutie, Lois and Stuart came and fetched David. For her six remaining years, Betty would treasure his Twillingate holidays and save his every scrawled schoolboy letter.

After 1952, her condition deteriorated alarmingly. Often she was bedridden for days, her sheets soaked in sweat, her suffering barely masked by a smile. In desperate hope Dr Olds combed the medical literature from Hopkins and elsewhere. Hopkins researchers, he knew, had tested a kidney filtering device as early as 1913. Sometimes faulty kidneys could be drained by tubes. Gordon Murray's recent kidney grafting experiments in Toronto tantalized him, as did Hume's and Merrill's transplant work in Boston that year.

Yet nothing convinced him that kidney transplants were safe, except perhaps between identical twins. Immunological rejection doomed almost every recipient. He dared not experiment on her—and in any case Betty had no twin. All anyone could recommend was a salt-free diet, low fluid intake and ample rest. Hal Upjohn, a 1953 summer student from Brigham University and heir to the Upjohn drug firm, got her some Thorazine and that augmented her sedatives and helped keep her meals down. It was no good putting her in hospital, in Twillingate or anywhere.

In February of 1954, she developed severe intestinal pain. Blood tests showed a turn for the worse. "I wish I'd hurry up and get better for John's sake as well as my own," she confided to Mary. "He is so good and patient and takes such good care of me, but I hate to be another worry for him." By June her legs were swelling badly, and in August she wrote, "Every little bit of exertion and I get a sickening pain in my chest." Her only happiness was that David was again home for the holidays.

On summer evenings she lay exhausted and watched the westering sun flush the world with salmon pink before dying beyond Green Bay. Through the open window she heard the *put-put-put* of boats coming in from fishing, the fluty calls of children playing, the chant of mothers calling them to roost; the sweet staccato of distant hammering, of screen doors slamming, of wood being chopped. On foggy nights the deep largo of Long Point's fog horn rumbled through her dreams.

Between sleeping and waking, she saw herself as a child again in Colorado, a young nurse in Baltimore, a young bride in Groton. She recalled magical weekends alone with John in the cozy Tilt, happy parties at the old Cottage with the Hardys and Grace Patten and Bob Ecke, lovely musical evenings at the Woods'. There had been picnics on warm hillsides redolent of crowberry and Labrador tea; hot August days picking blueberries and bakeapples until one saw them with eyes closed; long winter walks with Stell.

Soon, she knew, men would be digging potatoes, packing barrels of fish for Spain and Jamaica, piling wigwams of spruce and birch firewood. Soon too, curtains of pale pink and green fire over Smith's Lookout would herald winter. Long ago she had told Johnny she wanted to see Twillingate under snow. Now she no longer cared. "I dread the thought of the long winter," she wrote.

By early September the Olds household was in deep gloom. John had to work, but Stella spent every spare moment with Betty, bathing her, salving her bed sores, overseeing her medication and diet. Once a week she cooked a special meal. When David reluctantly returned to Windsor, the gloom deepened. From her first bad seizure on Monday afternoon, September 13th, to the lowering of the coffin at week's end, Stell had hardly left her friend's side. As the pale, bloated figure sank into semi-consciousness, John had asked Ned Facey to stay the night. From time to time Betty moaned, "No, no...," then resumed her hoarse, laboured breathing. Uncontrollable weeping racked John's thin frame. He was drinking steadily. Nobody slept. Around three in the morning she had slid into a coma that lasted until the next afternoon. Suddenly silence filled the room and she was gone.

That night, Stella had stayed upstairs with John. Coming down the next morning, she said, "Dr Olds won't be going to work today."

With John's permission Stella had washed and laid out the body and clothed it in a flowered grey Christmas dress she knew Betty liked. She persuaded him to view the corpse before the coffin was closed, but afterward he rushed sobbing upstairs and slammed his bedroom door. She went alone to the funeral service at the United Church and stood beside the grave in the cold wind while Reverend Baker prayed and led them in "Abide with Me." Afterward, mourners shuffled in and out of the Cottage. Numbly he accepted their condolences. Nina the housekeeper prepared a late supper but no one could eat.

Dr Maguire reminded John about sending telegrams and drafted the final one to Windsor:

BETTY DIED THIS AFTERNOON   LET DAVID KNOW

He had put "passed away," but John had barked, "She didn't 'pass away,' she died!" Stella wrote Mary two long letters. Mary wrote Betty's mother, Alice and the two set up a memorial fund among their wealthy friends. Cheques from a few dollars to more than a thousand started arriving and John had to decide on the most worthy use. Since the Hospital had long been a training ground for nurses and young doctors, they decided on a small but excellent medical library in Betty's name.

With the donations came many tributes. Said Dr Robert Ecke to Mrs Arms, "It was she who made Twillingate liveable. John's great work was more meaningful to many because of Betty's kind and warming influence. It must be a bleak place without her. I know you must sense a great loss and many will know a little how you feel. I hope it is not too late to add this small cheque to the fund."

At the end of September, John managed a one-page letter to his mother. "It is no use trying to tell you how I feel," he began. "It is awful. I haven't felt able to write before & I can't write much now." Not until early November was he able to face the cemetery. He got Stell to point out the grave so he could order a stone.

Many images burned in Stella's brain. The one that most haunted her was that of Betty feebly trying to lift a cup to her lips and saying, with a ghost of her old smile, "I'm all right yet, Stell." In the weeks that followed, she had no reason to go to the Cottage—though John begged her to come and she ached to help him and sometimes did. He seemed not to care whether he ate or what, and was content to live on beer. He tried going back to work, but tired easily and was often sick in bed. She noted that he was coughing more and that he sometimes spat blood again. When he came to work in a paint-spattered raglan, she felt strangely embarrassed. She got him to skip OPD and night rounds and to leave all but major surgery to Dr Taylor. She made him promise to drink and smoke less and to eat at least one good meal a day. Time and again, he told her that he could not stay alone in the house at night. When Mike Maguire offered to keep him company over Christmas, she breathed a sigh of relief.

That December two more events shook her world. Her brother Frank died and John asked her to marry him. "I like John very much," Stella wrote John's mother on January 8th, "but neither of us wants to be disrespectful in any way. I do know that John needs someone to take care of him. At present he is in bed with a heavy cold for a few days. He is awful lonely and I do all I can for him to keep him company. But if I keep going to the Cottage, people will talk...."

Mary gave her approval. As they did not intend to marry in Twillingate, the rector of St Peter's was not asked to publish the customary Banns of Marriage and few knew of it. When Mike Maguire returned to the Staff House after Christmas, John importuned her to live with him. To him it seemed simple. They were engaged. They were responsible adults. He needed her. If she loved him she would do it. She could not make him understand why such a thing could not be done in Twillingate, why her upbringing forbade it. Even if they married immediately, she told him, Twillingate would accuse them of violating Betty's memory. If they didn't, the Church would rightly condemn them for adultery. John laughed.

In January 1955, the Board voted to send Dr Olds back to Summit Park Sanatorium. The man was clearly ill; the uproar in town made it expedient. His leave would commence March 1st. Meanwhile, Dr Bennett would handle surgery and Dr Taylor would be Acting Superintendent.

John asked Stella to quit her job and join him. Surely, he argued, away from Twillingate's prying eyes, she would consent to live with him. Then when he was better, they would marry. Stella was in turmoil. These last few months had forced her to admit that she had always secretly loved him; now in a horrible way her fantasy was coming true.

And what of her job? Ever since earning her cap in St John's in the thirties, Twillingate Hospital had been her life. She had been Head Nurse since the early forties and in recent years John's anesthetist. She had fought with Violet Lillington over OR staffing; she had struggled with alcohol too, had provoked an aides' strike and been demoted for it. That was all behind her now. She would ask the Board for paid leave. With RNs scarce and funds tight, she doubted they would grant it. They owed her for a year's vacation; at least they should pay that. The Board urged her to reconsider.

The winter was among the mildest in years. Snow came in lazy flakes that melted on the paths. There were days so mild that men scraped their boats in shirt sleeves beside a harbour unbelievably blue. It reminded Stella of Sunday afternoons after church, when she and Betty would walk from the Cottage to Tickle Bridge and back, talking and laughing like happy children and it stabbed her to the quick. Now she walked alone, grieving for her brother, for her best friend, for herself.

Early that February, she told Chairman G. W. Clarke she was leaving the first of March whether they paid her or not. The Board could not pay, and in fact would go almost a year without one graduate nurse on staff. Gloria (Hawkins) Wells would become Charge Nurse that October, but it would be almost another year before Mrs Maurine Regehr, the first of several Mennonite nurses, would arrive.

Dr Olds and Stella left Twillingate on February 10th, for Gander, en route to New York. As Dr Maguire had just set up a practice in Gander, they stayed the night with him. Nervously she showed him her engagement ring. After a few days in Windsor, they travelled down to see the Hardys in Pomona. Summit Park admitted John, and Stella moved in with her sister Mildred on West 18th Street in New York. With Pomona less than an hour away by train, she could visit him almost daily.

Before leaving Twillingate, John had filled a forty-ouncer with ethyl alcohol for the trip. Stanton Hardy had briefed the Medical Director on John's alcohol problem and stressed that the Board wanted it brought under control. Dr Yeager forbade him hard liquor and cigarettes, but permitted two bottles of beer a day. John was installed in a small cottage on the grounds and settled into an invalid's routine. After the pace at Notre Dame Bay Memorial, it was a shock. He was cooperative and believed his stay would be short. Reading became his chief distraction, including the latest TB literature in the Sanatorium's extensive library. When common room conversation palled, he watched television, a novelty to him. "Saw Peter Pan & thought it fine," he wrote; "but my roommates all walked out on it."

He began to live for Stella's visits. She would arrive in mid-morning flushed and happy, eat lunch with him and catch the afternoon train back. Some days she brought a basket of pears or fresh grapes, other times a bag of cashews and peanuts or a bottle of wine, or some bakeapple jam from home. They talked of news from Newfoundland, of his latest X-ray results, of her experiences in the city and of their future together. Every few weeks Doug or Tutie drove them up to Windsor. John spent hours talking with his mother, now seventy-five. It was good to see David again. But he and Stell yearned for privacy, a getaway cottage somewhere, a Tilt.

Early in March the doctors were trying to disprove he had TB. "But I think it a waste of time," he told Mary. "I will certainly be here two more weeks, and a lot longer if they decide to do any operating." Later that month, fellow patient John Sopeck drove Stell and him to George's Mills, New Hampshire for a few weeks in a cottage Mary found.

In April Drs Yeager and Hardy said they wanted him to stay another four to six months and to take it easy for six more when he got home. "I would have liked to disagree with them," he said, "but would give the same advice to someone else." He asked Mary to send up a typewriter and drawing pens and to remind David "to send the big telescope." Dr Yeager arranged for him to study orthopedics at the noted rehabilitation hospital at nearby Haverstraw.

Meanwhile Alice Arms was promoting Betty's memorial fund and seeking a publisher for John. He had written two children's stories about baby seals and a magazine article about his trip to the ice; an artist was teaching him illustration. She worried about Stella, a nervous outport sparrow perched in New York City, needing a job but handicapped by her Canadian citizenship, too poor to fly back to St John's and get work, estranged from Twillingate, unwilling to leave her fiancé's side. Alice persuaded her to live with her and her brother Jim Joy on Perry Street. There at least she would have a bedroom of her own.

"I think Stella is very unhappy and I don't wonder," Alice wrote Mary.

> John does need her; he is sick and helpless alone; and as we know, when John wants a thing he *wants* it. He's got to get away for a rest, but says he can't afford a trip, except home. He *won't* go anywhere without Stella; she says he wants her there every minute. I *pity* Stella's awakening. Much as I think of John, he *is* different, and just now quite in love I guess. It might be [that] as John felt better, he wouldn't feel so in need of a wife. She says she will *never* go back to Twillingate without him....

Alice urged Stella to be sure that it was "not a matter of lonely hearts only." Prophetically she told Mary,

> My fear is that Stella will break her heart over some of John's indifference to her happiness...and [that she won't be able to] live up to his plans. Betty perhaps knew better how to cope with John—often a very loveable man, [but only] in small things.... The more I think of it, the harder it seems to me. John says, 'I don't think Betty would mind.' I know Betty loved Stella better than anyone else, and Stella was wonderful in her care and love for her. But what girl would be pleased to have her husband take another wife so very soon after her death? I think John's mind must be off—truly, I do.
>
> The people loved Betty so much there. I know he needs Stella right now—and she can't be with him unless married. Betty may have told Stella [to marry John]—who knows? She always thought first of others...Stella *is* a lovely girl, John a fine man; hope it all spells 'happiness.'

In June, Mrs Arms got a breathless call from Stella saying she and John were being married in Windsor next month. "Give my love to John," Mrs Arms wrote Mary, "and always shall I know he *can't* have forgotten Betty...." John gave Tutie a lot of money, saying, "Go buy Stell some clothes," and the two women spent a happy day shopping in New York. On the Fourth of July, in a small family ceremony at Grace Episcopal Church on Windsor Green, with Stella's sisters Mildred and Edith present, John and Stella were married. They honeymooned for three weeks at the New Hampshire cottage. Stella wrote that John was eating well. "I have not had to remind him to rest since we came here, and I'm so glad he is being a good boy. I just love this little cottage and am very happy here." John collected and mounted butterflies, moths and snails and made plans to paint them. He caught a raccoon and tried to tame it. The animal almost tore the cottage apart but Stella didn't mind.

After spending Christmas in Windsor, the couple returned to Pomona and she moved into his small apartment. On New Year's Eve, 1956, two former Sanatorium patients invited them to a party in Haverstraw. Knowing there would be liquor and hoping John would stay home, Stella declined. But John was keen to go. Because he had been obeying his beer quota, she held her peace. He promised to drive carefully and to return at 9:30 PM. By 10 o'clock she was pacing the tiny floor like a caged cat. Every few minutes she peered out the window. At 11:15 PM, as she was about to call the police, his car pulled in. When he stepped out, he could barely stand. Watching him weave drunkenly up the path, she wondered how he ever got home alive.

"Since then he has acted strangely, not himself at all," she told his mother. "So yesterday I had a talk with him and he admitted that he was not well enough to go back to Newf. He said he needed shock treatments. Last night he was awful: didn't sleep, jumpy, almost crazy—and I was almost crazy with him."

At 7:00 AM Stella telephoned Dr Yeager. John asked her to tell him he thought his nervous system was "shot to pieces, that he had just been trying to keep going but had finally admitted he was not being honest about himself and that he couldn't go on any longer." Dr Yeager immediately arranged for a bed at the Payne Whitney psychiatric clinic of the New York hospital and ordered an ambulance. John insisted on walking out to it on his own. Mrs Yeager took Stella home with her and then to New York to see John through his crisis.

"I am almost a wreck myself from worrying," she told Mrs Olds. "I've done everything I could think of for John, and it kills me to think that he is back in Hosp. again. He needs help, alright; I hope this time they will really get to work on him."

Surrounded by the vacant stares of real mental derangement, John came to himself. In February he telephoned Tutie to come and get him. He told her he refused to stay at the Clinic any longer, that they had not helped him at all, that he had cured himself. The Motts fetched him to Windsor that day.

His rapid recovery probably had a simpler explanation. His unaccustomed intake of hard liquor probably dragged him into a severe depression. The forced abstinence at the Clinic likely snapped him out of it. Moreover, his abject confession of helplessness must have been cathartic for one so fiercely independent. Above all, incarceration in the bowels of a huge city—the very fate he had fled to Newfoundland to escape—would have galvanized his will. In his last letter from the Payne Whitney he said, "I am through with New York *forever*."

Summit Park never did fully identify his lung ailment. Perhaps his bout with lobar pneumonia at age ten had left a shadow; perhaps it was a dormant tumor from his years of inhaling nicotine. At least he was no longer spitting blood, and, as Bud Young put it, they "strained the alcohol out of him." That spring his mother sensed a change. "I think I will give David the car," he wrote, "if he can sell it for anything worthwhile for his trip to Europe & then we will fly back by T.C.A. from Boston." It sounded like the brisk John Olds she knew, taking charge again.

John and Stell arrived back in Twillingate aboard the Gander mail plane on April 20th, 1956. The *Norseman* alighted on Hospital Pond and taxied almost up to the Cottage door. The shore ice was already rotten—one ski broke through when the plane took off—but many of the Hospital staff pressed forward to welcome them. More waved and cheered along the path, and flags and bunting flew in the town below. The Faceys and Ashbournes came to visit.

The Cottage, locked up for a year, smelled musty. Nina returned and the two women went through the rooms like a whirlwind, scrubbing, waxing, dusting, cleaning windows. A fortnight later when their luggage reached Lewisporte, Stella went and accompanied it home through the roughest sea she had ever experienced, more terrifying even than the summer lightning storms she dreaded. She never let on to the crew, however, and only told John about it as they moved the trunks and boxes up to the Cottage in the *Jeep*, dropping a few on the way. He snorted at her fears.

Stella repainted the rooms in pastel rose and green, her favourite colours. She had a linen closet put in, converted the guest room to storage space, added shelves here and there and refinished and waxed the hardwood dining room table till it gleamed like new. Meanwhile John's library sat in a score of carefully numbered cartons along the hall. For a time he refused to use the front door. "I didn't much blame him," she said. "To open the door and see the painters and everything upside down was awful."

The afternoon she and Nina put the house back to rights, Stell suffered violent headaches with vomiting, such as she had never experienced. She kept on working because she wanted his favourite room presentable before he came home at six. By 5 o'clock his books were in order on the shelves and everything was finished. John's smile of approval warmed her anxious heart. "His voice came back after the living room was all done," she told Mary. About her sudden illness she said nothing. John restored the greenhouse. When a late frost nipped her tomatoes and peppers, he got new plants and helped start an outside garden.

Their marriage had placated one set of gossipers but vexed another. While the first said it made an honest woman of her, "let bygones be bygones;" the second condemned her as an accomplice in violating Betty's memory. John laughed it all off.

Perhaps, had she felt bedrock under their marriage, Stella could have been equally nonchalant. But as they entered the narrower passages of domestic life, they discovered facades and insensitivities that surprised and pained them. She was a nervous and talkative person, not witty but considered good company. He could be charming and witty in company, but was often grumpy and uncommunicative at home, content to read or tinker by himself for hours. Gradually it dawned on them that all they had in common was their love for Betty, a fear of alcohol, and their professions. With Betty gone and John tolerably dry, that left only their work—and Stella had quit.

John always liked having guests. Sometimes—as with Sid Fisher—it was for intellectual stimulation, sometimes it was to oil the government machinery, but mostly he just liked company. Tuesday, October 2nd, 1956 was the day of Newfoundland's third provincial General Election since Confederation, with Smallwood's Liberals predicted to win once more. Again politicians were pumping hands and promising roads and ferries. As usual they shamelessly courted Dr Olds; his opinion carried weight throughout the Bay. Attorney General Leslie Curtis wired to say he would be in Twillingate on Monday, September 17th. Might he stay at the Cottage? Expecting a brief visit, John said yes, even though Nina was on vacation. Stella could find no substitute except a deaf girl from the Hospital, who as it turned out couldn't cook.

Mr Curtis stayed two weeks. The Saturday before Election Day, Jack Pickersgill was to join them for lunch. When 3:00 PM passed with no sign of his helicopter, Stella prepared a chicken and salad supper. When Mr Curtis sent word that Mr Pickersgill couldn't come after all, they ate it, whereupon the federal Minister showed up with five aides in tow. All she had left was cake and cookies and tea, which they ravenously ate. John thought it was hilarious. Stella, a good cook, felt angry and embarrassed. "I don't want to see Les Curtis any more for a long time," she told Mary after the politicians were safely on the coastal steamer *Springdale*. "He is elected again, so I guess we are clear of him for another four years."

Back in the saddle as Medical Superintendent and Chief Surgeon, though two doctors short and the many night calls broke his rest, John was coping well. He began to test eyes two nights a week, a job Stella thought someone else should handle. In fact, he needed the $150 a month it brought in. The Cottage renovations had been expensive, his mother spoke of laying off her maid to save money, and he was helping to support David at Yale.

That summer he had a new frame cottage built in a pretty cove just below Purcell's Harbour on Main Tickle, about a mile north of the original Tilt. Stella wanted them to go take a week's rest there and in November he consented. The weather was cold, but he installed a new oil stove and they were comfortable. Hoping to generate his own electricity, he built the first of several wooden water wheels and set it up in a nearby brook. It proved too small and the kerosene lamp stayed. He began to draw and paint again.

That year the newlyweds celebrated their first Christmas in the Cottage. Stella decorated with traditional sprigs of balsam fir over the doors and windows, and hung red fold-out bells from ribbons of twisted green crepe. She set up a table-top tree like Mildred's in New York. There were scores of pretty cards for the mantelpiece—but few from the Bay. The Olds family members sent her gifts, and Dr Parsons' widow Elizabeth, now Mrs Taylor, sent $25 for a wedding present. John gave Stell a fancifully wrapped electric frying pan, and she bought him a set of fine shop tools. "Now my Christmas is complete," he exclaimed when he saw them. The Hon. Leslie Curtis sent a Lazy Boy chair. "It is very nice," John told Mary. "Guess the Liberals are pretty worried about the next election."

They braved the staff Christmas party at the Hospital, where the outside guests included her brother John Manuel, now Chairman of the Board, Business Manager Hubert Vincent, Board Secretary Ern Clarke, and their spouses. Stella had prudently cancelled the customary pre-party drinks at the Cottage, so she invited them up afterward. Pointedly, her brother and the Clarkes declined. Stella went alone to the midnight service at St Peter's Church, leaving Dr Bruce and John playing *Scrabble,* "which John of course won."

Nina, expecting the usual flood of after-Christmas visitors and mummers, baked two large Christmas cakes and tins of cookies. Not a soul came, not even on New Year's Day. "Why is it no one comes to see us?" Stell cried.

"Because there's nothing here to drink," he grunted.

"Well, if that's all they come for, they can stay away!" She gave the extra cookies to the Hospital and wrote a long, sorrowful letter to Mary.

They didn't visit much themselves. The old camaraderie was gone. Yet John seemed content to putter at an upstairs table with his paints, tools and machinery. He would sit in his Lazy Boy, reading the books he got for Christmas and flicking cigarette ashes in the general direction of the tray stand. Despite assiduous vacuuming, a blue-grey smudge grew like a lichen on the new rug. "I don't care how much mess he makes as long as he doesn't drink," Stella confided,"—and he hasn't had a drink since he came home. Mother, he is so different…."

The winter of 1957-58 was on the whole a good one for Dr Olds. It began badly, with two doctors feuding and their wives threatening to pull each other's hair out. But he recommended firing one, the Board did so and peace was restored. In January the American College of Surgeons accepted him as a Fellow, something he had "always wanted but [had been] too lazy to get." By March the new Hospital letterhead listed him as "John M. Olds, MD, F.A.C.S." His new stomach pump worked so well that he sent a writeup to the *Modern Medicine of Canada*. In March the *Canadian Medical Association Journal* published his paper on Seal Finger. He performed one of his first cataract operations; three weeks later, he wrote, the 83-year female patient had regained 78 per cent of her vision and was still improving. And at year-end, the Social Register of Canada added his name to their list.

For Stella the winter was not so good. Like a portent, blizzards lashed the islands, followed by bitterly cold Arctic air that drove the mercury down to minus 20 degrees Fahrenheit for weeks on end. John exulted in such weather, but she hated it and was glad she had quit her part-time Hospital work the previous March. Hamilton Sound froze smooth and hard as a rink and for a time cars drove to and fro across it. The Cottage could not be kept warm. At night she was so cold they had to buy an electric blanket.

On June 14th Dr Bruce left unexpectedly. Two weeks later Dr Bishop, one of his ablest assistants, did likewise. Suddenly John was back to a wartime workload. Dr Halliday had stayed, but in surgery he was "near useless." He also overturned the Hospital Volkswagen and wrecked it. "This was in daylight & on a straight road," grumbled Olds, forgetting that he himself had overturned hospital vehicles more than once. "He didn't get hurt but should have."

The Board advertised in a British medical journal and over thirty applications came. Encouraged, Dr Olds struggled on. In the next two years Drs Liborio Garcia and Alex Smith arrived, and proved to be willing and cooperative. But the surgical load remained heavy. His lazy days at Summit Park seemed a distant dream.

That year his income tax bill was unexpectedly high and there were expenses connected with his new diesel *Land Rover*. He began testing eyes four nights a week. Stella was diagnosed as suffering from a duodenal ulcer, and after the operation she caught influenza which hung on for seven months. David was in college and John fretted about his career plans. On July 1st, 1958, Canada's new national health insurance plan came into effect, replacing his Blanket Plan. In 1959 his old friend Dr Wood died.

All this weighed on them both. Their only respite was an occasional weekend at the new Tilt. Even there, he constantly drew or fiddled with pastels or tinkered with his water wheels while she knit or read a magazine or beachcombed. She sensed in John a growing indifference. Frequently, the charming and respectful Pomona groom sneered at her opinions and suggestions. "What a silly idea!" he would snort, or "How could anyone be so stupid?" Betty, she knew, would have fired back as good as he gave; she could not stand up to him. Her stomach pains returned, she drank some, she began to rely on barbiturates. Her exuberant, chatty letters to Windsor dried up. Dr Olds told his mother she was "not herself."

Nobody seemed to guess that Death had planted a claw in her very brain.

Chapter Nineteen

Stella and Gloria

"Mother never gave up on John."
— Tutie (Olds) Mott

"Peace, perfect peace."
— Stella Manuel's tombstone inscription

In the fall of 1960, at the age of fifty-four, John Olds fell in love for the last time. The woman was Gloria Chisholm, a buxom, blue-eyed, 27-year-old whom the Board had just hired. After leaving rural Nova Scotia at seventeen, Miss Chisholm had trained as a nursing assistant and worked in the Maritime provinces. When she saw the Board's advertisement, she had served two years with the Department of Indian Affairs on British Columbia's northern coast. The Board also hired five Mennonite nurses from Western Canada.

Miss Chisholm felt drawn to older physicians and in fact had just fled a painful affair with a married doctor. John was attracted not only by her physical beauty but by a certain sense of woundedness, of spiritual questing. At first they chatted; later they arranged secret meetings. For him it was a love such as perhaps only the middle-aged feel, a bittersweet amalgam of winter in the bone and springtime in the heart. Betty he had loved with the intensity of first love. Stella he had embraced as a drowning man grabs a plank unable to float him. This love was like a joyful shout against the encroaching dark, a chance to redeem his harrowed life.

John had never been good at intimacy, did not know how to flirt. He was like an armoured knight who is content to sally forth to undo wrongs and then retreat to his castle, safe behind the motto "I must be independent." This sudden passion for a woman half his age surprised and pleased him. Church doctrine held no terrors for him. The clergy would judge him immoral, he knew. As a surgeon he had no illusions about conventional morality. To him loveless marriage was far worse. But he would not tell his mother, not yet.

By November they were having a full-blown affair. As the first snow whitened the town, wisps of gossip swirled down Hospital Lane, eddied in and out of tea parties and church socials, mingled with pipe smoke in net lofts and boat sheds. Friends whispered, "John, John, what are you doing?" He paid them no mind. He was too busy anyway.

When Stella confronted him, he did not spare her the truth. She was devastated. Her world, already shaken by the deaths of Betty and Frank, tottered. Stella Manuel, RN, Head Nurse, skilled anesthetist, was now merely Mrs John Olds, watering the house plants and jilted at that. She had tried working part-time, but her increasing migraines had forced her to stop for good. Paralyzing attacks of anxiety and depression assailed her. She obtained barbiturates from the dispensary and tried to medicate herself, but sometimes confused the dosages. Her walk became erratic so that people said she was on the bottle again. Her pleasure in homemaking had faded like the summer, leaving her marooned between her profession and a dream.

Had John remained the needy, penitent man of Pomona, her wound would have been less grievous. As winter's cold fogs and chilly rains closed in, the memory of that Fourth of July in Connecticut when they had laughed in a shower of confetti under rustling maples, she a shy bride of forty-nine, he a man reborn, seemed unbearably remote. She had known they could never have children; they would have each other. Now they didn't even go to the Tilt. He was taking someone else. She packed a suitcase and went to stay with a friend.

Within a week Stella returned. They fought, John with steely coolness, she with tears and broken dishes. On December 2nd he told his mother:

> Stell got very bad four days after returning & now she is in the mental hospital in St John's. If she ever does get better I see no possibility of her living here with me again. Whether the trouble is me or the environment or both, I don't know. Anyway I now feel that a divorce is more necessary for her even than for me, after she recovers. If she gets better I see no sense in her risking another breakdown by returning here.

Out of hospital again and staying with her sister Edith in the city, Stella resumed writing long letters to Mary and to Mildred in New York. She couldn't tell them the full story, she said, but "hoped everything would be straightened out someday." When Edith returned to work the Christmas break, Stella signed herself back in at the Waterford Hospital. "It nearly killed me," Mildred told Mary, "to hear her say there was no one to take care of her."

John continued to write his mother, but his monthly scrawl on Hospital letterhead barely filled two pages. After apologizing for not writing sooner, he reported on local weather or ice conditions, on Hospital doings and his latest invention. He told her he was sending his electrocautery holder idea

John at the wheel of the "King" in Windsor, Connecticut, 1907. [ddo]

Alfred Allen Olds—"Gramp"—with John and Lois, circa 1910. [ddo]

John at five. [ddo]

John and Alfred Olds in Home Guard uniforms, 1918. [ddo]

The former Olds family home, Windsor, CT, 1991.

Top: *The Olds' cottage at Black Point, 1920s. [ddo]*
Left: *John at the helm of* **Joloma I**, *Long Island Sound, 1920. [ddo]*
Right: **Joloma II**, *late 1920s. [ddo]*

JOHN McKEE OLDS
Windsor, Conn.

JOHNNIE, NIGGER

"Who can refute a smile?"
—Moral Philosophy.

Entered 1919.
1919-1920: Midget Basketball Team, Midget Baseball Team.
1920-1921: Midget Football Team, Midget Hockey Team, Midget Baseball Team.
1921-1922: Captain of Second Hockey Team, Darwin Club, Captain of Midget Football Team.
1922-1923: Second Football Team, Hockey Team, Second Baseball Team, Darwin Club.

Yale.

Forty

John's yearbook page from the Loomis Institute's **Loomiscellany**, *1923.*

Class of 1927 polo team, Yale University (John is at far right). [ddo]

Above: *Dredging gold with high-pressure hose near Fairbanks, Alaska, 1927. [ddo]*

Right: *John and a classmate on the Chatanika River, Alaska, summer of 1927. [ddo]*

Below: *Plan of the Johns Hopkins Hospital, downtown Baltimore, MD, as it looked when John Olds took his degree, 1927-31. The Medical School is in the upper left corner.*

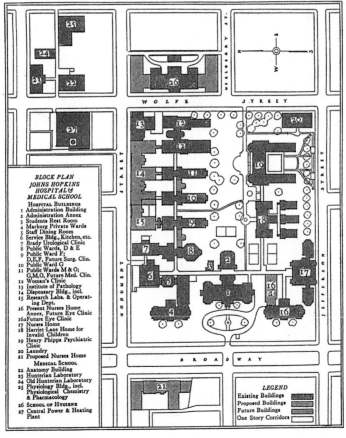

BLOCK PLAN
JOHNS HOPKINS
HOSPITAL &
MEDICAL SCHOOL

HOSPITAL BUILDINGS
1 Administration Building
2 Administration Annex
3 Students Rest Room
4 Marburg Private Wards
5 Staff Dining Room
6 Service Bldg., Kitchen, etc.
7 Brady Urological Clinic
8 Public Wards, D & E
9 Public Ward F;
 D,E,F, Future Surg. Clin.
10 Public Ward G
11 Public Wards M & O;
 G,M,O, Future Med. Clin.
12 Woman's Clinic
13 Institute of Pathology
14 Dispensary Bldg., incl.
15 Research Labs. & Operating Dept.
16 Present Nurses Home
 Annex, Future Eye Clinic
16a Future Eye Clinic
17 Nurses Home
18 Harriet Lane Home for
 Invalid Children
19 Henry Phipps Psychiatric
 Clinic
20 Laundry
21 Proposed Nurses Home

MEDICAL SCHOOL
22 Anatomy Building
23 Hunterian Laboratory
24 Old Hunterian Laboratory
25 Physiology Bldg., incl.
 Physiological Chemistry
 & Pharmacology
26 SCHOOL OF HYGIENE
27 Central Power & Heating
 Plant

LEGEND
Existing Buildings
Proposed Buildings
Future Buildings
One Story Corridors

Left: *John and Betty on their wedding day, September 3, 1932 just before sailing to Newfoundland. [ddo]*

Right: *Charles E. Parsons, MD, F.A.C.S., first director of Notre Dame Bay Memorial Hospital.*

Bottom: *The Hospital as it looked when John Olds first saw it as a summer student in 1930.*

Top: *Twillingate in the 1940s, looking southward from North Side.* [H]
Bottom left: *John's parents, Mary and Alfred, on their first Twillingate visit in 1936.* [ddo]
Bottom right: *The new Medical Director, circa 1936.* [ddo]

Fishing schooners in Twillingate Harbour, ready for Labrador. [tgc]

John ensconced in his favourite chair at the old Cottage. [tgc]

The Tilt

John and Betty's hideaway—the Tilt at Kettle Cove on the back end of South Island. [ddo]

Christmas dinner with the Olds: Betty and Dr Stanton Hardy in foreground; left to right: Pat Coady, Bank of Nova Scotia Manager; Jessie Smith, RN; Walter Baldwin, Dentist; Hazel Jeffreys, RN; Annette Hardy, RN; John at the head; Edith (Simms) Manuel, RN; Thelma (Groze) Christie, RN; Joe White, Hospital Director; Minnie (Newhook) Baldwin, RN. [tgc]

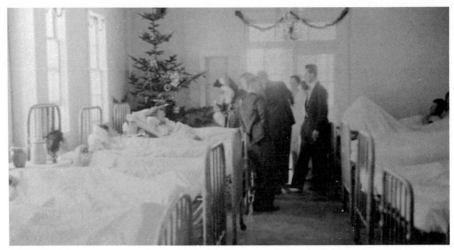

Dr Olds and his Directors making rounds, Christmas morning—note Olds' "King Suit." [tgc]

Bonnie Nell II. *(Inset: Captain Elijah "Lige" Dalley on **Bonnie Nell I**.)*

Dr Stan Hardy setting out on a winter call by dog-and-sled.

Victim of bone TB with daughter. [H]

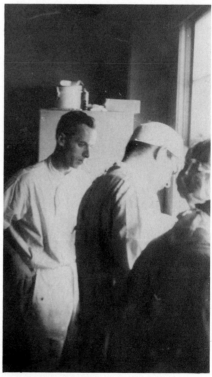

Dr Olds outside OR with Dr Rube Waddell. [H]

Top: *The morning after the February 1943 fire, looking north.* [tgc]

Middle: *Reconstruction of wing, with new Cottage in background.* [H]

Right: *David Olds in 1948, the year he went to school in Windsor, CT.* [ddo]

Betty, Mary McKee Olds and John, 1949. [ddo]

Howard Thistle   Billie   J Olds.   Harvest
                  John   fields
                                       1938

Top: *Howard Thistle, guide Billy John and Dr Olds, NW Gander River, 1938.* [jmo]

Left: *Captain Saul White by Ted Drover, 1946. (Used with permission)*

Right: *Ashbourne's schooner* **Bessie Marie**, *skippered by Saul White, coming home with a full load of seal pelts.* [ef]

Betty Olds circa 1952. [ddo]

Stella Manuel, RN in the 1940s. [H]

John and Gloria (Chisholm) Olds, 1962. [ef]

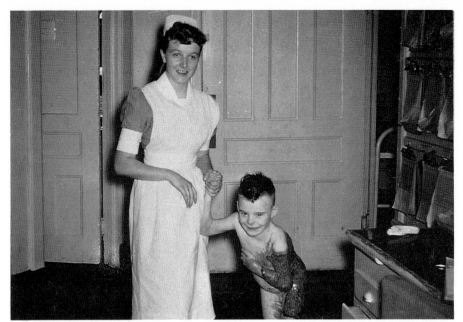

Cedric Mills, victim of scalding, 1960. [cm]

Hospital in the fifties, looking southeast: left to right, Staff House (with warehouses, workshop and boiler room in foreground and Cottage # 2 in background), wing (to rear) and main building (note low roof built by Ned Clarke after 1943 fire). [H]

In his late sixties, Dr Olds braves the icy Main Tickle waters. [ef]

John's sister Mary ("Tutie") and husband Douglas Mott, Maine 1987. [pc]

Dr Olds in his early seventies with Order of Canada pin. [ddo]

to the Hartz medical instrument people for appraisal, that he was writing a paper on a new way to safely drain hydrocephalic fluid from a baby's brain. He might ask about the Windsor weather, about Mary's health and David's finances, and sign off with the usual "Love, John." Of Miss Chisholm he said nothing.

Again it was a mild December. The Tilt beckoned. On weekends he took Gloria there in the *Land Rover*. To his lovestruck painter's eye, the familiar route across wet bogs, through scrub spruce and over grey bedrock ridges seemed transformed into golden meadows inlaid with pewter ponds, enchanted Christmas forests robed in green paisley, courts of sculptured Carrera marble. They parked by the heaving green ocean and beachcombed below icicled cliffs, their happy voices lost in the rote of the sea. All creation seemed to bless their love and mutual need. The discovery that their birthdays were only a day apart seemed to erase the gulf of years between them.

Twillingate buzzed like a hornet's nest poked with a stick. The monthly Board meetings, now chaired by Stella's brother John, became ordeals for everyone. However, even with the new doctors Alf Dennison and Alex Smith on staff, Dr Olds hardly had time to think about it. That year closed with a record inpatient load of 1,652—541 more than in 1955 and twice that of 1940. At year's end he could look back on 297 operations, procedures and deliveries, including eleven hysterectomies, a spinal fusion and over seventy appendectomies. In September he had done a second series of skin grafts on Cedric Mills of Moreton's Harbour, the young victim of massive scalding.

In January 1961, in spite of his warnings, Stell wired to say she was returning. John braced for a new confrontation but a blizzard intervened. "I feel very sad about the whole thing," he wrote Mary on January 25th. "But I know it is not best for us to try & live together again. I might be able to stand it but certainly wouldn't enjoy it, & she couldn't stand it very long." Again he was silent about Gloria.

He now asked Stella for a divorce. She refused. When she came back in mid-February, he moved to an empty apartment in the Dental Clinic. Bessie the new maid left. In late February the affair sparked an uproar among the aides and nurses. Head Nurse Carolyn Schwalzerndruber, outraged in her professional and religious convictions, asked John Manuel to fire Miss Chisholm and Dr Olds both. Chairman Manuel, equally outraged but with only hearsay to act on, hesitated. Unlike Charlie Parsons, Dr Olds had mastered his drinking and was doing superb surgery. Yet, if he didn't fire him all the Mennonite nurses might quit.

At a special meeting on March 7th, the Board moved to fire Miss Chisholm immediately and to request Dr Olds' resignation. Dr Olds refused, and reminded them that no staff member could be fired without his signature. He demanded her reinstatement on grounds of wrongful dismissal, and asked Secretary Ern Clarke to read aloud a carefully worded memo spelling out proper procedure. Just before adjournment, Secretary Clarke did so, but before the vote was taken Chairman Manuel asked Dr Olds to leave the room. Four voted for his dismissal, three against. The next day Miss Chisholm's dismissal was confirmed, Dr Olds received a formal request to resign and Dr Smith was unilaterally appointed superintendent. On March 13th Dr Olds wrote the Board:

> Though you gave me no reasons for asking for my resignation, I understand from Dr Miller that you have asked [this] on the sole grounds that local gossip & rumour accusing me of being involved in a liaison with Miss Chisholm.
>
> Firstly, I deny that there is anything in my relationship with Miss Chisholm to which anyone could take offence.
>
> Secondly, I consider that my private life is my own business & in no way concerns my employers, especially when, as here, it does not affect my work in any way. In my opinion any accusation, especially an unjustifiable one, which is levelled at my personal relationships does not constitute reasonable grounds for terminating my employment.
>
> Accordingly, I will not offer my resignation.
>
> Should you have any other grounds on which you feel justified in asking me to resign, please let me know them in writing as soon as possible and I will give them due consideration.

The next day, at another special meeting, Dr Olds outlined his duties, again stressing that all staff changes required his signature. "If you don't agree with my idea of the job," he concluded, "then give me *your* idea of it and we can come to some conclusion." He also reminded the Board that they could not fire him without three months' notice. The Chairman again asked him to resign.

His 55th birthday came and went. Early in April he was ordered to leave the Hospital by April 15th. He wired Attorney General Lesley Curtis and Deputy Minister Miller, stating his case. To his chagrin they sided with the Board, saying they had "heard some scandalous stories." Mr Curtis even implied that if he made a fuss he would be struck off the Newfoundland Medical Register and thereby barred from practicing in Canada—and perhaps in the United States.

John now realized that his only hope was the Notre Dame Bay Hospital Association. They had appointed the Hospital Board and they answered to nobody but the communities of the Bay. He would take his case to the people.

Unfortunately, Chairman Chesley Roberts was away. Quickly John located and briefed him. Roberts was sympathetic. With Frank Pardy, Walter Elliott and Dr Smith at his side, Roberts asked the Board to explain its actions. "The directors could give no sensible reason," Dr Olds told his mother, "...mostly that I was hard to get along with since I tried to defend 2 members of the staff from getting fired by improper procedure...." For the first time, he alluded to an "indefinite 'scandal' about a nurse."

As word of his dismissal spread, letters of support began to come in from Trades Union members and others. Three meetings later, however, the Directors still stood firm. Roberts then mustered a legal quorum of ten Association members and demanded a full meeting for Friday, April 7th. That night a blizzard lashed the islands, isolating Twillingate and hampering travel. Eighty people showed up—triple the usual number for a good night, and, in Dr Olds' words "more than ever belonged to the Association before." As the snowy parkas piled up outside the waiting room and the tension mounted, sweat beaded the foreheads of John Manuel and his dissenting directors.

Chairman Roberts called the meeting to order and stated its purpose. The Secretary read out a fistful of endorsements from New World Island and elsewhere. At the call, only four of the dozen directors present—John Manuel, Harry Ashbourne, Walter Facey and Ern Clarke—voted against Dr Olds. Chairman Roberts instructed Secretary Clarke to inform Dr Olds of the verdict by hand-delivered letter forthwith.

The next day all five Mennonite nurses threatened to quit. Mr Clarke dallied. "Other times when it was bad news I got the letter the next morning," John observed wryly. Not until April 13th, and only after several phone calls from Association members, did Secretary Clarke deliver the letter.

"Of course I didn't resign," he wrote a few days later, "as I knew a lot of people wanted me to stay. I couldn't figure out anything I had done to warrant such treatment. They have been mad at me ever since I similarly objected when Louis Osmond got fired by improper procedure." Then he said: "It is probably a bit premature to consider marrying again, but if you know anyone foolish enough to consider it let me know. There is no one here I would want."

Stella had stayed until the third of April, stripping the Cottage and Tilt of things she considered hers. She tried for a last reconciliation, but John refused. "If I had given in an inch," he wrote, "I would have been completely hooked again." Shortly afterward she sued for alimony and again refused a divorce. While awaiting a settlement, she sold her car. Back in St John's, she had her lawyer demand $355.44 a month, which John agreed to pay.

Having been fired, Gloria could no longer stay at the Staff House. In fact, the Board had warned her to leave town. For a while she lived at the local hotel. When this became untenable, John persuaded a friend across the island to take her in, after which she escaped to the Tilt for a short time. Waiting long hours alone for her lover to appear, she was a virtual outcast. He began to fear for her safety. One night, she wrote in her 1981 memoir *In Green Pastures*, they were debating what to do when a heavy fist rattled the cabin door. Standing there with flashlights was a male doctor and a Twillingate woman who ordered her back to the hotel. To face what, she had no idea. Men with guns? A lynch mob?

She had to face something worse: the righteous fury of an outport community protecting its honour and its own. Twillingaters had half forgiven John's earlier sins as a sort of family quarrel. This churlish treatment of a good and respected woman, albeit one of their own, infuriated them. They blamed him, but they blamed the outsider, the interloper, even more. They called her hard Babylonian names and left no doubt that Twillingate did not want her. A job was found for her in New Brunswick, Dr Olds arranged transportation, and in tears and anger she departed. The volcano subsided.

That spring the weather was as turbulent as his life. Every day brought snow or rain or fog. Northward and eastward a rumpled prairie of creamy drift ice stretched to the horizon and groaned against the black cliffs. All the sealing vessels were jammed; one of them sank as a helicopter lifted the crew to safety. Dr Olds returned to the Cottage and Bessie the housekeeper followed. Board meetings became more electric. The Mennonite nurses stayed but shunned him as if he had cloven hooves and a tail.

To restore normality to his life, John tried to tinker. Tutie got a letter asking for a piece of oil-proof rubber to fix an oil pump. At the Hospital he drove himself harder than ever. Almost every day he called or wrote his love, and every week pawed through the mail for envelopes bearing her generous, looping handwriting. If he found none, he was as downcast as a moonstruck teenager. People hardly knew what to say to him.

As an American citizen, he knew he could get a divorce in Reno, Nevada. At the May 2nd Board meeting, expecting Stella to sign the papers soon, he requested a month's leave. On June 9th his mother received a postcard from 125 West Liberty Street in Reno. Later he wrote of the divorce, of meeting his lawyer, of seeing Payute Indians and "many beautiful horses" in a parade, of attending his first wrestling match. He was enjoying the rodeo, making pastels of cows, mountains and sagebrush. Four weeks stretched to six, six to nine. He had to request extra leave and to borrow money from Mary. On July 14th the divorce came through.

The lovers were married in Reno that month and returned to Twillingate by way of Windsor on August 3rd. They found Gander Airport blanketed in blue haze. After weeks of drought, the coast from Carmanville to Wesleyville was besieged by forest fires that rampaged back and forth with every shift of wind. By day the sun hung like an orange Chinese lantern under a pallid sulfurous dome, to set each evening in colours more gaudy than usual. As the islands were considered safe, Twillingate overflowed with refugees. At night the southern sky glowed and flickered like the mouth of a distant furnace. Acrid smoke borne on hot southerly winds, sometimes hid the Harbour. The harsh odour of burning turf invaded every house. Even the Operating Room stank of it. Each night the Gerald S. Doyle radio bulletin reported more houses and stages burned, more communities evacuated by sea, more timber and wildlife torched.

Amid this confusion the couple slipped into their new life. With John Manuel gone and John Loveridge in his place, Board meetings became less tense. Dr Olds now attended as Chief Surgeon, not as Medical Director. The demotion troubled him less than he feared. "There are a lot of people I don't have to bother about any more," he told Mary, "& I can't say as I miss them." Occasionally he forgot himself. One afternoon, returning to work, he came up against the boiler room stack lying across his path. Junior Cooper had been hired to dismantle the rusting 54-foot pipe and had sensibly chosen a quiet noon hour to do it. He had skillfully lowered it to the ground and was preparing to haul it away with his bulldozer when Olds appeared. "Get that goddamed thing the hell out here," roared the doctor in his usual style. Hubert Vincent strode up to him, waved a ham fist under his nose and threatened to punch him if didn't leave. Dr Olds grunted and meekly walked around the obstacle.

That winter the harbour stayed open till February. In April *The Canadian Medical Journal* published his "Surgical Drainage of Hydrocephalus via the Thoracic Duct and Subclavian Vein," a preliminary account of the innovative procedure by which he had saved one of two otherwise doomed infants the previous year. He sent Mary a copy. When, later that month, US warplanes bombed Cuban air bases in preparation for an invasion at the Bay of Pigs, he was thankful David was back from Cuba and only a naval cadet.

Because of his nine weeks away, total procedures for 1961 fell to less than half the usual number. In the next few years, with more doctors on staff, it would go as high as 466. Again he was doing two or three operations a morning and supervising three or four doctors in minor surgery. With Alex Smith, Alf Dennison and Bob Garcia, he again had a strong team. His afternoons in Outpatients were proving unexpectedly pleasant. "Dr Hose, we'm so glad to see you back," the people said. In the evenings he resumed testing eyes. He was toying with a new idea to coax electricity from the sea.

Each in his own way, the four dissident Directors came around. Harry Ashbourne, it was said, spent the rest of his life trying to win Dr Olds' forgiveness. They needn't have worried; he almost never held grudges.

Gloria and Bessie did not see eye to eye on housekeeping and soon Bessie left for good. The couple spent many weekends at the Tilt, which she brightened with paint and curtains. In long happy letters home, he recounted the antics of their dogs Mago and Gwen and told of delightful encounters with baby foxes and other wildlife. That July they visited her parents in Nova Scotia. His ship of marriage seemed to have entered calmer seas.

Early in August of 1962, for no apparent reason, Gloria was seized with symptoms resembling those of extreme paranoia with manic-depressive overtones. Absurd jealousies suddenly inflamed her. She would wander down to the Hospital, create a scene and have to be escorted home. Guests at the Cottage might be accused of pilfering. As suddenly as these storms erupted, they would pass and she would again be serene and loving.

That November Les Curtis and Mr Pickersgill were in Twillingate campaigning in Mr Smallwood's fifth provincial election. John had a long discussion with Curtis, Alf Dennison and Alex Smith about committing her. Dr Dennison obtained her consent to undergo voluntary psychiatric treatment in St John's, and Curtis, Pickersgill and a nurse took her to St John's. On arrival, however, she began to behave normally and refused to stay. They wired John, and on August 16th he consented to have her detained.

"I feel so bad I am feeling sick most of the time," he wrote Mary from Twillingate on September 8th. "If she would only write or wire, it wouldn't be so bad. I still love her very much & have told her so repeatedly. What I fear is that my feeling may change in spite of myself, as I am pretty damn low." Five days later, writing from the Newfoundland Hotel, he said: "The situation is simply awful. They have very little hope of any worthwhile recovery. She is a peculiar type of case that has symptoms of several classifications but fits none, & there is no particular treatment for such. She is now taking Largactil (a tranquilizer) & is happy & contented."

John returned to Twillingate knowing she was for the time wholly indifferent to him. His letters went unanswered. Various drug regimes were tried with varying results, none satisfactory. Lithium she refused; she had seen too many patients go into convulsions, she said.

Thus began for both of them a torturous cycle of recovery and relapse, of fruitless visits to the Waterford for John, of fruitless homecomings for her, of searing separations and joyous reunions. Scenes of tranquillity succeeded scenes of violent discord. She was fanatic about cleanliness, emptying ashtrays even as people used them. Troubled by her husband's increasing use of painkillers like Demerol, she became convinced their home was being robbed, that it was a center for illegal drug trafficking, that the RCMP had bugged it. At other times she was equally certain John was romantically involved with other women—a suspicion not always unfounded. If John went to the Tilt alone, she would write notes to suspected females saying they could find him there. Once, in a tantrum, she tore up a Bible—an aberrant act since she professed strong religious feelings.

Because she was a large strong woman and formidable in her rages, people began to avoid her. Though a number of good friends remained loyal to them both, few visited their home any more except on urgent business. Periodically she would leave him, yelling "That's it, I'm never coming back!" He would beg her to return, she would refuse, and later relent. A few weeks later the cycle would repeat itself.

Mary was his lifeline. "I am surprised at myself as I have not even gotten mad at her, though she has hurt me very badly. For the record, I wish to state that I have never been anything but kind & considerate of Gloria—never bawled her out or started a row." Tutie vouched for this.

That first December after Gloria's illness began, John spent Christmas alone. He was fifty-six years old, confused and spent. Clumsily but sincerely he composed what is perhaps his only love poem:

> I came upon a beautiful bird
> Struggling with courage and pride
> In the confines of the snare.
> With clumsy love I attempted
> To set her free.
> New love renewed my life,
> But the net now bound us both.
> The mesh was tough and caused us pain which she
> Assuaged with love.
> Escape was won but at great cost.
> The lovely bird was wounded
> And could not fly.
> In mental anguish she turned love
> Into fearful hate, and black was white
> And white was black,
> And I was outcast to darkest doom:
> The lovely bird was snared again.
> This type snare was made of different twine,
> Of love and therapeutic skill.
> Deep despair and gnawing fear
> In a dark solitary cell.
> With directed care and courage of her own
> My lovely bird began to molt
> The poison from her mind.

As each ugly fetter dropped
There phoenix-like appeared a new
Resplendent garment of her soul,
Which touched me with its love and light
And freed me from my private Hell.
The light is lit and stronger grows—
Come spring with strong flight
Pinions secure, as one we
Will join in love and vernal
Migrant flock.

> To Gloria with much love,
> John, Christmas Day, 1962

That year, Stella was living alone at apartment #12, One Churchill Square, St John's. Away from John's abrasive presence and with proper medication, she had salvaged enough self-esteem to support herself by private nursing around the city. She liked the hours—4 o'clock to midnight—because she dreaded long evenings in her apartment alone. Her sister Edith lived not far away; she wrote letters to Mildred and Tutie, and now and then she visited relatives.

At Christmas Mildred flew up from New York to be with her and Edith. When a storm prevented her from leaving on the 31st as planned, she stayed for Edith's New Year's dinner. After the nine guests left, Mildred wrote Mary Olds, "we sat around just being lazy."

> I happened to look over at Stella, and she seemed to be trying to say something to me and—no sound. I went and knelt in front of her and asked if she felt ill and she patted my hands and smoothed my arms and smiled so beautifully and just didn't say one word. Edith flew to the phone and called the doctor. He was out, but she left word for him to come at once. It only seemed like a minute or two and her speech came back; but she couldn't remember what day it was and who had dinner with us, etc. After a while it all seemed clear to her and she seemed as well as ever. We almost forgot that we had called the doctor. When we were having tea, she looked across at me and said, 'I feel another of those turns coming....' We helped her to the couch. I sat with her head on my shoulder for a few minutes. The doctor came and at first he thought it was a stroke. Just as the ambulance came, Stella went into a very severe convulsion....

She died in hospital two days later. The autopsy revealed a grape-like cyst in the third ventricle of her brain. John was surprised when he heard the news and telephoned Lou Lawton to verify it. Her body, in a print dress pinned with a silver brooch under a jacket buttoned to the throat, lay for the customary interval at her brother John's home in Twillingate. Her other John never came—would have been unwelcome if he had—nor did he attend the funeral. She was buried in St Peter's Church of England Cemetery on the North Side, across from the Hospital where she and the only man she ever loved had served so long and well. The inscription said simply,

Stella Marion Olds, R.N.
1907-1963
"Peace, Perfect Peace"

For another decade and more, John and Gloria struggled in the black web of her recurrent nightmare. Together they learned much about fear and hope, of giving and receiving love. In the fullness of time, with better medication and care, Gloria's wounds began to heal. In a 1981 poem based on Psalm 23, she wrote:

> I discovered an isle in a make-believe world, a new world wedged between my soul and the choppy sea. I loved what I saw and no common man was to steal that precious gift God so freely gave. I would not exchange the pitfalls and sorrow for all the joys in the multitudes. I am happy and free. I have discovered green pastures.

With more staff, fewer responsibilities and someone to love, John's creative energy renewed itself. Through the late sixties and early seventies he would average over 300 procedures a year—in 1968 it was 466, in 1972, 414. People said he had mellowed. His weight went up to 142 pounds. He continued to drink, but not as much as in the past, and relied more on drugs.

One day years later, a friend saw Dr Olds and Gloria picking berries near the Tilt. Hailing them, he asked John how he was. Straightening his arthritic back, Dr Olds drawled, "Jesus, I must have picked at least a ton of berries in my lifetime since I came to Twillingate. I was married three times and every one of my wives loved to pick berries. Am I stupid?"

Part IV

Wing and Wing

Chapter Twenty

Gillett's Lye and
Other Horrors

"John never gave up; he never gave up till
the last breath."
— Grace (Patten) Sparkes

"**A**re you Hitler?" asked ten-year-old Ted Reccord of Gander Bay
around 1945, coming out of ether and seeing Dr Olds' face
looming over him. Children feared Dr Olds. Parents liked it that
way. "If you be naughty I'll send you to Dr Hose!" they said.
Howard Butt recalled the day of School Clinic: "The door would open, and
in would walk Dr Olds. I'd swallow. I was always afraid he'd turn on me.
To us he was the same as the Ranger or the RCMP." The tall gaunt man in
white would seat himself on the platform. One by one the youngsters,
nudged by teacher and nurse, would shuffle toward the unsmiling figure
in white. "And how are *you* today?" Dr Olds would say, lifting his terrible
stethoscope.

"Fin-n-e, Doctor...."

"That's gooood," he'd drawl, and proceed to check for TB, bad teeth
and skin disease, all of which he usually found in the school. On Clinic days
so many children stayed home "sick" that the Board finally had to hold them
at the Hospital.

Howard and his classmates would have been amazed to know that Dr
Olds was almost as nervous around them as they were around him. "He
was terribly shy," said Grace Sparkes, "hated to show affection." Nurse
Jessie Drover said the same: "John didn't know how to treat kids, how to
talk to them." Jessie's daughter Margo did rounds with him in Pediatrics.
"Even with the little tiny babies that couldn't talk, Dr Olds would lean over
the cribs and say, 'And how are *you?*' That was all. He'd never touch them
or make baby sounds at them."

But if a kid sassed him, he liked it. "When we asked one little boy what
the doctor had said to him in the examining room, he replied, 'Dr Olds said,

"Take off your goddam clothes!"' The nurses would get the little guy to repeat it. Dr Olds loved that."

It was well known that Dr Olds disliked obstetrics. It wasn't only the waiting. What upset him was mothers screaming and carrying on. "You should have thought about that nine months ago," he'd grunt.

A woman whom he had cured of barrenness had been wanting to show him her third child, a beautiful baby girl of six months. One day when Olds was completing a house call to her husband, she asked him to have a peek at the infant before he left.

"Why, is she sick?" he said.

"No," she said, "I'd just like you to see her, you know."

"Well, is she sick?"

"No."

"Then why would I want to see her?"

He did have a quick look before he left.

In his late twenties John wanted no children of his own. One day a nurse teasingly said it was time Betty had a baby. "My God," she said, "you'd think I had insulted him!" With his own son, John was strict, as Pop had been with him. He especially disliked what he considered emotional displays over trifles. One day when David fell and hurt his knee and ran to his mother, he ignored the boy's tears and forbade Betty to comfort him. Another time the housekeeper served cod for lunch and David wouldn't eat it. As John left for work, he said to the housekeeper, "Now mind, I'm telling you—don't give him anything else for dinner. He'll eat fish or nothing."

"My heart ached for poor David," she said, "going off to school with nothing for dinner...."

Shy and stern as he was, no doting father was more attentive once a youngster came under his care. "I remember little Christine who had leukemia," said Lorna (Bradley) Stuckless, a former aide. "A beautiful little person, she always had a smile for him. During rounds the other doctors and nurses would move on, but he'd hover around her bed. He would fold paper airplanes and play with her. Her death really upset him."

"There was this little boy," said Dr Fred Woodruff, "three parts dead, desperately ill, who had lost his leg just above the knee. When it became clear that he was recovering, what did Dr Olds do but measure up his leg and go into his workshop and make him an artificial one. With straps and so on. I don't know how many times he redesigned and lengthened it. And we used to call the little boy 'Stumpy' because he'd go stumpin' around on this leg."

Parents could rest easy about his abilities. Tor Fosnaes was ten when John took out his appendix: "I don't know if it is a record or not, but [it] was removed in about seven minutes from the time of the first incision...[including] sewing up, and the incision was about one inch long. It has stretched, but you can still see the mark of the one stitch that held it together." John was scornful of any doctor who made a longer scar for appendectomies, especially in a child.

Within days after John landed in Twillingate in September 1932, they brought him an unconscious seventeen-year old boy with two-thirds of his body broiled. Harry Pynn and Graham Manuel, camping up around Exploits, had mistakenly put gasoline in a kerosene stove. With his clothes on fire, Harry had run against the wind toward the water. The flames caught his shirt, scorched his upper body and charred his face, elbows and knees.

With the initial crises of dehydration and shock safely past, Dr Olds laid the unconscious boy inside a sterile tent in a room by himself, cradled on a metal frame he made with pads that touched only the unburned places on the boy's back. He placed a lamp underneath to keep him warm and sheets over the tent to keep it sterile. To prevent infection he coated the patient with Gentian Violet, the standard treatment for burns and scalds before antibiotics. Even Harry's sheets were washed in Gentian Violet.

"Everything in that room was purple," said Grace Sparkes. "When John saw a chance to do skin grafts, he did them on every part of Harry Pynn—legs and knees, and pinned the arms up, and so on. And when the part he had taken the skin from was better, he'd turn him over. He did all that by pinch grafting—a layer of skin; cover with gauze; let it grow in, then do some more. It got to the stage where Harry Pynn was conscious. He'd hear this cart coming down the hall, and he knew it was for skin grafting, and he'd start to cry. And John hated that. Sometime in May, when the boy was learning to walk again, John made him a walker so he could get around the Hospital."

It was years later before Grace saw Harry again. She was in Gander awaiting a flight when a fellow came along and said, 'Hi, Grace, how are you?' For a moment she stared at him. "Then I remembered there was a bit in his ear that John had not restored," she said, "and I knew who he was. He'd been overseas in the Navy and he was okay. But back then I didn't believe that he ever could live. I got to know him well because when he had recuperated enough I used to read to him. I recall we didn't know what colour his eyes were. The first time he opened them was in December—and they were as blue as the skies—little blue eyes shining in the purple."

For generations outport women had made their own laundry soap using lard emulsified in a mild alkali leached from wood ashes. By the thirties, scientific progress had brought them Gillett's Lye, a powerful alkali concentrate which was retailed in a tallish orange and white can. Parents, afraid their children might mistake its dry white powder for sugar, kept it well out of reach.

One summer afternoon in the thirties, 18-month-old Violet England was brought to him from Harry's Harbour, a fishing community fifty miles away in Green Bay. The infant had found a cup containing lye mixed with water and swallowed some. When the fiery taste made her drop the cup she stepped in the spilled liquid. "The run by boat from her home is [long]," recounted *The Twillingate Sun*, "and [Dr Olds] discovered that the child's esophagus was completely closed...." The *Sun* went on to tell how he dilated it by passing small catheters from stomach to mouth until she no longer needed a feeding tube.

> The child's esophagus is being dilated every three days and this procedure will...be continued for the next nine to twelve months. Violet is now eating well and steadily gaining in weight. About two weeks ago the child was moved from the Hospital to the doctor's residence and Mrs Olds, being a nurse, has taken over [her] care....

In February of 1935 eight-year-old Walter Cole of Carmanville also swallowed lye. It seared his mouth and esophagus like a red-hot poker. The dilatation procedure Dr Olds had used on Violet England was impossible—there was no esophagus to dilate. The lye had also damaged his trachea, or windpipe, impairing his breathing. The only options were to build him a new esophagus or to let him die. Feeding him intravenously, Dr Olds began to construct a tube of living flesh that in time might enable the boy to feed himself. Three months later he was extending it under the skin of the chest to connect to the stomach. "You'd put food in his mouth," recalled an aide, "it would go down the tube and you'd squeeze it into the stomach by hand. This was before the days of sulfa drugs or antibiotics or anything. It was a wonder Dr Olds got as far as he did...."

In the spring of 1936 and again in 1937, Dr Olds rebuilt the tube to allow for Walter's growth. One can scarcely imagine Walter's ordeal. He might have survived if he hadn't contracted pulmonary tuberculosis. In 1937 the only cure for advanced lung TB was radical collapse surgery and that was out of the question. Walter's last admission was on July 24th, 1937. On October 26th Olds wrote sadly, "Respiration ceased."

His most famous Gillett's Lye patient was Dougie Bath of Gander. Three years old when admitted with atresia or closure of the esophagus on March 4th, 1949, he was in and out of hospital for seven years. He had already spent seven months at St John's General Hospital when his anguished parents wired Twillingate. "Bring him out," Olds replied. He assured them Dougie could be cured if they would leave him for about a year, and then bring him back regularly for several years to correct for normal growth.

The patient's esophagus was more or less intact, so no skin grafting was needed. There was deep scarring all the way from his mouth to the cardiac sphincter at the top of the stomach, and the scar tissue kept growing together. The child was in constant danger of dehydration and starvation. Olds chose two-stage dilatation as the best treatment. For the upper portion he did a low tracheotomy—a small opening in the lower throat—and through it threaded a fine tube that came out of the child's mouth. For several weeks he pulled this tube very slowly back and forth for an hour a day. Then over several months he used tubes of increasing diameter, from pencil size to just over half an inch.

For the constricted lower esophagus he filled a small bag with mercury and had Dougie swallow it. Going down, the mercury became a thin flexible shoot. Coming up, the heavy liquid formed a bolus in the bottom of the bag and gently forced the esophagus open. Meal times were always preceded by the tube and bag routine, which made Dougie fret and cry. When the little patient learned to curse his tormentor, John took it as a good sign.

"Dougie suffered," said Mayme Hewlett, "and everybody else suffered too. I called him The Suffering Pet of Notre Dame Bay Memorial Hospital. It was an extremely bad treatment." One day Dr Olds came into her office hugging his thumb. "Doctor, what's the matter with your thumb?" she said.

"That little bugger Dougie Bath bit me!"

"Sir," she said, "if I was Dougie Bath I think I'd bite you too! Nothing would please me better than to hear that Dougie Bath was dead!" She didn't mean it, of course, but Dr Olds was furious. "Mayme," he shouted, "I'm ashamed of you! Dougie Bath will live, eat, and enjoy a good meal like you and me and the rest of us." Then he stormed out.

Lorna Stuckless worked at the Hospital throughout that period. "Dougie owes his life to him," she said. "Dr Olds would come down from his house and sometimes spend all night with him, just sitting there beside him to make sure he was all right. He did all kinds of little things to make him content—took him out for drives in the *Jeep*, or to play in the snow, or to Hospital Pond to slide around on the ice." The boy was first discharged in July 1949, came back the next fall for ten months, and then for nine days in August 1951. After that he returned only once a year.

"Many people described poor Dougie's screams," said Dr Woodruff, "but it worked. He made a perfect recovery. A nice cheerful young fellow. Became an accountant in the old Hospital. The story was still very fresh in people's minds in the sixties."

A few minutes after noon on May 6th, 1959, six-year-old Cedric Mills of Moreton's Harbour had just returned home from school registration with his mother. Some fishermen were barking nets on the beach across the road from his house, so while she went inside to make dinner, he lingered by the gate. Cedric had seen men bark nets before, but he never tired of watching the procedure. Like most outport children, he understood the purpose. It was so they wouldn't rot, he said to himself, and so the fish couldn't see them. Barking meant soaking them in wooden tubs full of boiling hot tea made from fir bark and spruce cones. The tubs were really sawed-off old barrels with rope handles. One tub might hold a cod trap leader, another the trap floor and a third the pound.

For a time he watched several men with hay prongs and sticks as they lifted the dripping, brown coils of linnet from the tubs and spread them along the beach to dry. Then he gazed at the big black iron pot belching white steam which disappeared as swiftly as it formed. The fire he saved till last. He envied the men whose mothers let them play with it, let them pile on driftwood and stoke its crackling flames and kick stray embers back under the pot with their boots.

"Boy!" yelled a fisherman. Entranced, Cedric had crossed the road to stand where he could feel the heat. "Get back before a flanker lands on you!" Startled, not looking where he was going, the boy backed away and tumbled into one of the steaming tubs. He went down until his right hand touched bottom. Rose to the edge. Slipped. Went down again. Regained the edge. Got one leg over. Then the other. Flopped, quivering like a dying trout, on the sand. All this time he had uttered not a sound. The fishermen had not seen his mishap. Trailing water and steam, Cedric started home.

As he toiled up the bank, the weight of his sodden, roll-neck Mary Maxim sweater dragged him back. Halfway across the road he fell. For the first time cried out. His older sister Alice came running and carried him dripping inside. The hot sweater was hard to peel off. She dried him with a towel, found a bottle of Gentian Violet and gently swabbed his angry red flesh.

"By now I was in quite a lot of pain and crying very hard," he said. "The only way they could quiet me was to go to the grocery store next door and buy me a pack of gum, which at that time was like a million dollars to a child. I can remember vividly the fishermen coming in through the door to see how badly I was scalded. As I was naked, I can remember being a little embarrassed."

Now they had to get him to Twillingate. The harbour was still jammed with rough ice, so the men took a handbar—two long poles with boards across for carrying dried fish—added quilts and a pillow, and set out. With a change of men to carry the load, they made good time. Stopping only to slake the boy's raging thirst, they carried him over rocky paths and through dense thickets about two miles to Western Head, where the ice was looser.

I don't know exactly how long it took to get to the Head, but someone had gone ahead and got a motor boat ready. Finally we headed out for Twillingate, six to eight miles away through rough ice and all. On the way we ran up on ice pans two or three times. They were so thick the fishermen had to push the boat through with their hand-gaffs and oars. When we reached the wharf in Twillingate they hoisted me up over and at last got me to the Hospital. Dr Olds was chief surgeon at the time but it was Dr Dennison who took and patched me up that day.

Gravely the doctors surveyed the unconscious boy. Three-quarters of Cedric's body had third-degree or full-thickness scalding. They could expect sudden swelling and other imbalances as his young body flooded the damaged tissues with plasma and fought infection. As the swelling and capillary dilatation tied up more surface blood, his blood pressure would plummet, and his pulse rate grow rapid and thready. Congestive heart failure was a real danger. If he weathered the dehydration and shock, there was still a strong likelihood of infection. His disability and scarring would be severe. His flesh, robbed of underlying tissue, unable to form new skin, would rally with thick scars, contracting the surrounding tissues like the skin of a prune. To move his arms or fingers would be pure torture. Dr Olds saw that only prompt and skillful skin grafting could give him a normal childhood.

I went into a coma for approximately three weeks, and wasn't out of danger for three months. I spent a year and a half in the hospital before I came home at all. Then I went back and forth for several summers getting more skin-grafts. When I first arrived I was so bad they couldn't let the sheets touch me. So they rigged a frame above my bed with the bedclothes on top. You can imagine what the under sheet was like when I turned over.

Along with removal of scar tissue, Cedric first underwent grafts on his hip, elbow and spine. Then, between July 13th and September 7th 1962, Dr Olds repaired old burns and freed his right shoulder. The final session entailed adjustment grafts to free his axilla or armpit.

At one time my right arm was sewn to my side to help straighten me up. I was bent over so much my fingers dragged the floor, leaving blood and pus behind. I didn't look forward to the nurses coming to change my dressings. They had to soak the bandages before they could remove them. Sometimes when they were in a bad mood I didn't get good treatment; but that didn't happen very often. They tell me I had 112 skin-grafts and operations. The soft place in the crook of my right arm is someone else's skin. All of the rest came from my own body, mostly my back and left side. After I improved I was the nurses' and doctors' pet and I became quite a character. I was spoiled rotten.

At first, said Nellie (Clarke) Pardy, "He used to go around all drawn out of shape, visiting the patients. I remember because it was when I had my veins done. He was bent right down two-double." Cedric recalled that his mother brought him school books so he could learn in the hospital. "I did well, and when I got home and went to school I took grades Primary and One in one year and could have done Grade Two but I would have disrupted the class. I have some vivid memories of my ordeal and some best forgotten. People have looked at me in astonishment as if to say, 'How did you survive?'" Cedric's last visit was on July 26th, 1963 and lasted only ten days. He later married, and became a successful fisherman in Bridgeport on New World Island.

One winter morning Lorna Stuckless' two-year-old daughter Barbara had to be rushed to the Hospital with severe stomach pains. After sleeping part of the night with her parents, she had awakened first and started playing with her mother's hair. In trying to open a bobby pin with her teeth the way she had seen her mother do, she accidentally swallowed it. Her cooing changed to screams and awoke Lorna. "I prayed the clip was a plastic-coated one and that it would somehow move without harming her," said Lorna. "I rushed her over to the Hospital and they X-rayed right away. Sure enough, the pin was in her little stomach. We were all scared that when it moved down it would puncture the intestine."

Dr Olds decided to give her barium so he could watch the object on the fluoroscope. "It's pretty damned nasty stuff,' he said. "Think she'll drink it?" Barbara did, and they stood her before the machine. As it started up Dr Olds said, "My God, what have you got here, a garbage can?" The screen showed not only the pin but two small metal discs, a spring and some other odd objects. Unknown to them, Barbara had been hugging her favourite Christmas teddy bear.

The barium pushed the bobby pin down a few inches, into the upper intestine. Here it lodged on an angle, pushing the bowel over. For two weeks the Stucklesses fed her thick porridge, bread, cotton wool—anything to envelop the pin and avoid surgery. Every day Lorna took her to Dr Olds. The pin never budged. One day he said, "Two more days and we'll have to operate." At first he couldn't find the hair clip. The enema had moved it farther down. When he did, all he had to do was push it out the anus.

Lorna was angry. "Didn't you have a portable X-ray machine you could have pulled in and made sure where that clip was *before* you operated?" she fumed. "We X-rayed enough," he shot back. "And you can thank the Lord above that I didn't have to cut the bowel. Don't let me hear another word out of you!"

On a stormy evening a week later, visiting Barbara during a snowstorm, Lorna wondered outloud whether she was well enough to take home. "You should know," barked Olds. "Christ, you've *lived* over here, haven't you, ever since she's been here? Take her home if you want; but first you come in here and sign this paper."

"I'm not signing any paper," she said. "But I'm gonna take her home."

"Well," he said, "*if* you can get home with her, fine and dandy. There's no cars running."

"At that time cars couldn't get right to the Hospital anyway," she recalled. "I'd been there most of the evening and it was really stormy. So I phoned home and had blankets and her sleigh brought over, wrapped her all up and went down Hospital Lane with her. It was as slippery as glass, and I thought, 'Oh God help me; don't let me break a leg and have to go back in there tonight!' So I took her home."

Some time later, their four-year-old son Paul fell off his bicycle. A month later she noticed he was still limping. Dr Olds had him walk down the hall while he watched. "Ahh, go on, woman," he said, "you're foolish. You're seeing things!"

"Dr Olds," she said, "I see him every day; I *know* there's something wrong."

"Okay," he said, "just to satisfy you, I'll X-ray."

By and by he came back, a different look on his face. "Yes, my dear, you were right. He needs to be in a cast for at least a year. You know that man from in the Arm, the fellow with one leg shorter than the other? Your son must have had some kind of accident to reduce the blood supply to his hip. But you caught it in time." He sat down beside her, took a piece of paper and drew everything out. The cast extended from armpit to ankle with a spike between his knees to keep his legs apart. In ten months it was so battered and chipped that she took him over for a new one. When it had been removed and his leg X-rayed, Olds came back waving the film and grinning. "You know," he said, "this is all right! He's all better. He won't need any more casts."

He had said a year; she was so glad she began to weep.

"What in hell you crying for?" he said.

"Doctor," she said, "there's tears of sorrow and tears of joy too."

"Well, get on home now."

One day the seven-year-old daughter of scrub nurse Elfreda Dalley fell on the school playground and hurt her arm. That evening she complained of pain, so next morning Mrs Dalley took her up to the Hospital. Nothing seemed wrong, so no X-rays were taken. The girl was known to imitate older children, and that week one or two other happened to be wearing arm slings. Her mother made her a sling and sent her back to school. Next morning she couldn't move her arm. When Dr Olds came back with the X-ray, he said, "She's pretty happy for a person with a broken arm."

"Right through that arm," said Elfreda, "there was nothing but an eggshell thickness. The bone was gone. It was so bad, he told me, that eventually her arm could have broken when she picked up a book. He said to me, 'Now, my dear, be prepared: her arm could come out in a bucket or it might come out all right.' He took chips off her hip bone and placed it in her arm and tied it up with Italian wire. She has a big scar right across her arm; she can't turn her hand over fully, but it worked."

As the Hospital was then the only place to take a sick animal, sometimes Dr Olds played veterinarian too—but not in the OR. "I don't recall ever treating a goat," he once told a reporter, "but I've treated dogs, cats, cows, horses and pigs." Said Nurse Margo (Drover) Evans, "If a pet got hurt and somebody loved it, he would help. Not that people were lined up in OPD with animals, but now and then it happened. We even had one in a plaster cast." One time he did a cesarian section on a dog.

Among his oddest patients was a chick which Muriel French of Moreton's Harbour brought in. "We kept a few chickens," she said, "and in 1948 one hatched out with four legs. The little thing couldn't walk." Muriel had been a patient of John's and knew him well, so she called him.

"Hell," he said,"bring it down."

"So I went down to OPD and he gave her a little anesthetic. I had the little thing in my hand. He snipped off the two extra legs and the chicken grew up to be a laying hen."

During the War, when Dr Olds routinely refused house calls because they took too much time, he once sneaked out to see a sick horse. In the mid-thirties Ern French had a thoroughbred riding horse named Molly Jo, the pride of Moreton's Harbour and famous all over New World Island. As Moreton's Harbour had no blacksmith, he brought her to Twillingate for Billy Bennett to shoe her for the winter. During the shoeing, she reared and snapped the bridle rope. It was tied to a circular lead weight in an iron ring on the floor. As she bucked, the sharp-edged ring severed her Achilles' tendon. With bright blood spraying the floor, the men roped and tied the terrified mare and knew she must be put away.

Someone said, "Call Dr Olds." The doctor got them to lay her on a sail and drag her to a flat place between the old Cottage and the Hospital. With scrub nurse Edith Simms applying open-drop ether—no easy thing, since too little would endanger them and too much could kill her—he sewed the severed tendon, closed the wound and applied a cast. While she was under ether they moved Molly Joe into the Hospital stable and secured her. During the night the terrified mare thrashed around so violently that she died. Nobody felt worse than John McKee Olds.

In the early sixties Gordon and Lorna Stuckless had a small dog with a foxy tail who was named Rally after his favourite brand of food. One day a school teacher accidentally drove over Rally. Lorna got Dr Olds to X-ray him and, cradling the dog in her lap, awaited the verdict. John returned and sat down beside her.

"Anyone love this dog very much?" he began, stroking its ears.

"Yes," she said, trying not to cry.

"Well, I'm afraid we can't put a cast on him, because his pelvis is broken in at least four places. But I tell you what. Take him home, put him in a comfortable place and watch him. If he pisses he'll be all right."

Back home, she laid him on his favourite blanket and kept watch all night. Just after daylight he urinated. "It was almost pure blood, but he urinated," she said. "After a few days I figured he'd be better off upright. So I took an old sheet and a broom handle and made him a sling—cut four holes for his legs and one hole for him to pee through, and hung him from a hook in the ceiling with his feet just touching the floor. Dr Olds said, 'Lorna, if it works you oughta patent it.'"

After a while Rally began to eat. Now the dog never liked Marvin the milkman and always barked at him. For three weeks he was silent. Marvin could park the truck in the driveway, walk to the door and deposit the milk without the slightest response. Then one morning in the fourth week, Marvin came and Rally let out one solitary yap. Afterward, said Gordon, Rally always ran at a thirty-five degree angle to his line of travel, but he ran for many years.

Chapter Twenty-One

He Had an Aura

"Surgery...is at once murderous, painful, healing, and full of love."
— Richard Selzer, MD
Mortal Lessons

"The two characteristics that struck me most were first, his great love for the people and secondly, his terrific natural ability as a technician. I haven't seen a better technician anywhere than Dr Olds."
—George Battcock, MD

One morning in March 1934, eighteen-year-old Max Gillingham of Clarkes Head, Gander Bay, was sleepily chopping frozen manure by lantern light in the barn. His father had roused him before dawn because they were going to harness the pony and haul firewood all day. Max had come home from the school dance only hours before and did not fully waken until the axe bit deep into his knee. Darius helped him to the kitchen couch, and, while removing the boot and socks and trying to stem the spurting blood, sent his wife running to the post office to wire Twillingate for a doctor. Dr Olds covered the thirty-five miles of sea ice and forest trails by dog team in just over five hours. He cleaned and bandaged the wound, left some morphine, saw one or two other people and left.

Darius forgot to mention it was a barn axe. A few days later when the wound festered, he sent another urgent telegram. Dr Olds couldn't come right then, and a storm followed. Max's leg ballooned from the knee down and went from hot red to clammy blue. Over fifty years later, his sister Mamie recalled the doctor's second visit. "He bounded up the stairs and lanced that leg. The blood went right to the ceiling. Aunt Alice was there and Aunt Effie, and when he had things under control he said, 'I'm staying here till he's ready to travel.' Aunt Effie laid rugs on the couch for a bed and he stayed overnight. When the fire went out she thought he must be cold and put a comforter over him, but he tossed it off."

By morning Max was pale and listless. Dr Olds got Darius to build a box for the sled. Some versions say the doctor now gave him a transfusion of his own blood before setting off with him for Twillingate. Others say he did the transfusion en route. Dr Olds' blood type was universal O RH negative; therefore he could perhaps have done so; but is more likely that he administered a unit or two of dried plasma or warm saline solution at the house, to prevent shock. All Dr Olds said afterward was, "I went down to see Max Gillingham twice in one week. The second time I brought him back. That was a bad trip.... We started with dogs, ended up with a horse—but mostly walked." There must have been other complications, for Max was still in the Hospital that August. Mamie remembered the family's visiting him there on his nineteenth birthday, because she wore a pretty new dress and Max said, "All eyes were on you." For years afterward he ran a general store in Clarkes Head, and walked with a limp.

Such tales abound in Notre Dame Bay. Not all are true, but even the taller ones have a grain of truth in them. The one about his self-appendectomy, for example, is half true—he directed the operation. The one about his keeping a kidney, connected by plastic tubes to its owner, alive in a bedside tray for a week, is also half true. George Grimes' renal artery was infected after kidney removal, so Dr Olds left a Kelly clamp, embedded in the sutured and bandaged wound, on it for ten days until it had healed enough to be trusted. The patient lay on his abdomen until the operation could be completed.

The story about his self-vasectomy *is* true. He performed it about 1944 with Betty's help because in her nephritic condition a pregnancy would have killed her. She administered the local anesthetic and he guided the scalpel by means of two mirrors. They did it at the Tilt and never told anyone until May 1974, when he remarked casually in a letter to Tutie, "I don't think I ever told you, but I vasectomized myself after Betty got sick; I have surely never regretted it." His mother never knew about it.

There are so many true stories, the others hardly matter. Even allowing for the inevitable magnification of a beloved personality over time, one is left with an uncommon resonance.

"I knew a fella, a retired serviceman from central Newfoundland, a farmer. He had this bad stomach and he couldn't get nobody to tell him what the trouble was. I was in bed there, and he was alongside, tellin' me his troubles. He was gone right to pieces, nerves was gone—thought he had cancer, see. "I said, 'B'y, when Dr Olds puts his hands on you, he'll make a good man of you, a new man o' you.'

"He laughed and said, 'I don't know, b'y.'

"I said, 'Never you mind, Sir; I knows about that.' He had the same symptoms, see, that I'd had with ulcers several years before. So Dr Olds had 'en out, and examined him, blood test and everything else. Then this morning he come in, leaned over to him and said, 'What have you been doing?'

"'I don't know. What do you mean, Doctor?'

"'What are you doing with yourself?'

"He said, 'I've been workin'; I'm a farmer....'

"He said, 'Your blood is like water.' He was run down, see; wasn't eating. And he used to be on the booze. He told me himself he used to drink a case and a half of beer every day. He used to come to Baie Verte, be there overnight. He'd be on the beer all day until they'd strip out his vegetables, and then he'd be too drunk to go home. Or wouldn't face the trip home—you know, too dark. He was a wreck.

"Dr Olds cut out the ulcers same as he did for me. He believed in cutting it out and get rid of it. Now they don't cut 'em out at all. That fellow come over to Twillingate in an old red van, barely able to drive. Dr Olds cured him and he drove back hisself."

Many came from beyond the Bay to be healed. Lorna Stuckless, returning from summer holidays by boat in the early sixties, got talking to a passenger and discovered he was from the west coast. "I'm surprised at you, Sir," she said, "coming to Twillingate when you have a new hospital in Corner Brook." He replied, "My dear, I'm not coming for the hospital: I'm coming for Dr Olds. Dr Olds is far ahead of what's over in Corner Brook."

A man came from Corner Brook with abdominal pain. Fluoroscopy revealed advanced stomach cancer. Dr Woodruff was there when John opened him. "It was an awful mess. The whole of his stomach was affected. Dr Olds removed almost the total mass of the stomach from the duodenum to the esophagus. He had a little bit left, but not much. Technically it was extremely difficult. He removed the spleen too and there was cancer all over the place. The post-op had just about every complication in the book. The patient developed some pneumonia; part of his wound broke down, then became infected. I really couldn't see that this chap had much of a chance," said Dr Woodruff in 1991. "He was at one stage just absolutely, diabolically ill. With good nursing and good support the patient eventually came through. A difficult feat. My wife's sister, a physiotherapist, helped him with breathing exercises. She said that Dr Olds would go in ten times a day—plasma, intravenous feeding, and so on. And as far as I know that chap is still alive in Lewisporte.

"We often got patients who'd been given up on by surgeons at other hospitals," said Woodruff. Dr Olds would always say, 'You want me to do something about that?' And they'd reply, 'Dr Olds, nobody else will touch it. Would you have a go at it? ' And he always would—with due preparation. An example of this was another Corner Brook man who arrived very sick and found that Dr Olds was on holiday. 'If I can only live till Dr Olds gets back,' he told Frank Pardy one day. After the operation, Mrs Pardy sent him up some fresh strawberries. He lived to a good old age."

Olds' most famous west coast case was that of the severely arthritic Mr Burridge of Bonne Bay, who in his own words was "buckled up just like a rattlesnake, drawed up in a ball." After going to his local doctor and three more in Corner Brook, he came to Olds in early 1954 "bent two-double with arthritis." He could hardly bend his knees or elbows or walk in comfort. He had been told he could go to St John's or to Montreal, but that it was useless to hope for a cure. According to them, he said, "I was good for nothing but the garbage can. That was the crump I was in."

His arthritis being quiescent, over the next few years Olds undertook a series of lengthening operations on the patient's ligaments. At the same time he freed the adhesions around his joints. In all, Burridge had thirteen operations in ten years. Woodruff met him in 1963 as a patient and "he was singing Dr Olds' praises. Miracle doctor! He still came back every two or three months to see him for a progress report and told me stories of how he'd found a new lease on life. Got onto treasure hunting with a metal detector made from an old minesweeper unit, was sure there was lots of buried treasure around town, he could climb; it was amazing."

Harry Layman Jr of Fogo was standing on the wharf in Twillingate one day, watching passengers board the *Clyde*. He noticed a man bent over and carrying a suitcase. Harry helped him aboard and said, "You've had surgery, haven't you?" The man said yes, he had been a sailor in England, and one night, returning drunk to his ship, he had fallen and hurt something in his belly. He had been to see doctors in London, Halifax and elsewhere and had submitted to over fifty X-rays, but was still passing blood and in discomfort. Dr Olds had taken one X-ray and said, "I can fix you but you'll need surgery." Olds discovered that his ureters were crossed and constricted—probably from birth, with the condition aggravated by his fall. Dr Olds uncrossed and cleared them and after some bed rest the sailor was going home cured.

Ernie Legge's story is as impressive for his determination as for Dr Olds' skill. About to be married, he was out turring when his gun went off accidentally, shredding his arm above the elbow. Twisting his shirt around the fiercely bleeding limb, he rowed back to Twillingate, arriving at the Hospital half dead. Olds amputated the arm with so few complications that Ernie was married that Friday, on schedule. Later he became a successful longliner skipper.

Peter Drake of Oderin, Placentia Bay was twenty-nine when a boat winch caught his hand in December 1946 and removed the side of his right hand with the fourth and fifth fingers attached. Olds repaired extensive lacerations, amputated his crushed fourth and fifth metacarpals and created a sleeve graft by attaching his hand to his body. On New Year's Eve, Dr Olds excised one end of the graft that had healed and started a tube graft for his third finger; on January 8th he removed half of this graft and a week later the rest. A fortnight later he finished the hand with a pinch graft from the abdomen and the man was discharged in April almost as good as new.

Another fisherman came in around 1950 with a gaping hole in his side where an engine flywheel had caught his clothes. "He worked on him for hours and hours," said an aide, "and used to stay with him all night. He had to graft skin to his side every so often to fill in that gap, that hole. Oh, it was fantastic what he did for that man." This man also recovered and went back to work.

Even in his seventies, just before he retired, The Old Man was still innovative. A man came from Moreton's Harbour with a permanently drooped eyelid. He could not see out of the eye, and he was in danger of going blind. Nobody else would touch it. "You'll just have to live with it," they told him. Dr Olds relocated a muscle so that it would elevate the eyelid. The man was ecstatic and, like the blind man in the New Testament, told everyone he met.

Before the War, when his case load was lighter and he had more help, Olds often made house calls around the Bay. He enjoyed these trips by boat, dog team or horse and sled, but by the sixties younger doctors were doing all the house calls. One cold sunny March morning in that period, however, when the sea was frozen to the horizon in all directions, a call came in from Tizzard's Harbour saying that an old lady had fallen and couldn't move her hip: "She's lying on the floor, can you send a doctor?"

Fred Woodruff recalled the episode. "Dr Olds had no surgery that morning and I remember his saying, 'Well, I'll go.' So he got in his Jeep and drove over the ice. Took someone with him and lots of blankets and I believe he took a mattress too. When he came back, here was this old lady, on a mattress, lots of blankets, very comfortable. He'd brought her back over the ice. And she hadn't had any breakfast.

"We checked her over," said Dr Woodruff. "She had blood drawn for hemoglobin and so on and cross-matched in case she needed a transfusion. We X-rayed her to make sure where the fracture was. And Dr Olds just took her in the OR and pinned that hip within three hours of falling. And she never turned a hair. And I felt that was complete doctoring, you know—over the ice, and bring her back, pin her, feed her—and everything was just perfect. And as my wife Mary said, the next thing he would turn around and do something quite different."

In Boston or New York Dr Olds would almost certainly have specialized in orthopedic surgery; in Twillingate he had to do everything. "When he first went there he would do anything but brain surgery," said Tutie. "He told Mother, 'You know, sometimes I have to go out and read up before I can do an operation.' Who could he ask? I mean, he couldn't have a conference with someone." Once when Fred Woodruff said to him, "I'm not sure what I can do for this patient," he replied, "You ought to say, 'If *I* don't do it, is there anyone better in the neighborhood?' You have to do what you can. They may not come back."

When Dr Lou Lawton arrived as a young resident in 1945, he was impressed by the surgical repertoire John had amassed in spite of not doing any official post-graduate training. "On a typical morning between eight and noon, he would do three to five operations ranging from minor to major. He would even do cataracts—although he didn't like to. He would fix a back and take out a stomach. Then he would fix a broken leg. He did all those different things which now they specialize in. If you asked someone who does cataracts now to take a stomach out, they'd say, 'Are you crazy? That's not my field.'"

In the early days, the people of Notre Dame Bay basically had the choice of going to Twillingate or to St John's. Dr Sheldon of New World Island was so convinced that Olds could do as well as anyone on difficult cases that it was years before he considered referring a patient to St John's. "Most people seemed to get on very well. The one area that perhaps I would question was cesarean sections. I think he never changed to the newer lower segment section technique, but continued with the classical method, an operation superseded years before. Yet he was young enough to have made the change. But there may have been some technical reason why he didn't. In some ways the older operation was perhaps a little safer in that it was clear of the bladder. I can remember vividly the first two occasions when The Old Man—he was then in his early seventies—couldn't do anything for a patient. It was a shock...."

Was Olds too fond of the scalpel? "Basically, he would tackle anything," said Woodruff. "Not because he wanted to, but because sometimes there was no alternative." As a result, Dr Olds acquired a reputation for cutting unnecessarily—being knife-happy. But he never operated impetuously or without adequate preparation. His colleagues attested that even for the commonest operations he would arrive first in the morning and read The Book—a beautiful surgical manual, probably from Johns Hopkins, which showed in photographic detail the layers he would meet as he went down to do the surgical repair. No matter how many times he had performed a procedure or what organ it was, they said, he always rehearsed in this way. So he always knew exactly what he would meet as he went in, and this freed him to deal with complications. "Far from being merely experimental," said Woodruff, "he had the courage to try when nobody else would."

A scrub nurse from the thirties said, "He did a lot of abdominals—appendixes, ovaries, cysts. But there were never so many hysterectomies as they do today—especially in young women. Then, there would have to be a really good reason, and they'd be up in their mid-forties or their fifties when he did. I think it's awful for them to have a hysterectomy that young. It affects your whole life. I've heard that Dr Olds was knife-happy," she said, "but I don't believe that. Sometimes he didn't know what was wrong. We couldn't do the scans and tests they do these days. Today they usually know just what they're going to find. But not in those days. He'd have to operate, and almost always he'd find something that was causing the problem."

Circumstances reinforced the notion that he cut too much. Most of his patients lived far from roads. Travel by water or over ice was difficult at best, and in spring and fall often impossible. Summer travel was easier; but except for Sunday afternoons after church in civil weather, catching and drying cod took every spare moment. People usually put things off until there was an emergency. Moreover, there was the lingering conviction that a hospital was a place where one went to die or to be cut up. "Dear Dr Olds," wrote a patient, "I been to your hospital several times but I'm not dead yet!" Olds once noted this bit of OPD conversation: "Oh, I knows that feller; he's the one was all cut to pieces up in Twillingate."

One day in 1939 Dr Olds made a house call through rough seas to a family who had sent word that their boy was ill. After examining him he said, "Your son has a bad appendix. You've got two choices—let me take him to the Hospital now, or let him 'bide here and die." After a brief family consultation the mother replied, "'E says he'll 'bide 'ere and die." Fortunately, the boy recovered.

This attitude was an old one, Dr Olds realized. Not long before the Bay was settled, hospitals in the Old Country had been merely asylums for poor and dying parishioners, places of death and decrepitude. By the mid-nineteenth century, hospitals had improved but still lost half their patients to post-operative infection. Said James Young Simpson, the Edinburgh surgeon who popularized chloroform after 1850, "A man laid on the operating table…is exposed to more chances of death than the English soldier on the field of Waterloo." Even after Joseph Lister introduced antisepsis, it took decades before abdominal surgery was at all safe. Surgeons still operated without rubber gloves until Hopkins' William Halsted introduced them in 1889. Dr Olds prided himself on his Hospital's low rates of infection and mortality, but his patients' medical fears were not wholly unfounded.

Naturally, when they did come he tried to make sure nothing else was overlooked— nothing that might flare up after they went back home. What worried him most was acute appendicitis in children over five and adults under fifty. His standard practice during abdominal surgery was to remove the appendix whether inflamed or not. Outport doctors called it the "Geographical Appendix" or "Island Appendix."

"The danger," said Dr John Sheldon, speaking of his own practice on New World Island before the causeway was built, "was that the ice would be in and the patient couldn't get to the Hospital. Given the situation, other physicians would have understood. The other thing along this line would be the combined operation, such as tonsils and piles simultaneously. That must have been the most awful awakening.... But one would be kept in the Hospital much longer for this than for just one. Olds once combined an appendectomy with a hernia operation. Ecke thought it very clever."

One timid young intern, later to become a well-known St John's surgeon, was greeted as follows on his first day: "This morning there's just a couple of small cases; you might as well do those. But there's an appendix as well."

"Sir," ventured the intern, "I haven't really done an appendix before."

"Well," said Olds, "that's what doctors do, you know—here, anyway." He assigned a supervising doctor and left him with, "So there it is; go on, do it." Later the intern proudly reported, "I did the incision, the drainage and the other thing, but the appendix had settled down. There's no pain, no temperature now, it's just great."

"Yes," said Dr Olds gently, "there's no problem *now*. But she happens to live on an island up the coast. And when she gets an appendix attack in February there's no way she's gonna get here. She's likely to die on that island."

Dr David Parsons came to Twillingate in 1953 from the Royal Victoria Hospital in Montreal. "After that winter," he recalled, "I came to appreciate...that he was not knife-happy, but doing what he could to *help* the people, to relieve them of their symptoms as quickly as possible. Regarding the Geographical Appendix—which was done not only in Twillingate but all around the Island—he'd say, 'That's fine. But wait'll you've been here in the spring of the year when the ice is coming in or going out. You can't get across. And that person is out there, and their appendix grumbles. Take it out.' He did the same with bad teeth. He had no financial motive. Under his Blanket Plan it didn't make any difference whether he did one case or twenty that day."

Dr Sheldon offered further insight into why some saw Olds as being knife-happy. "Patients were more or less self-selected and came to the Hospital confident that there was something wrong, something that needed doing, and that Dr Olds was the man to do it. His investigations would last a day or two and might include fluoroscopy or barium enema or an upper GIC—that's a stomach X-ray. And he would look at those films himself, review the blood tests and quickly decide whether there was serious disease. If there was, he would proceed either to a definite operation that was planned beforehand or he would do a laparotomy—an exploratory operation. And whatever he found, he would proceed to deal with it surgically. So most patients who went to the Hospital in those days *expected* to have surgery. As a family doctor I felt a great responsibility to make sure my referrals really needed surgery. That's what they expected and that's what they got."

During Olds' early years, most bone surgery in Newfoundland was done by the two Acker brothers, Drs Tom and Jack, who came from Halifax and put on clinics in Corner Brook and St John's. Local physicians unfairly nicknamed them "The Hacker Brothers." The two did mostly what doctors call "gross surgery"—rough orthopedics for bad cases. Most of what Olds did was by necessity also rough; but he was trained in advanced orthopedics. Between 1932 and 1960 he did 175 spinal fusions—not to mention twenty-four hip fusions and hundreds of knee, ankle and elbow procedures. To fuse a joint means to immobilize it with a bone splint taken in those days from elsewhere in the patient's body. It was his way of curing a bad back or a TB bone. Some of his fusions didn't work; but most patients were happy with the results. Their back no longer pained, the TB was arrested. But the St John's orthopedic community roundly criticized him for this.

Looking back a few decades, noted Newfoundland orthopedic surgeon Dr Edward Shapter could afford to be more objective. "I still see," he said in 1989, "people from Springdale, Roberts Arm and that area whose backs John fixed twenty-five, thirty or forty years before, who have worked all or most of that time. Now of course they've got a related problem, not of John's making. Sometimes their X-rays don't look the best," said Dr Shapter, "but they are very happy and the fixation is good. He took a TB spine or a painful back—it didn't make any difference—and he put it at rest. It got better. In the wintertime when the men weren't fishing he'd bring them in—the chronic low back pain, the injured worker, the fisherman who hurt his back in the summertime—and fuse them. The TB of course had to be done early; they couldn't wait for that."

Dr Olds used what was called the Hibbs Fusion, which he sometimes modified and called the Olds Fusion. It was one of the first ways, a simple technique now regaining favour. With the patient lying face down he cut a V-shaped groove down the spinous processes using a power-driven saw of his own design. With the same saw he took from the patient's tibia, or shin bone, a matching sliver about one-quarter inch wide—the length depending on how many vertebrae he wanted to fuse—dropped it in the groove, and sewed up the ligaments with sutures that would absorb. The whole procedure took him half an hour or less. How far up he fused the vertebrae depended on the extent of damage; sometimes he went above the hips, to the sixth or seventh vertebra or even higher.

Because he did only urgent cases, Olds needed no prolonged investigations and fine X-rays and specialist studies to show the disease in an early stage; it was usually beyond that. "Today," said Shapter, "we would treat such patients with braces and exercises and back education; weight loss, stop smoking, all that stuff. Olds would tell us, 'You're wasting your time. It's cheaper and easier and more accessible to do a fusion.'"

Sometimes patients came in excruciating pain from hip or other joints seized or deformed by calcium deposits. Dr Shapter recalled a fifteen-year old girl from Birchy Bay referred to him for leg surgery around 1967. "Olds had operated on her when she was nine and done a fine job on her leg. He was doing an arthroplasty—rebuilding a hip. This wasn't heard of in Newfoundland except in St John's. From the Smith-Petersen group in Boston he'd learned how to do what we call the cup arthroplasty—putting in a prosthesis. In other words, you ream out the hip socket, and make a steel cup to cover the head of the femur so the ball and socket can articulate without the bones rubbing together. He was advanced." And the reaming tools were of his own making.

Because Olds ignored accepted preventative and so-called conservative management, said Shapter, the St John's doctors misunderstand his work. They failed to grasp the social implications of what it was like to work year after year with a back pain that would put you in bed in the middle of the fishing season. Olds would do that fisherman tomorrow or the next day, put him in a cast and ask him to come back in four or five months. By then the back would usually be better. So people would travel far to see him. They came from Brookfield in Bonavista Bay, up to Badger's Quay, along the coast to the Straight Shore, right west to Bay of Islands. "I don't think Olds had any great regard for St John's medicine at the time," said Dr Shapter.

Not only patients sought him out. The medical students who arrived each summer from Hopkins, Harvard and elsewhere came as much to work with John Olds as to practice frontier medicine. Dr Cyril ("Skid") Walshe had heard of him in St John's even before he attended Dalhousie University's medical school. "I knew Lou Lawton had been there already. They said he was a very brave surgeon, a good surgeon with good judgment, that he would try things." Dr George Battcock of St John's had come to Twillingate in 1950 by much the same route: "I heard of him at Dalhousie. He was considered a good and experienced surgeon. Pat Whalen, a year ahead of me, was down there with him a year, also Bob Lawton...I thought it would be a good place to do a year's surgery, good exposure. His ability as a surgeon was remarkable. I haven't seen a better technician anywhere than

John Olds." Dr Battcock must have impressed Olds too. "George," he said when Dr Battcock was leaving, "you don't need to go back; you stay with me."

Newton E. Hyslop, a third year Harvard summer extern at Twillingate in 1960, recorded an incident he never forgot, and which, incidentally, proved that Olds could manage even vascular surgery when he had to.

> This past week I have had a chance to see the fantastic John McKee Olds at work. Alec Smith and I made a rather bad blunder when he and I were doing a vein stripping for varicose veins. Alec wished to isolate the femoral vein and catch the tributaries there, so we exposed the femoral triangle, but not clearly enough. And he began to tie off branches before everything had been anatomically demonstrated. In due time we tied and cut a rather large vein which I thought to myself too large to be the greater saphenous. When he called for the vein stripper, I thought the time had come to point out that the vein dipped rather deeply into the muscle tissue for as superficial a vein as the greater saphenous. I felt sure it was the femoral, the total great vein drainage from the leg. He hesitated, and then thought about it. Too late, we began to identify the structures and found that, indeed, we had ligated and divided the femoral vein.

> The call was sent for Dr Olds. And in the next half hour he did as beautiful a piece of vascular surgery in approximating the severed, delicate femoral vein as is done anywhere, I am quite sure. It didn't leak a bit when he finished. And the rest of the vein stripping was carried out in grand style by the master himself. We both felt chagrined...for it might have meant the loss of the leg.

Alf Dennison and Alec Smith had earlier called him "only a fair surgeon," but now they changed their minds. "Other surgery I have seen John Olds do," said Hyslop, "includes a cholecystectomy [removal of gallstones], mid-thigh amputation, resection of a neuroma [removal of a nerve tumor], several appendectomies and a handsome gastrectomy [stomach surgery]. He also does cataract removals, chest surgery (he's known for his skill in thoracotomies [lung removal] and thoracoplasties [rib removal to collapse TB lung]; people come from Corner Brook with its large hospital, internists and specialists in every branch of medicine for this and other surgery, much to the disgust of the Corner Brook doctors), and eye testing several nights a week, sending away the prescriptions for glasses to St John's."

"In the Operating Room he is a veritable lion," recalled Dr Hyslop. His reaction to minor as well as major annoyances is 'God damn it, Rose; why the hell can't you—? I've told you fifty times to do it this way!' Rose, his scrub nurse of many years, is used to being his buffer and rarely utters a word of reply. Outside the abdomen, to put it surgically, he is witty, charming and engaging."

Dr Raymond Yerkes of Harvard Medical School, another summer extern, told David Olds in 1992, "I was always very moved by your father. He certainly fits in somewhere with the 'caring crusty old cantankerous men' of the world. His skill and gut common sense amazed me. Your dad was [that rarity], the sophisticated frontier hero, man of all seasons, saint and sinner, scientist and pragmatist, who had guts to take on just about anything."

Dr Mike Maquire remembered such a case: "There was one fellow had a terrible pain in his face, what's called *tic douloureux*. It came from the fifth nerve, which is responsible for sensation along the side of the face. In those days there wasn't much you could do for it. Sometimes they used to inject the nerve with alcohol and this would sort of numb it. This man had been elsewhere to get injections and all. It didn't work.

"And I remember, Olds did the most radical thing," said Maguire. "He severed the fifth nerve where it goes into the skull. It was a big operation and a dangerous one. Now he could be criticized for doing this, but the fellow was delighted. He was going around with the side of his face all twisted up, but he didn't care. 'Eh, b'y,' he said, 'I got nar pain now!' I feel that in those days Olds was justified in doing it."

A nurse who worked with him in the early years said that while he was willing to experiment, "the patient always came first. He would try three procedures to see what was best. For example, hysterectomy—he tried vaginal once and the patient died from bleeding. He never did it again." Dr Walshe was with him from 1947 to 1950 and recalled Olds' first use of the suprapubic prostate method, that is, through the bladder. "We got a book out and read up on it and he said, 'Well, we'll try this fellow by the book.' And it worked out all right; there was less bleeding."

The rarity of malpractice suits in his day may have worked in his favour. If he erred, it was usually forgiven. At a dinner in his honour in 1974 he joked, "I only made one mistake: I once left a pair of small tweezers in a patient." She had come back complaining of abdominal pain when she bent over, and an X-ray revealed the reason. He said, "Well, you can tell the world, or you can let me remove it. It'll only take ten minutes." She cheerfully chose the latter.

Some called him a pioneer like Grenfell. While Dr Olds did pioneering work on medical insurance, TB surgery and Seal Finger in the Bay, he was not in the least like a medical missionary. While admiring the great man, he felt that Grenfell was perhaps only average as a doctor. He called his famous *Lost on the Ice* story "damned foolishness"—said the local people had told him not to go that day. And Olds certainly would not have allowed anyone to put scripture passages over the door of *his* Hospital, as Dr Grenfell had done in St Anthony.

When Dr Ted Shapter was growing up, his first feeling upon hearing about Olds was, "Well, here's this great god; what's he doing in Twillingate?" Later he understood. "His shyness and sheer workload made him avoid much dialogue with the patient. And the people had great faith. They used to debate in the 1950s who was more important—the doctor or the teacher. When it came right down to it, the doctor had a slight edge. And among doctors the surgeon was Number One. Even the anesthetist took orders from the surgeon. John Olds had an aura," said Shapter. "In some cases eighty percent of his success came from it."

Herb Gillett, Hospital Director from 1963 to 1981, said, "In his day J. M. Olds was Newfoundland's top surgeon. Dr Dinty Moore was one of the best in St John's. Forty years ago when I was in there on my honeymoon he said to me, 'You're fortunate to have J. M. Olds; I wish we had him here.' He undertook surgery that no other doctor would do. His infection rate was lower than in St John's. I knew this nurse Kyle that worked with him, who said that some of his surgery was fantastic. His hands, see boy, were just as steady as a rock. He was born to it."

Chapter Twenty-Two

Consumption

*"The Commissioners I think would be glad to shut
their eyes to the problem."*
— Dr Olds to Dr Charles Curtis

"I skated in the water. That's how I caught it. I was playing hockey on the harbour that winter, early part of January, and I went in the water. I got 'flu and I developed pneumonia. In the winter it was hard to get to a doctor. And I was using the old remedies—cod liver oil and everything—and by 'n' by I got so bad that I was drawed down on one side. So they took me to the Hospital. Dr Olds took X-rays right away. And he said to my dad, 'Your son is in hard shape. He's got TB; there's a big grey sore up on his lung. He's a sick boy.' I'll never forget that. He wasn't talking very loud; I don't think he wanted me to hear. But I was standing just clear, and I did.

"I went in there 119 pounds. I had double pneumonia, I had TB. But now we were taking thirty-two pills a day—PAS, that's what they were called. Big brown pills, almost as big as a small cent, oval. And we'd take a little white pill a day—New Drug, we called he. PAS and New Drug; we had a song made up about it. This and the streptomycin—that was a needle, every morning six o'clock, in the hip. They used to sterilize the needle and use it again; they had no money, see. Someone said they were getting six dollars a day from the Government for we fellers with TB, a special grant. Because there was a lot of TB people out there.

"When I started putting on weight, Dr Olds he was some proud. Every Sunday morning we'd get weighed. The aide would come around with this spring balance—a weighing machine on wheels—and weigh us all. And Monday morning that'd be marked on our chart, how much we gained. I gained seven, eight pound a week. I was gettin' better, see. And he used to come in Monday, 4:00 to 4:30 PM.

"'Boy,' he said, 'eight pounds—eight pounds in a week! And you're telling me the grub is no good!' We used to always complain about the grub, because it *was* bad.

"When I come out I was 200 pounds. In a year. The food wasn't good, but they gave us eggs cooked overnight.... I could eat a half-dozen of them! And porridge—you could turn your plate bottom up without it falling out, it was so caked. This is the truth. Anyway, I got fat, really fat. I never had a stitch of clothes to wear when I come out; everything was too small.

"When they discharged me, he come in my room. I was dressed. And he said, 'You're goin' home.'

"'Yes, Doctor.'

"He looked at me and said, 'Now, you've gained a lot of weight. That's hospital weight; that'll go off you. Go home, and don't do anything but walk around for three months. And then come back and see me.'

"So I went home. I was only home about a month and I had no money and my Dad had no money. I went in the lumberwoods for two months. And I come out—big, now, strong—had my muscles built up. I went up to see him. He put me up on the table, and when he sounded me he said, 'You're in perfect health and perfect shape. What have you been doing for yourself?'

"I stopped a little while. 'What've you been doing?' he said again.

"'In usin' the bucksaw,' I said, sheepish-like.

"Oh, he cussed me! But he sove my life, definitely."

Contrary to popular belief, *Mycobacteria tuberculosis* is not highly infectious. Although the bacillus is endemic in fish, amphibians, birds, mammals—notably cows—and man, compared to the common cold virus it is delicate and reclusive. Hospital workers who can take precautions seldom catch it—though in the old days of sputum cups and no masks, many nurses and some doctors did.

To become epidemic, the tubercule bacillus needs ideal conditions. Otherwise it behaves like a smouldering ember in the woods—fairly harmless until exposed to ample dry fuel and wind. To become epidemic, TB needs active carriers mingling with ill-nourished people in warm, crowded conditions, preferably coughing and spitting and sharing cups and utensils. This is almost a portrait of the Newfoundland outport kitchen of the thirties, especially in winter when people gathered around the *Waterloo* or *Maid of Avalon* stove for warmth and society.

If, under such conditions, there is moreover a shortage of hospitals, sanatoria and medical staff and a general lack of disease awareness, an epidemic is likely. And until social conditions are improved, it will, like a raging forest fire, be almost impossible to curb. This too describes Newfoundland during the Depression and War years.

Even before Dr Olds arrived in 1930, tuberculosis was the Bay's greatest medical challenge. Nowhere in North America save in rural Quebec was the disease in all its forms so entrenched and so virulent. Had antibiotics and social relief not arrived when they did, a whole generation of Newfoundlanders would have been crippled and lost. This wasn't romantic, Keatsian TB. It was a horrible, debilitating, spreading rot of the organs and bones, unstoppable until conditions were changed. It afflicted children, mothers, wage earners, old men. It frightened people in the same way cancer and AIDS would at the end of the twentieth century. In Susan Sontag's words, consumption was "intractable and capricious," an "insidious, implacable thief of life." They shrank from it in fascinated horror.

It was Dr Olds' fate to arrive just as this monster was rousing itself. And, though well aware that surgery alone could never eradicate it, he had to rescue as many as he could from its jaws. Until streptomycin arrived after the War, doctors could only advise rest, sunshine, fresh air and better diet. Misguided though it was, the prescription did some good in the early stages of the disease. However, the Bay had no regional prevention program before the Newfoundland Tuberculosis Association was formed in 1946, nor any detection system save the *Bonnie Nell* and Olds' clinics for babies and school children. He simply had to deal with TB cases as they appeared.

Except for the meningeal form—TB of the brain or spinal cord lining—all were long-term cases. The three most common forms which Dr Olds met were pulmonary or lung TB, bone TB (half as many) and abdominal TB. Genito-urinary, glandular and meningeal TB were the least common. By the time his patients arrived, their symptoms were usually obvious—spitting of blood, crippled limbs, night sweats. Sulfa and penicillin were ineffectual. Even cases discovered by stethoscope and referred to Twillingate were already entrenched. Until streptomycin became available, surgery followed by bed rest and vitamin supplements was often the only option.

Until the Corner Brook sanatorium opened in 1958, Dr Olds accepted all the cases for which he had room. In the worst years, forty to fifty percent of his beds were occupied by long-term TB patients, especially in the winter when he did most of his hip and spine repairs. Since most patients had no money, this put a big strain on Hospital finances. Fortunately, the Commission of Government recognized the problem in time and reimbursed the Board $5,000 a year under its pauper relief program in return for monthly case reports.

In September 1936 Dr Charles Curtis, Head Surgeon at St Anthony, wrote John Olds saying, "I told Mr Lodge the Commissioner, who was here on Saturday, that I thought tuberculosis was increasing and he doubted my statement. What do you think? Is it increasing in your district?" Dr Curtis also wanted to know about Twillingate's treatment regimes. In a two-page, typed response Dr Olds replied:

> The percentage of [TB] in the Hospital from 1924 to 1936 was 16% of the admission rate. During the year 1935-36 [it] was 27%.... The criterion

for admission may be different. However I feel that we have not been any more partial to admitting tuberculosis than [in] the past.... Of course, we see many cases which we do not admit, being too far advanced. The Commissioners I think would be glad to shut their eyes to the problem.

Pulmonary [cases are treated by] absolute rest in bed, some sort of tonic, possibly cod oil or anything to keep their appetites good and if possible a collapse of the lung, either a pneumothorax or a more permanent thoracoplasty. Bone [cases] are treated by cast, sunlight or artificial ultraviolet light and a fusion in all possible cases. I agree with you that tuberculosis is a tremendous problem. I see no way out of the difficulty along therapeutic lines. The economical condition has fallen so badly; home conditions have grown worse; the food worse; and until there is a return to at least the possibility of getting food I do not feel there will be any decrease in the incidence of [TB] no matter how much it is treated.

Of course the first line of defence was to excise the infected part. In 1933, with Dr Parsons away and Dr Goodwin assisting, he mentioned removing a TB thumb, a TB foot and TB lesions from a femur and an elbow. He also did four spinal fusions, and two hip fusions. He knew that movement abets TB. If the infected structure can be immobilized, the germ normally encases itself in a tubercle and goes dormant. This is why, with tuberculosis of the spine, for instance, he fused the affected vertebrae and put the patient in a back cast for several months. The patient lost mobility but the disease was arrested within a year.

Pneumothorax—periodic insertion of sterile air into the pleural sac to collapse the lung—was Dr Parsons' standard treatment for pulmonary tuberculosis. It was the same treatment which Dr Norman Bethune took while in Trudeau Sanatorium at Saranac Lake in upstate New York in 1927, and which he credited with halting his illness. Olds did seven in 1933. Dr Olds relied less on air injection after Parsons left, but he did use phrenico-tomy and phrenemphraxis, wherein the phrenic nerve which controls the diaphragm was cut or crushed, respectively.

Thoracotomy—actual removal of diseased lung tissue, usually from the lower lobes where collapse therapy was less effective—was not done rou-tinely in Newfoundland until after 1950. The first thoracotomies were performed by Dr Thomas at St Anthony using techniques he learned from Steele. Although Dr Olds did one in 1934, this is the only recorded instance. Since this was well before the technique had been perfected, perhaps the 1934 operation failed. There was a high risk of cutting the pleural cavity—but it avoided the mutilation of thoracoplasty. It would be in character if he abandoned it as too risky. However, he did a few after 1960, having perhaps studied the procedure at Haverstraw in New York State in 1955.

The most drastic lung collapse therapy was thoracoplasty—making a hole in the rib cage directly over the infected part. Dr John Alexander and his pupil John Steele had pioneered the procedure in the United States in the 1920s, and its leading proponent in Canada was Dr Edward Archibald of Montreal's Royal Victoria Hospital. Despite the high risk of cutting major arteries and veins, and the mutilation it caused in those days before physiotherapy, it was the most effective method available for advanced lung cases. The operation was performed in one, two or even three stages spanning several months, and it was done as a last resort. Newfoundland's first thoracoplasty was done probably in 1927 on a young fisherman at the Grenfell Mission Association Hospital in St Anthony by Dr Charles Lockwood of Pasadena, California. During the operation Dr Curtis asked Dr Lockwood if he ever had problems with the procedure. "Never," replied the doctor. Just then he accidentally nicked the subclavian artery and hot blood sprayed them. The nick was swiftly sutured and the patient lived to be an old man. Dr Curtis did some thoracoplasties, but it wasn't until after 1949, when his assistant Dr Gordon Thomas returned from studying with Dr Steele at Marquette University in Milwaukee, that St Anthony used this and other techniques routinely.

Thoracoplasty worked best when the lesion was confined to the upper lung and discovered early. Although a smaller set of ribs sometimes grew back to partly cover the space, the patient, even after the lung recovered, was left permanently slope-shouldered and hollow-chested on that side. However, faced with the alternative of interminable bed rest with no certainty of success, most patients counted the deformity worth it.

After 1935 is offset by a steady increase in thoracoplasties in Twillingate. Since there is no record that Dr Parsons used the procedure, all the early thoracoplasties done in Twillingate were likely Dr Olds'. The first two were done in 1934, and three more in 1935. The next are reported for 1939, 1940 and 1941, when he did one each year. These would be mostly one- or two-stage operations. Then in 1942 he performed four, after which the numbers rose rapidly. It is possible that until then he had never seen the procedure done. He may have gone to St John's to observe Dr Garrett Brownrigg, the only other surgeon then regularly doing this procedure in Newfoundland. At any rate, Dr Olds did seven operations in 1943, thirteen in 1944 and six in 1945. After the War, when he was no longer alone in the OR, the numbers increased again. He performed fifteen in 1946, twenty-four in 1947, forty in 1948, twenty-four in 1949 and twenty in 1950.

Laboratory technician Bud Young saw Olds' war on tuberculosis played out patient by patient, month by month in the delicate greys and blacks of hundreds of X-ray plates. Of pneumothorax he said:

You had to do it gradually—say 50 cc's today and 50 cc's tomorrow. The air stayed in the cavity and was left to dissipate on its own. With an apical lesion they might want to collapse the lung down to see if it would cure. And after it had been down for so long a time, it would gradually absorb air and expand. If the lesion was still there and was active, then he'd go in and do the thoracoplasty. And they'd do those in about three stages. First two ribs—that'd be one operation. Then they'd wait for a few weeks, and do the third rib, fourth, fifth, sixth or so on. And with the third operation they would do the bottom four or five ribs. Eventually they'd do all the ribs on one side; the patient's chest would be well down then.

It was a drastic operation but it worked. There's people going around Twillingate today who were done back in the 1930s. Often he'd only do the first stage. The most had two stages done. But in extreme cases—if the lesion was in the base of the lung—they had to do all three stages. You had to work from the top down.

Between 1941 and 1946, Notre Dame Bay Memorial Hospital treated over three hundred patients for TB. While pulmonary tuberculosis accounted for nearly half these, it represented only six percent of the deaths. Meningeal TB showed up only ten times, but in those days all cases proved fatal. Next to pulmonary tuberculosis was bone TB, accounting for 108 cases, of which fewer than one per cent died. After that came abdominal TB, genito-urinary TB, general thoracic cases and glandular TB.

After Dr Stanton Hardy left in 1943 he was unable to enlist and found work with the Lederle Drug Company of New York. The next year he sent Olds a dozen vials of penicillin, whose germ-killing properties Sir Alex Fleming had first recognized clinically in 1928. It was one of the first in a series of chemical antibiotics which were soon to revolutionize medicine worldwide. Twillingate started using it only four years after Chain and Florey figured out how to produce it in quantity.

"We had the first penicillin in Newfoundland for sure," declared Bud Young.

I remember the first dozen vials we had come. They were all crude, in a glass vial, sealed with flame on the top. No name on it. Enough to treat two patients, and only to be used in extreme cases—for streptococcus and staphylococcus. You had to find out which kind of staph you were dealing with before you could give it.

Stanton Hardy kept us going with that for a while. Then, two or three years later, they came out with aureomycin, the forerunner of all our broad-spectrum tetraclyclines today. Lederle was the first to produce it. Hardy sent about 1,100 bottles. That's how John discovered the cure for Seal Finger. I'd say we were probably the first to get aureomycin too. When I first came, Seal Finger was treated by amputation; not long after that, none of these people were being amputated because aureomycin was curing them. And John discovered this.

"We didn't buy this stuff from the drug companies," said Young. "We got it direct, sort of undercover, thousands of dollars worth, a thousand vials at a time. They were using it in the States, but there was still a lot of experimentation. This is how he got away with it. It hadn't been on the market very long."

In those days antibiotics were expensive. When streptomycin was introduced at the Sanitorium in St John's early in 1947, the daily dose of two grams cost $14.00. Only the well-off could afford it. One St John's citizen had to sell $1,400 worth of property to finance his TB treatments. Without their Lederle pipeline, Twillingate could not have afforded the new drugs either. "We got it for nothing," said Young, "and John sold it for thirty cents a dozen." He recalled how a prominent Twillingate citizen went to St John's, saw a doctor there, and was given a prescription for a new "wonder drug." The first thing she did on her return was to bring up this new drug to show Dr Olds. "So John took her into the pharmacy and pointed to maybe fifty bottles of the stuff." In 1947 or possibly the year before, Dr Hardy also sent a batch of the new drug streptomycin. Discovered by Dr Selman A. Waksman and others in 1943, it was the first drug to show real promise against TB. Dr Lou Lawton tried in 1945 or 1946 to obtain some through an uncle at the Parke-Davis drug company, but without success.

St Anthony received $7,000 worth of streptomycin in 1947. By 1957 this drug, along with its successors, was ousting thoracoplasty and other drastic lung surgery at Twillingate and elsewhere. In time these drugs brought about the closure of the sanatoria in St John's, Corner Brook and St Anthony. Although Olds and his colleagues performed twenty thoracoplasties in 1952, Twillingate's use of such operations steadily declined after that. From 1951 until 1957 they averaged only eight a year—one-third the rate for the preceding decade. In all, John Olds did or supervised a total of 211 thoracoplasties between 1934 and 1957.

In 1949, the year Newfoundland joined Canada, they were averaging 100 TB deaths a year. In 1955 the number was twenty and in 1965 only three. While the province's percentage of new active cases was still higher than the national average, by 1980 it was about on a par. This victory was the result of an immense team effort that held the monster at bay until more potent weapons could be deployed, namely streptomycin in 1946-47, PAS (para-amino-salicyclid) in 1948 and BCG or TB vaccine in 1951. That arsenal was completed in 1952 with the bactericide Isoniazid or Rimifon and in later years Ethambutol and Rifampin.

In 1950, at the 50th anniversary conference of the Canadian Tuberculosis Association in Vancouver, Olds praised the BCG vaccine and got this resolution passed: "Resolved that full consideration be given to the use of BCG in all the provinces, especially those where Tuberculosis has a high incidence rate."

Until those weapons came along, John Olds and his Twillingate team battled the dragon alone and without real hope. They did it surgically, by widespread testing on the clinic boats *Bonnie Nell I* and *II*, by school and well baby clinics and through educational efforts such as his take-home leaflet for former TB patients and his booklet *Tuberculosis: Prevention and Treatment at Home*.

In 1936, poverty was the chief accessory to the crimes of *Mycobacteria tuberculosis*. In 1944 Newfoundlanders ate a little better, but still knew little about their killer. At a public meeting that year Dr Olds declared, "TB cannot be cured out of this country; it has to be educated out." After serving as fleet doctor to the seal hunt in 1947 he told the Newfoundland Fisheries Board, "Most [sealers] are all right, but after returning to St John's I examined a steward who was dying of tuberculosis. He said he 'got on all right because he did not have to work hard.' Olds urged the Board to require a health certificate of every sealer in future. With characteristic understatement he added, "To have him handle food for two months was not to the benefit of those he served." To anyone listening in the House of Assembly or on Water Street, his meaning was clear.

Chapter Twenty-Three

A Very Fine Crochet Hook

"He would improvise, invent, make anything he wanted."

— Nurse Jessie Drover

When seventeen-year-old Bud Young reported for work at Notre Dame Bay Memorial Hospital the second day of 1934, he may have expected to meet a physician in a three-piece business suit seated in a studded leather chair behind a polished desk. Instead he found his new boss in the lab, kneeling on the floor in a soiled white smock.

> He had this big square tin can there, rigged up to a revolving cylinder with graph paper around it, and a hypodermic needle with ink in it to draw a graph. The can was open in the top, placed bottom up in a tank of water and suspended there by a string up over a frame. It contained pure oxygen, he said, and the idea was to breathe in and out of this can through a tube. As you breathed in—used up the oxygen—the can would sink, and when you exhaled CO^2, it would rise. He got me to try it, and explained that I was breathing through soda lime, which absorbed the carbon and returned only the unused oxygen. The needle touched the slowly revolving electric drum and ran up and down as I breathed, recording the difference between CO^2 breathed in and released. This is your Basal Metabolism Rate or BMR. He told me he needed it for diagnosing thyroid troubles, people with goiters and such.

This began a forty-year apprenticeship for the bright young man who was to become his pharmacist and laboratory technician. Working with Olds was more fun than school had ever been. They calibrated the BMR device together, adjusting it for barometric pressure, temperature, patient's age and so on, and using a slide rule to figure it all out. "His machine wasn't very scientific," said Young, "but it worked. In the extreme range it worked perfectly. He didn't invent it; he just built his own. In those days we had no money."

Until the fifties they couldn't afford pre-mixed medicines either. Instead, they bought the materials in bulk and prepared the simple ointments, rubbing liniments, cough mixtures and sleeping medicines themselves, storing them in some twenty labelled glass gallon jugs. Dr Olds showed the young man how to do it and later entrusted him with the pharmacy. There were no drug stores then; everything came in bottles, which people brought back for refills. One day while Bud was wrestling with the jugs and stoppers and little funnels, Dr Olds came in. "You know, Bud," he said, "there must be a better way." He took a two-holed rubber stopper, fitted one hole with a glass tube bent to a 'J' shape over a Bunsen burner, and put a hypodermic syringe in the other. "After that," said Bud, "you just stuck your bottle up underneath the spout and pumped it full. We rigged fifteen or so bottles of liquid medicine that way."

Vaseline, lard, zinc oxide and boric ointment came in large tins and had to be laboriously dolloped out with a spatula. Olds took a half-gallon bottle, bored a small hole in the bottom, and inserted a rubber bulb and valve off a blood pressure cuff. Upended on a rack and fitted with a sliding metal lid such as stores used for dispensing molasses, the jars gave up their contents with a few squeezes of the bulb. To refill them, Bud simply removed the bulb and poured the melted ointment in.

Dr Olds invented medical contrivances and instruments the way a jazz pianist improvises melody. Give him a box of metal and electrical scraps, a few nights to scribble and cuss and test, and he would usually produce either a working replica of something in a catalog or an altogether new creation. Some of his inventions, for example the *Technitron* from his first year at Hopkins, could have made him rich. Perhaps the pirating of his idea soured him on the inventor's life. He never troubled himself much about patents afterward, except for a moulded glass boot he designed for patients with peripheral vascular disease. It utilized an electric air pump and a hollow rubber sock to rhythmically squeeze the leg and promote circulation. Manufactured in the States under the trade name *Pavex*, it died a quiet death. The only money he ever earned from medical tinkering came from his own Hospital Board. In 1937 they paid him $100 for adapting a hazardous X-ray unit to remote control. Twenty years later, he got $1,000 for converting an X-ray unit from single-plane to multi-level imagery or tomography.

All John's tinkering was done in his spare time, usually at night in the winter. Before and after the War were his most productive times. Some of his things, like his wave power projects, were purely recreational, a way of unlacing the tightness of the day. Some of them, like longliner drive shafts for fishermen, were a service to the community. The medical innovations, however, were an outgrowth of necessity. Dr Olds' improvisations, inventions and economies, replicated throughout the Hospital year after year, saved thousands of dollars and hundreds of hours.

Most of his medical contrivances he built in the workshop under the Staff House. Big jobs he tackled in the Hospital's well-equipped machine shop opposite the Boiler Room. Occasionally he tinkered at home. The Grand Central Station of these branching lines of endeavour was his office. It looked more like the lair of an inventor than the sanctum of a physician. Visitors wondered if they had come to the right place. On his desk, business letters lay next to *Popular Mechanics* and *The Lancet*; cotter pins, IV tubing and hose clamps vied for space with voltage meters and an old typewriter. His shelves groaned under electric motors, pump impellers, a gutted crank telephone, a dismantled oscillating fan. To disturb the sacred clutter was forbidden. Nobody much cared to; the pickled bodies of a set of full-term, still-born Siamese twins floating in a jar on the filing cabinet seemed like sentinels.

For a man like that, Notre Dame Bay Memorial Hospital was heaven. Always in need, always grateful for the smallest saving in money or time, it mothered his inventiveness in a way Yale never had. Before one creation was finished, another was teasing his brain. Not all his ideas were original. Perhaps to revenge his *Technitron*, Dr Olds had no scruples about pirating from medical catalogs.

"The Drip," however, *was* an original. A scrub nurse who returned from training at Englewood Cliffs, New Jersey in 1933 said she had never seen or heard of one. A contraption for rinsing and draining the body after surgery, it began around 1933 as a couple of half-gallon jugs connected to the patient and each other with tubes and activated by gravity and suction and cuss words. Nurse Jessie Drover called it a nightmare. "It was supposed to deliver a little fluid, just a little, all the time," she said. "It would drip, but the thing was always going out of kilter. John would come down around 10 PM on rounds and he'd arrange it for however many drops he wanted overnight. And by and by he'd come back up, and the drip would be stopped, or slowed down, or going faster.

"'Who in the name of God has been fooling with this?' he would shout.

"'John,' I'd say, 'nobody touched it.'

"'Well,' he'd say, 'somebody touched it. It doesn't go wrong by itself.' The mere fact he'd invented it made it sort of sacred."

In 1936 he got Alfred to mail him the motor from an oscillating fan. Then for several years he fiddled with timer switches and valves, trying to build an electric stomach pump. Along the way he crossed The Drip with various species of intravenous apparatus. An early model employed a one-litre bottle on the floor beside the bed, and one slung from a metal IV tree, both connected by valve-equipped plastic tubes that alternately flushed and siphoned. His drips might contain saline solution, antibiotics, glucose or plain distilled water.

In the spring of 1956 he told his mother, "I have completely redesigned & rebuilt the stomach pump. It works fine & even has red & green lights to tell whether it is sucking or pumping without taking the cover off. Also it is much smaller." By fall it was running for days continuously without a hitch. He drafted a paper on it but never got around to writing or illustrating it. No picture of it is to be found.

Most of John Olds' inventiveness was focused on the Operating Room, where every movement saved, every instrument improved, every procedure refined could save time and human life. "Sometimes," said Nurse Drover, "in the middle of a procedure John would send a nurse downstairs to this bench piled high with junk. 'Bring me up so-and-so,' he'd say, and describe it. And you'd go down there, in a panic to begin with because he was so short-tempered, and look through all this stuff. Sometimes you'd find it, sometimes you wouldn't."

"They were afraid to throw anything out," said Nurse Edith Simms. "He'd always remember that little something that might come in handy. He was always thinking what he could do for someone, what different instrument he could make, some problem he was trying to solve. His mind was so active...."

That was in the thirties. He was not different in the mid-fifties. "He was always eyeing your dental instruments," recalled Dr Mike Maguire. "He'd ask that if you were throwing any of them out, to make sure you passed them along to him. You had a job to keep him away from them."

"Mayme," he said one morning, poking his head in the office door, "have you got a very fine crochet hook?" Mayme Hewlett itched to say, "Planning to take up crocheting, Dr Olds?" But she knew how much he hated doing cataracts, so she answered, "No, Doctor; but I could bring one in this afternoon. What for, may I ask?"

"To make an instrument for a bad cataract operation," he said. He had to cut between the coloured iris and the white of the eye, he explained, and hook out the slippery lens. For that he needed a long thin instrument. He had a hunch that a tiny crochet hook, using CO^2 to freeze the tip if need be, might do the job. Mayme brought one in. He modified the tip and it worked well. This instrument, combined with his device for holding the eyeball steady, gave him a workable system.

The unhurried ritual of scrubbing and gowning up before operations had been mandatory in respectable hospitals since the twenties. First you stood before long-armed taps and soaped your hands and forearms. Then you took a large brush from a bowl of disinfectant and meticulously scrubbed every part of the hands and forearms, not forgetting the nails and between the fingers. This consumed a good five minutes. After rinsing off the soap under an elbow-activated tap, you were handed a sterile gown and cap by a nurse with sterilized tongs. You had to be put them on without touching anything unsterile and needed someone to tie the gown from behind. After powdering the hands from a small gauze bag, you pulled on sterile rubber gloves, tucked your sleeves into the wrists, donned a sterile gauze mask, rinsed the gloves and were ready. Scrubbing up took only eight or ten minutes but Olds resented even that.

He streamlined it in two ways. The first was his Automatic Hand Washer, which squirted hot water and liquid soap into a set of revolving brushes and cleaned the hands in half the time. The second was a one-piece, one-size-fits-all knitted wool cap and mask which could be pulled on quickly with no strings to tie. He had the Hospital seamstresses make several.

Inside the Operating Room, one of the slowest activities was sewing up wounds, especially in confined spaces or with tough tissues. For the former he soldered a curved needle to a pair of tonsil forceps. For the latter he took a lesson from the cobbler and devised a tiny awl which could be pulled rather than pushed through. That still left ordinary suturing. For a gall bladder operation or cesarian section this could mean patiently sewing layer after layer, from the inside out, for half an hour or more. In deep wounds the surgeon had to trade needle for scissors, snip, pick up the needle and place the next tiny stitch, over and over. For one so meticulous as he, it took a lot of everyone's time.

"A sharp, immediately available instrument for cutting sutures would be a great saver of time and motion," he wrote. "Ordinarily the little finger has little to do in an operative procedure; but, fitted with a knife-bearing sheath over the distal phalanx, it would become very useful as a suture cutter."

With Dr Maguire's help he designed and made a spring-loaded ring of smoothly moulded acrylic resin. The knife, pivoting on a pin inside a stainless steel case, was made from a broken safety razor blade—sharp, inexpensive and easily replaced. By pressing the side of his ring finger against a nubbin, Olds could flick the blade out, cut, and return it to its slot by simply letting go. A nylon leash prevented losing it inside the patient. He used his suture cutter all through the fifties and sixties and made copies for his colleagues, including John Sheldon. "It was beautifully made and brilliant in its simplicity," said Dr Sheldon, who kept it as a memento of The Old Man. Dr Olds wrote it up for publication but again never patented it.

Operating in deep wounds presented a different challenge. The human hand, holding a scalpel between thumb and fingers, is a fairly bulky object to insert between bile duct and liver, or a tonsil and palate. Olds' hands were small, but he made his right hand less obtrusive by taping a scalpel blade directly to the forefinger. This not only freed his thumb and middle finger to part the tissues ahead of the blade, but gave him greater precision. For a while he couldn't find a reliable wet adhesive. Gordon Stuckless suggested the soft waterproof plastic tape used for sealing underwater engine fittings.

Money was almost as precious as time. Stripping varicose veins called for a wire soft enough to snake along the vessel's curving path yet firm enough not to kink. He could buy vein strippers from a catalog but saw no reason to. The operation was crucial to remove the large bluish, worm-like lumps which developed in the legs of some child-bearing women. The abnormally high pelvic pressures of pregnancy had damaged the valves in the delicate leg veins, leading to ulcers, poor circulation and even the risk of a fatal embolism from wandering clots. Instead of opening the leg, the surgeon threaded a thick, flexible wire along the greater saphenous vein's course from groin to ankle, tied the ankle end to the wire and slowly pulled its many branching roots out. Any remaining knotted small veins were excised later. The patient could walk on her bandaged leg within two days, because the body quickly established a new vein network.

When Angus Dalley suggested using soldering wire, Olds had him make up several three-foot lengths. A scrub nurse recalled seeing these strippers in use. "He had little knobs or beads to put on the ends, different sizes. After each operation you'd clean it and roll it up into a little package and put it in a little tin. When vein-stripping was coming up, we sterilized it that morning. All we had was very small sterilizer."

She also recalled his "bone nibbler," a pair of modified pliers with recurved handles that enabled him to extract chips of bone for grafting. He also designed a "grabber," a standard clamp with the tip modified to grasp a tonsil, kidney or other small organ for removal, cutting or sewing. For tonsillectomy—where teeth, tongue, cheeks, soft palate, esophagus and bronchial tubes all get in the way—he invented an apparatus to keep the tongue depressed and the cheeks expanded. It had a light to illuminate the back of the throat. "Unfortunately," said Dr Lou Lawton, "half way through the operation all of this might collapse and we'd have to start over." Olds also modified a pair of pliers into a hemorrhoid snipper.

Thoracoplasty required two tools, one to strip back the tough intercostal muscle enclosing each rib and one to sever the bone. He made the rib stripper from a bent file with a sharpened loop welded across one end. For cutting ribs he needed a pair of sharp pincers small enough to insert between the ribs yet strong enough to shear bone cleanly, preferably with one hand. A saw was useless because of the flying bone dust and the proximity of heart and lung vessels. He made his rib shears from two strips of black quarter-inch steel about a foot long, hinged like scissors near one end but with the tips bent 90 degrees downward and meeting with a precise, powerful bite. They differed markedly from the earlier Bethune Rib Shear, a long-handled, curved instrument resembling garden shears.

In 1939 Dr Olds bought one of Newfoundland's first electrocardiographs, the little "Cardiette" made by Sanborn in the States. Its use of electrodes on different parts of the body to register electrical impulses probably gave him the idea for his "Nerve Locator." One day he asked Martin Young to go look for an old crank telephone. "I got one from Mr Fred Loder," said Young, "and brought it over. Dr Olds told me to stick on a couple of wires with probes attached. So we rigged it up and tested it. My hand was too insulated by calluses, but I cranked it up and tried it on his own hand and he said it was okay. He used that a long time."

Olds doted on electricity. It was tireless and cheap, the perfect labour saver. In the fifties he developed his own electrocautery. Cauterization had been used since ancient times to remove unwanted flesh, stop bleeding and sterilize wounds. By the late 1800s the various crude and cruel instruments had coalesced into a heated needle. This was used not only to seal the cut ends of small bleeder veins but also to perform surgery too fine for the smallest scalpels. Dr Olds, tired of heating and re-heating an ordinary needle over a Bunsen burner, challenged Gordon Stuckless, a former patient, to come up with an electrical model like the ones in the catalogs. Soon the young electronics technician brought back a prototype. It was, he said, "something like a little arc welder—low amp, high voltage."

Gord installed it on the Operating Room wall and over the next few months they refined it. One day when Gord was screwing it back on the wall, Dr Alf Dennison came in. "We ought to test it again," said Olds, winking at Alf. Suddenly Gord's arms were pinned and Olds, grinning wickedly, was waving the cautery in his face. "Gord," he said, "I know you've been wanting to get rid of that thing," and pointed to a small growth on his lip...." A deft pass, a "Phytt!" followed by the reek of burning flesh, and the wen was gone. The Stuckless-Olds electrocautery became a permanent OR fixture.

During a fast-paced operation he might use it every few minutes. That meant keeping it hot—too hot to safely set down. In 1959 he got Angus to weld a piece of half-inch copper pipe to a scissor-handled towel clip. With this "Needle Holder" clipped to the patient's coverings, the cautery was always ready and no one need to hand it to him or burn their hands on it. He intended to have the Hartz people in the US make a prototype but never got around to it.

For spinal fusions he had to cut a groove in the spine's projecting knobs and insert a matching sliver of bone taken from the patient's shin. Meanwhile, he needed metal retractors to hold back the patient's powerful back muscles. He made his retractors from soft copper straps about a foot long by two inches wide, bent to any shape he needed. Designing the saw proved more difficult. He wanted the sliver to fit on the first try, which was difficult with the standard carpenter-type bone saw. His amputation saw was made from a steel file and too heavy. A circular saw was too dangerous. The ideal tool would be a tiny band saw with a blade hard enough to stay sharp without snapping under strain. He settled on the main spring from a Victrola phonograph. To turn it, he would need a flexible dentist's drill cable powered by a small electric motor on the floor, with a thumb switch on the saw.

As usual there was no money to buy a motor. One day in 1940, watching a woman hemming a bed sheet on the Hospital's electric sewing machine, he realized that its 220 V motor would do perfectly. Next day he handed Elijah Dalley a coiled gramophone spring and six new triangular files. "Lige," he said, "I'm going to make a bone saw and I want you to file fine teeth in this spring for about ten inches." He sketched the blade running around two small spools, a driver and an idler, like a belt on pulleys.

A few days later Lige brought back what he wanted. He used this rotary saw for years, not only for bone work but as a cast saw. It had one bad habit. Sometimes the blade ran off its rollers and whizzed across the OR. "The saw amuses me," wrote Bob Ecke. "The operator has the greatest confidence but the assistant is always apprehensive...." The other problem was with the laundry department. "Often," said Nurse Drover, "when the women would arrive for sewing class or to mend the laundry, the sewing machine motor would be in the Operating Room. Miss Eddy would come to the door and knock very timidly and ask the nurse, "Is Dr Olds through with my sewing machine motor? 'Cause the women are here for sewing."

The Hospital got its first X-ray machine around 1936, a small 15 milli-ampere [mA] unit with a rectangular fluoroscopic screen. They used it mostly for bowel or stomach work with barium and normally the patient stood. In 1948 the Board bought an excellent 200 mA machine. "If you take a standard chest X-ray," explained Bud Young, "and you see a shadow on the lung, you don't know what's inside there; you can't see the extent of it. You have to do what is called 'cutting' or tomography—taking X-rays at different levels. Then if there's a cavity the pictures will show it up."

The General Hospital in St John's was doing tomography at this time, but Olds couldn't afford the equipment. During his rest cure at Summit Park Sanitorium in 1955-56, he saw how he could modify the new unit for tomography. "He mechanized it," recalled Young, "changed it, cut it down, tilted it for bowel work, worked the 'scope with a foot switch, cranked the bed up and down, did every damned thing with it."

"We had so many TB cases," said Dr Olds, "where we wanted to locate the level of the cavity more precisely. I modified the unit so that you could use it for making tomograms of the chest. The new unit was more powerful but it was also much heavier. Using it for tomography required a second person to push and pull the machine through a certain distance in a certain time, such as twelve inches in three or four seconds while changing the angle of the tube. I used two electric sewing machine motors geared 'way down so they were powerful enough to move the buckey," he explained. "This time I didn't steal them from the women...."

Now Bud could orchestrate any motion by flicking switches. This eliminated hand-cranking and reduced radiation hazard. "I'd do as many as twelve shots of one patient, all from the control room," he recalled. "By this time we were all conscious of the danger. In the early years," he said. "Olds never used a lead apron or goggles. I'd prepare the patient and go get him when I was ready. He'd come in and sit down on his chair—no protection in the world." Perhaps the lung ailment which afflicted him in the fifties started in this way. His 1948 machine performed well until the new Hospital opened in 1974. Meanwhile the Board had purchased two portable X-ray machines and a powerful *General Electric* portable for bed-side use.

Dr Olds thought nothing of converting existing equipment, even expensive equipment, to what he considered better uses. Twillingate's Iron Lung was a case in point. The thirties and forties were haunted by fears of a polio epidemic like the 1916 US outbreak which killed six thousand people and crippled twenty-seven thousand. There was no vaccine against it. Each reported case in Newfoundland and Labrador send ripples of fear through every community. Remembering his mother's bout with polio, John carefully read all he could find about it. The mid-1940s outbreak in the Canadian Arctic convinced him that cold was no deterrent. On the other hand, poor people seemed less prone than the well-to-do. He could only advise people to boil drinking water in summer and to avoid crowded places.

Because polio of the upper body could paralyze the breathing muscles, scientists had been trying to devise a respirator. After Harvard's Philip Drinker developed the Iron Lung in the thirties, Lord Nufield of the British Government promised one to every hospital in the Commonwealth. One day in 1940 a crate containing what looked like a giant's metal coffin arrived on the steamer. The apparatus had a rubber-lined hole in one end for the patient's head. An electric pump alternately lowered and raised the air pressure inside, causing the patient's chest to rise and fall eighteen or twenty times a minute. In this way it could maintain respiration until the patient recovered.

Parked in a Second Floor corridor, Twillingate's Iron Lung was comforting to have around. However, when no polio cases showed up, Dr Olds began to mutter against it. One year later Bob Ecke wrote, "We have used ours a lot, but never for a case of paralysis. It was a gold mine of useful things: the machine was put on the tonsil suction in the OR; the rubber mattress is used on the delivery table; the rubber hose is on a blower in the X-ray room and we use the top as an extra bed when we're crowded."

After the War, there was a surge in trans-Atlantic air traffic through Gander. Experts feared the virus had entered through Gander Airport and might break out at any time. On May 18th, 1945, the *Clyde* brought a sick baby with symptoms very like those of infantile paralysis. John and Dr Ecke worked half the night to reassemble the Iron Lung. Fortunately, the baby did not have polio. The machine was left intact for the summer, just in case. It was still there when Lou Lawton arrived that fall.

"Then one day we went up," said Lawton, "and the Iron Lung had become a cystoscopic bed." John had already made his own cystoscope—a thin, tube equipped with a tiny light for examining the urinary tract and bladder—and one day he realized that the Iron Lung was the perfect height for the awkward procedure.

As John's brother-in-law Doug Mott once remarked, many of John's ideas exceeded his capabilities. Nonetheless, if he suspected expertise in someone else, he was quick to enlist it. One day in 1954 he summoned Dr Maguire from the Dental Clinic to join a heated discussion. The South African Bert VanderBerg happened to be good at orthopedics and he wanted to buy a hip joint reamer. "What does it cost?" Dr Olds had asked. "Forty dollars in the catalog," VanderBerg had replied, prompting Olds to say, "Ridiculous price!" At this VanderBerg had launched into a tirade about not having proper equipment for his work. When Dr Maguire came in Dr Olds said, "He wants to buy that for forty bucks. Think we could make one?"

"I don't know," said Mike. "Probably could. What's it for exactly?"

"To shave out excess bone in the acetabulum."

"I'm sure we could." Dr VanderBerg rolled his eyes and left. They set about designing it. In the morgue Mike took an impression of the cup of the hip joint, copied it in plaster and made a wax pattern from which to cast the final bronze article. "We'll have to make a casting machine," said the dentist.

"How to you make a casting machine?" said Olds.

"The best way, apart from pouring, would be to steam-cast it."

"And how do we do that?"

"If we take a piece of four-inch pipe and fill it up with wet asbestos or something.... No, fill it with dental plaster and sand, and then when that hardens, melt out the wax and heat the metal and drive it in with steam pressure...."

"Let's do it!" said John.

Like a couple of boys making bows and arrows, they got a piece of pipe, put it in a vise and started in with a hack saw. "Aw, hell," said Olds after fifteen minutes, "this is a lot of work—let's make an electric saw." A week later he came back with a contrivance made from bits of bed post, a flat iron to weigh it down and an automatic mercury cut-off switch. He set it up and they went to lunch. When they came back the pipe still wasn't sawn through, but by early afternoon, after several visits to adjust the angle and change the blades, Dr Olds brought Mike the required piece, who prepared a mould and cast the reamer. All this kept them busy for many evenings and attracted much interest both inside and outside the Hospital. The reamer worked beautifully. Dr VanderBerg was happy. Olds then designed and cast a counterpart instrument, a cup-shaped reamer to fit over the femur's head to smooth it before attaching a steel cap.

In time his shears, reamers and a few home-made instruments would come to rest in a display case of the Twillingate Museum. These relics of a more austere era by no means exhaust the catalog of medical ideas and things which Dr Olds, driven by necessity and inventive exuberance, produced during his half-century in Twillingate. As early as 1933, when he was fighting to save young Harry Pynn, he contrived a "patient lifter" to ease the boy's pain and to make it possible to change the sheets. An aide called it "a contraption of wood, bicycle chains, sprockets and levers fitted out like a forklift." This machine, if patented, might have saved many nurses from hernias and dislocated discs. However, he dismantled it and used the parts for something else.

"Down in that workshop, where he wouldn't let anyone in to clean," said Nurse Drover, "he also made wooden legs for people. He even made extra limbs for a little boy so that as he grew he could unscrew one and put on a longer one. The fellow wore those wooden legs until he was a young man." Many times Ivy LeDrew sewed padding for these prostheses. He made a leg for the husband of his longtime anesthetist Rose (Cooper) Young. He fitted George Hawkins with more than one wooden leg.

He improved on open-drop ether anesthesis—dropping liquid ether into a cone fastened over the patient's face—by vaporizing the anesthetic and feeding it through a rubber tube inserted up the patient's nostril. "It was simple," said Dr Maguire, "but it worked very well. Stella Manuel used to give all the anesthetics then. He taught her the method and she was a dab hand at it."

Among his most ambitious ideas was the "Womb Extender." As sketched on a page of looseleaf dated December 9th, 1972, it was to be a complete system for the transport and home care of premature babies. It consisted of a spring-mounted, ventilated capsule in which the infant would lie cushioned on air or water in a thermostatically controlled environment. When stationary, the capsule would be rocked gently to and fro by an electric arm linked to an eccentric gear. To simulate the mother's heartbeat he planned to rig a notch and tympanum on the same gear. Below the capsule he had sketched a side-hinged bathing platform which formed the top of a tiny cupboard holding a blanket, powder and diapers for the trip. There was to be a pair of back straps with special Olds buckles. Should the capsule be accidentally dropped, a detachable rollbar would protect the occupant. "Baby Continuer" and "Mechanical Mother" were alternative names he toyed with.

He also dabbled in research. In the late thirties he was already quizzing patients on their home diet and testing for ascorbic acid levels. He experimented with extracting Vitamin C from turnips and other northern vegetables and recorded the results. Some of his findings he published in *The Northern Medical Review*, a short-lived journal which he and Evarts Loomis, MD of St Anthony founded in 1943. In their single July issue he also had an article on the actinomycosis, a fungal infection causing "lumpy jaw."

Since 1945, Dr Olds had been advocating seals as a source of natural insulin. Although J. J. Abel of Hopkins had successfully purified calf insulin in 1926, the supply from natural sources was still unreliable. Olds saw great potential in seal insulin as well as a valuable by-product. During his two voyages to the ice he had hoped to collect pancreases, but the demands of doctoring the fleet, shooting seals and collecting Seal Finger material prevented him. He tried again in 1952 when his marine biologist friend David E. Sergeant went to conduct harp seal research for Dr William Templeman. Dr Olds wired Leslie R. Curtis to have Sergeant collect a hundred pounds and Sergeant persuaded the Eli Lillie Drug Company to analyze them. However, Sergeant was busy tagging over 200 whitecoats; a Mr Johnson of Job's Limited in St John's wanted seal livers for pernicious anemia research, and a drug company wanted adrenals. In the end he collected only twenty pounds of pancreases. It would be thirty years before the synthetic human insulin *Humulin* came on the market. Dr Olds, entering the most traumatic period of his life, abandoned the search.

Bud Young called his former boss "a great one to experiment but not very scientific." When tooth decay was rampant and few patients could afford dentures, Dr Olds mused about tooth rejuvenation. He captured a stray dog, pulled some of its teeth and kept them alive in saline solution with the idea of replacing them a week or so later. However, the dog escaped with what teeth it still had and took the secret with him.

Chapter Twenty-Four

A Great Reluctance to Stop

*"All you had to do to make Dr Olds happy was
give him a box of junk."*

— Dr Jesus Austria

Afortnight before Christmas 1934, after the first few inches of snow had fallen, people living near the Hospital heard, up by the Cottage, what sounded like a Model T *Ford* starting. Instinctively they pulled back the curtains. They saw not a motor car but a strange little vehicle lumbering down the hill with young Dr Olds perched on the seat in his white lab coat. Nobody in Twillingate had ever seen anything like it. The December 22nd *Sun* reported, "Dr Olds has invested in a snowmobile, and trial spins have been made on South Island."

The *Snow-Go* was the first of many land and sea machines which Dr Olds would build and test over the next few decades. Probably he had just read about Joseph Armand-Bombardier's new troop-carrying snowmobile, and immediately envisaged a smaller version. Ideas for snow vehicles dated back to the late 1800s, but Bombardier of Quebec was the first to successfully marry bulldozer cleats, a flexible track and skis. John, unable to buy or make the small driver gears and idler wheels for such tracks, had to improvise.

"It was a tractor type of thing," said Bud Young, "but instead of the iron tracks on a D6 or a D7, he made one out of pork barrel staves fastened crosswise. He built it on a sleigh, and mounted a *Ford* engine to drive it. There was a wheel in front and one in back, and the one in front pulled the thing along. It was probably chain-driven. I've been on the thing, but it was so long ago that I've forgotten. It would crawl over the snow, ten or fifteen miles an hour. He worked on it probably all winter, changing it. But he didn't get out of it what he expected, so he chucked it to one side and that was the end of it.

"That's how he used to do things," said Young. "He'd get something built and get it going and then he'd probably get tired of it. It was only a hobby. People would watch when he brought out a new machine, but nobody paid much attention to him. He was always doing something like that. He spent an awful lot of time in his workshop."

By the fall of 1938 the *Frank and Annette,* Twillingate's first motorcycle, was worn out. That winter Dr Olds scavenged it for a three-wheeled contraption like a modern all-terrain vehicle. He mounted the cycle's wheels and gear box at the rear end and put the sidecar wheel in front. For power he adapted an old outboard motor. It steered with a stick like an airplane and on a good trail moved along at twelve or fifteen miles an hour. Hitler's lightning tank attacks were in the news so he nicknamed it the *Panzer.*

Bob Ecke took a midnight ride on this vehicle that he never forgot. It was after a birthday party the Hardys gave him on November 24th, 1939. John and Betty were there, along with Lige Dalley, Bud Young and others. There was plenty of liquor and arguments and the night was exhilarating. John suddenly got the idea that Bob should spend the night at the Tilt and that he would take him there in the *Panzer.* "The *Panzer* has two bad habits," wrote Dr Ecke. "When you throw it into gear it is inclined to rear like a horse. And, once going, it has a great reluctance to stop."

Hazel Jeffreys wanted to come along for the ride, so Ecke sat on the front with both legs sticking out. When they reached Edgar Warr's, just before the Purcell's Harbour bridge, the right rear wheel careened off a rock. The *Panzer* leapt to the right and overturned with the motor running. "Hazel pitched out on her head and split her eyebrow," said Ecke. "There was that wild unrecallable moment when you struggle to preserve your bones without emotion. We untangled and I was surprised to find myself functioning. We pushed on to the Tilt, where I discovered I had lost the food for breakfast at the accident. We built the a fire and had a drink.... [The next morning], in pursuit of something to eat, I walked up the road to the scene of the previous night's debacle to find my breakfast useable, but run over...."

In March 1940 John wrote his mother: "We have a lot of snow now, but very little ice. I have had 2 trips with my dogs—Herring Neck and Carter's Cove—but around the Harbour I have used my snowmobile most of the time. It works well in a path but won't go through more than a foot or so of soft snow." A month later he said, "I took the snowmobile to Herring Neck the other day & had a good trip. The last time I took the dogs & skis it was very sticky on the way back."

His first homemade truck also appeared in the spring of 1939. "It was a big flat thing in the form of a car," said Bud, "just a flat surface with an engine on the front and a steering wheel. It had a seat with room enough for himself, that's all. It was powered by a ten HP *Wisconsin* gas engine with a rope starter. He could sit up on it and drive it the same as you'd drive a car. There was a lever for putting it in gear, and levers for shifting to high and low. He just built that thing for fun—same thing as a youngster making a go-cart. He'd probably drive that out to his Tilt, and it'd break down or he'd run it into a cliff, and have to walk back. He did everything with that, modifying it for summer or winter. One week it would have wheels on it, the next it would have tracks. People didn't make fun of it because he made it himself—a smart feller. A harmless hobby." The *Sun* found it newsworthy enough to cover in its June 3rd issue:

> Dr Olds has recently completed tests on a new motor vehicle constructed by him and Martin Young. This is a light truck, powered with an air-cooled engine and mounted on a modified automobile chassis. It has proven quite efficient, carrying moderate loads up fairly steep grades. One convenient feature of this machine is that the front end is so light that it can be easily lifted by two men and the vehicle turned around in a [small space].

Like auto makers of a later generation, John liked to resurrect the same frame in different guises. Nobody was surprised when his truck metamorphosed into a tractor. "It has a *Ford* rear end," he told his father, "and my boat engine & motorcycle transmission mounted over rear axel [sic], with a *Ford* frame which is shortened to give 5' wheel base. It is geared quite low—about 48:1 in low. So far we haven't gotten it out of the shop, but should in a day or so."

For years he had wanted a Hospital plane, but nobody was keen on his piloting it. His "Air-Sled" was the next best thing, a propeller-driven land vehicle resembling a Florida Everglades air-boat—which may in fact have inspired it. In essence it was an airplane propeller mounted on a horse sled. A Mr Minty who carved wind-charger replacement blades made the propeller from a block of knot-free white birch. From tip to tip it spanned about four feet and was beautifully balanced. "He mounted this on the front of the sled," recalled Bud, "and connected it down through gears to a Model A or Model T engine. He had it on the floor in what was the old Hospital power house down by the road, and Martin Young was helping him." Indoor testing seemed prudent, as an earlier model had reputedly broken through a fence and chewed up a potato garden.

After a year or two of work, they put the finishing touches on it and Olds started the engine. "He revved it up," said Bud, "and the blade was spinning like blazes and started to pull the sled over the floor. It picked up speed and went slam right into the side of the powerhouse, a cement block wall. And oh, it beat the blade all to pieces. And this was the end of that rig. If he'd kept at the design, perhaps put in a clutch, it might have worked all right. Still, it wasn't practical. He had no covering over the blade—a very dangerous thing. A propeller is all right in the air, but going down the road—good God, you couldn't have that. I suppose eventually he would have added one. But he threw that one aside too."

In 1962 the new dentist Dr Jesus Austria got a call:

"Jess, you doing anything?"

"No, Dr Olds."

"Come on down to the house. We'll build a boat."

"OK."

Dr Austria got in his car and drove over. "He had an airplane fuel tank there, like a big cigar. He'd already cut it in half. I asked him what he was going to do with it.

"'We'll build a catamaran,' he said. Ever since seeing a picture of a twin-hulled catamaran in a boating magazine, he had itched to build one. He got a four-by-eight-foot plywood, put it across the two half-cylinders, and we got it together. 'Now,' he said, 'it's ready to float.' But for some reason he abandoned it. Two years later I heard that Dr Woodruff took the boat to the cove by the wharf and tried to sail it. And apparently it folded up!"

This was not his first catamaran. A decade earlier he had tried to build one from a picture. "But," said Bud Young, "he had no idea what its bottom looked like. All he knew was that this boat, when it got going fast enough, would plane. This was what he wanted. He got a fellow Pardy over in Little Harbour to build it. It was only about twelve feet long and six or seven wide, but it had heavy planking. And the power was a 4 HP *Acadia* engine. Not much, but he figured that with the catamaran shape he would get a helluva speed out of it.

"After he got it all built and the engine installed and everything, he and Martin took it out in the Cove down there. He started it up: *chug, chug, chug*. And the damned thing only went about four miles an hour. That was the best he ever got. You need a lot of power behind you—a 50 HP outboard on a light boat, or something like that. It was a good idea, but he didn't have the right bottom contour and it was too heavy to begin with."

In the sixties he bought several aluminum speedboats. When arthritis made hauling them up too difficult, he rigged a truck wheel on a post set in concrete and used a gas engine to winch them ashore. To eliminate the problem of bailing them out every time it rained, he fiddled with built-in tarpaulins. A December 1972 notebook contains instructions for one made of waterproof cloth or plastic "attached to a beam on either side and fitted over the thole pins. Fasten to bow and stern and two or three side cleats; unfasten, fold and leave or stow." To save wrestling with heavy sails, he proposed an aluminum tripod mast with slots for sails equipped with sliders in the leech and foot. They could be hauled up and down by a halyard, doing away with troublesome loops and grommets....

In 1963 New York City's new hydrofoil commuter service between Wall Street and Long Island began. After that, none of his aluminum speedboats went fast enough to satisfy him. He pictured himself at the controls of a hovercraft, whizzing to Lewisporte in minutes. Deciding to build one of his own that winter, he read everything he could lay his hands on, from

Leonardo da Vinci through Enrico Forlanini and Alexander Graham Bell to *Popular Mechanics* articles on the latest models.

He chose submerged foils over surface foils because they were said to work better in rough water. He drew plans for foils to fit his new sixteen-foot aluminum boat and hired Fred Manuel and his son Alf to make and install them. For weeks, like a child before Christmas, he visited their shop near Manuel's store on the North Side to observe progress and suggest modifications. While waiting, he wondered how fast this thing would go. All Twillingate wondered. With Gordon Stuckless he set about devising a marine speedometer. They came up with a hollow tube running along the keel with a forward intake and a branch line going up to a dashboard pressure gauge. As the boat accelerated, the increasing water pressure would register on the gauge, which they would recalibrate from pounds per square inch to miles per hour.

At last the hovercraft was ready. Perched three feet off the floor on struts and foils in Fred's shop, it seemed poised like a gull for flight. Olds could hardly wait to get it in the water. Gingerly they lifted and carried it down to the shore and lowered it into the Harbour. A gaggle of children and onlookers collected, smiling and pointing. The faces of the older men clearly said between squirts of tobacco juice, 'Why take a perfectly good boat and put legs on it?'

But John was used to scepticism. He explained that the hydrofoil worked like an airplane's wing. Airplanes flew, didn't they? When the boat gathered enough speed the hull would lift clear of the water, lose its drag and surge ahead. The onlookers wagged their heads. A fine doctor, but perhaps a little cracked....

It never did plane. He didn't have enough motor. The foils were only a drag in the water. The boat would have gone faster without them.

Chapter Twenty-Five

A Dream of Power

"He thought he could put a wave machine off Long Point
that would light the whole of Newfoundland."
— Dr Mike Maguire

The day Mike Maguire arrived in Twillingate in 1953, Dr Olds invited him up to tea. As he rapped on the door that evening, the 24-year-old Irishman wondered what his new boss would be like at home. "Come in!" drawled a gruff, nasal voice. Nina ushered him into a dim room. At first he could see nothing, but as his eyes adjusted to the gloom, he saw Dr Olds over in the corner reading a book by a faintly flickering bulb. Then he heard a dry, whirring sound. In a small cage two white mice were running inside an exercise wheel.

"Read a lot?" said Olds.

"Yes," said Dr Maguire, "But not by that kind of a light."

"Well, these mice are working," said Olds. "They're generating the power for me to read by. Welcome to Twillingate! Here, even the mice work."

Twillingaters knew that John Olds loved to tinker with wood and steel and rubber, elements which behaved with the sweet predictability of physics and mathematics and which never bled or died. On that first evening, Dr Maguire didn't know this. "My God," he thought, "this fellow is crazy. However, he has a nice wife, it's a nice comfortable house and I don't have to stay all night." Later they had a lovely meal, for which John went up and dressed formally. Betty was helping out a bit, but she wasn't well. It was a lovely evening.

Soon Dr Maguire saw that his new boss was something of an inventive genius. "He was very creative, very inventive; interested in all the materials I had, what I did with them, what they were used for. And he was always looking for other uses for them. 'Dammit,' he said one day, 'where's my bloody pen?' A few days later he brought me a pen and a pencil and got me to join the two of them with dental cement so that they'd always be together. A simple thing like that."

He showed Dr Maguire a mat-board cutter from a sharpened shard of hacksaw blade, a device for drawing perfect spirals, and oil painting brushes which he had improvised from manila rope and spent rifle cartridges during his 1947 trip to the ice. He was thinking of inventing a kind of dark glasses which you can make as light or dark as you please, and adjust for each eye so you can have one dark and the other light.

Of all physical phenomena, none captivated John more than electricity. From his Hopkins tissue embedder to the electric back-scratcher of his last years, its invisible energy was seldom far from his mind. During his 1951-52 rest cure in the States he equipped the light switches in his mother's house with mercury-activated dimmers for her convenience. "He used a hypodermic needle to drip the mercury," said his brother-in-law Doug Mott. "When you'd turn the switch on, the mercury would close the circuit, and as it dripped through this needle it would take fifteen seconds or so till it turned off. The trouble was, the switches would get clogged up. After a while I had to replace them all. He had good ideas, but many were more than he could handle."

When Gordon Stuckless introduced him to the solenoid, it had been like giving a child a new toy. To Dr Olds the little electromagnet with the shiny copper helix that moved metal objects by invisible force was beautiful. Immediately he began experimenting. Gordon described one application: "It was just the switch out of a reverse current cutout on an old car—a 6 V battery and a 6 V relay. He fastened the armature to his camera, placed the camera up on a tree branch, and screwed on this relay. We had the micro-switch—a very touchy switch—with a lever attached to the push-button on the camera. A movement of one-eighth-inch would trip the switch. When a bird landed on the switch, *click* would go the camera. He took some beautiful pictures with that."

Somehow, the little solenoid revived an old dream. Back in the thirties, the Hospital used to have a water wheel for auxiliary power. The kilowatt output of its ancient generator had been ridiculously small, hardly worth the trouble of cleaning out the dead eels. For some time he had been thinking about the ocean as a source of energy. Watching the little solenoid click his camera shutter reminded him that any sort of motion could generate power if the energy was harnessed.

The sea had fascinated him since childhood. Walking to or from the Cottage, he rarely failed to stop and gaze out over Hamilton Sound or Burnt Island Tickle. It thrilled him to see distant longliners disappear among the sea's grey hills, to be lifted high moments later. Even in calm weather the waters were never still, never ceased to harry the cliffs. Somehow he must

Gary Saunders

tap that tireless pulse. One day he bet someone he could make electricity by wave action. "And he didn't want to have to pay up," said Tutie. By the time Mike Maguire arrived he was talking about it all the time. "He had a bug about wave power," said Mike. "Thought it was the project of the future, that he could put a wave machine off Long Point that would light the whole of Newfoundland...." It was to be his most quixotic venture.

While the theoretical aspects were straight-forward, the physical obstacles were daunting. His basic idea was to anchor a large float just offshore and to capture wave motion to turn a generator. Two things plagued him from the start. One was the perpetual shortage of materials. The other was the elements. His apparatus would have to withstand an environment subject to violent fluctuations of wind and tide as well as the seasonal action of ice. Any successful wave machine would require large float tanks, massive steel beams, big gearboxes. For the time being, he would have to keep things small.

The new Tilt became his headquarters. Main Tickle gave him a good reach of ocean—all the way to Greenland, in fact. He started work on his first wave machine in 1956. It was "mostly bicycle parts and most of a lawn mower," he told his mother, but he hoped to at least light the cabin or pump cooling water through the refrigerator.

His next few rigs used an oil drum for a float and a car generator. "I'd say he made a half dozen of these," said Gordon. "He'd take them down on the beach near his cabin. And if the sea got very big, they would beat up. You see, he left all his machines out. And either the biggest kind of a sea would come and beat it all to pieces, or the ice would carry it away."

A breakthrough had occurred around 1954 when *The Twillingate Sun*, Canada's only newspaper still being typeset by hand, retired its ancient letterpress. John, who had often stood and watched its great thirty-inch wheel slowly turning, took it home like a man who has found a treasure. For the first time he would have a gear large enough to give him a sufficient ratio, and strong enough perhaps to withstand the force of wind and wave.

Although the press made him more ambitious, it was to be years before he could harness it to his purpose. By then his salary allowed him to buy good materials. "He had a lathe," said Gordon, "an acetylene torch and a good assortment of taps and dies. He'd call and say, 'Come on over and we'll spend an hour or so at this.'"

He started using bought lumber instead of scrap wood. For floats he stopped using oil drums and started using aluminum boats. Securely moored but free to move up and down, a boat would serve as a convenient platform on which to fasten the apparatus he had in mind. Moreover, he could stand in it to work.

"His rigs were getting bigger and more powerful," said Gordon, adding ruefully, "and he was beating up more boats. But he didn't get discouraged, didn't seem to mind losing $300-$400 in the one storm." Drift ice was the greatest hazard. It churned back and forth through the Tickle every spring and fall, taking anything moveable with it.

He spent hours discussing strategies with Gordon, mulling over problems, drinking beer. How could they prevent the wheel from going backwards when the lever came down? How could they turn the generator faster? Where would he get a gear box with a big enough ratio? They spent many long winter evenings filling cigarette packs and the backs of envelopes with diagrams and notes.

When he was stymied or waiting for materials, he designed a weathervane and various gauges to measure the frequency and amplitude of wave and wind without having to leave the Tilt. One instrument used a gauge and float from the gas tank of an old car. Another used a long piece of IV tubing connected to an aneroid barometer in the cabin. His best wind speed indicator or anemometer utilized a plastic Javex bottle mounted upside down on a weighted, tilting spindle above a tambour or diaphragm in a tobacco can. He fastened the spindle in the middle of a horizontal bar that swung freely on a gimbal like that of a ship's compass. As the wind tilted the bottle, a piece of nylon suture pulled on the tambour, conveying an air pressure change through a length of IV tubing to a gauge mounted in the house. He liked his toys to be complex.

Dr Olds' best and last wave machine was built around 1965. "His biggest problem had been to get up enough speed," said Stuckless. "Then he found an old war surplus aircraft starter gear box—about a 100:1 reduction, I would say—a very strong piece of stuff. And then he used the same ratchet system that's used on the windlass of a schooner. It worked both ways: when it was going down it would exert power, and also when it was coming up. There was no lost motion. And that way, he got up enough speed to turn the generator fast enough."

He built a frame for the press, poured a cement base near the shore, and bolted and welded a frame in place. Just offshore, he moored his latest aluminum boat, a 16-footer fitted with four mooring lines and grapnels. "The idea wasn't original," said Gordon,"but the machinery, the get-up, was all his own. The speedboat went up and down and worked a lever on shore to drive the gearbox. The boat had enough leeway to go up and down with the lops—the bigger the better. Fastened to the boat he had a vertical wooden post attached to a big H-beam steel lever extending out over the cliff. He used the up and down motion of the waves to work that lever like the windlass on a schooner. The lever had springs to capture sideways motion and was attached to a ratchet rig—I helped him make it up—and to a generator and a fly-wheel." There was also a coil spring on the lever to act as a universal joint, and an idler gear to keep the drive chain tight.

They assembled the contraption. The last step was to fasten the overhanging arm to the boat post. After so many failed attempts, all he wanted was to charge a 6 V storage battery enough to light a single 40 W bulb in his cabin. He chose a day with a good wind and a three-foot lop. As the arm began to rise and fall to the rhythm of the waves, the great cog wheel began to turn and the smaller gears speeded up the motion until the generator shaft was fairly whizzing. Even in daylight, anyone could see the bulb glow. His old bet was won—but the loser had tired of waiting and even the winner was bored. When South Island got street lights in 1966, he got Steve and Ira Troake to hook the cabin up to town power. "This was his last energy venture," said Gordon, with the air of one who misses Don Quixote.

Chapter Twenty-Six

Hunter

*"Some of the best trips we had were when
we never got a damned thing."*
— J. M. Olds

Every fall in his teens Johnny Olds smelled of swamp. Strong soap was helpless against the faint odour of mud, methane and sweet musk he brought home at night. It was the distinctive odour of the trapper and skinner of muskrats.

Johnny caught the river rats for pocket money. He earned little cash, however, until an oldtimer taught him the proper way to skin and stretch their chestnut brown pelts without cutting or tearing them. It took a steady knife, a keen eye and a good stomach. Like most country boys, he examined his first carcass carefully. With the fur peeled away to the ankles and wrists, its darkly muscled purplish body reminded him of a midget boxer wearing gloves and slippers. He opened the stomach and poked through the rodent's last meal, a finely chopped salad of young cattail shoots mixed with bits of river clam. He traced the esophagus from mouth to stomach, studied the bright pink lungs and probed the tiny sac of amber liquid folded inside the rubbery brown liver. The tubes draining urine from the bean-like kidneys to the bladder intrigued him. He marvelled at the length of the veined grey intestines. Loomis never taught anatomy so well.

As he grew older, hunting replaced trapping in his affections. Knowing Johnny's fearlessness, his mother would peer out the windows at dusk until she saw her son's slender form striding up the hill, paddle or shotgun in one hand, a string of mallards in the other. "One Thanksgiving in his early Yale years," said Tutie, "a duck that he wounded flew to the other side of the river before falling. And he swam over and got it. You know, in November. The Connecticut River is over half a mile wide there. Came home shivering. Mother was a little put out."

The great fall hunting event of Notre Dame Bay was turring. A northeaster in November or December, not too fierce but spitting rain or snow, was ideal. On such days, rafts of murres, scoters, eiders and bullbirds appeared off Spiller's Point and Crow Head, flashing semaphores of white and black above the lops. Ancient seven-foot muzzle-loaders were lifted down from wall pegs and oiled. Fingers of powder, grams of shot, wads of tow were ramrodded home, and for weeks the islands and capes echoed to warlike sounds as volleys of lead shot flew and birds crumpled and fell to be scooped from the waves. Sometimes an excited hunter sent his pellets toward another boat, where they rattled against the planking or pattered harmlessly off cold-stiffened oilskins. Scores—hundreds of seabirds were downed on every suitable day. Women groaned at the mountains of pluck-ing and cleaning but rejoiced in the harvest of winter meat and pillow stuffing.

John took to it like a native. That was one thing Twillingaters loved about him. "Nights we'd have to call him in the thirties," said Jessie Drover. "Go down the hall, knock on his bedroom door—he used to sleep in the Hospital years ago—wake him up in time to go turrin'. He wouldn't set the alarm for nothing; if the wind was wrong—too stormy a morning—he'd say not to wake him up. So we'd ask one of the oldtimers, one of the patients: 'Skipper, what do you think of the morning? Is it a good day to go out turrin'?

"'Yes, yes, maid,' he'd say, 'I think 'twill be a good day, 'tis goin' to be a good day.'

"So we'd call him and say, 'Dr Olds, 'tis gonna be a good day—get up.' And away he'd go, up to Crow Head with the Doves, the Elliotts or the Sharpes; or to some other place for to spend a few hours shooting with the fishermen. He seldom went far; there was always a chance he would be needed back at the Hospital."

Twenty years later, he was still as keen as ever. "Out in the Bight with Stevie Young we'd go," said Mike Maguire, "shooting turrs and ducks. He encour-aged us young fellows to go, loved to see you enjoying what Twillingate had to offer. He'd have one big day a year. Stevie Young and he used to go in Stevie's boat. It was supposed to be a great honour. They would haul a few lobster pots, have a case of beer, go on a picnic. A day out, a big day. John never complained about Twillingate—he loved it. The only things he ever complained about was the Government and the mail."

Sid Fisher from Montreal went birding with him once. "He was shoot-ing murres, which I had never seen before. Even though I was a fair shot, I wasn't used to shooting in waves. He got a dozen while I was getting one or two. He was terribly pleased about that."

In November 1962 Dr Olds appeared on the doorstep of Jess and Felly Austria in Twillingate and said, "Ever have turr?" Both shook their heads. "Well then," he said, and swung three fresh birds into the sink. "I tried to pluck them," said Dr Austria, "but I couldn't. They weren't like the tropical birds I was used to in the Philippines. At last I gave up and skinned them. We also didn't know how to cook them then...they were awful!"

The day Mike Maguire arrived in Twillingate, Olds asked him if he'd ever hunted partridge. He told him yes, that in the west of Ireland they hunted upland birds a lot. "Well," he said, "the partridge season is open here."

"Is that right?" said Mike. "Are there partridge on this Island?"

"Oh yeah," he said, "lots of 'em." He told him about the willow ptarmigan and the rock ptarmigan. "Why don't you go and get a few tomorrow?"

So Dr Olds lent him his Damascus twist shotgun, gave him a pocketful of cartridges and told him to go up back of the Hospital on the road to the barrens. Next morning the young man borrowed a pair of rubber boots and set out. He had no dog, and after walking for many miles concluded that either there were no birds, or he wasn't hunting properly. Then a covey of partridge exploded in front of him and he knocked down three. Two of them he found quickly, the third took an hour. Disgruntled at what he considered a poor morning's shooting, he cleaned the gun and took it back to Dr Olds.

"Well," said John, "how'd you get on?"

"Ahhh, I only got three."

"What?!?" he said. "There's no damned birds on Twillingate Island!"

"He had sent me on a fool's errand," said Dr Maguire, "to make me walk across the island for nothing. But we had the birds for supper the next night. I suppose it was his way to help a single young fella like me, far from home, having to spend a winter in Twillingate, to survive."

And a way to take his mind of his own troubles.

Some years the drift ice brought seals close to land. By March month the seabirds were all eaten and everyone was sick of salt beef and salt cod, so the people rejoiced. Grabbing rifle, hauling rope and gaff, men went out on foot to hunt them for meat and sport. April 1940 was such a year. The seals were so close that the sealing fleet was in full view. "Ned [Facey] and I went out at 3:30 the other morning," John told Mary. "It was a long four miles before we found any, but we each got one. The dogs were a big help hauling them in." In 1954 he persuaded Dr Maguire to try it. "We would shoot them in the water or on the pans," said Maguire, "and then bring in the meat— especially the livers for himself, because they were full of Vitamin C. He didn't waste a thing."

His voyage to the Front in 1947 had versed him in the art of hunting adult seals. "At times the seals pay no attention and at other times will go off the ice in a flurry two or three miles distant. The going is always rough and it is necessary to take whatever cover the ice pinnacles afford. There is much running and jumping from pan to pan, zig-zagging to find a possible route. There may be from one to a dozen seals on a single pan. Once within range, the first thing any gunner should do is sit or lie down on the ice until he recovers his breath. The seals lie and doze with their heads pointing to the edge of the pan and often almost overhanging it, lifting them from time to time for a look around. They are not hard to hit at a hundred yards or so, but they must be hit in the head to kill them."

In the late fifties he sometimes went out with Gordon Stuckless. "Probably we'd talk about it the evening before. 'If 'tis a nice day t'mar, we'll go out.' I had a fast speedboat, small with a big engine, and during the winter I kept her down in Sleepy Cove. If he finished early in the OR—9 or 10 o'clock perhaps—here he comes and away we go, down to the boat. But I wasn't comfortable out sealing with him," said Gordon. "I'd be all bundled up in my warm clothes and he'd come just about naked; perhaps a pair of sneakers on and a little white jacket with no scarf and no cap. And to keep him from freezing, I wouldn't stay out very long. I don't believe he was so tough as he thought he was."

One day in November 1963 Dr Austria got a call from Dr Olds; did he want to go moose hunting?

"What do I need for that?" said Jess.

"Just your rifle and sleeping bag," he replied. The dentist went to the outdoor store, bought a bag for $5.00 and borrowed a .303 rifle. First we went to Millertown," said Dr Austria. "Bert and Milligan Pardy and Joe White came with us and we stopped at every camp and talked to everybody. In one of the camps an elderly man came up and said, 'Oh hello, Dr Olds! Remember me?' And Dr Olds said, 'Yes, I remember you; you're so-and-so.' The old man was pleased, really flattered. After lunch we took off again. I couldn't help asking, 'Dr Olds, how in God's name can you remember every patient you cut?'

"'Oh, I didn't know his name,' he said. 'I just read it off his safety helmet.'

"'We weren't seeing any moose, so we turned and went down to Noel Paul Steady. After supper he painted a scene there. Night came. I had this $5.00 sleeping bag and by two in the morning I was freezing. I got up and tried to start a fire in the stove. By and by Bert Pardy got up too. Dr Olds was muttering, grumbling. Bert said, 'What's the matter, Dr Olds—can't sleep?'

"'Godammit,' he said, 'how can I sleep when everyone is always moving around?'

"Next morning we got a moose. Afterward, Dr Olds and I were sitting there having lunch and the Canada jays were all coming around. 'Jess,' he said, 'Get some rum.' So I got some bread, soaked it in rum and threw it to the jays. Holy moly! The jay was getting drunk, having a ball!

"Dr Olds made a slingshot; but he couldn't hit it. Now, as a kid I had a lot of experience with slingshots. After I got the jay I said, 'What are we going to do with it?'

"'Put it in Bert's pack so he can tell his wife that's all he got,' said Olds. Joe White agreed.

"We all went home, me to Springdale, they to Twillingate. And when I came home the jay was in *my* bag. 'Oh, Mr White,' I thought, 'you didn't get me yet.' I went and mailed it to him C.O.D. When it reached Twillingate Joe was sick for a few days. Postmaster Wilson Manuel called him up: 'Mr White, you've got a C.O.D. parcel here and it's starting to stink.' So Joe went and got it. A year later when he was over to Springdale, he said, 'By God, did I curse you when I found out what it was!'"

Of that trip Dr Olds wrote his mother on November 13th: "We went way into the country, mostly on A.N.D. Company roads. I took the *Land Rover*, blew out 2 tires & had to get 4 new ones. The exhaust pipe got knocked off—got that welded—on the way back the generator burned out. We got one moose. I don't much like going this way. It is not as good as going in canoes up the Gander River."

To get to the river, sometimes they went to Lewisporte and took the train to Glenwood; other times they took the *Bonnie Nell* directly to Clarkes Head. Either way, they had the lovely overnight trip upriver to look forward to, thirty to seventy miles of rough rapids and quiet ponds, of sleeping under canvas on birch or aspen islands guarded by great white pines. Because there was no moose season north of Gander Lake in the early years, the guides always took them up beyond the Lake to the Northwest or Southwest branches of the Gander.

Dr Olds' first trip was in 1938, when the Government reopened the season on caribou. He and Rube Waddell hunted near Mount Peyton with Howard Thistle and Billy John. During and after the War, he often joined the annual moose hunting expeditions of Joe White, Ned Facey and Ern French. Magistrate Beaton Abbott came in the latter years, and because he was a teetotaller they put him in charge of the liquor.

By law each hunter had to have a guide. These they recruited mostly from Gander Bay. Over the years strong ties developed between each pair of men. "If I remember right," said Don Saunders of Gander Bay South, "the guides were usually my brother Brett, Mose and Finlay Downer and Harvey Francis. Nat Gillingham was another." Billy drowned in the Gander in August 1946, so in 1948 Don guided Dr Olds. "They came to Gander Bay on the *Bonnie Nell* and we went up the river from here. As usual we stayed the first night to the fishing camp on Third Pond Island. It was in November month."

"I remember it was windy—northwest, with flurries—and really cold. But what I couldn't understand was Dr Olds, with a sheepskin-lined coat thrown down across the thwart, was sitting there in a light windbreaker shivering. And wouldn't put that coat on. We were all dressed warm; he seemed just too stubborn to put it on.

"When we left the Bay, 'most everybody had the 'flu," Don recalled. "The second morning, I had a dose of it too. I was standing by a tree bleeding from the nose when Dr Olds looked out his tent door. 'What's wrong with you this morning?' he said.

"'Doctor,' I said, 'I've got the 'flu. You got anything any good for that?'

"'Yes,' he said, 'go jump in the river. You know, Don, if you treat a cold you'll have it for two weeks. And if you don't treat it, you'll have it for a fortnight. What the hell is the difference?'

"Ern had this old-fashioned radio, an old *RCA* with two big dry-cell batteries. He'd wake early in the morning while the other fellows were snoozing and he'd find this country music from Wheeling, West Virginia and turn it up full blast. Well, Dr Olds got up this morning, grabbed the batteries and slung 'em in the river. It was only for devilment that he would have the radio on that hour of the morning—just tormenting. But they never got mad with one another.

"Dr Olds wanted a caribou. After leaving camp we went across Gander Lake and up the Northwest Gander to a place called Greenwood Brook. There was an inch or two of snow on the ground when we set up our canvas tents. From there neither Brett nor I had ever been back to the open country where you usually find caribou. We knew roughly how far, but we weren't sure. So we decided to go back and see. Dr Olds wanted to come along. There was no trail; it was just through the woods. In places it was really thick. When we crossed the first little bit of open country—not the main lot we were looking for—Dr Olds was a bit tired. 'Brett,' he said, 'what you gonna do with that damned open country when you get there?'

"'Nothing,' he said. "I just want to find how far it is.'

"As it happened, there was a good sign of caribou right where we were, so Dr Olds decided to stay there. Brett went on; away he went and I stayed behind. It was chilly, so we made a fire. We were sitting around the fire yarning when Brett came back. We started back across this little opening for to come back to camp. When we reached the opposite side, I looked back and saw a big stag just coming. And he walked up till he saw or smelled the smoke. We were right in shot; so Dr Olds got the caribou. It had a good rack.

"We walked over alongside the stag and turned him up for to paunch him. Dr Olds gets down with his knife. And I, being young, forgot who I was with. 'Be careful, Doctor,' I said. 'Don't touch the paunch!' Meaning, be careful not to nick the intestines and taint the meat.

"He glared at me and said, 'You know, son, this is not the first belly I've cut open.'

"Myself and Brett took a quarter apiece and brought it back to camp, leaving the rest for later.

"Back at camp, Dr Olds was telling Ern about his big caribou—this great set of antlers he had in there. 'My guide here says he didn't think he was man enough to bring them out,' he said. 'Oh, I'll bring 'em out for you, doctor,' said Ern. Later Dr Olds took me aside and said, 'Don, what's the best way to make that bugger work? The most difficult way we can get him to bring that head out?'

"'The hardest way,' I said, "is to put it right up on his shoulders.' See, we had to come through the woods, through this young spruce. So the next day when we went back for the rest of the meat, Ern came with us. 'Oh,' he said when he saw the head, 'it'll be a breeze to carry that.'

"'Well, Ern,' said Dr Olds, 'my guide might have some suggestions,' and he gave me a wink.

"'Ern,' I said, 'the easiest way to carry it is up on your shoulders, same as the caribou do.'

"'That makes sense,' he said, and we hoisted it onto his back.

"He was okay until he got down in the thick woods. Ern was strong, and he would plow ahead until the antlers were caught up on both sides. He'd bend those young spruce right down, and when he'd stop they would spring back and drag him backwards. We kept him at that until he was just about beat. Finally I said, 'Ern b'y, try it *behind* your shoulders.' So that's how we brought the meat and the head back to camp. The head had thirty-four points."

When John returned, Betty wrote to David in Windsor, "Pop enjoyed their hunting trip very much and it did him good. Last night Stella & Ern and Pop and I had a caribou supper at Stella's. The caribou was so tender you didn't even need a knife. We all wished you were with us to enjoy it too. I like it much better than moose. The head that Pop bro't back is beautiful, and I daresay he'll get his way and have it over the fireplace."

In August 1979, John Olds sat for ninety minutes at his desk in the new Hospital and reminisced with Brett Saunders about those expeditions. The doctor was seventy-three and retired from surgery; Brett was seventy-five and retired from guiding and outfitting. After sizing each other up—"Are you taller than you used to be, or am I shorter?" said Dr Olds—they recollected their years together on the Gander.

Dr Olds: "That first trip in 1938, Dr Waddell and myself were very anxious to go. Howard Thistle was here as a long-term patient and he got Billy John and himself involved. Rube and I got a licence and we went up with Howard and Billy to the head of Gander Lake. And Billy walked the hell out of us up in the Harvest Fields. We stayed up there in Jim John's camp, and the next morning we went on a ways farther and saw some caribou and shot two and then we had the trouble of lugging 'em back. Billy said it was eighteen miles in and back. I knew it was damned far enough! I had eighty pounds to carry. And I never saw a bottle of rum go quicker than when we got back...."

It was on that trip, said the doctor, that he lost one of his fine leather riding boots. He had set them on the woodpile in the tent overnight, and the next morning one was gone. After they all searched in vain for it, Billy said, "Dr Olds, I s'pose if you can't find it you won't be needin' the other boot. How 'bout you give 'en to me?" Dr Olds eyed him for a long moment.

"Well, Billy," he drawled, "if it's no good to me it's no good to you either," and he slung it far out into the river.

"Next year Rube and me went again, and this time you came with us. Wasn't that the time we had trouble getting down the Lake, when you hollered that the following waves would swamp us, and I wouldn't stop the motor, and Ern was in front, and I sank the boat? The wave came over the stern and took the engine right off the transom. It was still running and the hot spark plug cracked when it hit the cold water. Ern was up to his knees and screeching and bawling. But we got ashore and bailed the canoe out and carried on without the motor. And then Rube wanted to make the train because he had to go down to Brookfield in Bonavista Bay."

Brett: "Remember the time you ate the piece of lynx?"

Olds: "Yes."

Brett: "One that was in trap for three weeks?"

Olds: "Oh, yes. That was good meat—excellent. It was like hare—not rabbit, but hare. You know, we'd been up there a couple of days and we had no meat. We hadn't had anything except beans for breakfast and I thought we should have lynx...."

Brett: "It wouldn't have been so bad if the meat was fresh.... 'Twas in a trap all that time...."

Olds: "The meat looked good, smelled all right."

Brett: "And remember the time we were coming downriver in canoe and there was a moose standing right in mid-stream at Long Angle Island? And Ern missed it? It was only sixty to eighty feet from him."

Olds: "You had to slow down, didn't you? To keep from ramming him?"

Brett: "Yes, I stopped and I was holding the boat against the current with the pole. I could have hit the moose with a rock. And he missed him with the second shot too. He had an automatic rifle, ten shots, and every one of them went somewhere else! And do you remember the night we camped at the Narrows and Joe White was up all night with a big gale of southeast wind? Stayed up the whole night, never went to sleep at all; I don't think he even went in the tent. He was nervous about the wind, didn't want one of those big birches to come down across it...."

Olds: "But you know, nobody was better on the water, probably, than Joe. Yet in the woods he wasn't worth a damn. You take him out of sight of the river and he was lost, never find his way back. Remember the time you parked him by a pond to wait for moose and he heard a noise—turned out to be beavers chewing down a tree—and when the tree fell, Joe's gun went off? That's the only moose he ever shot!"

Brett: "Oh, those were great times. Some of the best times in my life were those trips up there...."

Olds: "Oh yes, and some of the best trips we had were when we never got a damned thing. My recollections of those days are about the most memorable of my life and I'm sorry there is no way of living them again with that fine old crowd."

Olds: "The only active ones left of that crowd are you and me and Magistrate Abbott. Abbott didn't start till the last few years, so all the fellows called him 'Junior.'"

Brett: "Great country. I'd like to spend some more time up there..."

Olds: "Well, I only went up once after the bridge was put in. We drove up and put the boats in there."

Brett: "Yes, now you can drive within two miles of the Ballast Bed, only six miles from Gull River.... All changed."

Olds: "My son is a doctor in New York City. I wouldn't live there five minutes."

Chapter Twenty-Seven

Seal Finger

"Doctor, I can't tell you what's the cause of Seal Finger. But I'll guarantee you I can tell you what to do to get one."

— Captain Peter Troake

"Seal Finger, blubber finger, fat finger, speck finger, are all names for the same model of a very sore finger." With these words Dr Olds opened a talk to the Newfoundland Medical Society in St John's in May, 1967. They had invited him to speak on the topic because he knew more about it than anyone else in Newfoundland, perhaps anyone in Canada. Twenty years earlier, tired of amputating sealers' fingers and unable to learn anything about the ailment in North American medical literature, he had gone to the Front to research it himself. His findings had appeared in the *Canadian Medical Association Journal* in March 1957. While the precise etiology was still unknown as he spoke, he had at least narrowed the search and found a cure.

Like all northern outport physicians, Dr Olds was used to seeing fingers swollen by splinters and ripped by trawl hooks, wrists bladdered with "water pups," skin burned by engine exhaust pipes, hands and feet mangled by pulp saws, axes, winches and flywheels. Seal Finger was different. It appeared in the spring with symptoms like those of a bad infection that turned to a rapid bone TB. It occurred across the northern hemisphere wherever hair seals were hunted. Norwegian doctors had described the condition as early as 1907. For the one Newfoundland sealer in twenty who caught it, amputation was the only cure.

He recalled for the Medical Society how the late Dr A. J. Wood had introduced him to it in Twillingate thirty-five years before. "He had been dealing with them since he started practice there in 1907. He had tried all types of poultices—cod oil, onion, linseed meal, bard bread, soft bread, etc., and in combination; he had splinted them and incised them and then amputated them."

Olds went on to describe a typical case history:

"'Doctor, is that a Seal Finger?'

"'I don't know. Maybe. What do you find?'

"'It has been stiff the past two days and it pained last night.'

"'Did you cut your finger lately?'

"'No.'

"There follows an increase in swelling, pain and tenderness. The skin becomes purplish-red and shiny. Active motion becomes nil; passive is painful and limited. The whole hand swells. After the first week the pain diminishes, swelling of the hand decreases, but the finger looks the same and feels the same. You never get pus—nothing is changed by incising and the incision heals rapidly. General malaise is slight. At the end of another week there is little change. X-rays taken at this time show narrowing of joint space. Pain subsides rapidly and it is said that if left alone for four to six months the swelling will be gone and the joint solidly anchylosed in 30 to 40 degree flexion. I have never seen this phase as the patient demanded amputation as soon as the diagnosis was made so he could get on with the summer fishing with a sensible stump.

"No fisherman wants a stiff finger," said Olds. "It's very hindersome in his work, and it's cold. They'd lose a whole summer, waiting for it to get well enough so they could use their hand. So they demanded amputation so they could go fishing. It acts, clinically, like a very rapid TB in that it destroys the cartilage in the joints of the fingers. It was limited to one or two joints in the first or second finger."

One local sealer and fisherman who chose to keep his finger was Gus Young. "They wanted to take 'en off, see, but I didn't want that. It got swollen. There was once it was three and one-half inches around—I measured it with the tape measure. Very painful. Most people had them taken off. I was too contrary for that. So it finally healed up all right. I got a stiff finger for a souvenir."

Twillingate was in an excellent place to see or get Seal Finger. Since cod-fishing was a summer occupation, sealing had helped make the town a year-round community in the first place. As a source of mid-winter income in the 1800s, shore-based netting of southbound seals in December soon ranked with lumbering and furring. Later, Twillingate merchants began sending idle schooners and crews to hunt seals offshore during the spring whelping and breeding season. Twillingate came to rival Fogo as a leading sealing centre. With the advent of steamships in the 1870s, St John's took control, but the Crosbies and Bowrings still hired northern skippers and crews. As late as the fifties, the Ashbournes and Manuels of Twillingate still outfitted vessels.

Every sealer had his own notions about the cause of Seal Finger. Mr Young's opinion is typical: "It don't take very much, I believe. I might have knocked a little bit of skin off. I suppose something from the seal—handling the fur, or from the eyes—I don't know."

Captain Peter Troake put his own theory to Dr Olds. "I don't know, Sir, I can't tell you, what's the cause of a Seal Finger. But I'll guarantee you I can tell you what to do to get one. If you wants a Seal Finger, you go out and start to haul around them old seals—the ol' ones, now, not the young ones; them ol' hoods, them ol' harps, the three-year bedlamers which is coming up to the largest ones—and put your fingers in their eyes. Don't talk about cuts or scars; forget that. Put your fingers in their eyes, and you pull and strain and haul along a seal a quintal and a half or two quintals.

"'Tis not the eyes of the seals as far as I'm concerned; it's in the grease or the fat around the eyes, and it's the strain. You pulls your joints apart or strains your hand or something. We used to be always doing that, see. Every spring you'd come in, three or four fellows would have Seal Finger.... It's strain and something in the eyes doing it. What do you think?'"

"Eyes, my ass," said Dr Olds.

But he had no answers either. After his 1947 voyage to the Front, however, he made some educated guesses. "That year I made cultures of the seals' eyes, nose and hair as I shot them, and before anyone touched them. As expected, a variety of organisms was collected but none which clinically acted as does the organism causing Seal Finger. One of the bacteria showing up frequently was the staphylococcus. This has been cultured several times before from amputated Seal Fingers, both here and by Departmental lab. But as staphylococcus in its usual clinical manifestations acts so differently—boils, carbuncles, etc.—it was felt to be a contaminant.

"However, I cultured a staphylococcus from a Seal Finger under unusually good conditions and more or less believe it may be a causative factor. A man on the *Clarenville* developed a Seal Finger just before I left the ship and he was given sulfa drugs and hot compresses. When he returned to Twillingate, his finger had not improved. He continued on this regime for three weeks and the finger was worse. I then advised admission to hospital and amputation. On admission I started him on penicillin, and two days later the finger pointed (abscessed), which I had never seen one do before. (Penicillin is an active drug against staphylococcus; sulfa drugs are also, to a lesser extent.) Under a specially sterile technique I aspirated the pus from his finger and cultured it, and it was a staph, and with continued penicillin treatment his finger became well. One other man, from the *Bessie Marie*, had a Seal Finger and he got well on sulfadiazine.

"From cultures and the response to drugs, I almost begin to believe that the etiological bacterium is a staphylococcus; but it is a very queer way for a staph to act. However, I recommend penicillin treatment as soon as the diagnosis is made. Sulfa has apparently been effective in many, but it is nowhere as effective against staphylococcus as penicillin.

"It is a fact that only men engaged in handling seals (and in all probability old seals) develop this type of infection. Further, it is almost always limited to the first or middle joint of the first or second finger of the right or left hand. Thirdly, the incubation period is ten days or over. Without any remembered trauma or cut, a fusiform swelling appears in one of the phalangeal joints. Moderate stiffness is found, some redness but not too hot to the touch; no malaise or elevated temperature, [except] possibly one to three degrees Fahrenheit.

"Without treatment over a period of three or four weeks, suppuration may occur and there will be prolonged drainage. The end result is always a stiff finger due to the disintegration of the cartilage whether it drains or not, if the patient leaves it long enough. [The latter] is unusual as a stiff finger is a nuisance to a fisherman and he demands amputation so that he can get fishing as soon as possible.

"Clinically, it resembles a chronic arthritic condition simulating in many ways a tubercular infection. I have made many cultures of the infected finger on many types of media and had it done by others, and the offending organism seems to be small type coccus, possibly related to the bacteria that causes boils, carbuncles, etc.; but it certainly does not act that way clinically. At the ice I also made many cultures from the seals themselves; I would take a pocketful of culture media test tubes, shoot a few seals and before anyone else touched them, take cultures from the hair, the palpebral fissures (eyeslits) and the nose. Under such conditions, of course, many different organisms were grown but the small coccus was predominant.

"My theory, because of the distribution of the lesions on the first two fingers, is that in stowing the seals in the hold, the men move them about by inserting the index and middle fingers through the eye openings and thus rub the bacteria into the skin. Why no surface lesions are ever found has not been explained. There may, or may not, have been a history of a cut or scratch; but there is no sealer who does not have multiple small abrasions on his hands most of the time. Use of hooks for stowing pelts and wearing of gloves when handling seals is, I feel, the best preventive measure; but you try and get the sealers to use these precautions. But what is the loss of a finger? Few of them play the piano.

"Cures have been effected by sulfa drugs, later by penicillin, and still better by aureomycin. One year I treated thirteen with penicillin alone and eventually had to amputate four."

During his research Olds corresponded with anyone who might have a piece of the puzzle. Among these was the Norwegian Kaare Rodahl, who estimated that ten percent of the sealers working off Spitzbergen in 1950 were afflicted. As Chief of the Physiology Department of the Arctic Aeromedical Laboratory at Ladd Air Force Base in Alaska, Rodahl was, however, intrigued by the rarity of Seal Finger among Alaska sealers in the Pribilof Islands. So was Dr Olds. In November 1951 Olds sent Dr Rodahl a reprint of his paper on the hood seal from the November 1950 issue of the *Journal of Mammalogy*, and they began a correspondence. He also exchanged information with William Jellison of the Rocky Mountain Laboratory in Hamilton, Montana. Jellison noted that in 1950 a researcher named Waage had reported on the successful treatment of twenty-four cases of "sealer's finger" with aureomycin. Since Olds had already successfully treated patients with sulfa and penicillin three years earlier and was using aureomycin before 1950, it is unlikely he learned the treatment from Jellison.

In the spring of 1952 Dr Olds had another chance to go to the ice. David E. Sergeant, a marine biologist from England working on Newfoundland's harp seal fishery under Dr William Templeman, had come to Twillingate the previous December looking for seals and hoping to meet Olds. John and Betty had just gone to Windsor for a two-month holiday. Sergeant talked to Captain Saul White, read Olds' 1947 report to the Newfoundland Fisheries Board and invited him along that spring.

With Betty ill, John had to stay home. Sergeant sailed alone with Captain Wilf Barbour on the *Blue Seal*, and on his return documented a number of Seal Finger cases for John—including his own. He planned to do more seal research off Twillingate, he said, and still hoped to meet him. In May, Olds advised him that seals were scarce locally. The ice was well off, he said, and although it might come in again, Twillingaters "were hoping very much that it wouldn't. From what you say," wrote Olds, "I believe you had a Seal Finger, but you certainly were lucky to get out of the trouble with as little amount of medicine as you took. In the old days you very likely would have lost it." He never did meet David Sergeant.

In March of 1953 Professor E. G. D. Murray of the Department of Bacteriology and Immunology at McGill University asked Dr Olds to help supply cultures for seal research. When Olds outlined his work on Seal Finger, Murray became very enthusiastic and asked him to send an infected finger.

"By this time amputated fingers were in short supply," Olds told his St John's audience, "as a cure was possible if treatment was started before the joint was seriously involved. We were in luck the following spring. I saw one with the joint so involved that I could conscientiously advise amputation. This patient was unique in my experience—a housewife who had been helping her husband can seal meat. To try and eliminate skin contamination as far as possible, the hand and finger were scrubbed twice daily for 3 days, followed by merthiolate swabbing and sterile gauze. This procedure was done again pre-operatively on the OR table and a sterile glove was put on the hand in addition to the usual sterile draping. A rapid guillotine amputation was done through the mid-proximal phalanx, the rubber glove finger twisted over the stump, secured by a sterile elastic band, and dropped into a thermos bottle containing finely cracked ice and salt as no dry ice was available. The patient had no medication up to the time of amputation except routine preoperative morphine and atropine."

Murray received the specimen by air express the next day, June 16th, 1953. Knowing that various gram-positive bacteria had been identified or suspected, he suspected an organism related to *Listeria*. With fresh material from a Seal Finger patient available to him for the first time, the professor immediately set up standard tests using chick embryos and laboratory mice. In the end, however, he could only report that "...several organisms were isolated. One was thought to be a member of the genus *Nocardia*. Another organism isolated after several weeks of storage was a gram-positive rod which liquified Loeffler's serum medium. This organism was classified as a member of the genus *Corynebacterium*. It is very difficult to assess the significance of these isolates. None is a known pathogen and after such long storage and frequent handling...air contamination cannot be overlooked. At no time was an organism resembling a member of the genus *Listeria* or a member of the genus *Erysipelothrix* isolated."

Dr Olds concluded that possibly two or more organisms, generally considered non-pathogens alone, might be involved symbiotically. He continued writing to Professor Murray for several years and sent him a copy of his Seal Finger paper in the *Canadian Medical Association Journal*. Late in their correspondence, Murray sought his opinion on the widespread problem of hospital infections. Dr Olds had always prided himself on the cleanliness of his modest operating theatre, sometimes even refusing to send high-risk patients to St John's because of its known higher infection rate. Evidently, Professor Murray had heard of this and valued his opinion.

Summarizing for the Medical Society, Olds concluded, "Whatever the etiology [cause] of Seal Finger, I am sure the disease could be prevented. Sealers' fingers are tough and thick-skinned but are rarely without minor abrasions or cracks. I believe these to be the site of entry as there is practically never a history of a cut on the finger involved nor visible evidence of one.

"I also think there is a reasonable explanation for involvement of the finger joints and not the thumb. Seal pelts are heavy—up to 300 pounds—slippery when first removed, and stony hard when frozen. They have to be moved by hand several times before they are finally stowed in the hold, and there is only one good handle to use. The palpebral fissures are ideal for finger-holds, though the thin skin feels pretty sharp and rough, especially when frozen. Iron grab hooks are supplied for the purpose of stowing pelts but they are rarely used as bare fingers are easier to find. Gloves could be worn but they are no good for general wear and the universal knitted woollen mitt has only one free finger, which is not enough for a heavy pelt. More soap and water on the hands wouldn't hurt but isn't too practical a suggestion as water is scarce and you might not wash at the right time. No one at the ice gets good marks or promotion for cleanliness.

"My feeling is that aureomycin is the drug of choice. I have not used erythromycin or Albamycin T and it is possible they may be as good or better. None of them is of any use unless given before the joint is involved. From my experience, 16-18 250 mg doses of aureomycin given at 8-hour intervals has been very effective and capable of converting a tense, shiny, red, painful finger to its original state within a week or 10 days."

Did J. M. Olds find a cure for Seal Finger, as many grateful non-amputees liked to claim? He was certainly among the first on this side of the Atlantic to undertake original research on this disease. And, with his pipeline to the US drug companies, he may well have been curing patients with penicillin and aureomycin before anyone else. As usual, once he had found a way to avoid amputation, the topic became for him less urgent. He was a very busy doctor, his laboratory was primitive and other matters soon absorbed his interest.

Part V

Looking Aft

Chapter Twenty-Eight

Carmanville Nurse

"I was scared."

— Nurse Jessie Drover

Nurse Jessie (Troake) Drover of Durrell came to her lifelong profession almost by accident. "My sister Lil worked at Notre Dame Bay Memorial in 1926 and I went for two weeks to relieve someone on holidays. It was night duty, on the top floor where they had convalescents, mostly TB children in casts. Mamie Wheeler was in charge on Second Floor. After two weeks I was fully determined I had all I ever wanted of nursing. I had spent the two weeks rolling plaster bandages. They made their own then, for plaster casts. The plaster got in your nose, hair, eyes, under your fingernails, down your throat—everywhere.

"The only patient I remember from that time was one I took to be a pulmonary hemorrhage, which sent me flying down the steps at 3:00 AM shouting for Miss Wheeler. It turned out to be blueberry vomit and I got a dressing down. That fall I went teaching school, and around March had to go to Hospital for an eye infection. Dr Parsons kept urging me to go nursing. Finally I promised to try it again in the summer holidays; a bit of extra money would come in handy for teacher training in the fall. That July I went to work in the Hospital as a nursing aide and never looked back.

"Some of the new girls who came in as aides in 1928 were Meta (Chaulk) Osmond, Mary Young, Jessie (Smith) Dominy, Kit (Phillips) Churchill, Hazel Anstey, Marion Jeans, Eva Swyers and my sister Lil. We went into uniform, had classes organized, and began.

"The classes I remember best were in the OPD with a Dr Anderson. The mail used to come by dog-team, weekly or biweekly. Being at the mercy of winds, snow and ice, it was seldom on schedule. Unless it arrived late at night, the Postmaster distributed the mail when it came. So if we were in class and the lights came on in the Post Office across the Harbour, someone would say, 'Mail's in!' And Dr Anderson would say, 'Good—that's all,' and off we'd go.

"Top Floor was still the convalescent children's, with side rooms, one or two, for private patients. The children were mostly all in Bradford frames—one-inch pipe with moveable canvas strips—or plaster casts, and they soon learned to manoeuvre themselves like young seals. The cots were low, without side frames, and could slide back and forth. Because the children were there for so long, some for years, they were like a family. They shed their casts for larger and newer ones like old clothes.

"The nurses were all from Johns Hopkins then. A stint on Top Floor was more a social event than nursing. I remember one Southern girl who could Charleston like a dream and she made chocolate fudge the same way. We'd do anything Mac wanted done so long as she did the entertaining.

"I must mention the lighting system—the old water wheel that was turned on at night cut down on cost. To say it was dim would be a gross understatement. It was dismal, spooky. And since at that time we didn't have a morgue or a night orderly, a newly dead body was put in a room and we had to made rounds on the dead as well as the living.

"At first we used small lamps, later lanterns and flashlights. I remember using a lamp once while fixing a dressing on a young fellow, a second-day post-op appendectomy. He and I started laughing about something and the glass chimney fell off and he nearly hopped out of bed. A sure tragedy at that time—might have torn out his stitches. Or so we thought. Back then patients had to be carefully turned over and weren't allowed out of bed under a week or so.

"The staff all ate together. The roast was placed in front of Dr Parsons and he carved. If you didn't like farina pudding—a cheap dessert—you didn't say so. You ate your 'Welsh Rarebit' and counted yourself lucky to get away from a second helping. No point trying to argue with Dr Parsons; it was good healthy food and we needed it. But we didn't eat at the dining room on our afternoon off. There was a close family feeling about the whole staff—doctors, nurses, laundry workers, electricians, boiler room—all.

"The old bus *Twilly* was our picnic conveyance as well as ambulance. She rattled around the narrow roads to every crook and cranny on the Island.

"There was only one telephone. It was at the Pardys' in Little Harbour. Herring Neck would call this house, and you went over and called back to see what it might be. We had a southern doctor then, Rube Waddell. One time Rube was talking on their phone to a man in Herring Neck whose wife was sick. Rube needed to know whether to take the obstetrics bag or the other, so he said, 'Is she pregnant?'

"The fellow said, 'I don't know, Sir; I don't know what you'm talkin' about.'

"And Rube said, 'Well, Jesus—is she knocked up?'

"'Oh, no! No, doctor!'

"If you went to Twillingate as an aide, you got to know somebody who had trained outside and they recommended you. Ethyl Graham recommended me. There were five girls, including Edith Simms, who went to Englewood, New Jersey; I went to Montreal. So we were all landed immigrants. I left Twillingate on the first of January, 1930."

Jessie Troake came home in May 1933 as an RN and had just started work at the Hospital when Dr Parsons asked her to go to Carmanville. He had been concerned about the lack of nursing care around the Bay once navigation closed in the fall. The Outport Nursing and Industrial Association, formed in 1924, enabled outport women to fund local nursing care through the sale of handicrafts and other work. Parsons had helped organize a local support committee, hired a NONIA nurse, found a boarding house and set the fees. At the last moment the nurse couldn't come.

"Now this was my first time home for three years," said Jessie, "and I was reluctant to go." Dr Parsons said, 'Well, if you don't go, the work we've done up to now will fall flat.' Dr Parsons had lent me money to go in training; I had intended to be a teacher because I couldn't afford nursing. I felt an obligation, so I went. I went right out of training. Nowadays you wouldn't be allowed to do it. I had three or four days pulling teeth with Dr Olds—the shortest dental course in history—I had a crash course in obstetrics, et cetera, and that was it.

"I went down on the coastal boat as far as Change Islands—Dr Parsons went too because he had a meeting—and a man Waterman took me over from there. I landed in Carmanville on the coldest Christmas Eve on record. 'Twas dark when we got in and they just put me on the wharf. I had with me four or five Twillingate patients going home for the winter, my supply of drugs and my textbooks. I was scared. They just put the whole thing up on the wharf and left again. The water was freezing behind the boat as she went. Men came with horses and took the patients away and they took my drugs and everything. And by and by I noticed there was only one man left. I was just standing there, so I suppose he realized there was something wrong. I was wearing slacks, not my nurse's things. He came over and said, 'Did you come on the boat?'

"'Yes,' I said, 'I'm the nurse, and I don't know where I'm going.'

"He said, 'You come up with me, my dear, and we'll soon find that out.' 'Twas a man Blackwood.

"So they had a boarding house for me at Ernie Hicks'—Aunt Laura and Mr Hicks'. I always called her Aunt Laura, but him I called Mr Hicks. They had two daughters; they all went to the United States after, and their oldest daughter went into nursing at Englewood.

"Aunt Laura's parlour was my office. They had cupboards for me and I kept my medicines there. I didn't lock it. It was her house, and nobody was coming in and out. I was travelling one week out of each month; the rest of the time I was in Carmanville. I made calls, and people would come to see me.

"Sometimes I had to go out to Alder Harbour where Ted Drover's mill was. A woman over there had a bad heart, and every time she'd have an attack, they'd send the horse for me. And sometimes it would be so late I'd have to stay the night. Ted and I weren't serious then; but he had a gramophone, a Victrola, and he had opera, he had *Carmen*. All such music was new to me—Beethoven and *Peer Gynt*, and all this, and it was...oh, 'twas lovely. Ted was from St John's—born in Green's Harbour but grew up, lived his life, in St John's; St John's in the winter and Brown's Arm in the summertime. I've told Ted since, 'I married the place as much as you.'

"Now there was a sedative out at that time—I forget the name of it—but it was exactly the same size as today's aspirin. And I had this call to come back to Carmanville: Uncle Ernie was sick. Well, Ted took me over. I'm glad he did, because when I asked Aunt Laura what the trouble was, she said, 'I can't get Ernie to wake up.'

"And I said, 'Well, what have you been doing?'

"'He had the 'flu last evening,' she said, and I gave him aspirin. I gave him two every four hours like you do.'

"'Show me where you got the aspirin,' I said. She did—and it was this sedative. This is why Uncle Ernie was zonked. I was frightened to death. I said, 'Ted, come on in. We've got to get to work on him.' I gave him a coffee enema; I didn't know what else to do. We got him out of bed and we walked him and walked him, and walked him some more. Wouldn't let him lie down; I tried to keep him up and active. After a while, he started to come round. As soon as he could swallow, I started getting coffee into him.

"Now Uncle Ernie was a real outport man, with a Carmanville accent, which was different than Gander Bay's. 'Twas something like a Musgrave Harbour accent, where they soften their Rs. For example, Frank Mercer was the RCMP officer in Twillingate for a long time and his wife's name was Ada. In Carmanville she was always called Ada*r*. Well, they put Rs on like that, and flattened their vowels. So Uncle Ernie, in explaining to the people around, would say, 'I don't know what 'appened to me. I never 'ad the like o' that 'appen to me before. Lara gave me aspirin and I went to sleep and I didn't know anything until I woke up and the Nurse was walkin' me round the room.' And Aunt Laura would be over there with this smile on her face, knitting. Last time I saw her, I said, 'Aunt Laura, did you ever tell Uncle Ernie?'

"'Yes I did, finally,' she said.

"It was a severe winter, with deep snow that at times made travelling impossible. There was a lot of pneumonia and a couple of people died. We had only linseed oil poultices and we tried to get as much fluid in them as possible. That winter one of the first mercy flights took place. An acute appendix was air-lifted direct from Carmanville to St John's. Although the patient was my responsibility, the transportation had been arranged by a relative in St John's.

"If I got into trouble, I had to contact the Hospital by wireless. I hated obstetrics. I remember I had a very bad time—a woman who was in labour a long time. I think her squeals frightened me more than anything else. I wired Dr Olds, told him the symptoms. He wired back and said to do a decapitation. That means, as a last resort—to save the woman if you can't have a cesarean and the baby's head is too big to come down through—to crush the skull so the head could get down. If the mother died, the baby was going to die anyway. That frightened me completely.

"That winter, Harry French's sawyer went berserk. They wanted me to come up to Gander Bay, so I went. There wasn't enough snow to go through the woods by horse, and 'twas ice only around the shore, so we trekked all the way up, all around Frederickton, over boulders and between ballicatters and whatever. I was up all night with him until we got a policeman—there was no Ranger Force then—a Constable Bartlett who was in Musgrave Harbour. I don't know what was wrong with the sawyer. He might have had a stroke, or a brain tumor. We had an awful time with him. He was French's sawyer for years, a very well-liked man. He died; he didn't come out of it.

"I'll never forget as long as I live going through Frederickton. The church bell was ringing and there was some soft snow falling. And the lights in the church and everything....

"I should not have been there, just out of training with no experience except in a hospital where conditions were so different. But in Gander Bay we had no special difficulties. I remember only pleasant things in Gander Bay. People were so good to me. Wherever I went, they served me delicious bottled meat. They told me it was beef—yet I never saw any cows. Later I realized it was moose."

That spring Nurse Troake returned to Twillingate. She worked at the Hospital until fall, when she was sent to Musgrave Harbour at the east end of the Straight Shore. The Hospital still paid her salary and she still dealt directly with Twillingate. After that she worked as a Public Health nurse— "an enormous salary raise from $40.00 per month to $75.00!"

"I came back to Twillingate during the War, around 1943-44. Dr Olds was alone and the nurse doing outside work had been called overseas, so I ended up doing District work again, this time on New World Island and especially Herring Neck. How many times have I pushed off from Pardy's stage with Mr John Pardy, God bless him, making me take his mitts or oilskins or something to wrap around me. The more serious cases always went back to Dr Olds, either in person or in signs and symptoms, and always received the necessary consideration and advice. I wonder how he stood up under it all.

"At one period I was giving anesthetics, schooled by Joyce Scammell, and to this day I can think of no more satisfying sound than that of a patient under ether, and especially when J. M. Olds was in the abdominal cavity. If ever I prayed, I prayed then. I was in the OR when the Siamese twin was delivered by cesarean. The woman had been in labour across the Bay for several days and Ted brought her over. And whoever was giving anesthetics was gone, so Dr Olds called me. We were living in the old nurse's home and I remember I was frying pork chops. He said could I come over right away because he gave her a spinal, and you need someone checking blood pressure. The babies were full-term, and born dead. He had them in a jar in his office for years—an acceptable practice with stillborns in those days

"Looking back, so many things, small things, flash through my mind. One of the early patients, an elderly man with uremic poisoning, coming back from the brink. A young lad with intestinal obstruction taking his last breath, while we waited for the end—but took one more instead, and then another and another while we held *our* breath.

"TB patients coughing their lives away in prolonged agony.

"The sweet babies in the nursery with hare lip repairs; they always seemed more gentle, more vulnerable than other babies. The old woman who couldn't void on a bed pan and said, 'My dear, if I could only get down stage.' The comfort of having George Ings around in a crisis. The absolute puzzlement on the faces of medical students trying to take a case history—'What's *smurt?* [smart, or sting]. The vile coffee we made for J. M. O. in the morning when he used to go birding; he always asked for it but never drank it. The linseed meal poultices, mustard plasters, the 'Stomach Drip'....

"I remember we all went through the agony of a young doctor who mis-diagnosed an isolated diphtheria case until it was too late for the antitoxin to be effective and the patient died. It taught me early in my nursing career what tremendous burdens men carry who deal with life and death, and it made me sympathetic to their reactions.

"And I remember how nervous one of the doctors was when his wife was in labour. Dr Parsons told him to get out of the Hospital, so he took his gun and went up around Hospital Pond and shot a wild duck. I don't know what he was most proud of, his first son or his first duck....

"Miss Georgina Stirling, the retired opera star, coming to Sunday tea at the Cottage...her blouse was on inside out; she knew, but wouldn't change it—bad luck. She was a patient later when I was on nights. She couldn't sleep and we had some interesting chats....

"It was a life and time and place I wouldn't have missed. Sharing it all with dedicated nurses made it that much more enriching, and I mention especially Ethel Graham, Betty Olds and Stella Manuel.

"The small balcony off the wards was always in use when the sun shone. All the beds were pulled out and most patients were tanned beyond belief; this was considered good treatment for TB at the time.

"But I remember the balcony especially for early mornings. When the work was done—somebody else must have been making plaster bandages then, or maybe instant readymades had come—and before the patients were awake, I'd steal out and listen to the day awakening—the fishing boats put-putting up through the Tickle, the roosters starting to crow, the birds chattering to one another, the first sunlight slanting up over the hill, the lovely smell of dew on moss and blueberry bushes. It was a beautiful time. I loved Top Floor."

Chapter Twenty-Nine

An Education in Itself

"Hospitals are run by nurses."
— William A. Nolen, MD

One day in 1949 when most of the nursing staff was down to lunch, young Lorna (Bradley) Stuckless was taking pans of water around the women's ward so the patients could wash up. Suddenly a woman called out, "My dear, get me a bed pan quick! Get me a bed pan!" The new aide from Eastport hurriedly did so. "When I went back to collect the pans," said Lorna, "here she was still sitting on it. 'My dear,' she said, 'my baby is coming in the bed pan!'

"What a fright! I had no idea what was taking place. Both my mother and grandmother were midwives, but I really didn't understand the whole process. The RNs had warned me never to go to the doctors on my own, but I thought, 'Well, this time I don't care.' When I went out, Dr Olds was just coming out of Number Nine at the head of the stairs. He'd been in checking on Winnie Price, whose leg he had amputated that morning.

"'Dr Olds, come quick,' I said, 'there's a woman having a baby in a bed pan!' He spun round and came with me. On the way he said, 'Now, you take a screen and I'll take one.' So we went in and screened her. Then he said, 'Go get me the tray.' At first, being new there, I had no idea what he wanted. But I had kind of watched where everything was put, so I went to Number Seven and got the right tray.

"When 'twas all over, he said, 'How long you been here?'

"'Three days.'

"'Well,' he drawled, 'daaamed goood! I think you'll do it yourself the next time.'

"After that, he and I were kind of friends...he would notice me every time we passed as if to say, 'Very good; you did a good job.' A lot of the nurses and aides were scared of him, but I was never. He said to me once, 'Why are people scared of me?'

"'I don't know,' I said. "You're only a man, and I'm not scared of men.'

"'Good for you.'"

Lorna Stuckless was one of hundreds of young women who worked as nursing assistants at Notre Dame Bay Memorial from 1924 onward. Chronically short of RNs, Twillingate had to rely on well trained aides to bear most of its nursing burden. That year there were only 350 qualified nurses in all of Newfoundland, and it would be fourteen years before the province had a nursing school. Moreover, few nurses cared to work in Twillingate. For years the Hospital had met the requirements of the American College of Surgeons, but there was nothing it could do about the isolation, hard work and low salaries.

In the 1930s Twillingate got most of its nurses from John Hopkins. After the War this source dried up, leaving only a few former aides who had trained elsewhere and come back. Often in the forties and fifties Dr Olds was lucky to have a single RN on staff. When he did, they had to shoulder interns' duties—just as aides had to take on nurses' work. Under such conditions, few nurses stayed long. Those who did usually married and had children and had to be replaced. Like Dr Parsons before him, John Olds and his Board were always scouting for the brave few. By the fifties they were recruiting farther afield, in Canada and Asia and especially Britain where midwifery skills were taught. In February of 1965, the Board hired fourteen Filipino nurses.

In 1933 a graduate nurse at Notre Dame Bay Memorial got only $40.50 a month and found—room and board and laundry included. Dr Olds himself got only $50. Grace (Patten) Sparkes, who did both housekeeping and teaching, received the same salary as Olds. "Once," she recalled, "at a party at his house, John made place cards and on mine he put 'The Bloody Plutocrat.'"

Grace was a Newfoundlander from the Burin Peninsula. For a nurse from away, Twillingate was far more daunting. "Only three or four cars on Twillingate Island," wrote Thelma (Groze) Christie, who arrived from Toronto General Hospital Nursing School in March 1939. "Most of the fishermen on the Dole. Many suffering from tuberculosis. Bone surgery was a big item—often five or six hip operations in one room post-operatively. Patients with beriberi—very rare in the Western World. Dr Olds cured them by teaching them to eat their potato skins, bakeapples, lobster—all containing the vitamins they lacked, especially vitamin B^1. And all the time people would leave lobsters lying on the beach—wouldn't eat them. But every patient received one ounce of cod liver oil (they called it 'God Oil') daily, and vitamin B pills. He asked the staff to take the same.

"Our only way of receiving news was shortwave radio, battery operated. It seemed very inadequate after war was declared, as the only stations we got were London, Paris, et cetera. Patients had no way of hearing any war news at all. Dr Olds told all he knew about the Dieppe disaster, and one patient remarked, 'They'd better be careful or someone is going to get killed.'

Gary Saunders

"[The Hospital] was managed efficiently with very little money. No waste of any materials. Only one Registered Nurse on duty each shift. Local girls were chosen and trained by doctors and nurses to do most of the bedside nursing. The RNs were responsible for all drugs, for discipline and many of the special treatments." Though Miss Groze learned to like her new life, she was an exception.

After 1939 Dr Olds could see that his only solution was to train local high school girls as aides. He had already trained RNs and even one aide to be competent scrub nurses and anesthetists. These included Edith (Simms) Manuel, Rose (Cooper) Young, Elfreda (Kelloway) Dalley, and Stella Manuel. He did it by apprenticeship enriched with lectures, demonstrations and tests.

While training, nursing assistants wore a capless blue uniform. A "Blue" who studied hard and behaved well could expect to receive her cap in two to three months. Young women on kitchen duty wore green. In 1940, with the RN shortage getting worse, five blue aides, each with three years' experience, were asked to consider doing RNs' work. To signify their greater responsibility they were given a pink uniform and white cap. Thus began the era of senior or "Pink Aides." In 1942 a "Blue" earned $7.00 a month, a "Pink" twice as much.

Mildred (Scammell) Sheppard's first glimpse of hospital life came in the early thirties. For a young girl from a sheltered home, it was a shock to be exposed to so much illness all at once. "But I soon became accustomed to the life—though there were moments of homesickness, especially when I saw the Change Islands boat pulling out from Blandford's wharf. The room my friend and I occupied had absolutely no heat; in winter we called it 'The Bait Depot.' The visiting medicos were horrified and ordered a door cut directly opposite the hall stove, which brought a great degree of comfort.

"In those days there was nothing called an energy crisis; but we surely had one within the Hospital. Promptly at 11:00 PM, the regular lights went off and we reverted to the water wheel. This was augmented by kerosene oil lanterns. One particular night nurse, like Zacchaeus of Bible days, was so short that on rounds her lantern practically touched the floor. Later, flashlights replaced the lanterns.

"We often waited for days for our pay, then knocked timidly on the door of the Manager's office. Almost always he gave us sad tales of extremely low finances. We often came away with $5.00 'on account.'"

Florence (Burt) Ings finished school in 1937 and got accepted as a nurse's aide. "But no High School curriculum prepared me for the challenge. Learning about the Seven Years' War was one thing—I soon forgot the details anyway—but seven years' service with the hospital, even though I was a volunteer and not a conscript, was something I could not possibly forget. It was an education in itself. There were fourteen aides, five graduates and around ninety patients. We were diligently taught to care for them, always being supervised as we took each step to more responsible duties."

Said Frances (Cook) Rowsell, "Our hair had to be a certain length; to have it touching our collars was improper and forbidden. That was as unpardonable as using a safety pin to replace a missing button. Our surgical scissors—a must at all times—had to be tucked through two buttonholes at the back of our aprons. Our uniform consisted of the basic blue, over which we wore a starched white apron. A stiffly starched white collar and starched white cuffs were the finishing touches. Our white stockings were not nylon, but silk, and they wrinkled. The white shoes had to be cleaned daily."

Senior aides shepherded the frightened newcomers. Molly Arnold remembered her first weeks in 1940: "I had never been so frightened in my life! My [initiation] took place in Room Six under Floss Burt—kind, laughing Floss. How patient she was with me! My starched collar was beheading me, my shoes were torturing my feet and green soap and Lysol seemed to be turning my hands to splinters. By some miracle, she prevented me from harming any patient or myself. It took a while before I could conquer my fear. I remember making rounds with a little lantern. We were always reminded to keep it in good working order and *never* to shine it in a patient's face."

Alison (Loveridge) Bartle, who joined the staff in November 1939, remembered other rules. "Except in emergencies we were not permitted to speak or to raise our voices, nor to use first names while on duty. If we laughed too merrily we were reprimanded by the nurse on duty. As there was no lounge and our sleeping quarters were on Third Floor, this was quite a chore and we often sinned. Caring for the patients was of course our first responsibility. But first a raw recruit was shadowed by a senior aide and when possible by a graduate nurse. Whenever I showed signs of absolute panic, someone was always there to encourage me or to take over where I left off—or had not even begun. In time the patients didn't cover their heads or cringe when I came near. Often they'd cheer me on, saying, 'You'll get used to it.' I never did manage to view sickness and pain with objectivity and I don't think anyone ever does."

By the time Lorna Stuckless started work in 1949, most aides came from outside Twillingate. Their training had become a full-fledged course requiring up to a year. "Stella Manuel was there then. We had courses every week and exams to write before we got our cap, our blue uniform and so on. We learned at our own speed. In the first few months you got just a dress and apron; two or three months later, you got your cap at a little ceremony. After a few more months, or a year, you received your blue uniform."

Gary Saunders

Many Twillingate nursing alumnae mentioned Stella Manuel, who was Head Nurse from about 1940 until the 1950s. "Nurse Manuel called the roll at 11:00 PM," said an aide. "If discipline was required she'd take you aside in the linen closet. One time she recalled an aide who had left without washing the beds." Beds also had to lined up properly. Molly Arnold admitted that though they secretly rebelled at her strictness, "we learned things we shall never forget. We have her to thank for instilling responsibility. We marvelled at her dedication and we all remembered her one brief but important first rule: 'The patient must always come first.' Her main concern was not so much to keep us from making an error the second time as to prevent our making one at all. Our lives are richer because of her."

The Main Utility Room was "a stepping stone to future shock," recalled Mrs Bartle. "Its rows of bedpans and urinals had a sort of dubious splendour since they were a very present help in time of trouble. But the rows of curved basins looked harmless and the containers of green soap and disinfectants looked, well, interesting. And why was that giant toilet bowl called a hopper? It seemed a misnomer, since we and not it did the hopping. The sink seemed to be of giant proportions. And what was in the covered trays on the top shelf? I soon learned that they contained the 'fittings' for hot compresses and the wherewithal for that scourge of all patients, the enema. And that hissing monster was a *Primus* for boiling hot compresses. I boiled dozens, hundreds of compresses; but I hated the *Primus* and always approached it feeling it might blow up in my face.

"We all have our own memories of our attempts to emulate Florence Nightingale. Some are funny and others best forgotten. Like the first time I screened a patient and came bearing, if not glad tidings, then soapy ones. It was my 'solo sudsy,' or first unsupervised enema. After the usual preparations I stood there like the Statue of Liberty, holding the container. I wasn't saying 'Give me your tired, your poor'; I was saying (inaudibly, of course) 'Give me good results.'

"Suddenly the container slipped and it was decks awash! I never knew such a small amount of water could gush over such a large area. Before heading for mop and pail I had the presence of mind to put the poor patient on a bedpan."

Molly Arnold never forgot night duty. "With such a shortage of staff, we had only two aides and one graduate on the Second Floor and one aide on the first. On Second, one worked in the Wing and the other in the women's and men's wards. The graduate was of course in charge. Night duty began at 8:00 PM and ended in the morning whenever our work was finished—8:30 or 9:30, never at eight sharp. There was so much to do and so few to carry the burden. The endless compresses kept us going at a pretty fast clip. Then there were solutions to mix and countless other duties in the still of the night. Whenever there was an empty bed, how we longed to just lie down for a few minutes!

"If we were lucky enough to take a few minutes off, it was done more or less on the run. Many nights we had no time even to munch a biscuit or drink a glass of milk. Once a month we were permitted a 'night off' (night duty lasted a full month then)—which meant reporting in at midnight instead of at eight o'clock. The pay for night duty was $12.50 a month.

"To be posted to the First Floor meant a lonely vigil, made lonelier when the OPD bell announced an emergency. The bell always startled me and I always expected the worst. We looked forward to the graduate nurse's hourly rounds—someone to talk to for a few minutes. Daylight meant making mounds of toast for breakfast trays. After that we brought all the patients pans of water, then scoured the trays with green soap before returning them to the Utility Room shelves.

"Between 4:00 and 6:00 AM sleep did its best to conquer our defences. But there was always something to keep us on our feet, like a trip to the basement for ice—no ice machines then. We went down with our bucket and hacked away at a chunk until we had enough for various ice collars and for all the water glasses.

"I wonder how many unnecessary steps we made, by day and night, trying to figure out where a bell was ringing. No buzzers and lights then; each patient had a hand bell. We skittered around, frantically trying to hurry without seeming to—a neat trick.

"We worked long and exhausting hours for little pay. No off-duty recreation was provided. But many lasting friendships were made, both among the staff and between staff and patients. The patients taught us the meaning of courage."

In those days discharging patients from far away entailed more than having a car pick them up at the front door. Often the *Bonnie Nell* took them home on its regular Bay run. The *Clyde* or its successor *Northern Ranger* commonly blew its whistle in the Bight at 2:00 or 3:00 in the morning. "What a commotion when the *Clyde* arrived unexpectedly and Dr Olds decided to discharge five or six patients," said Mayme Hewlett. "This might be their last chance before navigation closed. While they were being hurriedly made ready, including bills and discharge papers, Hodge Brothers would be called to ask the Captain to delay one hour because there were patients going north or south as the case might be. Then the difficulty of getting teams, either horse or dog, to take them to the steamer. Often at this time of year no car was available and certainly no road was plowed. One could see George Ings bundling them on the sleighs, administering the last rites, so to speak, by tucking in their blankets and giving last instructions. With a wave they were off, and George could be heard shouting to the teamster: 'Don't forget to bring back the blankets!'"

Gary Saunders

Entertainment was strictly homemade. Some, like Dr Olds, were content with Twillingate's simple pleasures. A day at the Tilt was popular. "We had but to ask for the key and he passed it over," said Janet (Earle) Hori. "There was a stove, table, some chairs and bunks and a few books—but no telephone. The sough of wind in the gnarled trees, the hiss of surf on the beach and the cries of gulls soon banished hospital tensions. The view was superb. It was the site of many fabulous parties, of corn beef and cabbage 'scoffs,' wiener roasts and invigorating ocean swimming."

Rita (Boyd) Rios liked sitting on a blanket on the hills behind the Staff House. "I really enjoyed the view," she said. "Or getting our money together for a taxi ride. Or walking to the stores, to Colbourne's cafe, et cetera. And of course the many trips to Al Green's little store in the Hospital basement. Unlike Florida, Twillingate had those marvellous winter days with simple fun such as walking or frolicking in the snow. Occasionally a boat load of us would go in to Lewisporte, or put on a Hospital play. I enjoyed playing Trixie in *Deacon Stubbs*.

The Hustler's Club was not primarily a drama group. It also organized teas and helped with church suppers and sales of work. Its plays, however, became an annual highlight. "We started practicing after Christmas," wrote Janet Hori, "and staged our performance in the early spring right after Lent—we did not indulge in such frivolities during the Lenten Season. From the money earned we bought such items as a refrigerator and dishwasher for the Diet Kitchen and various instruments for the Operating Room. We thought of this not as work but fun—or, at worst, a labour of love. It was *our* hospital. That made all the difference."

An old piano in the sitting room on the first floor of the Staff House became a magnet. With Bud Young as the capable pianist, there was step dancing with the carpet rolled back, and group singing of such songs as "Home on the Range." Mrs Bartle liked to hear George Ings and Meta Wiseman sing 'Summer Land,' one verse of which went:

The sun will never set, in Summer Land;
No eyes with tears are wet, in Summer Land;
No shade of dark'ning night will shut the view from sight;
Nor e'er becloud the light, in Summer Land.

"Who will forget Christmases at the Hospital?" mused Mayme Hewlett. "The filling of stockings on Christmas Eve, receiving the many packages from outsiders for the patients, the delicious turkey dinners at which all the staff sat down as one family, the pleasant evening at the Cottage with Dr and Mrs Olds. And, finally, Christmas morning, when the late Joe White became the jovial Santa Claus, to the delight of both patients and visitors." One year Joe danced so energetically that he tore his Achilles' tendon and ended up a patient himself.

And the Olds were noted for their hospitality. Thelma Christie, arriving only two weeks after the first Cottage burned, remembered being welcomed to their makeshift apartment on the top floor. "It was in that house, listening to Betty's records, that I became interested in classical music. They also received many new books by mail, which we were expected to enjoy with them. We had our own community at the Hospital."

In such a friendly atmosphere, pranks were inevitable. Because they helped ease tension, Dr Olds mostly turned a blind eye. At three o'clock one morning Pauline (Young) Thomas and her girlfriend rang for the duty nurse. When she came downstairs, she saw a pale thing circling and moaning in the dim hallway. Much to their amusement, she screamed and raced back upstairs. The ghost was a big floor polisher under a sheet.

Occasionally a prank turned sour. Off-duty nurses and aides were supposed to be back by 10:30 PM and in their rooms by 11:00. No men were allowed in at all, even on the first floor. Later there was a small lounge where they could see a boyfriend until 10:30 PM—but never in their room. The nurses found ways around the curfew—kept watches on the matrons, put dummies in their beds—that sort of thing. One aide, annoyed that certain nurses were abusing the curfew, stayed out with a doctor until after 11:00 PM. Next day she was fired, and the doctor's salary stopped. Dr Olds protested and began paying her out of his own pocket—she was needed in the OR. After a month she quit. Her doctor friend then quit too. A year or so later the Board paid him, but not her.

Nurses from larger hospitals often remarked on the heavy responsibilities placed on Twillingate's nursing staff, and on how well the local trainees coped. Mary Esau arrived as a novice nurse in 1958. "I was overwhelmed at the responsibility in that hospital. It was a fantastic education. To this day, doctors ask me where I learned this or that and I tell them, 'probably from Twillingate doctors.'" Linda Facey was surprised that Dr Olds invited RNs to join him and his assistants on rounds and encouraged them to join the discussions.

What was it like to work with Olds? "All of us had a healthy fear and respect for him," said Florence Ings. "We all wondered how he could keep going during World War II when doctors were in even shorter supply than nurses. He gave such personal and dedicated care to patients. Often in the middle of the night he could be seen coming to the main desk to check on the patient's progress, even though he had done so several times during the day and evening.

"One evening I had just catheterized a patient's bladder and was on my way back to the Wing Utility Room. I was going full speed ahead with the tray and, rounding the corner, found myself on a collision course with Dr Olds. It was too late to slow down or go in reverse. He received the full force and contents of the tray. I managed to squeak, 'Oh, I'm very sorry Sir.' His reply is best left unrecorded."

Pauline (Young) Thomas was working alone on the children's ward with fifteen kids. "Suddenly I got a stabbing pain back of my ear, so I laid my head on one of the beds. Didn't know anything before someone poked me and said, 'You working here or sleeping here?' What a fright!—Dr Olds!"

Elfreda Dalley noted his respect for the sensibilities of female patients—and perhaps for the power of gossip. "He would never go to see a female patient without having a nurse with him," she said. "He wouldn't even talk to a woman without another woman with him."

He respected strong women. "My sister stood up to him," said Muriel Small. "She was a good nurse. She took him by the slack of the pants one day because he was being nasty to her. 'Now turn around here, John,' she said. 'What's wrong with you? What have I done?'

"'Hell, nothing,' he said."

"On duty he was firm," said Nurse Christie, "not easy to work with, even harsh. Off duty he was okay. He was a wonderful bone surgeon and one of the greatest doctors I've ever known—a very special personality which I cannot explain. My reaction to Dr Olds as a person was immediately positive. He was a quiet man, very pleasant at our first interview—professional and friendly. He was a man of few words, very rarely bad-tempered. He was not a churchgoer—said there was no need to go. He demanded respect and always got it. I feel privileged to have known and worked with the Olds family for eighteen months—the most interesting of my nursing career."

In these days of institutionalized medicine, the words of nursing aide Ann (Frank) Haines are timely. "All those Pinks and Blues who learned on the job nonetheless gave expert nursing care. They truly cared. That is what is lacking in our nursing care here and perhaps everywhere. One doesn't really do one's best unless one cares about each patient. And it's hard to care when you don't know people and their families."

Graduate nurses felt the same way. "Twillingate Hospital will always have a special place in my heart," wrote Ella (LaFever) Peters, "for it was there as a new graduate nurse that I found out how much nursing meant to me." Rita Rios, a veteran of various hospitals, said in 1974: "No place stands out in my mind with fonder memories and warmer affection than does Twillingate Hospital.... We got along well together, we had a lot of fun, and we enjoyed our work. In many cases the patients even enjoyed being there.

The mutual love and respect was in itself outstanding—qualities one seldom finds in some places of employment!"

Although Nurse Christie enjoyed Twillingate, by September 1940 she felt it her duty to enlist. "When I told Dr Olds I was resigning to get back to my own country, he said he couldn't understand why anyone would want to go to Canada, when Twillingate had all I could ever want. I am inclined to agree."

Chapter Thirty

Scrub Nurse

*"Even if I'd got a chance to work with a nice doctor,
I wouldn't have."*

— Elfreda Dalley

To ordinary folk going under the scalpel, the surgeon was God. Taken from their familiar world, stripped, probed, photographed, starved, shaved; wheeled through echoing halls to a glaring cell smelling of disinfectant; ringed by people in white or green who whispered and grunted in monosyllables; knowing they were about to be drugged, disinfected and cut open, they needed a god to wield the knife.

Standing at the god's elbow day in and day out, the scrub nurse saw another reality. Though she had never cut down through fat and muscle, she had followed every move of hands that did, had passed every scalpel, clamp, retractor, suture, swab and pad. She had rinsed amniotic fluid and blood off the surgeon's glasses, handed out iced coffee between operations, heard the grunt of dismay when the toad-like tumor came into view, felt the sag of defeat when a patient expired. She knew all too well that the surgeon had feet of clay.

Dr Olds' first scrub nurse was Betty. She worked with him from 1932 until 1937, when David was born. He cussed her when things went wrong but she forgave him, knowing whence it came. Afterward she ran the Hospital's housekeeping department, scrubbing only when no one else was available. His other principal scrub nurses were Edith (Simms) Manuel, Rose (Cooper) Young and Elfreda (Kelloway) Dalley.

Edith Simms succeeded Betty in the OR. She found Dr Olds "a clever man who knew what he was doing; but he had a bad disposition, a short temper, a short fuse. The more serious an operation, the more intricate, the worse his disposition. A mastoidectomy was no problem. Something new like cataracts upset him. He wasn't too bad with bone surgery—spinal fusions, for example—what he called 'clean' operations. But in the abdomen there was so much you could accidentally snip. You couldn't see very well because there's a lot of organs down there, all sort of together. He especially didn't like to work on fat people.

"I scrubbed by his elbow all the time. He'd start at 8:00 or 8:30 AM and work until 12:00 or 12:30. Lots of days he'd be at it for all day till the evening. Most days he'd just do surgery in the mornings and have afternoons for Outpatients downstairs. I had to get out the instruments he needed and sterilize them. It was hard to know what he wanted. I'd try to find out the night before; the operations were listed in a book. If we had a heavy day coming up, I'd get up at six and go over and pick out all the instruments. We used a Coleman stove then to boil them on—put them on a tray and set them down in this big boiler.

"The patient was lying on the table, all covered with sterile sheets except for the operation opening. We'd have to drape all that on first when he came. And then this little tray—like a dinner tray it was—would go in over, on wheels, and lie on top of—not on—the patient. That held the instruments he needed right at the beginning. Then they'd be thrown aside. When he'd get into the operation, there would be clean ones. The first ones would be called dirty, where they had gone through the skin. You can never sterilize the skin; there's always perspiration. And then there'd be the different swabs for whatever blood would come right away.

"I'd just be there, handing out things. He'd just put out his hand; you'd have to put the right one in it. Sometimes you didn't know what he wanted because you didn't see, and you'd have to ask. If it was the wrong one he'd swear out the big one. So you'd try another, and that might be the right one. But a lot of the time he didn't know what he wanted himself. And if he didn't say, you just had to watch what he was doing. When the operation was over, everything was great. We all relaxed. Watching him, assisting him all the time, I could have done an appendectomy any time. If I'd had the education and the money, I think I would have tried to be a surgeon."

Of the three principal scrub nurses, Elfreda Dalley of Durrell scrubbed for John Olds the longest, twenty-two years in all. Actually, she had been a nursing assistant when Olds put her in training under Rose Young in 1942. "He just judged what you were. If you could take the pressure, you might go in the OR." Elfreda left in 1947 to marry Angus Dalley, came back in 1962 and stayed until arthritis forced her to retire in 1979. To work that long with a surgeon, helping him through ten thousand and more operations, is to know him uniquely well.

Surgeons are notoriously difficult and Olds was no exception. Mrs Dalley never quite got used to his habit of cussing her. More than once she threatened to quit. "After 1942," she said, "doctors were scarce. Students would come, get frightened to death and go home. We had one girl in Emergency, but no RN. No; if one came to work in the OR she would never stay; 'twas in one door and out the other. Because he was so wicked. If you asked what he said, if you didn't hear it the first time, you damned well heard it the second, because that time he roared. Or he'd answer with a grunt.

"The first time I scrubbed in with him he said, 'I'm taking you on trial. You watch what I'm doing.' That's all he said: 'Watch what I'm doing here now.' I'd never seen a patient opened before. That was the first test. If he wanted anything, the circulating nurse would hurry out and get it. He'd say, 'I don't want it tomorrow, I want it today!' You had to be smart. And you couldn't take it personally, because he'd swear on you all the more. You had to learn fast; you couldn't help learning. The OR technicians who come out now, they'd never work with Dr Olds in this God's earthly world. Everything was rough then, and you had to be rough to take it.

"First when you got in there, he'd come and watch you scrub up. You'd shiver with fright, didn't know if you were scrubbing right. You had to scrub just so: clean your fingernails first, do your hands as you went up, go up a little bit farther, up to your elbow. You couldn't let any suds run down over your hands or they wouldn't be sterile. Then you'd come out and someone would dress you. He had his own gowns; his were white.

"In there, you had to listen, make sure. He was very tense in surgery. His patient was very important. He'd mumble something, and you'd think it over: what *did* he say?

"'Well, are you stupid?'

"'No, Sir; I just don't know what you said.' It was just the way he was; after surgery he was okay.

"If there was big surgery on—say a gastrectomy up first thing next morning—I'd go down and say, 'What do you want for the morning for instruments?' He would grunt. That's all you'd get. I'd say, 'Dr Olds, I've got to know what you want tomorrow morning. What kind of sutures will you need?'

"'Well, godammit,' he'd say, 'you've seen me use them enough to know!'

"So you'd have the various kinds lined up on the table. And you had your scalpel ready, and your different blades. He used a Number 23 and a Number 15 blade. And if you passed him the wrong one—supposing you only had the one handle—that went on the floor. Then you'd have to grab that and go and clean it and put it in alcohol for a few minutes and use it again. If you passed him, say, a hemostat and he wanted an Allis clamp, he'd stick out his hand again. And if you passed him the wrong thing again—everyone gets confused sometimes, especially when they're new— it would also go to the floor. The hand would go out again.

"'Dr Olds, Christ,' I would say, 'I don't know what you want!' It made me so frustrated. More than once I went down to his office and said to him, 'I can't scrub any more.' And I would cry.

"'Yes you *can* scrub,' he'd say.

"'No,' I'd say, 'I can't do it; I can't cope with *you*.'

"'If I can cope with you, you can cope with me.'

Some of his cussedness was a test. His longtime secretary Angela Jenkins noted it. "I think he would ask me for something just to be contrary, knowing I didn't have it," she said. "I wouldn't put it past him to do that, not at all." One time he sent a young nurse hurrying from the OR to fetch a Y-shaped glass tube. With George Ings' help she found it. Rushing back out of breath, she slid it across the counter to him. He failed to catch it—or didn't try—and the tube splintered on the floor. Instead of the violent outburst she expected, he merely shrugged and said, "That's okay; I've another one here." Most of the time, said Angela, he was "totally wrapped up in his patient and forgot everything else—total concentration."

Angela recalled George Dalley's initiation as an orderly. "Olds took him in the OR this day, all gowned up and everything. They were doing a procedure and he asked George to pass him something. The poor guy didn't know; he'd just come in off the street, as it were. Dr Olds hit the ceiling and George said, 'Look here now; I just came to work in this goddam place. How do you expect me to know everything that's here?' Right from Day One he took absolutely nothing off him. Not like me."

"You know," said Elfreda, "He'd almost never had an infection with his surgery. He was very strict; you had to be just so. If he thought you were careless, 'twas 'Go!' I remember my first night call. It was only just the doctor and the circulating girl—no doctor assisting. So the scrub nurse had to scrub and assist, both. It was an emergency cesarean section. I was frightened right to death—what in the world were we going to do?

"Anyway, I got the things ready, hoping to have them in line so he wouldn't say, 'What in hell have you got there?' All he said was, 'Get the patient ready.' Ten minutes to get the patient done—that's all you ever got. We had a major tray, minor tray, emergency tray, plastic tray and a TNA tray—tonsil tray. That's all we had. If there were two or more operations that day, you had to sterilize between procedures. The circulating girl would wash them while you were doing up the patient—putting the adhesive, plaster and everything on. Before the patient was wheeled out, she'd have them on to boil again. Our new sterilizer was a high voltage thing that could do them in ten minutes. So by the time everything was straightened out, the instruments would be ready again. Often we never had time to clean the floor between operations.

"I've seen us do ten operations in one day—and two of them were nephrectomies or kidney removals. Gastrectomies were something else. For those he'd do a lot of suturing. Perhaps he'd have to cut two-thirds of a stomach out; cut so much out and join the ends. And that would be sewed over and over and over. There was linen, there was catgut—things are changed now—but that's what we used then. Linen and catgut were put there to stay, to gradually dissolve. If you didn't get that doubled for him, and the right kind, that would go on the floor too. And after your surgery was over, where's your needles? You had to count them before you started or you wouldn't know.

"See, he didn't have to thread needles then. They came already threaded. The needles were curved and you took them from a needle holder. After he was finished, this was the problem. You were keeping track of the instruments and trying to count your packs, trying to count your needles. You'd have them all lined up, but he'd probably take half a thread and pull, and do some other thing with it.

"There you were, five full needles and one gone. Perhaps that other one was thrown up on the patient's head part. This is where he'd throw his needles, up on that top sheet—and there they stayed. If you were handy enough to get it, all right; if not, it would fall on the other side of the patient. Sometimes when he needed another instrument you would be at the head looking for a needle. And he'd say, 'Get the hell down here; I don't want that what you're looking for up there. I want a clamp.'

"For the cesarian section I had six needles when we started. And one for skin suture, a straight needle. The others were curved. So after surgery was over, 'twas rush to get the baby and rush to get all the sutures in and water everywhere and everything up in your face so you couldn't see. Then he'd give you the baby to pass to the nurse, who would take it and go out.

"And now you're helping to sew up. And you'd have to cut his sutures for him, pulling back the muscle until he was ready to let go. You'd have to let go each vein or blood vessel that he'd clamped with a hemostat. If you didn't let that go in time for him to burn the edge with the cautery, God help you. More than once we got our fingers burnt. You had rubber gloves on, and if the electric needle touched the glove—phtt!—it's gone right through! You'd have to go and put another glove on top. Your hand was in his way, see, and he wouldn't tell you to move it. 'If you want to take a burn, you can.' That was his attitude. You had to hold the hemostat until he burned the vessels that were going to stay closed after the operation. He'd never tell you anything as he was going. You'd see it, but as far as you knew, it was French. If you took your hemostat up quick you'd be all right.

"The instruments were taped on the patient's stomach or wherever Dr Olds was working. Nowadays, they keep those on the tray. He would have these on a tray at first, yes; but later he wanted them laid on the patient. As for the other things—so many hemostats, so many Allises, so many pick-ups—all these different instruments that you would need—Badcocks and all those things for the stomach, your stomach clamps and all that, was kept back on your table, because the tray couldn't hold it all. You were supposed to know all the instruments. If we didn't, he called you damned stupid. He would hold out his hand and if you didn't have it he'd stop, look at you and grind his teeth.

"After that first section, he went down in his office and sat down, sat down and waited. So when I checked, I didn't have all the needles. One was missing. I looked everywhere, cleaned the garbage buckets, checked the padding, the packs. During an operation he wouldn't wait for me to count the packs—the pads to soak up the blood—you did that while he was sewing up. If you happened not to have the right one, he'd say '*I* haven't got it.'

"The missing needle scared me. I thought, 'My God, suppose it's gone in the patient. What am I gonna do? I can't go home.' I looked for an hour, alone there in the OR. Finally, I went down in the office and said, 'Dr Olds, I'm missing a needle.'

"'How come?' he said.

"'I don't know,' I said. 'You were throwing them around and I just can't find it.'

"He went up the stairs three steps at a time to the OR with me close behind and he pointed and said, 'There it is, in the corner.' He knew right where it was because he *threw* it there. That's why he waited in the office—to see if I was honest enough to admit it was lost.

"'That's a dirty trick,' I said.

"'I did it to try you.'

"Nothing ever turned my stomach, ever; but lots of times I used to shiver.

"'Why are you trembling?' he'd say.

"'Because I'm afraid of you.'

"'Christ Jesus,' he'd say, 'suppose I said I was afraid of *you*?' Sometimes he made it funny, more times he'd make me shiver. After a hard operation, he'd go out and then the Emergency crowd had to take it, since OR was finished. This tension he had, they got the steam from it; *somebody* had to get it. Even if nothing went wrong, he'd still be fussy. He'd go to the Office and just grout at them.

"If he wanted something from the Pharmacy, you had to tell the circulating girl to go and get it. He used to mumble through his mask, and if you didn't get what he wanted he'd say, 'Did you tell her?' And I'd say, 'Well, Dr Olds, I didn't understand what you said.' Then he'd roar it out, like a roaring lion.

"See, it was this patient on the table that was his problem; *you* didn't matter, not you. He didn't care if he burnt the hands off you. 'You be careful with that patient! 'Elfreda,' he used to say, 'one move from you—if you move that retractor—it could be the end.' And that used to make me kind of scared. He was tensed up with his patients. Every one was important to him. In surgery there was no such a thing as certain people—everyone was special. And if a patient didn't pull through, OR closed. Nothing was done. I only saw one time when a patient died under anesthetic, and that was a man from Change Islands.

"And you dare not make a noise when you walked. At that time we had no OR sneakers. If your shoes squeaked he would say, 'Get those goddam things off!' And you had to be quiet for every operation, not just the major ones. Silent. No talking. Just the sound of him clicking his instruments, and us breathing, watching what was going on, helping. And listening for his orders.

"'Just keep your eyes on this.'

"'Keep that goddam thing still; don't go shaking!'

"How could you keep from shaking when you were afraid? In the early years I would come home nights and say to my husband, 'My God, Ang; I've got deep surgery tomorrow. What'll I do?' There was nights I never slept. We had to take night calls; we never had any time off. But afterwards I got so used to him I didn't dread each day.

"The longest operation I remember was three hours and a half. That was a thoracoplasty—removal of ribs for TB lung. When the TB was on the go—about two years it was raging—he used to save those operations for the wintertime. When the boat traffic was down and things were quieter, he'd take his TB patients in, do their lungs in the wintertime. They would be in casts for a while, about six weeks."

The seasonal nature of travel meant that Olds had to schedule elective surgery according to where patients came from. This was especially true of boat traffic in spring and fall. Unless it was an emergency, several people from one place usually travelled together. So in Outpatients he would try to see one group at a time, from farthest to nearest. That way they could be discharged together and get home sooner. It saved them time and money, and allowed the boat owner to get on with his work.

"Say the boat come from Barr'd Islands," said Mrs Dalley, "you'd finish that load before the next. And if there was someone going for surgery, they'd post that on the OPD door. The OR nurse would go down and see what surgery there was in and what had to be done. One time we had two Mrs Wheelers in, one for a nephrectomy, the other for a hysterectomy. We brought in one of them and when he came in he said, 'Who the hell is she?'

"'This is Mrs Wheeler.'

"This is not the Mrs Wheeler I want *now*,' he said. 'I want the *other* Mrs Wheeler." I never once knew him to make a mistake in his patients. He'd look at their face in OPD and he'd remember them. Otherwise there would have been mistakes. But he looked at his patient's face.

"He was a terrific surgeon that was hard to work with. Still, you liked the man. Although he was hellish to work with, he had a nice disposition. The swearing was the worst part. But if I went down to OPD and said 'Dr Olds, I'm through scrubbing for you; I just can't keep it up; the tension is too much,' he'd say, 'Forget it—swear back at me. When I swear on you, you swear right back.'

"'Dr Olds, I can't do that....'

"'Why the hell can't you?'

"'I just can't. I'm not going to scrub any more for you.'

"'Elfreda,' he'd say, 'don't be such a goddam fool. You come on in with me tomorrow morning and you swear at me.'

"He was something to work with. I've worked with good doctors, but never a man like this. I learned a lot, appreciated a lot, and I'm glad I decided to work with him. I used to go to bed and wonder what was going to happen to me next day—whether I was going to be killed or what. Lots of nights I lay awake, wondering; in my mind I was getting the table ready, getting the instruments ready, getting the sutures lined up. Even if I'd got a chance to work with a nice doctor, I wouldn't have. I would have felt out of place.

"Dr Lou Lawton used to laugh at me, tease me. 'The Old Man is in a helluva mood this morning, Elfreda,' he'd say. And I'd say, 'My God, Dr Lawton—stand by me.' But his bark was worse than his bite. You had to stand your ground."

Did he never praise her? "That would have been nice," she said. "But you never got that kind of talk from him. You were just supposed to do better and better. You never knew when you were doing good—never had any good days." Yet after fifteen years he paid her the ultimate compliment. "One day in 1962 I was calling about a job for my oldest daughter. He was just leaving for Moreton's Harbour and he said: 'Well, I don't have a job for her, but I have one for *you*.'

"'For me?'

"'Yes. You come up tomorrow morning and get your uniform from Miss LaFever; tell her I said you're to go in the OR tomorrow morning.'

"'Oh my God; how can I do that?'

"'Well, you do as I'm telling you.' And with that he left on his call.

"So I went up to Miss LaFever, the Mennonite Head Nurse was there then. I told her and she said, 'This is news to me.'

"'I was just told to come and get a uniform to go work in the OR.'

"'Well, I'll give you a uniform, but I don't know what this is all about."

"I began to think, 'Am I losing my mind, or what's happening to me?' But I went up in the morning and went to him and said, 'You know, Miss LaFever doesn't know I'm here.'

"'She'll goddam know it when I come up.' From that time on, Miss LaFever was perfect. She hadn't been told; didn't even know he knew me.

"After fifteen years I was rusty. But everything came right back to me. We'd go up around seven in the morning. He'd start his surgery around eight, sometimes at 7:45. We would get off when work was done—sometimes after supper. I'd get home probably five or six, and have to go back at seven for surgery again. I've known me to come home at one in the morning.

"In those times we had no Central Supply Room. We had to fold up our linen, do it up in packages and then do a forty-five-minute load, enough for surgery. In a big brass drum, to sterilize it for the next morning. We had seven big drums, so that if anything came up in the night, everything was in one of those drums, sterile. And the trays had to be done before you left. You couldn't just go off duty four o'clock; you had to have everything ready. Now they don't have to do that.

"When I went back to work, the children all promised to do something. 'If everybody does their job,' I'd say, 'then I won't have to.' One washed the dishes, one made the beds and one tidied up. When I came home, I had nothing to do. All my children were like that; they all knew what they had to do. We had a good family that way.

"When the students started coming from St John's, they were shocked. They never realized we had so little. The doctors would come in; the girls would bring them into what we called the Sterilizing Room where we had everything to, and he'd be in the next room. Everybody could see him doing his surgery. The table was there. You just walked a few steps and there it was—the Operating Room, the Theatre, we called it. Just two rooms."

There were some light moments. Once when they were preparing a child, someone tipped over a tray of instruments and made a terrific clatter. The boy on the table laughed so hard, the nurse thought he was going into convulsions. The kid explained, "But you tipped over the forks and knives!" She remembered a big black book in which Olds recorded patients' sayings.

After an operation, Olds' assistants often faced another ordeal. After working hard for an hour or more in masks and gowns under the big hot light, everyone was thirsty. The Hospital had no water coolers, but in the basement one could get ice cubes. "He'd come up with a big jug of ice water—and he with his bloody hands. He'd put his hands in the ice and drop them in his cup. Well, now; everybody else wanted ice too. But after this, nobody would touch it. Sometimes when Rose and I were working with him—one assisting and one scrubbing—he'd reach over and put ice in our glasses for us. We used to drink it. 'Rose,' I'd say, 'we're gonna die for sure after this.'

"And she'd say, 'If Dr Olds doesn't kill us, we'll die anyhow.' So we used to pretend we didn't notice.

"He drank iced coffee. Dinnertime, if we had time, we'd take perked coffee down in the ice bin for him. To this day I can't sit down and enjoy a coffee...."

Being on her feet so much, she suffered from bunions. The day after having some removed, she scrubbed in bedroom slippers. "I know your feet are good today," he said. After she got arthritis in her legs, she still kept working. Sometimes it got so bad she would fall to her knees. "Elfreda, I don't know if you're going to the Cross or no," he would laugh. At last she had to take a year's leave. On her return, Olds advised her to retire. "I don't want you to fall and have to replace your hip," he said. So in 1979 she left on a disability pension.

"It was really interesting. I'm glad I worked with him. I worked in the OPD too, but I'd much rather be in OR. And if I could still work, and he was up there, I'd rather work with him than with any other one. Dr Dennison was good. Dr Lawton was good. Dr Lawton used to torment me, call him The Old Man, but he was one I could talk to, discuss things with if we had a serious day. I used to say, 'For God's sake, don't call him The Old Man! You do, he'll kill you.' But he liked Dr Lawton; he was the first doctor that he had after the War."

When he moved up to the new Hospital, where he had more people to help him and more free time, she would sometimes visit him. "'You know, it's funny,' he'd say to me, 'in the old Hospital we were all one big happy family. But when we moved up here, everything went to Hell's flames.' That's the words he used. Yes. Because in the new Hospital he was no longer in control.

"To me he was a father. If I wanted to know anything, I'd always go to him—even after he retired. I felt relaxed with him. I could sit and tell him anything. There was no such thing as wanting an appointment. I'd go up and wait till he'd come. He'd come out of OPD and take my hand and say, 'Lord Jesus, Elfreda, come in my office and we'll talk.'

"'Dr Olds, what kind of a mood are you in today?'

"'A hell of a mood. Why, Elfreda?'

"One morning I went there and this nurse came in. 'What are you here for?' she said.

"'Well, for a reason.'

"'You're not supposed to be here.'

"'We'll wait until Dr Olds comes and then see, eh?'

"'All right, but you're not allowed to be in his office.'

"'That's fine; I'll take the consequences when he comes.'

"'He came and I said, 'Dr Olds, I'm not supposed to be here, you know.'

"'Since when?' he said.

"'Just now. The RN said so.'

"'Don't mind that,' he said. 'If I was in my prime, things would be flyin' round here.'"

Chapter Thirty-One

Cussedness

"A lot of the timid nurses just scurried like mice."

— Nurse Jessie Drover

"'T'is a Sunday afternoon," said Harry Layman of Fogo, "and the waiting room is packed—twenty or thirty aboard a trap skiff on a fine day, up to see the Doctor from Herring Neck, Fogo and Change Islands. That was the trend. The only time they had off was Sunday; he had no Sundays off.

"Rex Willis is there from Fogo; he'd been to Doctor Olds before with a back problem.

"'You're Rex Willis,' he says.

"'Yes,' says Rex.

"Now Olds has been working on a sick horse for several hours and the horse has died. His arms are bloody to the elbows because he hasn't had time to clean up. He's not only disappointed, he's hurted over losing that horse. And he isn't fit to look at, he's a mess.

"And Dr Olds says to Rex, 'Didn't I tell you to come back in six months for a checkup?'

"'Yes,' said Rex, humble-like, 'but I took a box of Dodds Kidney Pills....'

"'I don't give a good goddam if you took a *barrel* of kidney pills; I told you to come back in six months!'"

A Gander Bay guide and friend of his had just endured a harrowing fifty-mile boat trip to see him for his injured hand. Olds noticed him in the Waiting Room and growled, in the hearing of all, "What in hell's the matter with you?" The embarrassed man shot back, "Nothing, Doctor, nothing at all," folded his arms, and sat fuming.

His cursing was legendary. "Very foul-mouthed to work with," said a colleague. "A thing he didn't learn at home, I can tell you," declared Tutie. "Nobody used that kind of language at home. When Bill Card of Loomis heard what language John was using in the Operating Room, he had it out with him. I don't think it made any difference."

"Yes, he used a lot of cuss words," said Dr Mike Maguire. "And although he tended to use certain standbys, he was a creative curser, he had a vocabulary. 'Goddam' was his biggest one.'Christ Jesus' was another. But there was nothing serious in them. It was quite harmless, really."

Melvin Woolfrey recalled an incident where Olds cursed an aide in his hearing. "Betty was Head Nurse then, and she jawed him for cussing the girl. So the next day when he met her he said, 'Betty tells me I cussed you a lot yesterday.'

"'Yes, you did.'

"'Well,' he said, 'I'll cuss you again tomorrow.'

"He wasn't vexed," said Melvin. "He might have been *stirred*, you know." A scrub nurse agreed: "I wouldn't say he was angry *all* the time. It's just that his mind was so active."

Nurse Felicitas Austria sometimes did anesthesia for Olds. "We enjoyed each other but he cursed like crazy. One time I said, 'Dr Olds, I just heard you swear.'

"'You swear too,' he said.

"'No I don't.'

"'Yes you do.'

"'No, I never do,' I said. 'You don't hear me saying what you just said.'

"'Yes you do swear—in Filipino!'"

Secretaries dreaded the blast of his tongue. "Audrey was one who never did get over her fear of Dr Olds—never," said one. "Even now, the mention of his name sends cold shivers over her. He chased her with a hammer one time. She was working in the business office and there was only one phone. Dr Olds was wanted on that phone, and he was up in the workshop. Audrey, terrified of him as she was, had to go up and tell him. She went up and stood in the door. And when she told him, he turned around with the hammer in his hand and chased her right down across the ramp. Was it a bluff? Who would chance it? Audrey didn't want to."

After thirty years as his secretary, Mayme Hewlett was given a farewell dinner with many complimentary speeches. When Dr Olds' turn came he rose and said, "Ladies and gentlemen, I have nothing to add," and sat down. Some time later a canvasser dropped by his house. He gave some money and impishly said, "You should go see Mayme, you can count on her for a generous donation." When the canvasser relayed this to Mayme, she replied, "Tell Dr Olds I have nothing to add!"

Angela Jenkins was his personal secretary in the sixties. "It was hard to know *what* he believed. He was that humble he used to make me sick sometimes—unless it was all just a put-on. I don't know how I ever stuck it. I was only to be there six months, as a clerk-typist in the business office.

All of a sudden I became Dr Olds' personal secretary. This was from day one. Nobody told me I was going to be someone's secretary. And I was foolish enough to stay.

"A guy in the lab made a point of coming in every single day and saying, '*He'll* soon be back; you don't know what you're missing.' He had me shaking in my shoes before I even *met* the man. And once I did meet him, I wanted to turn around and go right back to Conception Bay.

"I got the job because his bell rang and somebody told me to go answer it; they didn't want to. When he rang that bell—it more a buzzer than a bell—you heard it all over the front of the building. Say he wanted more paper in his desk. He'd ring the buzzer and you had to jump. He expected you there before his took his finger off the button. You'd go in, and he'd point to the empty drawer and bark: 'See that? Look!!'

"We used to get mad at each other. Mr Vincent used to do his income tax, and when he came over for Dr Olds' things I had to have everything ready. If there was anything missing, the roof was raised. Dr Olds used cuss words that lit up the whole place. One time Dr Olds lost a bank account. It was income tax time. He knew he had it, but couldn't recall where—whether it was in the States or Canada or where. I kept all his receipts and all his bank statements and all his everything. He had a personal file, he had a patients' file, he had all these different files and he'd just heave it in the basket and expect me to clear it out and to make sense of it. And he blamed me. But I'd never heard tell of it, didn't know what he was talking about. Well, we had an awful goings-on over that.

"Same with typing. He chased me out of his office one time—came after me with his fist. He used to handwrite everything then—wouldn't use a dictaphone—and would read everything he wrote after I typed it. I was writing a letter to American Motors in St John's about his *Jeep*. He always dealt with them for his cars and I did all the correspondence. I went in and he was swearing.

"'Christ Jesus, look at that!' Over and over.

"Finally I asked, 'What? What is it?' He jabbed his finger at the sheet I'd just typed and said, 'That should be an 'L,' not an 'I'! Do you think you'll ever wake up?' I went to leave, and he put the fist up. And he came after me with the fist, and I faced him because I didn't dare turn my back on him. I groped for the door and when I found it I turned and ran. I went to my waste basket, found his crumpled original letter, marched back and spread it out on his desk. "'Dr Olds,' I said, 'maybe your pen slipped there, but that's certainly no 'L.' And furthermore, if you'd write so a person could read it, you would find that your letters would come back perfect!'

"After that, I had very little trouble with him. If he cussed on me I cussed him back, and if I didn't want to do something I'd tell him so. After that I didn't mind him whatsoever. Once I stood up to him, it was okay. He seemed to respect anyone who stood up for themselves. Others—they lived in dread of him till the day they died.

"Joyce Grimes took nothing off him," said Angela. "Told him just what she thought of him. Anything she wanted to say to him, she said. Not like other people; they'd almost whisper. Joyce worked for Versa Foods at the Hospital, and one time she was flying to Labrador City to see her daughter. Versa's cheques used to come in every two weeks. She was planning to go the next day, but her cheque hadn't come. One day she was going up in the elevator and he got on. 'Dr Olds,' she said, 'I'm going to Lab City tomorrow.'

"'Oh?' he said.

"'And if I don't get my cheque this afternoon you're gonna have to lend me the money to go.'

"'Well, I daresay,' was all he said. Joyce was dead serious. If she'd said it flippantly, it would have been different. As it happened, the cheque came on time. But she would have got the money from him."

"You had to come back at him," said Bud Young. "You had to get up against him. Soon as he saw that you weren't afraid of him, you were all right—no trouble then." Dr Olds liked to tell the story of a young man who, at the wheel of the doctor's speedboat one time, ran through a net and snarled the motor. Pale with terror, the boy had turned to Olds and begged, 'Don't kill me!'

When teenager Patricia (Baird) Bonasera of Twillingate came in with acute appendicitis one midnight, she refused ether and insisted on spinal anesthesia. They argued and finally struck a deal: she would let him give her ether if he would not strap her hands down. Afterward he said to her father, "That damn kid of yours is case-hardened; how do you live with her?" Clearly he liked her.

As Angela Jenkins discovered, behind the tyrant's mask was a shy, gentle person. Visiting the Austrias after they moved to Springdale, Dr Olds admitted he didn't want to walk down the street "because so many people would know me." Edith (Simms) Manuel said, "He wasn't someone that could sit down and talk to people. At home he'd be sitting with a book. All kinds of books; he had a big library. And he wasn't one to have friends come in sometime and yarn, the way Newfoundlanders do. No, that wasn't his type at all." He didn't like to show his feelings, said Grace Sparkes. On her wedding day he sent this telegram:

YOU OLD FOOL—CONGRATULATIONS

Dr Olds couldn't understand it when people weren't interested in their own bodies. "He didn't like it when people just lay there," said Lorna Stuckless.

"But if they asked, 'What did you do to my leg?' or 'What did you find?' he'd sit down and talk to them and draw pictures for them." If an examination revealed serious illness, however, he had real difficulty in breaking the news—especially if he had mis-diagnosed it in the first place. "I showed him this hard bunch on my hand," said a Gander Bay woman, "and he said it was only water and would go away." When it got worse, he had it X-rayed. "He came into the room and paced up and down and looked out the window," she recalled. "Whatever it was, he didn't want to tell me." At last he stopped, turned to her and said, "Have you ever had TB?"

"'Not that I know of.'

"'Not as a child?'

"'No.'

"'Well, you've got it now.'

"'Oh, Doctor, I feel so relieved,' she said.

"'Why in hell would you feel relieved at a piece of news like that?'

"'I thought I had cancer.'

When Melvin Rideout was in Twillingate with TB, a male co-patient whose toes had been frozen was anxiously awaiting the doctor's verdict. At last Olds came in and said, "I've got bad news for you." The man's heart sank. "What is it, Doctor?" Olds came and sat on the side of his bed. "I've got to amputate those toes." Expecting much worse, the patient allowed this wasn't so bad.

"Perhaps," said Dr Olds. "But I've got to cut 'em off just below the knee."

One Christmas a group of his staff came mummering to the Cottage. When one of the nurses, hardly able to see out of the eyeholes of her mask, stumbled at the door, he remarked, "I hope to Christ you don't come in with a broken leg." And on the bottom of her examination report he always wrote, "Eat more"—because she was so thin.

"He was very possessive," said Angela. "If you were Dr Olds' patient, he didn't want you seeing anyone else. As the newer people started to come in—Drs Garcia, Woodruff and Dennison—it would have hurt him if patients had left him for one of the other doctors. And if he wasn't there and his older patients had to see somebody else—well, they wouldn't believe what the other doctor said, anyway. They'd have to come back again and see Dr Olds. That happened more than once."

Dr Lou Lawton agreed. "John was rather jealous of his status in Twillingate. He wanted to be the kingpin. If somebody came in and they said, for example, 'I want to see Dr Hastings,' that would irritate John."

Why would someone with Dr Olds' genteel upbringing and fine education, who dressed formally for supper guests and knew how to be gracious and charming, sometimes play the boor with simple folk? Overwork and shyness aside, was it also condescension? Sometimes it seemed so. Did he forget that he had fled urban living to be with just such people, whose wit and skill and courage he admired?

The real reason was nearly always exasperation. Vanity and stupidity he could not abide, and he hated malingering. One day a patient got out of bed and came down to Olds' office.

"'What are you doing in here?' said Olds.

"'Oh, Dr Olds,' he said, 'I got a wonderful gas.'

"'That so?'

"'Oh yes, Doctor.'

"'What kind of gas you got?' growled Olds. 'Propane gas or butane gas?'

"'No—pain gas, Doctor,' he said, retreating hurriedly."

Servile behaviour annoyed him too. When he saw Newfoundlanders doff their caps to merchant, clergyman or banker, his Yankee blood simmered. But when they did it to him, he half enjoyed it. He told his father so.

In fairness to Dr Olds, most Newfoundlanders of his day expected roughness in a leader. A Botwood teacher recalled seeing several fishermen from Pike's Arm being so treated. They had brought their trap fish to Carter's premises in Herring Neck and were riled by what they considered unfair culling. When Joe White confronted them, their spokesman said, "Your man 'ere is cullin' our trap fish too 'ard. A lot of the fish in that pile oughta be in dis one, an' we fellers won't stand fer it no more." Joe snatched up one of the supposedly good fish, a large thick salted summer cod as tough as leather, grasped it in both hands and said, "Yes, a lot of your fish is in that pile, and probably a lot more *should* be. And if you don't like it you can take your goddam fish elsewhere." With that he ripped the fish in two and flung the pieces over the wharf. In fact, their trap fish probably was inferior, since jigged fish got better care. The men accepted the price. They were likely in debt to Carter's anyway.

It was no accident that Joe White was one of Dr Olds' best friends. They were cut from the same rough Victorian broadcloth and felt it was legitimate to talk and act so. As the boss of Notre Dame Bay Memorial—and in some ways of Twillingate too—John Olds considered it his right. As he had already won their respect, most accepted this without question.

There was also in that time and place a certain round repartee between doctors and patients that is rare today. Arriving to examine a man reputed to have a serious bowel problem, he was told it was only hemorrhoids after all. "God," he snorted, "I didn't know you only had a pain in the ass!" On the same Sunday that Rex Willis got blistered, Alfred Barnes of Fogo was there for lumps on his face. Olds took a look and passed him over to another doctor, who took a skin sample. As Mr Barnes started down to the wharf, the OPD window flew up and the doctor called out:

"Mr Barnes?"

"Yes Doctor?"

"Are you working these days?"

"Yes," he said, "I works at Earles."

"Well now, if I were you I wouldn't lose any time off work. Just mail me your head and I'll fix up your face and send it back to you in the mail."

"You kiss my goddam ass," said Barnes.

Anything that wasted his time also raised his dander. One day in Outpatients a man said,

"'Dr Olds, I have a child and I think she's deaf and dumb.'

"'Oh? And where is she?'

"'Back 'ome.'

"'You mean to tell me you came here—Sunday afternoon, twenty-odd miles by boat—to tell me there's something wrong with a child of yours back home? Well, she may be deaf and dumb, but she's not half so dumb as you!'"

"It was all according to what mood he was in," said Mayme Hewlett. "When you consider it, some mornings he did five operations in a row, and then perhaps an emergency ruptured appendix right after dinner, and then saw thirty or forty patients in OPD. From that time until 5:30, if he was irritable and snapped your head off, you couldn't much blame him. He had reached the end of his tether."

Did he have a sense of humour? For years Angela Jenkins didn't think so. "There was one guy Paul that worked in the Business Office, who, even though he had shaved in the morning, after lunch he'd have a five o'clock shadow. One afternoon a girl who worked there got some cotton wool and stuck it on his face. And Dr Olds gave them what-for—the girl, and Paul too for 'being fool enough to stand there and let her do it.' Most people would have just laughed." On hearing that he collected patients' witty sayings—what he called "OPDisms"—she was surprised.

When Dr Jesus Austria decided to set up a dental practice in Springdale, he asked Olds for a letter of recommendation to the Lions Club there. Handing it to him, John said, "I don't know, Jess...I just wrote it to see what my name is worth there." Then he brightened: 'Now I can refer patients to Jesus or to Austria!'

One can sympathize with the girl who has just learned she is pregnant:

Olds: "Are you married?"

Patient shakes her head.

Olds: "Who's the father?"

Patient does not answer.

Olds: "Tell me; we need it for our records."

Patient: "Nobody, Sir."

Olds: "Nobody? I see. Another baby Jesus."

One can also perhaps sympathize with him, having to break that news to so many naive young women.

Olds: "And what do you find?"

Patient: "I finds a sort of funny feeling in my stomach, something like there was a butterfly fluttering around in there."

Olds: "I see. Did you feel it flutter in?"

Patient: "No, Doctor."

Olds: "Well, you'll damn well feel it flutter out."

Sometimes he couldn't resist a practical joke with friends. To a new father in Moreton's Harbour whose wife had previously borne two sets of female twins he sent this telegram:

BABY GIRL BORN THIS MORNING STOP MOTHER
AND DAUGHTER DOING WELL STOP
NO CHANGE IN PREVIOUS EQUIPMENT

An aide remembered an OR prank. "Don was a real devilskin, you know. He would climb up the radio tower over there on the Lookout with no fear whatsoever. And he was always playing tricks on people. But he had to go in for surgery. And while he was in the OR they taped his whole scrotum and everything right to his leg. And when he came out of anesthetic and they were alone, he said nervously, 'Dr Olds…what happened down there?'

"'Well, Don,' says Dr Olds,'I had to cut it off, that's all.' Olds knew who he was dealing with, of course. But it frightened the living daylights out of Don. The guy's wife was a bit of a case too, and Olds teased him, saying, 'What's she gonna do now?'" Yet Dr Olds disliked dirty jokes. "I never once heard him tell a filthy story," said Dr Maguire. "Never. It wasn't in the man." He got away with such pranks because he knew everybody and they knew him. A young mother took her son in to ask Dr Olds whether he thought the boy had bowed legs. After examining him he told her, "It's nothing; don't be so foolish. Take a look at his grandmother."

Sometimes the tables were turned. George Ings, the orderly, wore white hospital garb like the doctors. Many patients knew Olds only by name, and now and then one of them would say to George, "I wants to see you, Dr Holds." And George would say, "Wait a minute; I'm going to surgery now," and stride off briskly, chuckling to himself.

Once, calling on Eric Facey's invalid father on North Side, Dr Olds stopped to play with the boy. While showing the doctor his toy truck, Eric yanked on it and cut Dr Olds' finger. "Well," said Olds, sucking the cut, "the little bugger drew my blood before I had the pleasure of drawing his."

Humour or no, the nurses feared his tongue, his scowl. "We dreaded making rounds with him," said Nurse Jessie Drover. "It was a nightmare, that's the only way to put it. If you had a second doctor with you that was approachable, you kind of got him off in the corner afterward, and got Dr Olds' orders through him. A lot of the timid nurses just scurried like mice whenever they saw him come on the floor. We all knew the reason for it. He had such tremendous pressure on him that, like everybody who has pressure, he got irritated when things went wrong. With him it was a little more than irritation. "But I found that if you had to call him in the night, for any reason—if something went wrong and you called him out of bed, when he came down he was like a lamb. He was pleasant; you could ask him any question; he was just an entirely different character. In the night, he was just like a lamb."

Chapter Thirty-Two

Teacher

"It was primarily because of his inspiration that
I chose medicine as a career."
— Gilbert Ross, MD, former Chair of Neurology,
Syracuse University; 1954 summer student

"**I**t was an exciting, busy, intimate place when Dick Mirick and I first saw it as students in the summer of 1934. Dr Parsons had just left and Dr Olds was holding it together by sheer will-power. Jolly, exuberant Grace Patten was the house-keeper…. Edith Simms and Hetta Young ran the OR and that was no picnic. I can still feel my eyes "smurt" as I assisted Olds…sterilizing was done by *Primus* and the fumes vied with the poured ether…."

Thus Dr Robert Ecke, younger brother of the 1930s film villain Albert Dekker and Dr Olds longtime assistant, began his memoir for the Hospital's fiftieth anniversary publication in 1974. A Hopkins graduate, Dr Ecke worked with John from 1937 through 1942 and again in 1947 and 1948.

After World War I, hundreds of young men and women from America, Canada and Britain volunteered to do professional and menial jobs in Newfoundland and Labrador. They were popularly known as W.O.P.s— Workers Without Pay. Among them were doctors and nurses doing their summer practicum. During Dr Olds' four decades, many journeyed to Twillingate from schools like Hopkins, Harvard, Brigham, Syracuse; from Toronto and McGill, and even from the United Kingdom.

"The student," said Dr Olds, "thought it a privilege to pay his own travelling expenses and work for nothing. It was mutually a beneficent arrangement—the student learned some practical medicine suddenly, and relieved the resident staff of many routine duties during the busy season." Three Junior or Senior medical students would arrive in June, to be replaced by three more in mid-summer. Originally each team stayed six weeks; around 1950 this was stretched to ten. Until 1941 most students came from Hopkins—three dozen in all. After the War, Harvard and other schools displaced Hopkins. In all, 292 medical students, interns and residents worked in Twillingate between nearly 1934 and 1977. Most returned home, completed their training and took up careers. Some, like Stan Hardy and Robert Ecke, came back to help John. None of them ever forgot that remarkable summer. In the words of 1935 student James Seaman, "This period of my life demonstrated what the practice of medicine should ideally be." A few wrote about their experiences.

When Ecke returned in 1937 as an MD, he found a Hospital that had lost none of its verve. "The contract system of prepaid medicine seemed to bring more patients, especially on Sundays. The *Bonnie Nell* had been commissioned. Lige Dalley, the skipper, looms large in my recollections. I had a kind of hero worship for him. I died a thousand deaths in those autumnal North Atlantic waters but he was rarely perturbed.

"The whole early Twillingate scene comes alive in my head.... Patient care was the important thing and on that subject and on many others, John Olds' word was law in Notre Dame Bay. But medicine is medicine and somehow the miracle—a fine hospital on a rather remote island in a bankrupt country during the Depression—was taken for granted.

"The thing that made it all wonderful and beautiful was that the Hospital was in Twillingate. The island situation made travel an important consideration. The snowmobile had not been invented, there were no causeways and no ferries. The hill behind the telegraph office rose stark and clean against the glorious sunsets without the tall communications tower. The deep-throated fog horn on Long Point urged caution on the sea. Herring Neck was half a weary day away. A quintal of fish was worth a barrel of flour. There was plenty of good, thick salt cod and corned meat and capelin and in the autumn there were seabirds and caribou and moose.

"I am not sure I would want again to cross the Main Tickle by the skip-and-copy method, nor would I go again on the ice across the ship's run to Fortune Harbour. I like to remember making my way by dog, pony, ski and foot all the way to Carmanville and back to Horwood in one day. To cross Gander Bay in the cold and dark was like being on a tread-mill in hell.

"A thousand images swarm about me—Hazel Jeffreys, crisp, pretty, slim and smiling, radiating calm and comfort on the wards at night; Rube Waddell soaking his boots in cod liver oil to make them water-proof; the beautiful, gracious Betty Olds as head nurse or as house-keeper or presiding over those many, many meals at the Cottage. Bud Young, busy in the laboratory, starting his long, loyal service to the hospital. Stella Manuel teaching the aides or making tea in the nurses' home and giving me tatting lessons (I got quite good at it). Joyce Scammell, dressed for a Girl Guide picnic, furious at having to pour ether for an emergency.

"Crowds of patients on Sunday in the OPD. Hurrying to get the mail onto the *Clyde*. Rube Waddell collecting eggs for a Christmas egg nog. I missed the Christmas when Joe White snapped his Achilles' tendon while playing Santa Claus on the children's ward...the Christmas when Santa broke his leg.

"The Hospital had loyal friends...Father Casey, Joe White, Billy Earle of Change Islands, Bert Pardy, Ned Facey, Malcolm Simms the telegraph operator in Herring Neck, Chaulkers of Cobb's Arm. There were many more—[especially] Jessie (Troake) Drover and her husband Ted. They took me in at Alder Harbour during a storm and Jessie made a terrible trip with me on an OB call down the Straight Shore when no sensible vessel should have been out. Jessie taught me how to make pie crust when we miraculously got back."

The first Harvard Medical School contingent of third-year students arrived in 1949, lured by Dr Ed Murray's report of his previous summer with Olds. They recruited Clement Hiebert, Arnold Nevis and Jerry Foster in 1950. Next summer Shillito, Pittman and others came. Shillito explained the recruitment process in the October 1954 *Harvard Medical Alumni Bulletin*: "Each winter a little notice appears on the Vanderbilt Hall bulletin board, enticing volunteers to seize parka and stethoscope. The Twillingate "alumni" do the recruiting, fan the wanderlust in the hearts of susceptible HMSIIIs, exaggerate no more than the average fisherman, show colourful photographs, look appropriately wistful, and, when an eager group has finally been assembled, sit down in closed meeting and [decide] which of the dozen or so applicants may go. Dr Murray alternately fans the spark and restricts the blaze."

In August 1951 Shillito, Stan Gianelli and Joe Wilber left for what Shillito called "the land of the squid and the cod" to relieve Al Anderson, Jim Pittman and Howard Rasmussen. Getting to Twillingate was half the adventure. "Flying was the only practical choice. About $156, round trip, bought a seat on a Boeing *Stratocruiser*, a delightful machine...with overseas delicacies. Apprehensions were pleasantly dispelled before the ship levelled off at 17,000 feet.

"At last Newfoundland's barren south coast loomed up at us like the face of the moon. Four hours after leaving New York, we descended the ramp in bright sunshine at Gander. A friendly voice inquired, 'You're from Harvard, aren't you?' We met Dr Harold Wood, their second in command at Twillingate. The Trans Canada Highway had been cut, but no more. At the Gander River we drove onto a log raft and slithered across cold black waters in the moonlight. Already, home seemed far away!

"Next day in Lewisporte we boarded Ted Drover's 40-foot, inter-island ferry and set out between beautifully wooded shores into a crystal blue day. Soon we were taking tricks at the wheel, and snores from the adjoining cabin announced that Ted had complete faith in our knowledge of these waters. Fortunately we had purchased two charts in Boston....

"The staff at NDBMH was quite large—four doctors for 130 patients. Dr Olds was assisted by Dr Wood.... Bob Lawton and Craig Loveys were at the intern level. We were shown to our quarters in the Staff House, which towers above the Hospital and serves as home for nurses, attendants, maids, doctors and medical students. We shared two rooms on the first floor, which was also reserved for some of the more senior nurses.

"Such a pleasant change from Vanderbilt Hall! In addition to obvious social assets, we enjoyed flickering electric light from one of the island's few generators, plenty of hot water, clean linen and, on Sundays, breakfast in bed. A ramp at the end of our hallway connected with the second floor of the Hospital, making night calls easy. Since there were no phones in our rooms, the girls thought twice before rousing us. One of us spent some time in bed with a dead squid because his custom of sleeping in only pajama tops forbade his flight in the presence of the enterprising nurse who employed this method of reveille!

"After a welcome from Dr Olds and his wife, we toured the Hospital and made plans to divide the patients equally among us: TB and pediatric wards to one, male medical and surgical to another, female medical and surgical to a third. Next day, work began at nine. By custom everything ceased at dinner time for one hour, resumed until "tea-time" about 5:30, and then stopped for the day.

"Between 9:00 and noon, anywhere from two to six procedures were undertaken daily in the OR. Dr Olds was undaunted by the nature of a case, and the same team was likely to perform gastrectomy, laminectomy [removal of part of neck vertebra], tonsillectomy, appendectomy or pelvic surgery in the same morning. We first assisted at the start, then did the appendectomies and tonsillectomies assisted by Bob or Craig, if available, or by Rose, the scrub-nurse, if they were busy. One nurse anesthetist administered open-drop ether; any of us gave spinals....

"Twenty or thirty out-patients were seen daily by at least three of us. Between cases, the OR team helped out in gown and gloves. Our lessons in dentistry came early and were brief and to the point. The OPD rang continually with the half-stifled groans of someone parting almost painlessly with a well-set tooth or a long-neglected root. We averaged close to 300 teeth apiece during our stay.

"House calls were always different, and as a rule never turned out to be what the chief complaint implied. In preparation for the awesome day when we would find ourselves alone and far from advice, we carefully packed and repacked the two black bags—the general kit and the obstetrics kit. The *Merck Manual* always went along, for its prescriptions if nothing else. We might be called to any spot on the Twillingate islands, and to any of the several nearby islands. The Willis wagon or a taxi provided transportation on the home island, fishing boats elsewhere. Often a long hike through the woods was necessary.

"Giannelli disappeared for a couple of days because storms prevented his return; Wilber was long overdue in good weather, which was puzzling until we learned that he had stayed on another island for a wedding.

"Wherever the doctor arrived, he was swamped by requests. Only our successors knew what we missed; but our limited diagnostic acumen turned up pneumonia, tuberculosis, cholecytitis [inflamed gall bladder], acute glomerulonephritis [kidney inflammation], cancer in various forms, diabetes, congestive heart failure, incomplete abortions, deficiency diseases, scabies, post-measles encephalitis, ulcer, psychoneurosis and of course pregnancy. My first home delivery was enlivened by the two-year-old daughter watching through the foot of the bed, thumb in mouth, while the five-year-old son and his cronies peeked through the bedroom window....

"Night calls occurred too, for a distraught mother usually waited till Father came in from fishing before a boat was sent. After a cup or two of jet black Newfoundland tea, it was a pleasure to ride back in crisp, clean air under Northern Lights...."

Clement Hiebert, in his presidential address to the New England Surgical Society in Montreal in 1988, remembered his own initiation. "The time: 4:00 AM. The place: a rocky path in front of a fisherman's cottage on Twillingate, an island off the northeast coast. Icebergs loomed in the bay, and I shivered, partly from the chill of the night and partly at the prospect of my first home delivery. My doctor's bag had been carried by my father on innumerable house calls in the North End of Boston before I was born and now, more than two decades later, its cracked leather interior still smelled of ether and iodoform. The bag had been tested aplenty. Not so the new hands that carried it. As I walked up the rocky path, I hoped the baby would arrive before I did.

"Minutes later, the child was born in an upstairs room illuminated by a faltering flashlight. Anxiety gave way to relief, but it was short-lived. I laid the flashlight down, rummaged in the shadows for the cord, and was startled to grasp instead a tiny foot. For an instant I thought it belonged to the child just delivered.

"'Twins!' I announced soberly.

"'Oh, dear,' responded Mrs Pardy, 'do I have to go through all this again?'

"I thought, 'Do I have to go through all this again?' Why hadn't I paid attention to Duncan Reid's lecture on difficult obstetric presentations? In the delivery of a footling breech, was the critical manoeuvre flexion of the neck, or extension? And what if I guessed wrong? Would this child die for my falling asleep during a third-year lecture?

"Mrs Pardy decided the issue by squeezing her baby straight out. Again, relief. And again, embarrassment. As I set about the details of tying off and wrapping up, Mrs Pardy asked about 'grease' for the babies. I was new to the Newfoundland dialect, and innocent of the local practice of oiling the skin of newborns. I interpreted it as a request to say *grace* for the twins. After that got sorted out, I tucked a baby under each arm and retreated down narrow stairs to the kitchen, where children and relatives had gathered around the stove; that is, all but the father, who was outside, operating in the pre-dawn light on a pile of codfish. "Ecstatically I called over, 'You have *two!*' He barely looked up as he asked, 'Are these your first?' Two weeks later I gave him open-drop ether anesthesia for a strangulated hernia. I do not recall his asking me then, 'Is this your first?'

"One learned never to ask, 'What is the matter?'...Instead it was: 'What does she find?'

"'Oh, Doctor, she 'as a wonderful hake in 'er stomach.'

"We encountered rickets, scurvy and much tuberculosis. Tuberculosis was the dreaded word then, much as cancer is now; virtually every household had seen it. We became ambulance drivers, dentists, family physicians, pharmacists, X-ray technicians and public health officers. Most of all, we were surgeons. Think of it! As third-year students we did appendectomies, cesarean sections and tonsillectomies, and we extracted countless teeth besides. After that, holding a retractor for an intern's first appendectomy during our fourth year at Harvard Medical School seemed pretty dull."

Dr Hiebert appreciated Olds' method of teaching the importance of careful diagnosis. "Before an operation Dr Olds insisted that we affirm our diagnosis by dropping a quarter in a box for what he called the 'Education Fund.' Only if that diagnosis were correct was the coin returned. The box filled altogether too quickly. One day I asked Dr Olds to what purpose the fund was to be put. 'That's for your education, son. So you will remember never to make that damn fool diagnosis again!'"

Students also learned to appreciate the skill of locally trained workers. In 1962 Miles Novy and his Harvard classmates filled in for Bud Young while he was on vacation. "We took the X-rays, operated the pharmacy and did the EKGs and the BMRs, gaining increased respect for this man who did the lot with single-handed efficiency. Our wives, too, became active in many hospital activities, distributing oral Sabin [polio] vaccine to children in outlying areas, serving as nurses on many of our house calls, assisting on the pediatric wards and in several deliveries."

Dr Mike Maguire was no student when he came in 1953, but overnight he became one. Arriving from Ireland to run the new Dental Clinic, he found his building ready but nothing installed. The evening before, at the Cottage, Olds had said, "Come see me about the Clinic tomorrow." So the next afternoon Mike presented himself and said, "I'm ready for work, Dr Olds, but we'll have to get the fella in to put it together."

"You're the fella," he said.

"Well," said Maguire, "I don't know how to do it."

"I'll get you a couple of hands off the *Bonnie Nell*, and an electrician, and put them to work."

"Well, that's very fancy equipment. I wouldn't want the responsibility," said the young dentist. Olds grunted and left. The promised help showed up, and, between visits to OR and OPD for advice and direction, they put Twillingate's first dental clinic together.

Mike's next lesson in self-reliance came a few days later. Dr Olds had insisted he come along on daily rounds. Tagging along on the fourth day, listening, trying to attune his Irish ear to Olds' mumbling Yankee accent and the patients' rapid West Country idiom, they came to the bed of a nine-year-old girl. Thinking he heard "dental problem," he edged closer. Dr Olds asked him to examine a massive cyst on her jaw.

"You look after that," said Olds. Maguire gulped but kept quiet. After rounds he said, "Dr Olds, that's a very large cyst and there's very little bone left. If it's done improperly, she could have a pathological fracture."

"It's your problem," he said.

"It's *not* my problem," Maguire replied hotly. "I'm a dentist, not a surgeon. We should send her to Montreal to a specialist."

"Will you pay for it?"

"No; isn't there a dental surgeon in the area?"

"No."

"Is there one in Halifax?"

"Yes, there is. Will you pay for that?"

"No, I can't."

"Here, we do it ourselves."

"Well, I've never done one and in all honesty, I can't."

"Got any books?"

"Yes, of course, but...."

"Go read your books," he said.

They did the operation next morning, the older man looking over his shoulder, directing each move, standing by. The girl made a full recovery.

A week later a telephone lineman fell and fractured both jawbones and split his chin bone. "Your problem," said Olds gently. Again Dr Maguire got out his books. They wired the jaws together. A month later, X-rays showed everything in order. From then on, with Olds at his elbow, Dr Maguire performed many such operations.

People over forty usually came to the Clinic with a mouthful of rotten teeth. One day Mike said to Dr Olds, "Where do we send for dentures? Where's the laboratory?"

"There is no laboratory."

"Well, there's one in St John's."

"Yes, but it costs too much. The best thing to do is to get a fellow and train him."

Twillingate had movies in the Orange Hall once a week—Roy Rogers and Dale Evans, Hopalong Cassidy, Batman, The Three Stooges. During intermission a notice was flashed on the screen:

DENTAL TECHNICIAN WANTED
TO TRAIN
APPLY AT THE HOSPITAL

From the applicants they chose and trained young Eric Simms. After that the Clinic produced its own dentures, bridges and the like.

"Sink or swim" was Dr Olds' teaching philosophy. When Dalhousie Medical School graduate Dr Louis Lawton arrived, he had already spent a year at the St John's General Hospital and one in Toronto, but still felt he needed more surgical experience. Dr Olds had him in the OR next morning. "The first thing on the list is a gall bladder," he said. Dr Lawton explained that he had never done a cholecystectomy, that he'd rather assist. The next was an appendectomy. "Are you going to do this?" said Olds.

"No," said Lawton.

"Well, what did you come here for, if you're not gonna work?"

Dr Lawton did the appendectomy; John assisted. In the next two years he got a great deal of surgical experience.

Twillingate had movies but no organized sports or other recreation. Since the June contingent of students arrived near the start of lobster season, Dr and Mrs Olds would have a lobster feast for them. But first there were lobster races on the kitchen floor. The numbered crustaceans were supposed to travel a couple of inches before going in the pot. Students placed bets, and the contests took all night. Each year's scores were recorded in the "Lobster Book." Dr Olds also had a long-standing bet with all new students that they couldn't swim the icy harbour as he had done years before. Hiebert won it in 1950 and Pittman in 1951. Shillito declined, preferring the warmer ponds.

Most evenings they spent in one another's rooms or with the young nurses and aides. Old jazz records, or a community singsong around a piano or organ, whiled away free time. Olds lent them the key to the Tilt, where they slept, read, drank home-made beer with only wind in the trees and surf at the doorstep to break the stillness. They jigged cod. By August Shillito and Wilber had eaten too much fish to enjoy catching more, but squid jigging sounded intriguing. It was fun, said Olds, quoting Art Scammell's famous lines with a glint in his eye:

> But if you get cranky without a silk hanky
> You'd better steer clear of the squid-jiggin' ground!

"The double-ended jet monstrosities are readily hooked," wrote Shillito, "but the sport begins when the head end breaks water...a stream of several ounces is directed at the holder of the line with sufficient force to carry twelve feet or so into the air. Drowned or startled, the novice relaxes...and allows the line to dangle, whereupon friend squid loads again through the still-immersed tail and fires until hauled clear or allowed to sink back under water. Thoughtful squid reserve their charge of ink for this moment. We spent one very wet thirty minutes landing thirty squid. Fried, they resembled Lobster Newberg and old inner-tube."

The bird life was amazing. In the late fall they rose at 5:30 AM to shoot turrs and partridge. But through the summer there were expeditions to nearby islands. "Sunday, July 22nd," noted Jim Pittman, "Week ago today I took 14-year-old David Olds and rowed down to Capt. Pierce's Rock looking for terns' nests—found freshly broken egg (not in nest) and dead baby tern, but no nests. Also two baby spotted sandpipers—caught and photographed them, & took pictures of the nearby mother.

"Then, rowed back past the beautiful stony beach on Trump Island, where we had lunch & saw the sparrow hawk catch the young robin & almost lost the boat in the rising tide; past Trump Island, across Friday's Bay, past Black Island and Duck Island, around Vincent's Point into the Main Tickle, up the Main Tickle to the Tilt, where we landed for 20-30 minutes & had supper of steak, potatoes and lettuce with Harold and John Wood and Brian; then pulled a lobster pot, put in an extra thole pin we had cut at the Tilt so that David and I could both row at once, & rowed past Purcells Harbour."

They went on to explore the top of Main Tickle Gull Isle. Here they found more sandpiper nests, counted nearly 200 common tern nests and saw American pipits around the freshwater pools. Rowing past Gunning Point and Clam Rock Head, the sea like glass but with a big ground swell foaming against the rocks, they passed the finger-like rock which Twillingaters call "The Naked Man" and entered the fifteen-foot tickle between Twillingate South Island & Spillers Island. "Downward," he wrote, "[was] the clear cool green water & the white bottom with its rocks, sea anemones, urchins, starfish & plants. Upward, the cliffs and sky...."

The scenery *was* engrossing. From spring to fall they marvelled at the parade of icebergs. They dared each other to dive off Burnt Island's sheer cliffs. For months after returning home, they were haunted by images of limpid air and bottle-green sea depths, of sea-dazzle after storms, of humpback whales chasing capelin. In downtown Baltimore or Boston, they still envisioned the vivid tans and burgundies of bog and barren, the lavender fire of dancing northern lights over Hamilton Sound.

Among the few former students who saw the islands in winter was Bob Ecke. Always a good observer, his eye seemed keener during medical crises. "I found a very frightened young boy, just getting over the acute stage of rheumatic fever. I persuaded him to come to the Hospital. It snowed all the way back and the SS *Sagona*, anchored in Seal Harbour for the night, was very lovely with its blaze of distant lights." The next spring, returning on foot from a house call, he was stopped by "the dark blue of Burnt Island and Long Point [which] framed a piece of peacock blue sea. Against the lighter sky, a schooner was beating in with all sails set...."

After a patient dies from TB meningitis, he writes, "It seems to me that sunsets here have a delicacy of colour not gained anywhere else in the world." Assisting in the Operating Room at dawn, he sees "the sun [break] out from in back of us, making the far shore of the harbour stand out in gold relief against the grey. A glorious rainbow out from Long Point...beautiful and gone in a minute...." Walking to Jenkins Cove one evening at dusk to visit a woman who has cut her finger with an axe, he admires "a fantastic arc of sheer gossamer flame, of pale translucent green, festooning across the zenith—the best northern lights this fall." He arrived to find that a neighbour had charmed the blood away.

Something like Dr Ecke's passion infuses the words of many Olds' alumni. They had brushed the rough gown of a greater reality, but did not know it until they returned home. It led Ecke to abandon a lucrative New York residency and return to Newfoundland in 1937. "My bond called for six months as an assistant resident and a year of residency," he wrote. "Well-meaning friends had talked me into this. 'It's time,' they said, 'you gave up this silly wandering around among those Newfoundlanders. You've got to settle down, you know, and open an office.'

"[The hospital was] designed to be a citadel of private medicine. Three-story columns graced the entry, marble floors softened the suffering of the sick and impressed the visitors who sought the spacious lobby. Off to one side, a broad hallway led to the ducal lair of the director-owner, who sat behind a Florentine desk in his palazzo venezia office with its forty-foot ceiling. As we used to gather cosily in the green room after or just before operations, I would listen to the words of wisdom: 'You know (adjusting the mask), you have got to soak these birds. If you don't charge them generously, they don't think you're any good.' Or 'We'll have to get out and find something else to do. I haven't done a mastoid in a month. This sulfa stuff will put us out of business.'"

Each morning, scrubbing up, Ecke watched the ships in the harbour ten floors below. "Each tug that nudged its bigger brother into the stream separated me a little more from my bondage until...my soul was won back to me. It was the work of an hour to have in hand the notice that, 'At his own request, Dr R. S. Ecke is relieved from further duty.'

"Now," concluded Ecke, "I can't walk past one of those discreet suburban offices without a shudder. I can see through that tapestry brick veneer and the iron-grilled downstairs doorway into the reception room with its chrome furniture and magazines very carefully kept up to date by a charming receptionist. It brings back my ulcer."

In Twillingate, said Shillito, they were "suddenly liberated from the text and the clinic, confronted with people instead of patients. "It was a voyage into the rapidly disappearing era of the old family doctor, where, for a few short weeks, we basked, undeserving, in the respect earned for this title by men such as John Olds."

By the late sixties, most students came from the United Kingdom. The Hospital paid their fare and gave them a small stipend. Beatlemania reigned, and many wore long hair and beards. To Dr Olds, increasingly irritated by arthritis, by the imminent demise of his beloved old Hospital and by the unpleasant prospect of retirement, these young people seemed Neanderthal. The aging lion tried to overlook their brewing beer in Staff House bathtubs; some things he could not countenance.

One morning two British students met the Old Man on First Floor East. Angela Jenkins, picking up forms in OPD, witnessed the encounter. "As they sauntered down the corridor, he hauled back and looked—just watched till they got out to where he was. He looked at their heads. Their hair was stringy and not very clean. He said, 'If you two have any thoughts of coming in my Operating Room like that, you can goddam well forget it!' And he would not, Sir, even with caps and the OR garb on, let those two boys inside the OR!

"It wasn't just the hair. Back then a lot of the UK students came for a holiday. The Hospital paid their way. They didn't come to work, so they didn't care. It was very evident. Being such a nose-to-the-grindstone-person himself, he could not tolerate this. To him, a lazy medical student was the lowest form of life on earth. In the old days they had a lot more responsibility."

Many former Olds students returned years later. Clem Hiebert made his own sentimental journey in 1980. One of his twins had died, but the surviving brother sought him out. "He is a handsome fisherman," Hiebert told his Montreal audience in 1988. "His parents had named him after me—not 'Clement,' but 'Hiebert,' in a land where *h*'s are not pronounced. The island had changed, thanks to a causeway…. Dr Olds was then living, still at work, as cussedly original and independent as ever. The dusty hospital lane had been paved and his old Hospital replaced and taken over by the Canadian government.

"[Although] the new hospital has an annual budget of $2 million, fewer patients are cared for now than in 1950 when Dr Olds was the sole practitioner with a total budget of $50,000! The chief surgeon was a woman.

"'Did you train her?' I asked.

"'No, but I delivered her,' he replied.

"I sit in the nurses' station," Dr Hiebert concluded, "where the resident makes sign-out rounds by touching each chart as he recites to his replacement, 'The gall bladder in 308 is okay. Check the 'lytes and the cardiac indices on the cabbage in 310.' Brownian movement around computer terminals has replaced the doctor's lonely walk up the path to the fisherman's cottage. I think of Dr Olds sitting on his horse in a snowstorm, compass in hand, making his way across the frozen bay to see his patient. I recall that summer under the northern lights with Jerry and Arnie. And I remember the dawn when Mrs Pardy got twins, Twillingate got two new citizens, and a fledgling surgeon got a cup of black tea."

Chapter Thirty-Three

Bedside Manner

"One of the hard things to learn in medicine, even harder
to teach, is what it feels like to be a patient."
— Lewis Thomas, MD

"**I**f Dr Olds was there, we were safe," said a Twillingate woman in her seventies. "He knew just what your problem was, where your sickness was, what to do for you. And night after night he slept in the Hospital. He had a little room there, and if there was any patient that was serious and he was worried about them, he'd stay in this little room and check on that patient right through the night, on the hour.

"He had this great big long flashlight. You'd hear him scuffing in across the ward with his house coat on. Well now, if anyone couldn't sleep through the night and there'd be a couple of them talking, whispering to one another and the door would come open, they'd say, 'That's Dr Olds!'—and there'd be silence. He'd come in, shine the flashlight around. He'd scarcely ever come by himself; he'd have the nurse with him. Even if you were in the examination room he'd still have this nurse. He never came alone.

"He was always there when you woke. The last operation I had—they put you in this little recovery room until you woke up—I had come through the ether. They checked my pulse and everything was all right, so then I was put out on the ward. That night at six o'clock, when I woke up again, I heard him calling me. When I opened my eyes, I looked right in Dr Old's face. And I said, 'Oh my, I'm some proud to see you.'

"He said, 'You're all right.' You know? That feeling you have? Some people were so afraid to go under ether. Dr Garcia gave the anesthetic then, but I'd always ask if Dr Olds was there yet. And he'd come in: 'I'm here, me son,' he'd say to Dr Garcia, 'I'm here.' And once you'd see him with that smile, you'd go out just like that. You had an easy mind; you knew he was there and that he'd take care of you. In eight or ten days I was ready to go home.

"I was never close to him—not for to joke around with him—like some who were in there eight or ten months or more. He was *so* serious, you know. He never had much time to talk to anyone other than about their sickness. He was never friendly like that. He always had that grumpy look onto him. And if you went up there for examination—well, everything had to be perfect and you had to have your clothes off, all ready for him. He couldn't wait, because he had so many lined off to see him. If you weren't ready, he'd just swear and go on to another one until you were.

"He was kind. But now—he was a bit rough. You wouldn't let on that he was hurting you. You couldn't say anything, wouldn't howl or anything like that. He wouldn't like that. When I went in there I said, 'This is it. He's the doctor; he knows what he's doing so whatever he does is okay with me.'

"There's no doctor nowadays, you know, you can put your trust in like you could him. He'd neglect his own self for his patients. Because he didn't have his meals properly, and he couldn't get his regular sleep. He wasn't thinking about himself at all; he didn't care about himself. 'Twas his patients—that was his whole life. Whatever he could do for anyone, he'd do it. You don't see the doctors now doing that; they haven't got time to talk to you. He was an excellent doctor. His equal is not around. They had such a confidence into him that whatever operation he did, it was satisfactory.

"You wouldn't settle for a young student; oh no. The minute you knew that Dr Olds was around, well, you'd have to see *him*. If you went there and got someone else to examine you, you didn't have an easy mind. He forgot more than those doctors will ever know. I wouldn't go up there now for an operation; you couldn't pay me enough money. I can't trust to the doctors…there wouldn't be enough anesthetic in the Hospital for to put me to sleep."

Jessie Drover, Hubert Vincent and others knew how he earned such extravagant trust. "I remember one night in the 1930s," said Nurse Drover. "I'd just come home from Montreal's Royal Vic, where everything had to be penned and signed and a doctor certainly didn't call you by your first name. And everybody was saying 'John' to him. It was kind of strange, coming into that. I was sitting in the dead of night, a quiet night, doing charts at the desk. I didn't know there was a soul around.

"All of a sudden I heard these footsteps pounding up the stairs fast. And before I saw his head appear he said, 'Jess, there's not a goddam bit of sugar in that man's urine!' He'd been down there all night working on a diabetic. And all of a sudden he let out this cry, just like a youngster seeing a Christmas tree. He'd found the trouble and now everything was okay…."

A 1930s scrub nurse said, "I've seen him sit on the floor outside the door all night long if there was somebody very sick. He might just have a little doze, but he'd be listening to their breathing."

"I tell you," said a former male TB patient, "'twas no trouble to see him at night by your bedside if you were sick. He'd come down and check on you and catnap outside. His patients were everything to him. He was really heart and soul into it. And there was no such a thing as turning anyone away. They used to come in boats and on the steamer. He'd try to see every one the day they came. Sometimes they'd have to stay overnight down to Stockley's.

"You know, he used to walk that corridor. My wife was down there once, and there was a girl from here had an operation on her lungs. There wasn't too many of those done then. And that night he never closed his eyes. He paced the corridor outside of her door, and kept going in to check on her."

A male patient from New World Island said, "I was there in the Hospital one time and I got real sick. And Dr Olds must have thought the doctor that was looking after me was a bit careless. My temperature went up to 104 degrees, my pulse was beating 150 or 160 and I was semi-conscious all night. He came into my room perhaps eight or ten times. I'd just feel his finger on my pulse; he wouldn't speak. Just feel the pulse. He didn't do much sleeping that night. He was like that with everybody."

"Every evening he'd take his rounds," said Melvin Rideout. "There'd be two or three doctors and a nurse with him, and we used to have our charts laid on the bed—not like it is now. He always had a five-cell flashlight. If he was in a good mood we could tell, because he'd be hitting you on the toes in the bed. 'How are you this evening?' he'd say. When he wasn't hitting you, it meant he'd had a hard day or he was in a bad mood. If you got sick in the ward, he'd come on out of the Operating Room, cap and everything on. When we saw him comin', full o' blood, we were frightened to death!"

"I've never seen it before," declared Angela Jenkins, "on any job, the kind of dedication he had for his patients. He'd get up any hour of the night—it didn't matter what time he was called out of bed; he didn't care. Gerty Hammond told me about this old lady around eighty years old. She had her appendix out sometime in the afternoon, and then during the night—she was a bit senile—she picked out all the stitches. When the nurse went in to check on her late that night, the sheet was soaked with blood. She pulled down the sheet and everything was gaping open. So they just called Dr Olds. He came back in, took her back up in the OR and stitched her up again. And the nurse said there wasn't a word out of him.

"On rounds the doctors would talk to the patients. We had this one lady from Shoe Cove who was in quite often. She always made sure she had enough knitting to last for the winter because she always planned on staying. A lot of our patients then did that—no one to look after them at home. But if they died in the winter, you'd have to keep 'em till spring to get them home. The Hospital supplied caskets—the carpenter used to make them, also little white ones for babies.

"This lady would be up at six o'clock in the morning, she'd have rollers put in her hair, and by the time rounds would start at eight, she'd have her hair all combed out, have her beads on, and lipstick and everything. Sitting up in bed. And as soon as Dr Olds would come through the door, she'd be right down, and almost dying, and panting. Then, as soon as his back was turned, up she'd come, sir; doing her hair, the works!

"He always remembered patients." said Angela. "My father was operated on for kidney stones at seventy-one years of age in St John's. I was sort of morbid over it. One day I was asking Dr Olds about the procedure. 'Oh,' he said, 'who's having that?' I told him, and mentioned that my father had never been in hospital before. And for *years* after that, until he retired, at least once a week he'd say, 'How's Pop?' Never met the man in his life, but he'd always come in and ask, 'How's Pop gettin' on?'"

There were some who perhaps needed to see him, but who hated to impose. Ivy LeDrew cooked at the Hospital for thirty-nine years and knew Dr Olds well. "They got along famously, really doted on each other," said Angela. "She knew him from the beginning—from the kitchen, far removed. And she was never afraid of him. He was soft spoken to her and of her." One morning she told her assistant Mabel that her side was bad again. Unknown to her, Mabel went up to OPD and told Dr Olds. "I'd been up there before," said Mrs LeDrew. "They told me when I got the pain again to come up. Anyway, I didn't. The next morning I was sewing in the staff kitchen and he came and sat down to the table. I said, 'Like a cup of coffee, Doctor?'

"'Yes I would.'

"I got the coffee and he said, 'You had a pain in your side yesterday morning?'

"'It wasn't severe enough for me to come, Doctor.'

"'Well, Ivy,' he grinned, 'next time you can keep it.'

It was widely rumoured that John Olds more than once gave his own blood to save a patient. This is true. Lab technician Bud Young confirmed it and so did Dr Lou Lawton. In those days Twillingate Hospital did not maintain a blood bank, but kept it "on the hoof," calling in local donors as need arose, checking blood type on the spot. Sometimes this system was too slow.

Olds was a universal donor, Type O RH negative. One night he rushed down from OR and said to Bud Young, "Bleed me," then hurried back with the transfusion to complete an operation. On that occasion the patient died, but on another he saved a life. In 1946 X-rays had confirmed a large TB cavity in the lung of a person from Cottrell's Cove. John had collapsed the lung by thoracoplasty. Around two in the morning, the patient went into severe shock and a nurse roused Dr Lou Lawton. "I called John." said Dr Lawton. "He came down, and we decided on a blood transfusion. He woke Bud

Young and got the patient grouped. John decided he would be the donor, and got up on the OR table. By today's standards our blood-taking apparatus was necessarily a bit primitive. You took a beaker, put in some anti-coagulant, put a large needle into a vein and let the blood run into the beaker under as sterile conditions as possible. When you had enough, you covered it with a sterile cloth, took it to the patient's room, poured it into a flask and ran it into the patient by gravity.

"So John got up and I took the blood. At around 400 cc's I suggested 'That's enough.'

"'No,' he said, 'take more.' So we took 500 to 600 cc's and transfused the patient. The man came out of shock and recovered. We finished at four or five in the morning. I was pretty tired, so I went to bed. About eight o'clock there was a knock on my door. A young ward aide stood there saying, 'Dr Olds is down in the OR and he wants to know where are you.' I thought at least he'd take an hour or so off. I went down and we proceeded with the normal routine for any other day. A very, very tough man; very wiry, very tough."

From the earliest years, Olds was concerned about the lack of occupational therapy for longterm patients, especially children and those with TB. When Grace Patten had arrived as a lab technician in 1932, he got her to double as a teacher for the TB children who were in casts. Likewise in 1936 he had persuaded Grenfell worker and artist Rhoda Dawson to give art lessons to the younger patients.

"I had never met him before," Rhoda wrote in 1990, "and our meeting was somewhat sudden. I wanted to stop in the town till the last boat, and paint. He there and then said I could stay at the Hospital for the winter, work with the children for my keep and paint the rest of the time. So I stayed—but only for two months. As the only paints I had were my own, I didn't let the children use them more than I could help, but of course one could always buy cheap drawing books in the town. I mostly played games with them. I found that children in Newfoundland and Labrador in those days had no idea of games. So with bedridden kids I had to invent the most idiotic games and they seemed to enjoy it; but what they really wanted was for me to go away and leave them my paintbox."

In April 1947 Olds was finally able to hire a full-time occupational therapist. Soon the TB patients were doing leatherwork, carving, model ship building, quilting and other crafts. The enthusiasm spread to other wards. Stamp collecting and jigsaw puzzles were added, books were borrowed back and forth. "If he saw a spark of promise, he would always encourage people," said Mike Maguire. "A patient was sketching once and this really delighted him. Every day he'd go up and see what she had done."

He himself was always teaching. When Melvin Rideout and his seventeen young friends on the male TB ward discovered that Dr Olds was a walking encyclopedia, they plied him with questions. "We asked him everything—girls, sex, everything."

"We had a school teacher there, and we'd get him to ask, because he had the right kind of language. And Dr Olds would tell us. 'Well,' he'd say, 'what else are you coming up with?' But when you asked him something about your *sickness*, he didn't want to tell you. He told us that if we began to dwell on that, we might never recover.

"One night when we felt better, a friend of mine from Boyd's Cove had a few rabbits sent up. We had our own hot plate—the Hospital food wasn't good—so we cooked it in the ward that night, hoping no-one would notice. Unknown to us, Dr Olds was doing an operation upstairs. And when he opened the OR door, he smelled onions. 'Christ Jesus,' he said, 'there's only two people in the Hospital cooking tonight, and that's Melvin Rideout and Stewart Thompson!'

"He came in with his apron on, right full o' blood. By this time we had all jumped back into bed. Well, you talk about a tellin' off we got. He gave us the biggest raking down. He wanted to know how we cooked the rabbit without getting out of bed. I was only eighteen or nineteen years old and frightened to death. But it wasn't about the rabbit; it was for disobeying the rules. We weren't supposed to be out of bed for a year. When he was leaving—we were out in the sun porch part where there were only four beds and two of them empty—he looked back and said in a low voice, 'Stew, you got any more rabbits?

"'Yes, Doctor; I've got two more down in the fridge."

"'Can I have one?' he said. That was Dr Olds."

At sixteen, Gordon Stuckless was working for Ted Drover on his passenger boat. One cold day in November, tying up at the Twillingate wharf, he slipped and fell overboard. He had just recovered from a bad case of measles and soon landed in hospital with pulmonary tuberculosis. He was put on complete bed rest for a year. To a bright lad just completing high school, this seemed like an eternity.

Gordon had sailed once or twice with his trader father around Newfoundland and Labrador, and this became a bond between him and Dr Olds. "That winter," said Gordon, "he spent hours and hours with me in the TB ward. He knew navigation; he had all the books on it. I wanted a Captain's ticket, a Master's. We made a cardboard sextant, glued mirrors on and shot the sun. Though he had no ticket himself, he taught me enough that in 1953 I went to St John's, wrote a Temporary Master's Home Trade ticket for Newfoundland waters, and passed."

John also liked to share his large library. If he thought a patient was interested, he would drop a book or two on their bed. When Lorna Stuckless felt depressed after her gall bladder operation, he came and said, "Here, read this; it'll cure you.' The book was Heluiz Chandler Washburne's *Land of the Good Shadows: The Life Story of Anauta, an Eskimo Woman*. Anauta, the young Inuit widow of a white furrier, had in the early 1900s passed through Twillingate seeking her father. When Lorna was about to be discharged, Olds persuaded her to stay the weekend and comfort Alison Bartle, another depressed gall bladder patient. "Tell her she can live without the damned thing," he said.

He believed in explaining things to the patient in language they could understand. When he was travelling on the *Bonnie Nell* in 1937 a fisherman came aboard and said, "Doctor, you got to come ashore and see Grandmother."

She told him, "Doctor, I feels like my stomach is all bate togedder." Suspecting constipation, he gave her a mild laxative and said, "Perhaps you don't have enough grease." She understood, and had no more problems of that kind. Before any major operation, he liked to outline the procedure to the patient and their close relatives. Sometimes they didn't want to know. "Well," he'd say, disappointed, "I'll do it tomorrow then." Such total confidence weighted heavy on him. One old lady, recounting a serious operation to Mayme Hewlett, said, "My dear, it was cut here, cut there, cut everywhere."

"And were you nervous?"

"Nervous, my dear? When Dr Olds told me he was going to take care of me, I felt just as safe as if I was in God's pocket. "

"The hardest time was Christmas," said Melvin Rideout. To try to cheer the patients, Dr Olds and his Directors got the various Twillingate churches and organizations to donate to a fund. On rounds Christmas morning, they gave every patient a present. "Dr Olds would come in," said Melvin. "He had Sandy Claus for us—Joe White. And Uncle Dave White, who used to drive the taxi, brought a big bag of candy and oranges and everything." After Olds' 1939 visit to meet the young King George VI, he amused everyone by wearing his suit of morning clothes, the famous "King Suit."

One year after Christmas rounds an elderly patient from Herring Neck complained that he'd had "nar bit o' Christmas this year." It turned out he meant cake, cheese and sweet red syrup, so Dr Olds got Janet Hori to fetch some. That evening he asked the man whether he had enjoyed Christmas. "Sure did, b'y," he replied. "But the cheese warn't as good as we gets from Joey White's shop."

If he lost a patient he was always shaken, and would talk to the relatives to comfort them. "Sometimes in private he'd curse," said a friend. "He'd get awful bad. Feel that probably he ought to have done a better job. I don't know; you couldn't do a much better job than he did, in the circumstances."

When the patient was a close friend, he wept. He wept when Billy Earle the Hospital plumber died, and the same with Elijah Dalley. "He fell across a bed and cried like a child," said Angus Dalley, "saying over and over, 'I've lost my best friend.'"

"He had no bedside manner whatsoever," said a long-term female patient. "Yet I can't begin to describe the hundreds of times, at any hour of the night, he came to see me. Perhaps I'd be disturbed—and here he'd be, taking my pulse. Just the fact that he'd be there, that he was present, made you feel so much better, so much better. Up until my last interview as a patient, he looked at me and I think he remembered every detail and every pain I ever had...."

Chapter Thirty-Four

The Man Himself

"I suppose a person would call him...selfish—
but with his patients he wasn't."
— Tutie (Olds) Mott

"He was a good man, a charitable man, very
generous and kind."
— Dr Mike Maguire

Ever since Twillingaters could remember, Harvey Sharpe had been their purveyor of fresh cod tongues. Harvey had haunted stagehead and wharf since boyhood, collecting them to sell to anyone who craved the fresh, ivory white delicacies. Harvey meted them out with a pint measure and did a good business all summer.

One day Dr Olds and Sid Fisher were down on Ashbourne's wharf, chatting with a schooner captain, when Mr Sharpe happened along with his pail. John bought a quart for supper and the vendor jotted the sale in his dog-eared notebook. Suddenly Harvey smiled and said, "Well, Doctor— you just bought my millionth cod tongue!"

"That so?" said Dr Olds, a little drunk. "Harvey, any man that's sold a million cod tongues deserves a medal!" An hour later he sent a telegram to Premier Smallwood recommending that Mr Sharpe of Twillingate be decorated for his achievement. "John and I had great fun cooking up that telegram," said Fisher. As an afterthought, Dr Olds sent one to Prime Minister Louis St Laurent and another to Queen Elizabeth. Only Joey Smallwood congratulated the cod tongue champion.

In the mid-1930s, when Grace Patten informed John and Betty that she was leaving in one month, they urged her to stay. As the date for her departure neared, he hid the key to her steamer trunk so she couldn't pack. "John," she said, "I just *know* you've got the key to my trunk! This won't work, you know; if you don't give it back I'll just leave the trunk here." Two or three days before the steamer came, he threw the key down in front of her and said, "Here, damn you; if you're going, you can have 'em."

One day an inpatient named Mrs Boone wrote out a message to her husband:

FEELING TERRIBLE STOP HAVING A HEART ATTACK EVERY DAY
STOP COME AT ONCE.

When an aide took it to the Hospital's front office to send, Olds chanced to see it. Knowing his patient very well and that her husband was a busy man, he reworded it to say, "Feeling much better." When Mr Barnes replied that he was pleased at the news, she was mystified.

One winter during World War II a group of US Coast Guard personnel, coming from Lewisporte in an amphibious *Weasel*, broke down and had to abandon the costly machine on the ice off New World Island and hitch a ride to Twillingate. "You didn't leave it there, did you?" said Olds in mock alarm. "With no-one guarding it? That could be stripped for salvage before morning, you know. People around here would consider it fair game." The Coast Guard fellows hastened back and spent all night on the ice with it.

Though fond of having the last word, Dr Olds didn't mind being put down if it was done in style. One day Mayme Hewlett needed some cheques endorsed. She found him in his workshop, scowling through a cloud of cigarette smoke at a piece of metal tubing.

"Dr Olds, would you sign these cheques?"

"I can't and I won't!" he grunted.

"I see," said Mayme. "Well, if you can't sign them, at least make your mark."

"Mayme," he laughed, "I'll sign 'em if you'll take 'em to the bank!"

He enjoyed making small bets. Anything would do, even a faulty cigarette lighter. "Will it go on the first, second or third try, or not at all?" he'd say, collecting fifty cents as often as not. He'd play hockey on Hospital Pond with Reverend Alex Smith and a bunch of other men and lay bets on the outcome. He once bet someone he could produce electricity from ocean waves. Every year he bet the naive summer students they couldn't swim across Twillingate Harbour—a pretty safe bet, since he had shivered for an hour after swimming it with young Grace Patten in 1932. When Joan Thompson and Rube Waddell left for St John's in 1939, John bet Bob Ecke and the Hardys that the two would marry there. He didn't collect his winnings because Rube had already let him in on the secret.

During the thirties and forties he and his cronies played "Dole Poker," the maximum bet being $2.00. Anyone losing that much could still play but no longer bet. One night David was playing long past his bedtime and Betty kept trying to pry him away. "He can't go now," said John, "he's winning!"

He read hungrily, averaging a book a day. He ordered regularly through the Book of the Month Club, and when they didn't have a particular title, he got his mother or Tutie to mail it and bill him. When his books arrived late or wet, he complained bitterly. He preferred non-fiction, especially natural history, but read some novels. Despite the loss of his medical library in 1939, at his death he owned nearly four thousand volumes. He also kept up with *Lancet, Scientific American, Popular Mechanics, National Geographic,* and several other popular and scientific magazines.

When John invited Jesus Austria and his wife Felicitas over to tea in 1962, without warning he handed Mrs Austria a book. "Here, read this," he said, "it'll be interesting for you." The title was *How to Raise Ants.* She had no idea why he chose it.

Anything he read stuck with him. Once when he and Mike Maguire were disputing some point of philosophy, he said, "Hell, I can prove it to you. See that book up there? Take it down and look up page so-and-so." Mike found the passage within two pages of where Olds said it would be. Dr Maguire discovered when he lived with him in 1954 that Olds not only took a book or magazine with him to the bathroom, but commonly read, shaved and relieved his bowels at the same time.

The only time he did not wish to be disturbed was during supper. Only in a dire emergency would anyone call him then. He was fond of that hour and kept it almost religiously, at least while Betty was alive. He usually went home around six, had a beer or two and then a formal supper. He wouldn't say grace or bless the food; Betty would do that.

He also loved foul weather, the stormier the better. "At his house up behind the Hospital the wind used to really whistle," said Maguire. "He had a good fireplace. He'd put on a nice fire and sit back enjoying the cosiness. One stormy night I struggled up over the hill to his place for supper. We had a couple of beers and were eating Gander Bay caribou and talking about some peppers he was growing in a pot, when in came Nina. 'Dr Olds,' she said, 'there's two men at the door wants to speak to you.'

"'What do they want?' he said.

"'I don't know,' she said, 'but they said it's urgent.'

"'Damn,' he said, and rose from the table. Nina had closed the door, but at that moment it blew open, a squall of wind came in, and the two fellows standing there said, 'Jesus saves.'

"'Goddamn it,' roared Olds, 'he'd better save *you!*' And he jumped up and took off down the hill after them. They were Jehovah's Witnesses. Leaflets were flying in the air. He was in a terrible rage. He came back muttering and panting and settled back into his dinner."

"Had John been in the Armed Forces he would have been killed," said Dr Lou Lawton. "He didn't seem to perceive danger the way other people do. For example, he made some kind of air sled to take him over the ice. It had a big airplane propeller with no cover over it, so that if he happened to fall backwards—that was it." He said some of his friends went and broke it up because they figured it would kill him sooner or later. The main reason his Directors refused to get him an airplane was that they figured he would crash it and kill himself.

He liked to show visitors the lighthouse on Long Point, whose lofty cliffs had no guard rails in those days. John would walk out to the edge, stick the toes of his shoes an inch or two over and yell back, "Come on out; you can't see anything from in there!"

"He had no fear of rough water or anything like that," said a Moreton's Harbour fisherman who sometimes ferried him around to see patients. One stormy night this man had to fetch him for his own father. In Friday's Bay the sea was running so high he couldn't risk landing in Gillard's Cove on the South Island, but chose a safer spot and walked across the island. When he and Dr Olds left the shelter of Shoal Tickle on the return trip, the water was seething white. Deciding it would be suicide to attempt the exposed westerly route around Berry Island, the fisherman set a more southerly course for Tizzard's Harbour, about three miles distant.

"Where you headed?" yelled Dr Olds above the roar of wind and water.

"Tizzard's Harbour."

"Hell, I don't want to go to Tizzard's Harbour," he said. "I want to go to Moreton's Harbour!"

He was notoriously tight with Hospital money and supplies. "He had a budget," said Dr Lou Lawton, "and got upset at any waste." Dr Lawton lived in the new Staff House from 1945 to 1947. Though the building had a furnace, by January his apartment was so cold he had to wear an overcoat. One bitter night, watching the curtains billow in the draft, he thought, "This is ridiculous." Taking a jug of water, he poured some into the horizontal window seams, where it immediately froze and made an effective seal. Then he got adhesive tape from the supply room and sealed the vertical seams. Just as the room was becoming tolerable, Stella Manuel looked in to ask how he was coping with the cold. Word spread that he had the only comfortable room in the place. By and by Dr Olds showed up. "How'd you get your room so warm?" he asked. Dr Lawton told him. "Did you stop to think how much that tape cost?" said Olds.

In Mike Maguire's opinion, John felt that the Hospital should be supported completely by the people and for the people. "In some ways he was a communist. Even the plumbers and carpenters didn't get much pay. He wasn't being stingy; he just felt they should do this for society—their own society. He considered that a day out shooting turrs with a bottle of rum and a case of beer was a big fringe benefit, enough to keep anyone happy."

Once, during his holidays, Dr Maguire took two summer students on a weekend boat trip to Herring Neck, Boyd's Cove and down Dildo Run. "It'll be good for the students to see the coast," agreed Olds. On the way, the propeller shaft broke and Leo Donahoe had to tow them back, which took an extra day. Since he was still owed some holidays, Mike asked leave to go to St John's, adding that he would get the shaft fixed while there. "No," said Dr Olds, "three days off is enough."

Repeatedly he warned the staff never to throw out anything remotely useful. Hypodermic needles were sterilized and reused. "It wasn't that he was mean," said Maguire. "But he'd been there so long and had done so much with so little, he felt it was his own place. He was the king. And in some ways he ruled it with an iron fist—the Hospital and even the town to some extent. Everything revolved around the Hospital, and what he said was law."

In fact, John Olds was by nature generous. One weekend at the Tilt he did a painting of Smooth Cove. When Ern French's sister Muriel saw it, she impulsively said, "I like that one. Can I have it?"

"Why, certainly," he said. "If you want it, there it is."

"Many a man years ago," said Herb Gillett, "would go to him and ask him to back a loan at the bank. Which he would do. God only knows how many of those he backed." People came to him for help with sending a son or daughter to college. He bought uniforms for, and lent money to, staff aides who wanted to go study nursing. A young doctor friend came down from Labrador to get married, but couldn't afford the boat and train fare from Twillingate to Grand Falls. At that time John was broke too, but he remembered that David had just sold a bike. He borrowed the money and gave it to the doctor. He once showed his brother-in-law Doug Mott a shotgun taken as collateral on a loan. "John lent the fellow a lot more than the gun was worth," remarked Doug. He lent David and his Twillingate school friends Jim Young and Jim Cooper money to start a playtime grocery store, and gave them used rubber gloves for balloons. Among his papers was a note which said: "Dr Olds, I would rather owe you money than anyone else."

After he and Gloria moved into the new house on Main Tickle near the second Tilt in 1969, he donated the cabin to the Girl Guides. He let Peter Pelley borrow his speedboat and outboard motor whenever he wished. He gave Gordon Stuckless all his *Popular Mechanics* and *Scientific American* magazines when he was done with them.

After the Hospital fire in 1943, the Board acquired a powerful new pump. A crowd of onlookers gathered to watch its test run. Suddenly the hose sprang free and the heavy brass nozzle slammed against Steve Young's face. Dr Olds was unable to save the young man's eye and the father always blamed Olds for the mishap. John got him a 1938 Plymouth and Steve soon had Twillingate's first regular taxi business.

And he lent the Hospital money. "Very few people knew he was doing these things. "He didn't talk about it," said Dr Fred Woodruff. "You would hear about it from someone else." In the early years he was almost indifferent to money. Secretaries were told to deposit his salary cheques and to remember when his insurance premiums and investments came due. Except for cash to buy a new boat or pay David's tuition, he didn't seem to care what they did with them. There were times, especially after Betty's death and his remarriage and divorce, when he had to borrow from Mary. Years later he admitted to being foolish about personal finances in his youth. In the early sixties, when the Trans-Canada Highway was being pushed across the Island, he and two other fellows bought some war surplus bulldozers and trucks and successfully bid on highway construction contracts. "I made more money at that racket than I did at the Hospital," he once told Tutie.

Some of his old fiscal exuberance returned after he married Gloria. One day Gordon Stuckless was working on electrical equipment at the Hospital. "You've got a new car," said Gordon.

"Yes," grunted Olds, "The Missus bought that Monday."

"Volkswagen, eh?"

Olds snorted in disgust. A few weeks later, he drove the Volkswagen to St John's on business and Gord, who wanted to buy a Chrysler *Valiant* station wagon, went along. They went down to City Motors. "And here was this *Barracuda*," said Gordon, "a big poshy car. Beautiful sleek looking thing, like a submarine.

"'How much is that?' said Dr Olds to the salesman. And buddy tells him the price. It was a lot of money then.

"'Well,' says Olds, "I'm going to have that one. Can we take it out for a little run now?'

"'Sure,' says the salesman. So we took it out, and came back. 'What'll I do with *that*?' asked Olds, pointing to the Volkswagen. 'Normally we don't take new cars on trade-in...how many miles?'

"'Oh, less than a thousand.'

"And I don't know whether he *gave* the man that car," laughed Gordon, "or what he did; but he climbed in the *Barracuda* and went on."

People said he was shy, which was true; but shy was scarcely the correct adjective for so commanding a personality. More accurately, he had a low threshold for foolishness. He enjoyed staff parties but avoided Twillingate's social functions. "His idea of a good party," said a close friend, "was to boil up a feed, have a few drinks and tell stories. When invited out he'd say, 'Betty, let's go to the Tilt!'"

In the early years Dr Wood's wife used to put on "Musical Evenings," during which she would play the piano and everyone would sing. Always she invited John and Betty, and always he tried to escape. Early one night he phoned Nurse Drover at the Hospital and said, "Jess, I'm invited to another of Mrs Wood's goddamned *evenings* and I need you to rescue me. Around eight o'clock, you call and say there's an emergency." When she called she said, simply, "Your fifteen minutes are up."

"Okay Jess, I'll be right there," he said, made his excuses and escaped home. He played this game for years.

After attending the 1939 Royal Reception in St John's, Betty and he got invited every year to the Governor's Garden Party. After a few years he left the invitations unopened. The secretary would wave it under his nose and say, "Dr Olds, you're supposed to return the RSVP...."

"I don't want to go to that foolishness."

"Look, you should go...."

"If you think somebody should go, *you* take the ticket and *you* go!"

It was the same with convocations. After Memorial University bestowed an Honourary Doctor of Science on him at its 1970 Fall Convocation, the Board of Regents kept inviting him back. Again he dropped out. To him it was all a big show, a waste of time and money, and besides he was too busy. When Herb Gillett successfully nominated him for the Order of Canada in 1969, he probably underestimated the difficulty of getting the candidate to Ottawa. Soon after returning home, Dr Olds received a letter asking him to return the medal by registered mail because they wished to replace the ribbon with a lapel pin. Olds ignored the request. "Too much money," he muttered. "Lot of foolishness!" The gold medal lay on his desk until it was buried in mail. Finally Angela Jenkins mailed it back.

Even getting him to attend local functions was a chore. In 1949 the Hospital celebrated its twenty-fifth anniversary. Betty (Ashbourne) Facey, after whom the *Bessie Marie* was named, had to make him go home and get dressed to join the other distinguished guests on the platform. He voluntarily attended the opening of the new Dental Clinic in 1954 only because Mike Maguire was a friend, and it marked an important advance in medicine for the Bay. Standing there with Premier Smallwood, Leslie R. Curtis and Jack Pickersgill, he almost seemed to be enjoying himself.

He hated public speaking. His standard retort was, "You know I can't talk, and I'm not going to, either!" At a medical conference in St John's, a bit under the weather, he gave the shortest speech anyone there had ever heard. "Gentlemen," he said, swaying on his feet, "Why?" and sat down. As a respected Twillingate figure, however, he could not avoid some public exposure. When asked to add his blessing to Twillingate's new government wharf he said only, "I think enough has been said about this wharf." He disliked the annual fall Memorial service at the Hospital steps, when old soldiers and young cadets would parade and pay tribute and he and his Directors would add their blessings. One year the weather was hot and a young cadet fainted after Olds spoke. As Dr Olds whisked the unconscious lad aside he was heard to mutter, "Too bad you hadn't fainted before."

Yet he could speak well in public. When Memorial University's Family Practice Unit held its October 1981 workshop for cottage hospital workers in Twillingate, they enlisted him as closing speaker. After the Friday evening banquet of fresh turr, moderator Fred Woodruff introduced Dr Olds. The Old Man rose stiffly, ran his fingers nervously through his mane of curly white hair, cleared his throat and held them spellbound for over an hour with an account of early medicine in the Bay.

Floss Ings, who knew him first as a neighbour and later as a co-worker, said, "Everybody was alike to him. He treated rich and poor the same. If he came in the kitchen and you were cooking something, he'd take it right off the stove. He was a real down-to-earth person."

"I never met a man who won my affection so quickly," said Sid Fisher. Dr David Parsons recalled him as exceedingly tolerant and forgiving. "No matter what anybody said about him, he'd always have a good word for them—even some of those doctors over in Corner Brook who spoke ill of him. He'd look on the best side. It didn't make any difference. And no matter what a mess I made of something, he would come and very gently point out where I'd gone wrong. I only heard John Olds say anything derogatory about one person and that was Dr Swanker, the one who left him in the lurch in 1944."

"If you're ever down in Connecticut," he'd tell visitors, "be sure to stop and see Mother." She once joked, "I never knew Windsor, Connecticut was on the way to so many places."

What did John's family think of him? His mother adored him, believed in him, understood him deeply. Pop and Lois frequently misunderstood him, seemed to admire more than love him. Tutie, eight years younger and a child when he left for Yale, regarded her big brother with a mixture of awe and pride, but hardly knew him until years later. Of the siblings she was most like him in temperament. After Pop and Mother died they corresponded regularly.

"He was different than the others in our family," she said. "None of us went the route he did, to isolate himself like that. Father wanted him to be a rich doctor in Hartford, wanted him not to go to China. The only time we saw him in the early years was when Poppa went up there. They went in 1936 and 1940, and Mother went twice after that, in 1948 and another time, to take David home. John wanted him educated in the US...he just felt David wasn't getting all he needed in Twillingate. He didn't say 'Would you like to have David come and live with you?' He just said, 'I'm sending him down.' That was the way John did things.

"John didn't seem to have any feeling for family. In many ways he was very cold. In Twillingate when he would come in to tea on an afternoon, he would go off and read and Betty would entertain. There may have been some shyness there, but he didn't suffer fools. And he wasn't much for small talk. Lois was only a year younger than John, but he wasn't close to her either. He didn't seem to want to hear anything about us after he left home. Mother just lived for letters from him. And all the time, my father was trying to get him back. He paid no attention to Poppa at all. John had to do everything the hard way."

"John always told the truth," she said, adding perceptively, "sometimes he avoided telling it; but when he did, it would be true. Whatever he wrote down would be absolutely true. I guess he was a pretty good husband, in his way. I suppose a person would call him self-centered and selfish—but with his patients he wasn't. And not with his life. Look, he gave his life up there."

Raised by a Christian Science mother against a backdrop of Episcopal, Presbyterian and Congregational doctrine, John as an adult attended no church. Yet he gave to each Twillingate denomination more or less equally. "I keep a pew in all of them," he quipped. When Ivy LeDrew collected for the Salvation Army he usually gave her a generous donation, not because he especially liked the Army, but because he liked her. He welcomed the local clergy into his home, and when Father Kelly from Norris Arm visited Dr Maguire—then the only Roman Catholic in the town—John invited them both up for dinner. Discovering that the priest had been a Japanese prisoner-of-war and spoke Chinese well, he plied him with questions about the country, the government and the work of Dr Norman Bethune. China had been his second choice after Newfoundland, he said.

After David was born, Betty wanted him baptized in the Church of England. John said no, he wouldn't go; he didn't believe in that at all. Betty then got the minister to come to the Cottage and baptize their son, and John accepted this. "Certainly he wasn't demonstrative in his religion," said Maguire, "but he was no agnostic either. His sense of morality was probably different than mine in those days. For instance, he was pro-abortion. But I'd say he was a God-fearing man."

While John had little use for organized religion, he did not hold the beliefs of individuals against them. He and Mike Maguire enjoyed long, heated debates about what Maguire called "the pros and cons of chaos versus order. One night when we were a wee bit in our cups, I asked him whether he believed in God. He said, 'I believe in the God that heals wounds.'" He told Herb Gillett once, "I believe in the God who knits the two sides of a wound together—only I wish sometimes He'd help a little more." Little David, watching John make something in the workshop one afternoon, asked if he could make some skin. "No, son," said his father, "only God can make skin." One night when Betty and David were visiting the Faceys, the six-year-old boy saw a rubber plant and asked how rubber was made. Betty said, "When we get home we'll look it up in the *Book of Knowledge*." Back home, they decided to ask Pop instead. Making a game of it, Betty urged David to think up a question Pop couldn't answer.

"So they started in," said Betty. "He asked how to make glass, wine, tobacco, tin, etc., etc.—and of course John answered it all. Then David said, 'How do you make bone?'

"And John said, 'Only the Lord knows that.'

"And David, with a twinkle in his eye, said, 'Yes, and He never told you—so there's one question you can't answer!'"

If Mary McKee Olds had any doubts about her son's religious beliefs, her first visit to Twillingate in 1936 with Alfred had dispelled them. She saw a young man selflessly healing the sick and revered by them. Perhaps she thought of the words of Jesse Fell, who said of his friend Abraham Lincoln that his beliefs placed him "entirely outside the Christian pale. Yet...his principles and practices and the spirit of his whole life were of the very kind we universally agree to call Christian...."

The outside world knew Dr Olds as Walter Earle of Fogo did—as the tough, hard-spoken, hard-drinking boss of Twillingate Hospital. One day when Walter was a patient there he overheard a conversation which shattered that image. The man in the bed next to him had come from Montreal to see Dr Olds about a serious back problem. After looking at the X-rays, Olds came and sat on the bed. "My friend," he said, "there's three persons involved here. Among the three of us we might be able to do something for you."

"And who might they be, Doctor?" said the man.

"You, me and God."

In Twillingate John found his God. "I liked the water and the country," he said, "and I very quickly came to like the people." On the rare occasions when he journeyed home to Windsor, he soon grew restive. "The best part of the trip from Connecticut," he once declared, "is the last 10 miles to Twillingate." When a reporter asked him why he came to Twillingate for one year and stayed for over forty, he replied, "Because I liked it."

Chapter Thirty-Five

Naturalist

"Six crows feeding...Now very fond of Rice Crispies...."

— J. M. Olds

Loomis' Darwin Club had taught John early to be a scientific observer of Nature. Among his favourite Twillingate phenomena was the capelin "scull," which he had watched almost every June since 1930. Every year he wanted Betty to cook some capelin—though she was not fond of them herself. In 1936, when his family was visiting, he pestered her so much that she retorted, "All right! Tutie and I will go out this afternoon and get some capelin. And I hope we drown. And if we do, it'll be on your head!"

His interest in capelin went beyond food or curiosity. These little fish, he knew, had helped nourish the potatoes he ate for supper and the dogs that took him on winter house calls. More importantly, they were the main spring food of northern cod. Their arrival signalled not only the onset of the fishery, but hinted at its success and supplied the early bait. When the capelin scull failed, all Notre Dame Bay suffered. For these reasons he had since the early sixties been thinking about breeding them. "He spent a lot of time trying to hatch out capelin eggs," said Dr Woodruff. "He used to collect them and put them in a miniature aquarium with wet beach sand and keep them at the temperature of the sea. And although he changed the water regularly, he never could hatch out those eggs. This frustrated him and he talked to all kinds of people about it."

Among his personal papers is a letter dated June 21st, 1963, from his friend David E. Sergeant, now with the Arctic Unit of the Fisheries Research Board of Canada in Montreal. In it the biologist thanked him for his letter of June 14th, with specimens of capelin eggs and naturally hatched larvae. "Your very interesting observations on the hatching period for capelin—20 days or so—agree well with Dr Templeman's of 15-17 days. The exact time would vary with temperature." He went on to cite a useful paper by Templeman and told him how to obtain it.

People often brought Dr Olds marine specimens to identify. It was a task he enjoyed. In 1950 a strange fish appeared dead on the beaches. It was slender and silvery, about a foot long, with a thin bill on its lower jaw. He made coloured sketches and sent them to the Fisheries Research Board of Canada in St John's, who told him it was *Scomberesox saurus* of the Saurie family, and that sometimes it got chased inshore by predators. Its common name, skipper, was derived from a habit of skittering across the surface when disturbed, they said, and it was related to the flying fish. In the spring of 1963 another unknown fish appeared, this time in fishermen's nets. Deep-bodied and herring-like with large bright scales, it was tasty but full of small bones. He sent a preserved head and some scales to the fisheries people. Dr Templeman, Director of the station, identified them as shad, *Alosa sapidissima*, a very large member of the herring family only occasionally taken in Newfoundland waters.

As part of his ocean dabbling in this period, he bought a neoprene diving suit with an air tank. When the sea was civil he poked about in shallow coves, collecting sea anemones and other curiosities. Soon, however, the mechanics of scuba diving distracted him. Tired of pumping the flippers up and down, he began to design a pedal-driven propeller. The prototype consisted of a gear box with rack-and-pinion gear to make the pedals turn a shaft and propeller. The gears gave him some problems. Since aluminum was too soft, they had to be steel; but steel, added to gearbox and axles, weighed him down behind. And the contraption was slow. To gain more RPMs, he would have had to add more weight. Moreover, the propeller must be kept small to avoid cutting his suit. When he operated near the bottom he bumped his knees. In the end, he abandoned the idea and let the younger doctors play with his gear. When the Girl Guides held their first meeting at the Tilt, they found his badly cracked scuba suit hanging on a nail.

"When we were putting the radio station on the hill back of the Post Office," said Sid Fisher, "he was curious about what we were doing, and took the opportunity to pick my brains. I explained about VHF radio, and that we were putting a multi-channel network for telephone, telegraph and teletype from Gander to Twillingate and on up the coast. John and I talked and talked. He was drinking at the time, so he would get a little incoherent before the evening was over; but next morning he was fine.

"I couldn't talk literature or music with him; always we talked science. Though he didn't know much physics, he would put problems to himself and solve them. Often they had to do with atmospheric pressure and temperature. He'd walk up the stairs in his house and say, 'Now Sid, am I at a higher pressure or a lower pressure?'

"'A lower pressure.'

"'No, I'm not,' he'd say, 'because there's a pressure inversion here.' He had determined this with a barometer. This was the kind of thing that he caught me on. He didn't know much geology, however. He wanted to know about the geology of Newfoundland. When I got back to Montreal, I dug out some books and sent them to him."

As a sailor he was interested in navigation, which led naturally to a study of the heavens. "He used to talk a lot with Eric Facey about astronomy," said Dr Woodruff. "I remember their having long, great arguments in the new house he built near the Tilt. They would argue about the lighthouse lights and were always poring over star charts."

"We went sailing a few times," recalled Dr John Sheldon of Virgin Arm. "He was thrilled, loved every minute of it. Out there, we talked. He told me about a place where he used to dive off, a high dive from one of the cliffs in Twillingate. But the moment I shall never forget was off Cottrell's Island early one spring. It was a really cold but sunny day, and we passed a big iceberg. He reminisced about the time when he had got close to such a berg and fired at it with his rifle and the iceberg had exploded—just shattered into smithereens. He couldn't believe it. One bullet had finished it! He recalled that moment with intense pleasure."

He had a special fondness for wild birds. When someone gave him a camera, he found a way to combine tinkering and bird-watching. Too impatient to shiver in an outdoor blind for two hours, he contrived ways to photograph them from inside the house. When store-bought remote shutter release cables proved too short, he devised his own. At first he used air pressure. With the camera mounted on a back-board near the feeder, he strung a long piece of intravenous tubing into the house. To the house end he taped a rubber bulb from a discarded blood pressure cuff. To trip the shutter he had levers attached to a tiny piston on the camera. When a bird landed at the feeder, he pumped the bulb and a pulse of air did the rest. Later he found that a hypodermic syringe worked better, and later still he rigged a solenoid switch activated by the bird itself.

Bird-watching led him to recording his observations. Notebook lists of hospital supplies and medical ideas now mingled with jottings about the wildlife outside his winter windows and along the Tickle. "Six crows feeding," he wrote on December 20th, 1972. "Now very fond of Rice Crispies, bread & toast. Have fixed remote control camera to photograph them." In 1974 he wrote: "Crow sun-bathing in light fall of fluffy snow. Crow plowed a ditch maybe 10 metres long, throwing snow with wings & much jumping. Watching him with binoculars at about 300 metres for about 15 minutes."

On the same page is a note from January 22nd, 1975: "My crows are still on welfare, but seem to be getting tired of Hospital toast; in spite of very bad weather they haven't eaten any in two days—[they] just look at it." He noted that Main Tickle had frozen Dec. 26th, adding that he "walked on ice Dec. 29. Temp. -17° F; 2 fox tracks coming ashore by our house."

Ever since his excitement over Halley's Comet at age four, he had always kept an eye peeled for anything unusual. Even on hunting trips, said Gander Bay guide Harvey Francis, he collected insect specimens in pill bottles to take back home and identify. More often than not, the bottles gathered dust on a shelf in his cluttered office. Not until his late sixties was he able to pursue natural history in the field. Even after he retired in 1976, he still spent part of each day at the Hospital. Older patients sought him out; many refused to see anyone else. They would keep him busy well into his seventies.

As the Hospital added more staff and his workload eased, however, he found time to study not only the crows at his feeder but the cinquefoil on his lawn, the blue mussels on the shore, the microflora of the ocean. In time he could squander a whole afternoon watching the doings of squid or terns. In August 1976 he observed two huge sunfish: "Never expected to see any in these waters; saw two (one with David aboard boat, later one—a beauty— with Eric Facey in John Sheldon's sailboat)." On August 31st he noted: "Squid—large number 10-20 yards offshore, visible and audible from house; stayed 1/2 hour. No wind 4:30-6:00 PM. One gull swimming in midst, very nonchalant. Only 2-3 boats squidding at causeway, where there have been many all of August—81 present on one occasion at least. Catch has been only fair: price $1.60-$2.00 dried." A year later he noted on the same page: "Squid fairly plentiful. Price up to $3.50 lb dried."

"In September 1980," recalled Dr Fred Woodruff, "Dr Olds had been very ill with pneumonia—in fact, he'd been in hospital for a short time—and was now home. And as is very common after pneumonia, he was quite depressed and still not eating and looked very tired. I used to visit him at home and talk with him, but he wasn't very interested in anything. He had tried a little walk around the Harbour, shuffling along, very weak. After I left his house one day, driving home past the pond, I saw this huge beaver and behind it a smaller one. The larger one had a stick in its mouth. I thought, 'Dr Olds would like to see this.' So I went back and said, 'Would you like to come for a little walk?'

"'Oh I don't think so, Fred,' he said.

"'I've got something to show you that you'll really like—a beaver, close up.'

"'Really?' he said, brightening.

"Getting him out of the house in his weakened condition was quite a performance. But I got him into the car and drove up the side of the road. The larger beaver was still there. Dr Olds said, 'That's the biggest damned beaver I've seen in many a year.' And then *both* beavers came up, right by the side of the road, and looked at us. He stood for a long, long time admiring them. And he insisted on walking back down the road to see if they'd been building anywhere. That took about twenty minutes. Then he got back in the car and I drove him home. It seemed to liven him up." After he got better, John gave the Woodruffs a fine drawing of the scene, done from memory.

Although he never lost his love of wild animals, toward the end, he became increasingly engrossed in the smaller forms of intertidal life, their shapes and colours, their seasonal comings and goings, their bizarre life cycles. The summer of 1981 was especially fruitful. On July 3rd he carefully listed the relative abundance of sea fauna near his house. For a man of science his spelling is bad, but his eye is still sharp: "Barnicles 10; Winkles [periwinkles], 5; Crabs, 0; Muscles [mussels], 2; Anemenoe [anemone], 0; Whelks, 3; Starfish, 1; Urchins (or Whore's Eggs), 1; Sea lice [scuds], 1; Limpets, 0; Cunners, 0; Eels, 0." The next day he mentioned having seen only "three stearins [terns] all last year," but went on to record eighteen sightings between July 2nd and July 4th, followed on July 8th, 1982 by "5-6 stearins, morning & evening."

To collect ocean plankton, he rigged a pair of women's panty-hose with a floating hoop to hold the waist open and guy wires for towing. In the fall he would putter about the Tickle in his little boat, trailing the plankton net and occasionally bending over to clear seaweed or jellyfish. "The pteropod *Limacina*," he observed, "by the release of dimethyl sulphide, causes a bad smell in codfish that eat it." He was especially interested in the luminescent plankton that glowed pale green and blue in a boat's wake on October nights. Back home, he tried to recreate their eerie light inside darkened fish tanks. Having read by mouse power in the fifties, perhaps he meant to read at last by plankton glow.

Chapter Thirty-Six

At the Last Going Off

"I think it really hurt him when he had to stop surgery."
— Angela Jenkins

In the fall of 1969, Dr and Mrs Olds moved into the new bungalow that Angus Dalley built for them on the highway near his second Tilt. Early on the morning of October 7th, 1971, walking in from the parking lot to the old Hospital, he heard a new sound from the hill above. It was the roar of a bulldozer starting up. The Newfoundland Engineering Company of St John's, with a contract for $1,650,000, was starting the foundation for a new hospital. One foggy night in March 1972, with the wind in easterly, he was putting away the lawn mower when he heard the faint bellow of the new fog horn over on Long Point. Painfully he straightened up to listen. He stood there for a moment, curly white hair moving in the wet wind, then grunted and closed the garage door. On Guy Fawkes Night 1973, driving home from work, he met a lot more cars and trucks than usual and realized that Western Construction, after two years and six hundred thousand yards of fill, had finally finished the Main Tickle causeway. It was harder to sleep after that.

In March 1974, the staff gave him a birthday party. "I know it was his 68th," said Angela Jenkins, "because we had one of these cards that you dial around till you get to the right year—I thought I'd never come to 68. Of course it had to be done without him knowing. He never wanted a hulla-baloo about his birthday, never. I once put a card on his desk and he almost hit the ceiling. Just a silly little thing, something like 'Birthdays are like baths—you have to have one every year whether you need it or not.' He went right off the deep end. He disliked recognition of any kind.

"'Well,' we said, 'he's not going to be able to do anything about this one.' This was all done on the spur of the moment in the morning. 'Now Ivy,' we said, 'how fast can you bake us a cake?' Pretty soon, Ivy sent up this warm chocolate cake. We gathered a crowd in the BMR Room and put these little tiny birthday candles on it. We tried to get him in. He was really busy out in OPD, so we got Dr Woodruff to coax him. You know how fast those candles burn down, and all this mushy chocolate cake.... So Dr Woodruff went out and said, 'John, we've got an emergency out in BMR; can you come and give me a hand?' We waited and watched those damned candles burning right down to the icing. And everybody was saying, 'Is he coming? When is he coming? My God, he'd better come on. Look at the mess the cake is in!'

"Finally, in he comes. And everybody yelled, 'Surprise!'

"'Christ Jesus!' he said, and tried to bolt. But three of us blocked the door. We weren't going to let him out and that was it. After a couple of minutes he settled down. Joan Dennison brought over two wine glasses; we gave him one and Jim Drover had the other. And the rest of us drank out of those plastic portion cups or pill glasses. Just to be on the safe side, we stood right by the door with our little bit of cake and candle wax and our portion cup of wine."

That same year, after some twelve months in a nursing home with her mind wandering, his mother died. She was ninety-four. Alfred's death in 1943 had afflicted him far less. She had nurtured his life, been his steadfast correspondent for nearly sixty years, never given up on him, always understood.

On May 4, 1976, sick in bed and reading Dr Lewis Thomas' *The Lives of a Cell*, he took a scribbler and started writing. This surprised him, he said, "because I am practically always too lazy to write anything. I made no specific diagnosis," he continued, "but woke up at 2 AM & couldn't sleep any more till around 8 AM, after taking such medication as Furinal, Valium 10; & have one hell of a backache and general malaise with no fever & very weak—with some nausea & no headache but considerable generalized muscle ache, no diarrhea or constipation or sysuria; no desire to move & less desire to even attempt to go to work. I did not pretend to make any other diagnosis than the extremely unmedical &/or scientific one that I was sick....

"I slept most of the day, resented such attentions (and which required, admittedly, little exertion on my part) as having my wife take my blood pressure and & insist on taking at least one of the ordinarily palatable drinks like orange juice, milk, tea, coffee, 7-Up, tomato juice, etc., etc.; and, worst of all, straightening the bed. I now realize what tortures nurses do to patients up in the Hospital.

"Well, today I am some better but surely don't feel like working. I am 70 years and five weeks old & I expect to recover enough to continue work in the Hospital tomorrow & do whatever surgery & whatever duties are necessary. So I have no premonition that I won't recover."

He then went on to tally his inventions, but tired of it after a couple of pages and went back to Dr Thomas.

John Sheldon: "In his last five or ten years, when he had slowed down a lot, he'd get me to come in to his office. And he'd ask me about various old people around the Arm, former patients for whom he obviously felt tremendous affection. Which they might not have realized. And I loved to sit and talk to him about them. And on my return I would tell them how Dr Olds was asking about them. That meant a great deal to him. Because socially, apart from one or two people, he didn't have much contact with them any more except when they were sick.

"I've often wished I knew Dr Olds better, that I'd spent more time with him. Because he had so much to give and he was so interesting to talk to. But when we were separated by water, you didn't get down to the Hospital very much—and when you were there, you were busy."

Fred Woodruff: "He just did what amounted to a geriatrics practice. Came in the mornings for two or three hours. There were always patients who wanted to see him. And he had time to see them. But because he was now well into his seventies, they used to limit his appointments."

Mike Maguire: "He knew everybody in Notre Dame Bay and Green Bay, he'd been there so long. That's the finest kind of doctor you can have—not some young doctor who knows hardly anything about you, but someone who's known you for years. Because with the older family doctor you have a complete picture, like on a computer."

Angela Jenkins: "In his late years he liked people to yarn. He'd go into his office with his buddies and they would yarn and yarn all day long. Only certain people had the nerve to go in there—like Pete Pelley for instance. Pete came and went whenever he liked, wherever he liked. If Pete wanted to go up to OR and talk to Dr Olds, he did. That was Pete. They were great buddies. And Herb Gillett. And Peter Troake. They'd sit and yarn. And you'd have to go and interrupt them—though he wasn't too pleased about that.

"And later he used to come in my office and sprawl on my chair with the pipe going. Sometimes he talked and sometimes he would just sit there and grunt now and then. He had some severe back problems—probably bone cancer. Some days he could barely walk."

Peter Troake: "When I'd go up to the doctor, in his latter days when I had the arthritis, he used to come and examine me. And the poor brute was worse than I was. 'Pete,' he'd say, 'I got the arthritis something shockin'.' And he'd sit down alongside me and we'd chat about the seals and talk about the fish. We had so many conversations—talked about everything, because he *knew* about everything."

Melvin Woolfrey: "I was a friend of his, but not a close friend like Joe White and Ern French and they. They were buddies. He was superior to me, you know. But I used to go there every month for four years for my blood pressure checkup. Sometimes he'd say, 'Melvin, come back in two months' time.' So I had occasion to talk to him lots of times. Because in the last couple years he didn't work after dinner, I'd be nearly always the last patient. And he'd sit down to yarn about old times and people we knew and shipwrecks and the like o' that.

"And there was one story he liked a lot. 'You know, Doctor,' I said, 'there was a feller up in Moreton's Harbour years ago when I was a boy, he was a dwarf, a small feller. His parents took him to the doctor about it. When they asked him what the doctor told him, he said, 'The doctor told' me I wuz a w'arf. ' 'A w'arf?' said his father. 'Tis a wonder 'e didn't say to build a stage on 'e!'

"Anyway, crowd of us, Sunday, went down on the Government Wharf to see the old *Clyde* come in. You wouldn't miss that, not for the world. And we were out in an old boat, a schooner's punt they called it, and Angus—that was the small feller's name—was with us. And when he was gettin' up over the wharf—the wharf was sort of steep, and railed so you couldn't stand upright—Angus fell overboard. We all laughed. Joe Knight, his uncle, had to go down and haul 'en in. But before he did, he shoved 'en under again just for devilment. Angus crawled up over the wharf, streaming wet, and when he got on top he said to Skipper Joe, 'You old bugger, I wouldna got wet if it hadn't been fer you!' Nobody expected Angus to speak like that to his uncle.

"Dr Olds had a wonderful laugh at that."

John Sheldon: "Before he retired, he didn't have any pension or anything. It was there, waiting for him, but he was on salary. The Government said, 'You've got to retire.' They cut off his salary, and for his last years he was on his own, just getting his pension. Then he worked on a fee-for-service basis at the Hospital, same office and everything, and would bill the government for the people he'd seen. He was in heavy demand and had a heavy case load. Which meant that his bills were high—higher, in fact than his salary had been. So in a way, he got back at the Government for forcing him to retire.

In August of 1979 he sat in his office for over an hour yarning with my father, Brett Saunders, about their hunting trips together. Near the end of their conversation Brett asked, "When you gonna retire?"

"I don't know, Brett," he replied with great weariness. "'Most any time now, I guess."

Angela Jenkins: "He had to be forced. He fought it tooth and nail. I don't really know how it happened, because there wasn't much said about it at the time. But rumour had it that he developed something like Parkinson's Disease; he had a slight tremor, and I think the Hospital Board really had to get on his back. Everybody feared that something might happen.

"I think it really hurt him when he had to stop doing surgery. He came in for all day for a while, then he just tapered off and left just before dinner. And there were days when that man came in to see patients, that he could barely walk, his back was so bad. Arthritis they said it was, but we said he knew from the beginning that it was cancer of the spine. He would never even hint this publicly. But to see him walking.... It was terrible, especially after watching somebody for so long, to see him just go downhill so fast. But he was working, really active. He was in every day, seeing his patients and busy as could be. I think he came just for something to do in the mornings...."

On the morning of March 4th, 1980 he came to Gloria in his dressing gown, pointed to his bare midriff and said, "What do you think of this?" A swelling had appeared, and the pulsing was strong enough to feel. "Aneurism, I think," he said, and she agreed. He was rushed to James Paton Memorial Hospital in Gander. The diagnosis was abdominal aortic aneurism. Three days later, he was taken to the Health Sciences Centre in St John's, where he underwent vascular repair. The diagnosis included pneumonia, chronic obstructive lung disease and osteoarthritis of the spine. His seventy-fourth birthday came and went. He was discharged April 3rd.

"Finally made it home," he wrote Tutie on April 13th, "& am now running on plastic tubing. The aorta and iliac arteries are replaced & doing alright so far. The lymphatics on the left side are still leaking but seem to be slowing down. While this racket was going on, the high school was getting named after me. Gloria officiated in my stead & did a very good job." On May 17th he wrote: "I am extremely lazy now & am not doing anything— some days are better than others—but none really good."

In September of that year he told his sister, "I can't say I am getting any stronger; feel fairly well sitting on my ass. Still taking TB pills, 4 kinds, but doubt it's doing any good." By October, a few weeks after Dr Woodruff showed him the beavers, he was feeling much better and went back to work part-time.

On October 13th, 1981, Cooper Construction started demolishing the old Hospital. It was done against Dr Olds' express wishes, for he believed it would make an excellent home for old people. He had even convened a meeting of the five main churches to discuss it. But nothing had happened and now he had no time or energy to pursue it.

The flattish timbered roof that Ned Clarke had thrown up after the fire of February 1943 was easy to dismantle. The next two storeys of six thousand and more concrete blocks—hand-made while John was finishing Loomis, blackened by the fire of 1943, were harder to dislodge. The blocks had weathered thousands of storms and absorbed the groans and laughter of countless patients; but the swinging steel sphere soon laid them flat. The most stubborn was the 5,000-square-foot poured concrete floor. It clung to the pickaxed bedrock as though part of it. The Dental Clinic came down the same day.

In the fall of 1981, the new hospital had a strike of lab and X-ray technicians. Finally they were legislated back to work, no better off and short five weeks' pay. That November, in one of his last surviving letters, he told his sister, "Next week support staff—aides, maids, laundry, etc.—are supposed to go off. Patients seem to be the last concern of anyone...."

On December 15th Frank Pardy noted in his diary: "The old NDM Hospital is completely torn down and not a vestige remains. The site is being levelled off for landscaping." From the Harbour one would never know the structure had ever existed. Higher up, overlooking the site, a long brown slab-like structure had taken its place.

Jessie Drover: "When he was really sick with his back, I had an old aunt over here and he and I used to go over and see her. I didn't realize then how sick he was; it was just before he went to St John's. They had taken the old Hospital down and 'twas all cleared off, and they were going to put a memorial there because it had been a memorial hospital. He was very sick but he said, 'I asked them to put a tennis court there so it would be of some use. I didn't want some damned monument stuck up there. For that reason,' he said, 'I didn't give 'em one red cent.'

"'Well, John,' I said, 'you may be sick but you haven't changed.'"

Louis Lawton: "I kept in touch with him; used to visit him every year in Twillingate; when he was in hospital he'd usually phone. Or someone would call and say he was in St John's and I'd go and chat with him. When I saw him that last summer in Twillingate I noticed a fairly definite decline. Because he always read a tremendous amount. He could discuss many things—geology, art—he certainly kept informed in spite of his relative isolation. And that interest was going."

When he could no longer go outdoors, he stationed himself in his favourite chair, in sight of the bird feeder and the Tickle. With a drink on his right and his pain-killers nearby, he read and watched TV and sometimes sketched. For days he went without speaking. One morning he said, "You know, Gloria, this can't go on much longer."

At times he became terribly confused and agitated. One day Gloria asked him to fix the washing machine. He puttered at it; when she went to use it the next day, she found he had tied it up with string. In October of 1984 they moved to a house in Twillingate.

A swelling appeared on his forehead. He appeared not to notice. "John, you have a bump on your head and it's growing," said Gloria.

"Is that so?" he said.

"Yes, and you really should have that looked at." He never bothered.

On August 8th, 1985 he was rushed from Gander to the Health Sciences Centre with a fractured right hip. He had fallen while trying to get out of bed. On admission he was confused and dehydrated. There were swellings on his forehead and on his right hand. Investigation revealed extensive metastatic disease—cancer. The physicians were unable to identify the primary malignancy site. An orthopedic surgeon plated the subtrochanteric fracture of his right femur. To relieve intense pain he was given radium therapy.

Jessie Drover: "He was in St John's at the hospital and he called us up. He wanted some paper and pencils and stuff. Margo and I went down. He was grumbling about his pills and this and that, so one of the doctors went in and said, 'Now Dr Olds, tell us exactly what you want.' John said, 'Jesus Christ, look, I get this at two o'clock, and this at six o'clock, and this is for another time. Is that too hard for you to accept?'"

Muriel (French) Small: "The last day I saw him, he was in the Health Sciences Centre in St John's. I shook hands with him; he knew me. And he was very sick. I said, 'I'll see you in Twillingate'—knowing full well I wouldn't."

Melvin Woolfrey: "He was good friends with Ted Drover, Jessie's husband. A fellow who worked at the hospital told me once that Ted used to write Dr Olds pretty often, till he got so bad that he couldn't any more. On his last letter he said, 'Dr Olds, I won't be writing you any more. But when you land on the other shore, I'll be there to catch the line.'"

Louis Lawton: "The second time, he was taken from Twillingate to Gander and then to St John's. In St John's they took him first to the Health Sciences Centre and later to the Palliative Care Unit of St Clare's Mercy Hospital. At Health Sciences they were giving him radium treatments. He was in great pain and asked me to get him pills, which of course I couldn't do. People in Twillingate felt badly that he was not brought back there, where he could have been cared for with less pain and shunting about.

"At the last going off he had TB, he had cancer—which had perhaps metastasized from the lung to his bones—he had a lot of back problems. But it was the cancer that finally killed him."

In his last hours, he was unconscious. Dr Lawton, David Olds and Eric Facey took turns at the death bed. On Friday evening, September 6th, a few hours after being moved to St Clare's, alone with David, Dr Olds died. When Eric put "passed away" in the obituary, David remarked, "Pop wouldn't have said that." Eric nodded, crossed it out, and wrote "died."

When he was four, Papa had promised him Halley's Comet would return in 1986. Johnny missed it by only five months and three days.

He gave his body to the medical school at Memorial University. Dr Eric Pike did the dissection. There was no autopsy. The remains were cremated. Twillingate held a memorial service.

On an overcast, windless Sunday morning two years later, as the bells of Twillingate's several churches called to each other, a gaff-rigged sloop tacked slowly out of Twillingate Harbour. The *Monica Talbot* carried its owner Eric Facey, Eric's mother Marie, Dr David Olds and David's wife and daughter. It also carried a small hardwood casket. Off Burnt Island Tickle, in a flat calm, they opened the box and sprinkled the ashes of John McKee Olds on the North Atlantic and said goodbye.

Moments later, a breeze sprang up and filled the sails: a free wind home.

Afterword

Gary L. Saunders

The idea of this book came while I was interviewing Dr Olds in 1979 for a biography of my father; Dad had guided him on Gander River hunting trips years before. I had not seen Dr Olds since he examined me at age eight. Now white-haired and weathered, he reminded me of a thoroughbred horse—alert, intelligent, wise. At seventy-three he was still working several mornings a week.

That interview sparked in me an unaccountable need to know more about this man. When I wrote him the next year to broach the subject of a biography, he was gravely ill. We corresponded briefly in 1984, but by 1985 he was gone, taking his stories with him.

Two years later, the idea still nagged me. Unfortunately, J. M. Olds kept no journals and seldom saved letters. To build a solid biography without them was impossible, yet taping his older colleagues could not wait. In 1987 I explored the prospects with Dr Olds' long-time associate Raymond "Bud" Young. Eric Facey agreed to compile a list of possible contacts and lent me two boxes of memorabilia. Tentatively, I taped Captain Peter Troake and a few others. In November of 1989 I rented a house in nearby Crow Head, took two months off work and taped and transcribed fifteen of Dr Olds' older colleagues and patients.

Still worried about the scarcity of primary documents, in autumn 1990 I visited Dr Olds' only living sibling, Mary "Tutie" Mott in Maine. That visit produced a family tree, some photographs—and a pleasant surprise. John had written home regularly ever since his teens, and his mother had saved every letter.

In January 1991, fortified by a Canada Council grant, I took six months' unpaid leave and interviewed a dozen St John's doctors who had worked with or known Dr Olds. That May, David Olds showed me his father's family home and haunts in Connecticut and released several hundred letters. He also sent a copy of Dr Robert Ecke's wonderful unpublished journal of the early Twillingate years.

Now my book was under full sail. As I wrote, I tried to imagine the Notre Dame Bay of John and Betty's early years. It wasn't easy. Thanks to Confederation, causeways and modern communications, the isolation and poverty had been largely banished—good riddance. The seal fishery was gone—a mixed blessing. Its great sail-proud schooners and crews had vanished—a loss. The cod had fled—a tragedy. Almost the only abiding benchmarks were the land, the sea and the people.

And the weather. One afternoon during my 1989 sojourn, after three weeks of Indian Summer, a sudden snow storm there knocked out the power. As dark and cold enveloped my quaking ranch house, I found some black spruce firewood under the deck, made a blaze in the Angel Stone fireplace and cooked my simple supper. While the blizzard raged, I wrote a few impressions by firelight:

> Twillingate, Toulinguet—a lovely name for a town and its pair of islands, seven miles from heel to prong with nothing between them and Greenland but a waste of ocean. One would be hard pressed to find a more weatherful place. Wind...forever sighing along the wall, keening under the eaves, driving boats to harbour, lashing the sea feather-white, riming the windows with salt. The sky...benign and sparkling one minute, drizzling the next, prone to celebrate with extravaganzas of lemon, orange and magenta before the day goes down to velvet dark. The sea...mutable as quicksilver, its distant rote the bass accompaniment of all life here.

Next morning my plate glass window framed a Hiroshige landscape of snow-covered white roofs stepping down to a pewter grey sea. In 1932 Betty Olds had told John she wanted to see Twillingate under snow. I knew what she meant.

What drew me to Dr Olds and Twillingate? It is hard to say. No doubt my hypochondriac mother, always worried about TB and diphtheria and polio, had something to do with it. So did his mystique. Growing up in Gander Bay in the forties, one heard his name all the time.

"Perhaps I'll go to see Dr Hose."

"You need to see Dr Olds."

"Dr Holds he saved my life...."

To most adults in Gander Bay, he was simply the good physician. To my childish imagination, he seemed more Robin Hood. For a time I too wished to be a doctor.

As so often happens with biographers, I started out a naive admirer, discovered darker truths and in the end embraced a larger reality. May my readers come away as enriched as I.

Clifton, Nova Scotia
May, 1994

Appendix of Honours

"An unusual event by any medical standards, where two whole days were dedicated to one doctor...an outpouring."
— Dr Warrick, 1990, commenting on
October 2, 1970—"Dr Olds Day"

1950 Specialist Certificate, Royal College of Physicians and Surgeons of Canada—General Surgery (December 8th).

1950s Honourary Membership, Newfoundland Sealers Association; Certificate of Achievement, Canadian Sealers Association.

1963 Silver Caribou presented by Jim Strong from people of Green Bay at annual Hospital Association Meeting; also made honourary director of Hospital. (Dr Olds later told his sister, "It appears I am being accepted into the community again.")

1966 Canadian citizenship on Tuesday, April 25th in Citizen's Court in Twillingate before Magistrate Jack A. White of Gander, who said: "Generally, it is the person concerned who is happy to become a Canadian citizen. While this is still true, I am sure that Canada must be happy today, for it is not every day a nation gets a citizen of the status of Dr Olds. His name and medical service are legend in Newfoundland. He has all the qualities of a Schweitzer, but needs comparisons to no one, for he is a great man in his own right. He has always belonged to us in Newfoundland in heart. Now we can acclaim him as our own in fact. And so he is ours and joins our medical greats—Keegan, MacPherson, Anderson and all the others."

1967 Centennial Medal, 100th Year of Confederation (July 1st).

1969 Appointed Officer of Order of Canada. Citation: "Medicine—practicing: For his services over many years as Chief of Medical and Surgical Services, the Notre Dame Bay Memorial Hospital, Twillingate, Newfoundland" (Appointment June 27th, investiture April 21, 1970 at Rideau Hall, Ottawa). Olds wrote his sister, Tutie, "The Ottawa racket was interesting. We went to Gov't House in our monkey suits, got presented with the medal, milled around a while & had a few words with Trudeau...."

1970 Dr Olds Day, October 2nd: Provincial Holiday honouring his 40 years' service to Newfoundland. Honourary chairman Premier

Joseph R. Smallwood. Many tributes, culminating in presentation by Twillingate Chamber of Commerce of a cheque for $14,400, representing "Operation Appreciation" pledges and contributions from people of Notre Dame Bay toward Medical Library Endowment Fund, set up by Chamber at Dr Olds' request that year in lieu of personal cash award. Dr Gordon Thomas brought greetings from the International Grenfell Association and the people of northern Newfoundland. "One of the highlights," recalled Dr Warrick in 1990, "was a testimonial pledge from each family, all assembled in large binders and brought on stage in the Twillingate arena—no other place would do for the huge number who came.... At dinner about 16 men and women spoke, and spoke well. There were messages from all over the world: the British Medical Association, the American Medical Association, national and local associations—I've never seen anything like it. The point was made that it was the *people* who inspired Olds to stay there for that long and to never leave them. Whether good or bad, he was *available*—a big thing in medicine. My impression was that the people really revered this man."

Honourary Doctor of Science, Fall Convocation, Memorial University of Newfoundland. Citation by Dr John Hewson: "Concern for one's fellow human beings can be, for certain extraordinary individuals, a consuming passion, a magnificent obsession. Transcending mere altruism, such concern is no longer simple virtue; it becomes the full realization of self through the service of others: it is the pursuit of all that is worthwhile in life for any single individual. And this is why it reminds us of the passion of creative Genius: of Michelangelo crouching for four and a half years on his scaffold in the Sistine Chapel—that peculiar human paradox of fulfilment through negation, through total devotion of self to an absorbing and all-consuming task.

"What else but such a passion could cause a man to spend a lifetime in the service of his fellows on the rugged Northeast coast of Newfoundland? Certainly not the money, at a starting salary of $50 a month. Certainly not the climate, which has ruined the health of not a few. Certainly not the living conditions with the inconvenience and claustrophobia of life on a small island. And certainly not the working conditions, when there is an unending struggle just to maintain ones' place of work, and every minor improvement is a major triumph over adversity. Not to mention the travel by dog sled and open boat, and the hard times of economic depression.

"It is remarkable in itself that John McKee Olds has for forty years brought the Christ-like figure of the healer to simple homes and distant settlements in a small, far-off corner of the world. What is even more remarkable is that only four years after his first arrival from the United States, and still only fresh out of medical school at Johns Hopkins, he accepted the heavy task of Superintendent and Chief of Surgical Staff in a hospital burdened with heavy liabilities and threatened with closure. Many good souls in such a predicament would quite simply have gone down with the ship. But in the midst of these trials he suffered the loss of his house and his medical library through fire, and four years later the hospital burned. At about this time he was the only medical practitioner on the whole Northeast coast of Newfoundland, from Bonavista to St Anthony. He not only continued his work, however, and rebuilt the hospital, but also devised a sort of minor Medicare system and extended his services to the outlying areas by means of a travelling clinic set up on board a boat. Instead of the medical services being eroded by the times and the conditions, they were expanded out of all proportion to the size and status of the hospital.

"One would have thought that an overworked doctor confronted with successive calamities would have enough to keep him occupied. But he spent five weeks at the ice with the sealers one spring in order to make first-hand observations of the painful infection known as Seal Finger. The common treatment for a finger so infected was amputation. John Olds analyzed the infection and devised a suitable treatment. The publishing of his research and findings has subsequently saved many hands from disfigurement. It is not surprising that he has, in his own lifetime, become something of a legend.

"Often asked why he stayed in Twillingate, he has always replied: "Because I liked it." We take the liberty of interpreting this supremely simple and modest answer to mean that he has enjoyed in Twillingate a life of magnificent achievement. Mr Vice Chancellor, it is to celebrate that achievement that I present to you for the degree of Doctor of Science, *honoris causa*, John McKee Olds."

Fred W. Rowe, Acting Premier "Tribute to Dr John M. Olds" in Newfoundland Government *Bulletin*, November.

Royal Canadian Legion (Twillingate Branch No. 21) "Friendship Award," its highest citation: "In grateful appreciation of the outstanding contribution made to the development of goodwill and comradeship" (June 24th).

1971 Named Honourary Life Member, Newfoundland Tuberculosis and Respiratory Disease Association (27th annual meeting, May 3rd); granted Honourary Life Membership, Nfld (and Canadian) Medical Associations, St John's (October).

1972 Named a Fellow, Royal College of Surgeons of Canada (September 23rd).

30-minute CBC Television Documentary, "Go See Dr Olds."

1976 After opening of the new hospital, September 24th, Dr Olds wrote: "I was very embarrassed at the excessive praise heaped on me by Premier Frank Moores, ex-Premier Joey Smallwood &, even worse, by Herb Gillett, Chairman of the Board. However, I got out of it without making a speech, and Frank Moores got so carried away he let me cut the ribbon instead of doing it himself; he must be a good politician."

Mr Smallwood, master of hyperbole, declared: "I would say, that in the entire twentieth century so far, Dr John Olds would have to be regarded as one of the half-dozen greatest human beings in Newfoundland. The man is outstanding; I mean he ranks with the greatest of them.... with Grenfell, with Dr Curtis, with Sir Robert Bond, Lord Morris, Sir William Coaker. He was a very great Newfoundlander, not by birth but by adoption, a great humanitarian, a great human personality, who, with all his greatness, never ceased to be a genial, friendly, very human being. " The Honourable Edward Roberts, Minister of Health, said: "We will never see a man who will make a greater contribution to our people than Dr Olds."

1977 Silver Jubilee Medal commemorating coronation of Queen Elizabeth II.

Certificate of Appreciation, Notre Dame Bay Memorial Hospital Association Board of Directors (May 11th).

1978 CBC National Radio Program. Olds commented, "It was awful & I will never do another & didn't want to do this one." (October).

1979 Senior Membership, Canadian Medical Association.

1981 Plaque from Hospital Directors "In Recognition of 50 years of Devoted and Distinguished Service to the People of Newfoundland and of Notre Dame Bay in Particular."

Plaque from education officials "On the Occasion of the Official Naming of J. M. Olds Collegiate, in Appreciation of a Life of Outstanding Dedication and Service." Accepted on his behalf by Mrs Gloria M. Olds (March 22, 1980).

Tribute by Ned Clarke in *Lewisporte Pilot* on his 75th birthday (March 27, 1981).

1982 Article in fall issue of *Newfoundland Quarterly*: "Prominent Figures from Our Recent Past: Dr John McKee Olds," by Paul F. Kenney.

1985 Premier Peckford paid tribute to the late Dr Olds in Executive Council (September 10th).

Memorial Service at Notre Dame Bay Memorial Hospital with tributes from Dr Fred Woodruff; Dr L. E. Lawton, Registrar, Newfoundland Medical Board; W. Earle, Chairman, Board of Hospital Trustees; H. W. C. Gillett "for the people of Notre Dame Bay"; Dr D. D. Olds; Eric Facey and from the Department of Health on behalf of Dr H. Twomey, Minister. Clergy were Reverend Mr. O. Dawe, Pastor W. Burton and Reverend A. J. Hoddinott. Scripture reading was Psalm 139: 1-12, 17-18, beginning with "Lord thou hast examined me and knowest me," and concluding with, "How deep I find thy thoughts, O God, how inexhaustible their themes! Can I count them? They outnumber the grains of sand; to finish the count, my years must equal thine." Hymns: "Rock of Ages" and "The Lord's My Shepherd;" Anthem: "Amazing Grace." (September 28th).

1987 Dr J. M. Olds Memorial Scholarship for Twillingate and area students pursuing medical or health-related study.

Appendix of Illustrations

"A sharp immediately available instrument for cutting sutures would be a great saver of time and motion. Ordinarily the little finger has little to do in an operative procedure; but, fitted with a knife-bearing sheath over the distal phalanx, it would become a very useful suture cutter."

— J. M. Olds

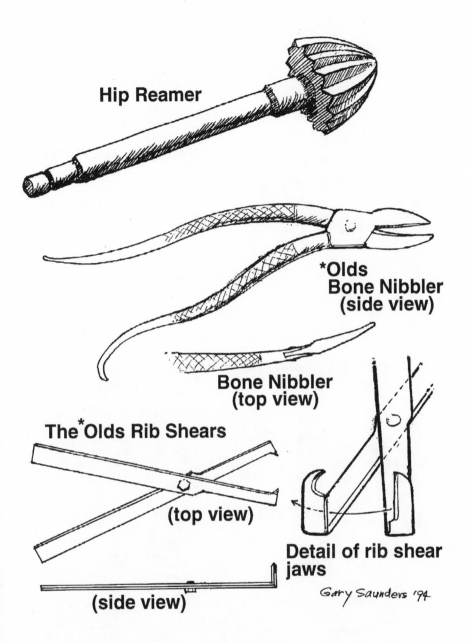

Hip Reamer

*Olds Bone Nibbler (side view)

Bone Nibbler (top view)

The *Olds Rib Shears

(top view)

Detail of rib shear jaws

Gary Saunders '94

(side view)

* Dr Olds' designs—the hip reamer is not his.

Suture Cutter

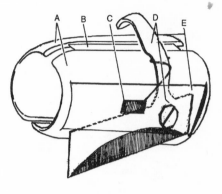

A - Acrylic resin sheath consisting of two halves.

B - Metal spring embedded in and uniting the halves of A, and permitting adjustment according to size.

C - Attachment of simple wire spring for automatic return of blade to sheath.

D - Lever and blade holder (with blade) secured by screw.

E - Metal slot enclosing blade and holder—here with blade exposed.

Pencil drawing by Olds of Gander River.

NORTHERN
MEDICAL REVIEW

| VOLUME 1 | JULY 1943 | NUMBER 1 |

Printed by LONG BROTHERS

St. John's, Newfoundland

Cover, premiere and only issue, *Northern Medical Review.*